KU-531-521

SUSANNA LONGLEY

THE WEEKEND
GARDENER

COLLINS & BROWN

20073812

MORAY COUNCIL
LIBRARIES &
INFORMATION SERVICES

635

First published in 1998 by
Collins & Brown Limited
64 Brewery Road
London
N7 9NT

A member of the Chrysalis Group plc

Copyright © Collins & Brown Limited 1998
Text copyright © Susannah Longley 1998

All rights reserved. No part of this publication may be reproduced, stored in a retrieval system, or transmitted in any form or by any means, electronic, mechanical, photocopying, recording or otherwise, without the prior written permission of the copyright owner.

Editorial Director: Sarah Hoggett
Art Director: Roger Bristow
Photography: Sampson Lloyd
Additional photography: Geoff Dann, Mark Gatehouse
Illustration: Vanessa Luff, Martine Collings
Diagrams: David Ashby

1 3 5 7 9 10 8 6 4 2

British Library Cataloguing-in-Publication Data:
A catalogue record for this book is available from the British Library

ISBN 1 85585 939 4

Printed by Paramount Printing, Hong Kong

Contents

Planning Your Weekend Garden

WHETHER WE LIKE it or not, most of us are 'weekend gardeners', fitting all of our gardening efforts into a few precious hours along with other domestic chores, such as shopping and housework – and, of course, relaxing with family and friends. But having only a limited amount of time shouldn't entail any lowering of quality. It simply means that you have to tailor the garden to suit your own resources and requirements.

The Weekend Gardener is designed to help you do just that. A lot of practical gardening books are over-ambitious: they seem to assume that everyone wants to go back to the drawing board, ripping out established plants and temporarily installing a cement mixer in their place while the entire site is relandscaped. *The Weekend Gardener*, on the other hand, recognises that few people have the time, energy or resources for this. Instead, it encourages you to look for ways of enhancing what you already have through a series of small, manageable projects that you can carry out at a time that suits your timetable.

Start by asking yourself a series of questions in order to work out exactly what you want from your garden:

How much time can I spend gardening?

If you're limited to just a few hours each week, then you need low-maintenance designs, easy-care plants that suit the situation in which you plant them, and projects for which the basic groundwork can be done in a matter of hours rather than days. All the projects in this book fall into those categories, leaving you time to relax and enjoy the fruits of your labours.

Quick and easy
Tailor your gardening projects to fit the time you have available. Containers are a quick way of bringing instantly mature plantings to your garden.

Garden for pleasure!
Gardening should be fun! Whether you enjoy pottering around for hours (above) or prefer quick-and-easy, instant results, such as planting a container (right), use the projects in The Weekend Gardener *to help you plan your garden so that you get the maximum enjoyment out of it.*

What aspects of gardening do I enjoy?

Do you like pottering around, getting your hands dirty and putting in different plants for each season – or would you prefer to establish a core of permanent plants that, once planted, need very little upkeep? Do you find mowing the lawn a good way of relaxing after a hard week's work – or does the thought of having to spend your precious Sunday mornings cutting the grass discourage you? Make a list of the activities you do and don't enjoy, and use it as the basis for revamping certain areas of your garden, if necessary, so that you can get the most pleasure out of your gardening. Before you embark on any of the projects in this book, check the Project Planner and Maintenance boxes (see pages 10–11) to see what you're getting yourself into – and if you don't like the sound of it, don't do it!

How do I plan to use my garden?

Is it primarily a place to relax? If so, attractive, planting schemes that are easy to care for may be your top priority. Or is it somewhere for the kids to play? In that case, a large grassy area, surrounded by robust shrubs

THE WEEKEND
GARDENER

Design a garden that suits your needs
Rather than being a slave to other people's ideas of what a garden should be, make sure that your garden fits in with your tastes and lifestyle. Whether you want it to be a horticultural showpiece with luxuriant herbaceous borders (above) *or a place to relax and enjoy the sunshine* (left) *is entirely your decision.*

and ground-cover plants that can withstand trampling from young feet, might be the best answer. Again, make a list of your personal priorities, rather than copying designs that do not fit in with your family's needs.

Be prepared to adapt your garden to suit your changing circumstances. Once the kids have grown up and left home, you can plant over the play area or pave it to create a stylish-looking patio. If you retire from full-time work, you will probably have more leisure time – and the carefully nurtured herbaceous border that you've always dreamed of is suddenly within your grasp. The projects in *The Weekend Gardener* give you plenty of scope for quick-and-easy changes that will transform your garden in a short space of time.

What constraints does my garden impose?

By choosing plants that naturally thrive in your garden's conditions – shade-tolerant species for a shaded site, for example – you are making life a lot easier for yourself as a weekend gardener, since happy plants require less maintenance. The Gardening Basics section (pages 12–51) shows you how to analyse the soil and other conditions that prevail in your garden. Each project makes it clear what conditions it is designed for. If you decide you would like to use plants other than the ones suggested, the plant lists on pages 182–185 are a useful starting point. Supplement this information by consulting a good plant reference manual before you

buy anything, and also check the label that accompanies potted plants.

Armed with a checklist of your own gardening priorities and conditions, you are now in a far better position to assess which of the projects in *The Weekend Gardener* meet your needs.

Planting plans to suit your garden
The Gardening Basics section (pages 12–51) explains how to analyse the conditions that prevail in your garden, so you can choose plants and designs that will be successful.

7

About This Book

THE WEEKEND GARDENER begins with a short introduction to basic gardening skills, which covers techniques for improving your soil, sowing seed, planting everything from bulbs to trees, watering and general maintenance such as staking and pruning. Use this section as a handy reference source whenever you're unsure about how to do something. The step-by-step projects in the book refer you to the Gardening Basics section for information on routine gardening tasks.

The Gardening Basics section ends with The Weekend Gardener's Calendar, which tells you what routine gardening tasks you should be doing throughout the year. When you're short of time, planning ahead to maximise what little time you have is essential. Get into the habit of checking this calendar every month, using it as a reminder of what you need to do. Carrying out the right task at the right time will save you time in the long run: prune a shrub at the right time of year and you'll keep it looking neat and tidy and encourage

Gardening basics section
The Gardening Basics section (pages 12–51) sets out in an easy-to-follow format all the essential practical information that you are likely to need as a weekend gardener.

Step-by-step photographs
Step-by-step photographs and instructions make routine gardening tasks easy for everyone to follow.

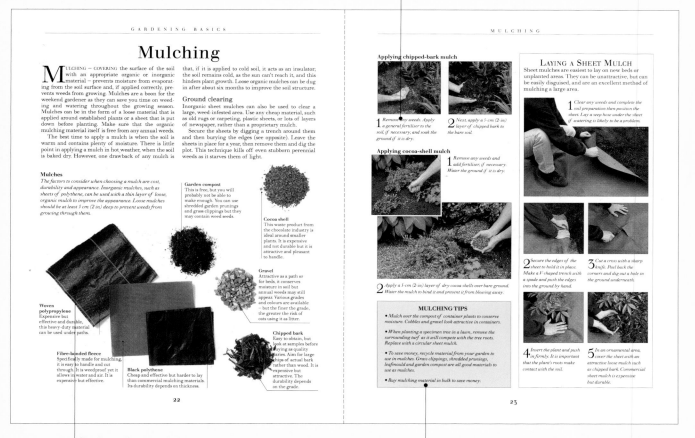

Tools and materials
Colour photographs of gardening tools and materials are included throughout, so that you can devise your own weekend gardener's tool kit.

Tips
Useful tips are displayed in special feature boxes for easy reference.

bushy growth, but leave it for a year or two and you'll find that you have a much larger task on your hands. By planning your garden maintenance in advance, you can spread tasks over several weekends rather than trying to blitz everything in a single day at the end of the growing season in preparation for winter.

The core of *The Weekend Gardener* is a series of project-based chapters with a unique cross-referencing system to help you decide which projects are most appropriate to your own garden. All the projects are designed to be achievable within one weekend at the most; many take only an hour or two.

Each of the first five projects chapters begins with a series of questions setting out common gardening problems. Some of these problems relate to aesthetic or design points (for example, "Is your lawn a harsh, geometric shape?"), while others touch on horticultural considerations (for example, "Do you have a mature tree under which nothing grows well?"). You are then referred to a specific project or projects that will help you to answer the question. Use these pages for both practical help and as inspiration; they are intended to open your eyes to possibilities that you might never have considered.

Question-and-answer pages
These question-and-answer pages are a unique feature of The Weekend Gardener. *By setting out typical problems that many people encounter in their gardens, they are designed to help you choose projects that are appropriate to your own situation.*

Typical gardening problem
Questions set out typical gardening problems or situations that you might encounter in your own garden.

Ideas for Improving Walls, Fences and Hedges

THE EXTERNAL boundaries of your garden – the walls, fences and hedges – provide the basic framework against which all of your plantings are seen. They also have a practical effect on the micro-climate of your garden, creating shelter and shade and therefore influencing the types of plants that you can grow. When you choose plants, you need to think not only about factors such as shade, but also about aesthetic considerations – how your plants will blend in or contrast with the boundaries in terms of their colour and texture.

Something that many people overlook is that walls, fences and hedges can also be used as internal divisions – separating a patio area from the rest of the garden, or creating a secluded corner where you can enjoy the afternoon sunshine.

The questions on these two pages are designed to help you pinpoint ways in which you can improve existing boundaries, or create new ones, in order to enhance your garden. Each one is backed up by a step-by-step project that includes suggestions for plants that you might like to use in your own garden.

? Does your garden feel too open?
Set up boundaries within the garden to create a separate 'garden room' or a series of 'rooms' and make it more interesting to walk through. *Right*: This garden sanctuary is created by 2.1-m (7-ft) high yew hedging. The petunias and potted marguerite daisies match the striking statue. SEE *A Garden Divider, page 110; Formal Hedge, page 114.*

? Does your front garden fence look dilapidated?
With a minimum of practical skills, you can create an informal fence that also makes the perfect frame for plants to grow on and around. SEE *Front Garden Boundary, page 118.*

100

? Do buildings enclose or overlook your garden?
Raise the height of boundary walls and fences (be sure to check any local bye-laws) and grow climbers up them to make them look more attractive. *Above*: A trellis, covered in the beautiful *Rosa* 'Handel', increases the height of the low wall and prevents the garden from being overlooked. SEE *Raising the Height of a Wall, page 104.*

? Is your hedge an expanse of single colour?
Plant a flowering hedge or train a succession of flowering climbers through an evergreen hedge to give seasonal variety and colour. *Above*: The colourful splendour of this beautiful garden overflows into the hedges. The clipped, dark-green yew cone is enhanced by the flame-coloured nasturtium. SEE *Adding Colour to Green Hedges, page 108; Informal Boundary Hedge, page 112.*

? Do your bed and border edges look untidy?
Plant a miniature hedge to define the edges. *Left*: This miniature box hedge makes a neat edging to the bed and hides the bare rose stems. Alpine daisies and catmint cascade over the wall in front of the hedge. SEE *Defining Your Beds, page 116.*

? Do you have a fence or boundary that is bare and boring?
Use trellis panels to break up a blank wall area and train climbers and wall shrubs through the trellis to soften the edges. If the wall gets the sun, you can create a scented sitting area. SEE *Enhancing a Bare Wall, page 102; Plants for a Sunny Wall, page 106.*

101

Quick-and-easy answers
The solution to each question is a quick-and-easy project that you can carry out over the course of a single weekend.

Cross-references
By following up the cross-references, you can turn to a project or projects within the chapter for help in solving your gardening problem. Sometimes there are several options open to you.

ABOUT THIS BOOK (cont.)
Each project features an illustration that shows you what it will look like once the plants have reached maturity. The introduction to each project tells you the situation it is suitable for and the benefits it will bring. Many projects contain Alternative Plantings so that you can adapt the design to a different situation or colour scheme. Not everyone has the same requirements, but *The Weekend Gardener* gives you the flexibility to adapt designs to suit your own situation.

Once you have decided which projects you would like to do, read through the project to be sure you know what's involved before you start. This is important: not only do you need to know how to carry out the project, but you should also be aware of what you will need to do to maintain it. Draw up a shopping list of tools, materials and plants – and you're ready to begin!

The final chapter gives ideas for building a garden around a specific theme. The four shown here are the most popular types of themed garden – herb gardens,

Projects for the weekend gardener
The Weekend Gardener *contains around 50 projects to improve your garden that can be completed within a single weekend; many take only an hour or two. All are clearly set out with full step-by-step instructions.*

Plant lists
The plant lists (pages 182–185) should be your first port of call if you want to check whether or not a particular plant will work in the situation for which you have chosen it.

The benefits of each project
The introductory text sets out the benefits each project will bring to your garden and, where appropriate, includes useful practical information on such topics as plant choices and garden design.

Specially commissioned illustrations
A full-colour illustration depicts each planting scheme once it has reached maturity.

Plant photographs
Colour photographs show the suggested plants in close-up detail for ease of identification.

PLANTS FOR DIFFERENT PURPOSES

Plants for Different Purposes

BEDS AND BORDERS

Creating a Focal Point
SCENTED LILY AND ROSE ARBOUR

A FREE-STANDING ARBOUR or arch swathed in flowers brings several benefits to a garden: it can be used to divide the garden into separate areas, to frame a striking view, or to distract attention from an unattractive one. Beyond these, it provides a focal point – a dramatic, eye-catching feature that makes a strong design statement.

You can make your own arch, but it is far easier to buy one in kit form from a garden centre. There is a wide range to choose from – in wood and metal – and to suit all budgets. Once you have made sure that the arch is well anchored in the ground, you can start to train climbing plants to grow up and around it.

An arch is a particularly effective way of displaying such scented climbers as roses or honeysuckle, since you benefit from wafts of perfume every time you pass through it. Some rose varieties, particularly if they are trained over a wall or solid surface, are prone to mildew in humid conditions. However, growing them over an arch can help prevent this problem, since air is able to circulate freely through the plants' stems.

Fragrant pink and white arch
This arch is smothered in fragrant pink roses, while pots of lilies clothe the base. Geraniums and sweet violets cover the ground and help to minimise weed growth.

1 Pink rambler rose such as *Rosa* 'New Dawn'

2 Madonna lily (*Lilium candidum*)

3 Pink climbing rose such as *Rosa* 'Zéphirine Drouhin'

4 *Geranium* x *magnificum*

5 Sweet violet (*Viola odorata*), shown here in flower in spring

150

wildflower gardens, woodland gardens and water gardens – though there are, of course, many other types of garden that you could treat in this way and this section should inspire you to come up with your own ideas.

Finally, you will find plant lists that tell you which plants grow best in particular situations. If you want to substitute other plants for the ones suggested in *The Weekend Gardener*, or if you want to devise your own planting schemes, your first step should be to refer to these lists. They will save you a lot of time ploughing through more detailed plant reference books – although, of course, you may want to use such books to supplement the information given here.

If you carry away just one message from this book, it should be that gardening is fun – and to achieve this, you need to make sure that your garden works for you, not the other way round. Decide on your own personal priorities and adapt your garden, if necessary, to allow you to make the most of your precious free time. Above all, enjoy being a Weekend Gardener!

Maintenance
Maintenance tips tell you how to keep each project looking its best.

Time scale
The Time Scale tells you roughly how long each project takes, so that you can plan your weekend accordingly.

Tools and materials
The Tools and Materials list sets out all the equipment you need for each project, so that you can make sure you have everything you need before you start.

CREATING A FOCAL POINT

PROJECT PLANNER

● MAINTENANCE

• *Weed regularly.*

• *Water regularly, especially in warm and dry weather.*

• *In spring, sprinkle fertiliser around the base of the rose plants.*

• *Use old tights to tie the stems of the climbing rose to the arch. Wind the plant stems around the arch as they grow.*

• *Deadhead roses as they fade, snipping off their stems to just above a vigorous leaf joint.*

• *Prune* Rosa *'New Dawn' after it has flowered. Unwind the stems and cut each one that has flowered back to its main stem (see page 42). The other rose used here (*Rosa *'Zéphirine Drouhin') is a climber and need not be pruned regularly, though unwanted or dead stems can be removed in spring.*

• *Remove the pots of lilies once their flowers are over and replace them with pots of other flowering plants.*

• *In autumn, remove dead leaves and other debris, and apply a mulch of bark chippings to the soil.*

PLANTING ALTERNATIVES

Golden arch

For a predominantly gold- and cream-coloured planting scheme, substitute the plants listed below for those shown in the illustration.

1 *Rosa* 'Golden Showers'

3 *Rosa* 'Madame Alfred Carrière'

4 Lady's mantle (*Alchemilla mollis*)

5 Heartsease (*Viola tricolor*)

TIME SCALE 1 DAY

Tools and Materials
Arch kit • Post holders • Driving tool for post holders • Sledgehammer • Mallet • Spirit level • Fork • Manure • Spade • Bark-chip mulch

1 *Decide where to position your archway. Measure your site roughly so that you can make (or buy) an appropriately sized archway.*

2 *Assemble the sides and top of the archway following the manufacturer's instructions.*

3 *Insert the first metal post holder into the ground. Fit the driving tool over the post holder and use the sledgehammer to knock the holder into position.*

4 *Lay one side panel on the ground to help you check where the second post should be positioned. Drive the second post holder into the ground in the same way as the first one.*

5 *Insert the first side panel into its post holders, knocking it in with a mallet. Lay a crossbar on the ground to help you position the post holders for the second side panel and insert the post holders as in Steps 3 and 4.*

6 *Insert the second side panel into its post holders, as in Step 5. Use a spirit level to check that the tops of the two side panels are level with each other, tapping them with the mallet if necessary.*

7 *Fit the overhead crosspieces into position. Check that they are level. Make any necessary adjustments by tapping them with the mallet.*

8 *Fork over the soil around the archway, incorporating manure so that the ground is well prepared before you plant.*

9 *Plant one rose at each side of the archway. Plant geraniums and sweet violets around the base of the archway for ground cover.*

10 *Water well and cover the soil with a layer of bark chippings.*

11 *Position a container of Madonna lilies on each side of the archway.*

131

Clear, step-by-step instructions
Easy-to-follow instructions take you through the different stages of each project step by step.

Alternative Plantings
Many of the projects feature Alternative Plantings, allowing you to vary the suggested planting scheme to suit your own tastes and requirements – changing the colour, perhaps, or adapting the plants from sun-loving species to shade-tolerant ones.

GARDENING BASICS

Basic but beautiful
Using a few basic gardening techniques and some careful planning, you can create a garden to be proud of in a relatively small amount of time. These glorious colours and strking textures look effective, but need not be difficult to achieve.

Getting to Know Your Garden

UNDERSTANDING THE conditions that exist in your garden – whether it is sunny or shaded, sheltered or exposed – and identifying the type of soil you have is the key to successful gardening. Plants that like your garden environment are more likely to thrive and less likely to succumb to pests and diseases.

How sunny or shaded is your garden?

Most gardens have both sunny and shaded areas. First, determine which parts of the garden catch the sun and which are in shade: the amount of sun or shade that your garden receives can change throughout the day and with the seasons. Next, make a note of the spots where your garden offers shelter from wind or where it is completely exposed. Observe and keep a log about the different parts of your garden throughout the year.

With this information, you can position each of your plants in the most appropriate situation.

Which type of soil do you have?

Plant roots need a balanced supply of moisture, air, and nutrients, but the amount of each that is available to them depends on the soil type. There are a number of different types of soil and there may even be variations within your garden. The most common types are shown below to help you identify them.

The ability of a soil to hold air and water depends on the origin and size of its particles. Most garden soils contain particles derived from rocks or other minerals. Simply rubbing the soil between your fingertips will give you some idea of the size of the particles. Large particles, such as those found in sandy soils, feel gritty.

Soil types

Gardens, even in the same locality, can have very different soils. There may even be differences within your garden. Here are the most common soil types.

Peaty soil
Peaty soil is usually dark, wet and acidic. It can produce excellent plant growth, but often lies wet in winter and dries out quickly in summer.

Clay soil
Clay soil is fertile and retains water. The particles are small with few air spaces. If worked when wet, clay soil can become compacted, which makes it harder for plants to grow. When hot, the surface of the clay can bake hard.

Loamy soil
This is the ideal soil for plant growth. The soil contains clay, so it is fertile, and sand, so it has good drainage.

Sandy soil
Sandy soil has large particles with lots of air spaces between them, making the soil light and easy to work. Water drains quickly through the soil, carrying with it water-soluble nutrients. The soil is dry and the fertility level is low.

Alkaline soil
Alkaline soil can be sandy or clay. Its chemical content (it is comprised of limestone) makes it harder for some plants to extract nutrients from it.

If the particles are very small, the soil feels smooth. A soil that can be moulded into a ball is either loam or clay (see below). A few soils, such as peaty soil, have so much organic matter present that the size of any mineral particles is not relevant.

You can learn about your garden soil by handling it. Sandy soils will not stick together in a ball shape, while soils containing clay can be rolled into a ball (see below).

Making a soil ball

1 *Knead the moist soil in your hands and work it into a ball. If it has a texture like putty and forms a ball, the soil contains clay.*

2 *Roll the ball into a sausage shape and bend it around to form a ring. If this can be done, there is a high clay content (over 35 per cent) in the soil.*

How well drained is your soil?

In addition to assessing your soil's particle size, you must also establish if there is a water source near by. In winter, dig a hole up to 60 cm (2 ft) deep. Fill the hole with water and cover it if rain is forecast. Note how long it takes for the water to drain. If the water drains away within 24 hours there is no drainage problem. If the soil is poorly drained, the hole will still contain water after 24 hours. In a free-draining soil, water drains in less than an hour. If more water seeps into the hole, there must be another source of water near by.

Plants vary greatly in their tolerance to waterlogging and to dryness at the roots. If your soil is very wet or very dry, it will greatly affect the types of plants that will establish unless you take steps to improve it.

How acid or alkaline is your soil?

The acidity or alkalinity of your soil also affects the sorts of plants that you can grow in your garden. Most plants prefer a soil that is slightly acid (pH 6.5), but there are exceptions, including rhododendrons, camellias and some heathers. Other plants are able to tolerate more alkaline soils; these are sometimes known as 'lime loving'. Well-known lime-loving plants include aquilegias, clematis, marjoram and veronicas. Most soils are between pH 5.5 and 7.5. In practice, you may not need to know the pH value as many test kits simply require you to match the colour of a liquid with a description, such as 'slightly acid'.

TAKING A SOIL SAMPLE

You can get a rough idea of whether your soil is acid, alkaline or neutral by using either a simple test kit or a soil meter. Test each bed or area separately, and take several readings at different points in each bed, averaging them out to obtain an overall reading. Conduct the test before adding manure or fertilisers and always use clean tools. A soil meter has a probe that allows you to take readings directly from the soil. Test kits can be cheaper and more reliable than basic soil meters.

1 *Lay bamboo stakes on the surface of the soil in the shape of a W. Take a walnut-sized sample of soil at each end of each stake. You should have five samples to mix together.*

2 *Discard any stones or weeds and put the soil in a clean dish. Break up any lumps with your fingers and mix the sample up well.*

3 *Half fill the test tube with soil. Add water to fill and shake well. Allow the soil to settle, then take the soil reading.*

4 *Match the colour of the solution to the colour chart that is provided with the kit. The description or number next to the closest colour match tells you the pH value of your soil.*

Improving Your Soil

YOUR SOIL'S CHARACTERISTICS may limit the plants you can choose for your garden. However, there are lots of things you can do to improve your soil. Good-quality soil is a major asset, and it is worth preparing your soil before you begin planting. Soil that contains the correct balance of water, air and nutrients will reduce the amount of maintenance you need to do and improve the performance of your plants.

Concentrate on improving the topsoil – from the surface down to one spade's depth – as few plant roots penetrate much deeper. Digging uncultivated ground will open up the soil, making it easier for plant roots to establish. If your topsoil is shallow, add soil improvers (see pages 17–19) each year. When planting trees and shrubs in shallow topsoil, dig a deep planting pit and fill with topsoil (from another part of the garden or bought in bags) so they can root deeply.

If the soil is very poor quality, clear the topsoil and replace it with new soil before purchasing your plants.

You should see the benefits of improving your soil within a couple of years. Although annual applications of rotted organic matter will still be needed, the plants themselves will contribute to the soil. Plant roots can prevent light soils from getting washed away. Dead plant material can be collected and turned into compost, then returned to improve the soil.

Digging and raking tools
Tools for working the soil need to be durable, easy to clean, and comfortable to use. It is worth paying extra for good-quality tools.

Hand fork
Use for weeding and cultivating the soil around established plants.

Trowel
Use for planting small plants, such as perennials.

Soil rake
Use for levelling outdoor seedbeds and breaking down clods of earth to a crumbly texture.

Garden fork
Use for breaking up and preparing soil. It can also be used to improve lawns (see page 77), move garden debris, and turn compost heaps. Smaller border forks are also available.

Spade
Use for preparing soil and digging planting holes for trees and shrubs. Border spades have a narrow base and are easier to use in established beds; they are also lighter.

Soil profile

Soil consists of horizontal layers of different materials. Most plants occupy only the topsoil, so soil improvers, fertilisers or lime should be applied to this layer.

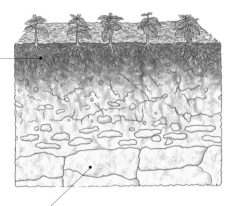

Topsoil
This is the fertile layer in which plants root. It contains organic matter and micro-organisms, critical for growing healthy plants. The topsoil should be at least one spade's depth.

Subsoil
This is often lighter in colour and coarser in texture than topsoil. Avoid mixing subsoil into topsoil as it lacks organic matter and micro-organisms.

Soil improvers

There are many sources of organic matter that can be used to improve the soil structure. Garden waste can be recycled as compost or leafmould. You can use any leaves except conifer clippings, to make leafmould. Pack the leaves into a large black plastic bag, and moisten if necessary, punch a few holes in the plastic bag, and store for two years. Leaves rot slowly, so compost large amounts separately.

You may need to supplement garden compost or leafmould, as it can be difficult to make large quantities.

Alternative sources of organic waste include local stables or mushroom farms. You can also buy specially prepared bagged products from garden centres.

Prices vary greatly, so shop around if you have large areas of soil to treat. Consider the convenience of each product: some of the cheaper sources need to be prepared months in advance or are available only at certain times of the year or in bulk quantities.

Apply soil improvers generously. Spread a 5-cm (2-in) layer over the bed, then dig in. Some materials also add nutrients, but the amounts vary and are not usually declared on the packaging.

Commercial soil improvers that you buy from garden centres or mail order companies can also be used, although you may not want to for ecological reasons. These are usually a blend of waste products, such as poultry manure and bark or peat. The products are often alkaline, so check the packaging for advice if you want to use them around acid-loving plants.

What soil needs

Topsoil should contain mineral particles, such as clay and sand, and lots of humus. Humus is formed when micro-organisms break down plant and animal material. It coats the soil and makes it easier to cultivate.

By digging in rotted organic matter you add air to the soil and produce humus. The soil will then hold moisture without becoming waterlogged. You should do this regardless of your soil type. As the humus decomposes, add bulky organic matter each year. If your soil is very acid or alkaline, you can help to redress the balance by adding particular soil improvers.

Improving alkaline soils

It is not easy to make alkaline soil more acidic. Adding peat helps to reduce acidity, while some nitrogen fertilisers, such as sulphate of ammonia, can make soils more acidic. Choose plants that thrive on limestone and grow acid-loving plants in containers of peat-based soil.

Improving acid soils

A slightly acidic soil (pH 6.5) is ideal for lawns, fruit and many other plants. Very acidic soils (pH 5) can still grow certain plants, for example rhododendrons, camellias, heathers and blueberries, but by adding lime (calcium carbonate) to reduce the acidity, you can grow a greater range of plants. This can be done at any time, except when manure is added or just before or after planting. Spent mushroom compost (see page 19) is also a good source of lime and organic matter.

Adding lime
Apply 100–200 g (4–8 oz) of lime (calcium carbonate) per sq m (sq yd). A convenient time to do this is when digging the ground in the autumn. Dig or rake the lime into the soil. Test the soil the following spring to see if it is less acidic.

Improving peaty soils

A peaty soil, which is already acidic, does not need extra organic matter. However, you will need to add lime if you want to grow vegetables, as they prefer neutral or slightly alkaline soils. Peaty soil can be hard to re-wet, so irrigate before it dries. Placing a couple of drops of liquid detergent in the water helps the soil to absorb moisture. Add extra fertiliser in the spring.

MAKING GARDEN COMPOST

Making compost is an excellent way of recycling household and garden waste. Buy or make a bin. The minimum size to generate enough heat is around 1 m (3 ft) square. Add material in 30-cm (1-ft) layers and water if dry. Add an activator between each layer to speed up the breakdown of the material. Activators include sulphate of ammonia, calcified seaweed, nettles and comfrey leaves. Finish with a layer of garden soil. Shop-bought bins come with a cover, and if you make your own bin it will need a cover, as heavy rain could turn the compost into a slimy mess.

1 Use a variety of materials to make compost, adding each in 15-cm (6-in) layers. Turn the material over with a digging fork every couple of months to speed up the decomposition process.

2 Cover the top layer of material with a waterproof sheet.

3 After three to six months the compost will be ready. Either dig it into the soil as a soil improver or apply on the surface as a mulch.

DO NOT COMPOST

The following should be excluded:

- *Food with grease or fat. Meat or fish waste.*

- *Coal ash from fires (wood ash can be used in small quantities).*

- *Diseased plant material, particularly if infected with viruses.*

- *Annual weeds in flower or with seedheads. Perennial weeds in flower or seed or their roots.*

Home and Garden Compost

Home-made compost is the most economic type of soil improver. Many materials from the garden and home can be recycled into garden compost. Here are the most useful:

Fruit and vegetable waste
Use cooked or raw waste, tea leaves, coffee grounds and egg shells.

Pet litter
You can use hamster and rabbit litter but not cat and dog.

Newspaper or cardboard
Shred and wet to help them break down.

Green prunings
Use from bedding plants, dead heading, cutting down herbaceous plants. Woody prunings should be shredded first.

Hay, dry grass
Grass clippings are suitable if dried first or mixed with other material.

Dead leaves
These can be added in small quantities.

Nettles
The leaves and stems are useful for activating the compost.

Other Organic Soil Improvers

These are available in larger quantities than garden compost, and are invaluable for conditioning the soil.

Farmyard manure

A valuable soil improver but do not use fresh or it can scorch new roots. Fresh manure should be piled up (away from open water and children) for six months to a year before use. Horse or cow manure is the best for gardens; chicken manure can be very strong and gives off ammonia.

Bark

Composted or chipped bark is a waste product from wood mills. It can be used to open up soil structure. Shredded prunings have similar properties. All are best composted before use.

Spent mushroom compost

This is what commercial growers use for raising mushrooms. It is a mixture of horse manure, peat and lime. It is a good soil improver for vegetable growing and helps to reduce acidity in the soil.

Improving Drainage

To open up air spaces in all soils, dig in rotted organic matter. For heavy clay soil, dig in horticultural grit (or gravel – see also page 124). It is expensive and can be hard work but, unlike adding organic matter, it only needs to be done once.

Horticultural grit

Horticultural grit (at least 3 mm /¹⁄₈ in in diameter) can be used to improve a poorly drained soil. Grit is heavy to move around so have it delivered.

Digging in horticultural grit

1 *Aim to add a wheelbarrow full of grit for every 2–3 sq m (2–3 sq yd). Place in piles over the bed.*

2 *Dig the grit in well. Horticultural grit will make an immediate and permanent improvement to the drainage of your soil.*

DIGGING

Digging can be hard work, but it is extremely important to do if you have compacted or clay soils. Breaking up and turning the earth creates air spaces within the soil, making it easier for roots to penetrate the soil and grow. At the same time, you can bury any weeds that are present and add organic matter to improve the soil.

When digging topsoil, do not bring a lot of subsoil to the surface, as it lacks organic matter and is not fertile. Heavy clay soils are best dug at the beginning of winter. The exposed clods can be broken down by winter weather to a crumb-like texture, which is ideal for making seedbeds or planting in spring. Never dig or walk on the soil when it is wet and sticky: it may damage the soil. Lighter soils can be dug at any time but, as with all soils, leave at least one to two weeks after digging to allow the soil to settle before planting.

Single digging

1 *Dig out the first trench to one spade depth. Keep the spade straight and lift the soil out into a wheelbarrow or outside the area to be dug.*

2 *As you dig the second trench, this time put the soil into the first trench. Continue until the whole area has been dug. Use the soil from the first trench to fill the last trench.*

Single digging is a very thorough method of digging an area. Remove any turf and divide the area into equal-sized trenches about 30 cm (1 ft) wide. Start in a corner and work standing on the next trench. The diagram below shows the correct order for digging.

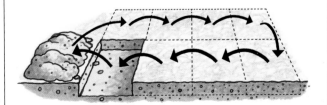

Feeding and Weeding

FERTILISERS ARE PLANT foods. Unlike bulky soil improvers, which are added in generous amounts to improve the structure of the soil, fertilisers are concentrated, so apply them as directed on the packet.

There are three major nutrients required by plants: nitrogen, phosphorus and potassium, often abbreviated to N, P and K. Fertilisers that contain all three are known as general or compound fertilisers; they also often contain smaller quantities of trace elements. You can compare brands by looking on the fertiliser packets for the NPK figures. The percentage contained and the ratio between the nutrients is important. For example, an evenly balanced fertiliser promotes leafy growth, while a higher proportion of potassium encourages flowering and fruiting.

There are lots of brands of general or compound fertilisers available. Some, such as blood, fish and bone, can be used all around the garden and tend to be the cheapest. Fertilisers for specific parts of the garden, such as lawns, roses and containers, are expensive but are more convenient to use. For example, you can feed and weed your lawn in a single operation using a 'weed and feed' preparation. Many container fertilisers include slow-release nitrogen, which needs to be applied once only at the beginning of the growing season.

Some gardeners prefer to use organic products, which are derived from either animal or vegetable sources. Both organic and inorganic products produce similar plant-growth results.

Applying fertilisers

Follow the manufacturer's instructions carefully. Wear gloves and wash your hands after each use. There is no need to dig in fertiliser as watering or rain will wash it into the soil. Dry fertiliser can scorch foliage, so brush it off or dilute with water. After applying dry fertiliser, water it to make it available to the plants.

ORGANIC FERTILISERS

Fertiliser	Description	When to apply
Blood, fish and bone	This is a powdery mixture of fast- and slow-release nutrients. Use to promote general plant growth.	Apply in spring and through the growing season. It is difficult to apply in windy conditions.
Chicken pellets	These pellets provide fast- and slow-release nutrients. Use all around the garden for general plant growth.	Use in spring and throughout the growing season.
Seaweed meal	The slow-release nutrients and trace elements boost root and leaf growth.	Apply in spring.

INORGANIC FERTILISERS

Fertiliser	Description	When to apply
Balanced general fertiliser	An all-round, fast-acting fertiliser with equal amounts of N, P and K. Available as granules and as a liquid.	Apply in spring and throughout the growing season.
Lawn fertiliser	This fast-acting product promotes grass, leaf and root growth. It is often sold combined with weedkiller.	Apply in spring and the growing season. Some lawn fertilisers have different spring and autumn formulations.
Rose fertiliser	A fast-acting product, high in K and trace elements. It promotes flowering in roses and other shrubs.	Use in spring and throughout the growing season.
Slow-release plugs	Fertiliser is held within a membrane that opens up and releases nutrients as the temperature rises.	Insert into compost in spring.
Tomato fertiliser	This fast-acting product, high in K promotes the growth of flowers and fruit.	Apply throughout the growing season. It is used for flowering and fruiting plants.

Weed control

A weed is any plant that you do not want. Weeds can make your garden look unattractive and they deprive your chosen plants of nutrients, light and moisture.

Using weedkillers

Perennial weeds are difficult to control. Preparations containing glyphosate will help but several applications may be needed. For best results use before flowering. Many formulations are available, including ready-mixed spray guns and stick applicators. These are worth considering as you do not have to handle the chemical.

Path weedkillers can be applied with a watering can fitted with a dribble bar to distribute the liquid quickly and evenly. Use a can that is not used for watering plants. Weeds between paving slabs can be removed using a special weeder or a penknife.

Lawns often need to be treated with commercial weedkillers (see page 75).

Hand weeding

Remove the whole root system and throw in the dust-bin. Use a hoe to remove annual weeds. Hoeing is most effective when done on a warm, windy day, as the weeds dry out naturally on the soil surface. Annual weeds that have not flowered can be composted.

Weeding tools

A variety of inexpensive hand weeding tools is available for tackling weeds.

Handfork
Useful for digging out deep-rooted weeds in borders or vegetable plots.

Daisy grubber
Useful for lawns with a few large weeds.

Onion hoe
For those who like to kneel down and hand weed small areas.

Dutch hoe
For controlling annual weeds between plants.

Paving weeder
An alternative to using a path weedkiller on small areas of paving.

WEEDING TIPS

● *Do not leave bare patches of earth for weeds to colonise. Instead, use ground-cover plants or mulch well.*

● *Before planting, clear the plot of weeds. It is easier to weed unplanted ground than to weed between plants.*

● *Start weeding in early spring: weeds are easier to eradicate while they are young. Remove weeds before they seed.*

● *Weed regularly. Constant weeding when weeds reappear will eventually bring them under control.*

● *Dig out deep-rooted weeds. Try to remove as much of the root as possible.*

● *When using weedkillers, follow the instructions carefully and be prepared to reapply.*

Using a daisy grubber

Insert the narrow blade down near the root and pull it up. The weed, root and all, should come out without leaving a large hole.

Using a paving weeder

Push the weeder backwards and forwards in between slabs to sever the weeds. Inset: Use the hook end to pull out the severed weeds. Put all the pieces of weed in the dustbin.

Using a Dutch hoe

Annual weeds that grow between plants can be kept under control by regular hoeing. Use the hoe with a skimming action over the surface of the soil.

Mulching

MULCHING – COVERING the surface of the soil with an appropriate organic or inorganic material – prevents moisture from evaporating from the soil surface and, if applied correctly, prevents weeds from growing. Mulches are a boon for the weekend gardener as they can save you time on weeding and watering throughout the growing season. Mulches can be in the form of a loose material that is applied around established plants or a sheet that is put down before planting. Make sure that the organic mulching material itself is free from any annual weeds.

The best time to apply a mulch is when the soil is warm and contains plenty of moisture. There is little point in applying a mulch in hot weather, when the soil is baked dry. However, one drawback of any mulch is that, if it is applied to cold soil, it acts as an insulator; the soil remains cold, as the sun can't reach it, and this hinders plant growth. Loose organic mulches can be dug in after about six months to improve the soil structure.

Ground clearing

Inorganic sheet mulches can also be used to clear a large, weed-infested area. Use any cheap material, such as old rugs or carpeting, plastic sheets, or lots of layers of newspaper, rather than a proprietary mulch.

Secure the sheets by digging a trench around them and then burying the edges (see opposite). Leave the sheets in place for a year, then remove them and dig the plot. This technique kills off even stubborn perennial weeds as it starves them of light.

Mulches

The factors to consider when choosing a mulch are cost, durability and appearance. Inorganic mulches, such as sheets of polythene, can be used with a thin layer of loose, organic mulch to improve the appearance. Loose mulches should be at least 5 cm (2 in) deep to prevent weeds from growing through them.

Garden compost
This is free, but you will probably not be able to make enough. You can use shredded garden prunings and grass clippings but they may contain weed seeds.

Cocoa shell
This waste product from the chocolate industry is ideal around smaller plants. It is expensive and not durable but it is attractive and pleasant to handle.

Gravel
Attractive as a path or for beds, it conserves moisture in soil but annual weeds may still appear. Various grades and colours are available – but the finer the grade, the greater the risk of cats using it as litter.

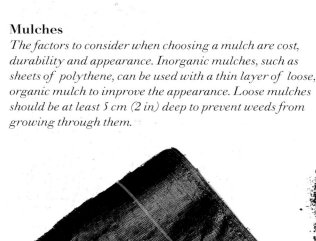

Woven polypropylene
Expensive but effective and durable, this heavy-duty material can be used under paths.

Fibre-bonded fleece
Specifically made for mulching, it is easy to handle and cut through. It is weedproof yet it allows in water and air. It is expensive but effective.

Black polythene
Cheap and effective but harder to lay than commercial mulching materials. Its durability depends on thickness.

Chipped bark
Easy to obtain, but look at samples before buying as quality varies. Aim for large chips of actual bark rather than wood. It is expensive but attractive. The durability depends on the grade.

Applying chipped-bark mulch

1 *Remove any weeds. Apply a general fertiliser to the soil, if necessary, and soak the ground if it is dry.*

2 *Next, apply a 5-cm (2-in) layer of chipped bark to the bare soil.*

Applying cocoa-shell mulch

1 *Remove any weeds and add fertiliser, if necessary. Water the ground if it is dry.*

2 *Apply a 5-cm (2-in) layer of dry cocoa shells over bare ground. Water the mulch to bind it and prevent it from blowing away.*

MULCHING TIPS

• *Mulch over the compost of container plants to conserve moisture. Cobbles and gravel look attractive in containers.*

• *When planting a specimen tree in a lawn, remove the surrounding turf as it will compete with the tree roots. Replace with a circular sheet mulch.*

• *To save money, recycle material from your garden to use in mulches. Grass clippings, shredded prunings, leafmould and garden compost are all good materials to use as mulches.*

• *Buy mulching material in bulk to save money.*

LAYING A SHEET MULCH

Sheet mulches are easiest to lay on new beds or unplanted areas. They can be unattractive, but can be easily disguised, and are an excellent method of mulching a large area.

1 *Clear any weeds and complete the soil preparation then position the sheet. Lay a seep hose under the sheet if watering is likely to be a problem.*

2 *Secure the edges of the sheet to hold it in place. Make a V-shaped trench with a spade and push the edges into the ground by hand.*

3 *Cut a cross with a sharp knife. Peel back the corners and dig out a hole in the ground underneath.*

4 *Insert the plant and push in firmly. It is important that the plant's roots make contact with the soil.*

5 *In an ornamental area, cover the sheet with an attractive loose mulch such as chipped bark. Commercial sheet mulch is expensive but durable.*

Buying Plants

THERE HAVE BEEN SIGNIFICANT improvements in plant labelling and presentation over the last few years. However, buying plants can still be bewildering. To help, use the chart on pages 26–27.

Nowadays, most hardy plants are available all year as they are sold in pots or containers. This means they can be planted at any time of year as they have a rootball to support them. However, the easiest time to plant is in spring or autumn as they will need less watering. The freshest stock is usually available in spring.

Plants are often sold bare rooted, which means they have been grown in a field rather than in pots. Bare-rooted plants are usually less expensive, but extra care is needed to protect the roots.

Buying good-quality plants
Most plants that have been recently delivered to garden centres are good quality and will establish well in your garden. Choose fresh plants that have plenty of young leaves or buds.

Flowering plants
When buying plants in flower, look for specimens with plenty of buds.

Plants with large foliage
Be sure that all the leaves are unblemished and intact.

Small pots
Plants in small pots dry out easily and need a lot of nutrients. Buy the freshest plants possible.

Bushy plants
Choose a stocky specimen that has lots of foliage and flowers.

Foliage colour
Look for leaves that are a healthy colour and avoid any that are mottled or have unnatural yellowing.

Plant names

Latin plant names are extremely useful for finding out more about the plant in reference books. There are two parts to a Latin name. The first tells you what genus (plant group) a plant belongs to. This, together with the second part, tells you the species; plants of the same species share most characteristics. If a non-Latin name in quotation marks follows, it indicates that this is a slight variation from the species. It may have been specially bred to produce a different flower colour or to have a different habit. For example, *Thymus* ('thyme') *vulgaris* ('common') 'Silver Posie' (a specific variety).

TIPS FOR BUYING HEALTHY PLANTS

Where to buy
Buy plants from an outlet that has a high turnover: fresh stock is invariably more healthy than older stock. Department stores, DIY stores and even petrol stations sell plants, but not all know how to look after them, or have the appropriate storage facilities. Retailers specialising in plants and gardening, such as garden centres and plant nurseries, do have that expertise and usually have a much wider range of plants for you to choose from.

Fresh plant
This plant is a well-branched, stocky specimen with a healthy colour and lots of foliage.

Older specimen
This tall, leggy plant has been on sale too long: note the roots on the surface and the poor shape.

Inspect the plant
Before you buy, always make a point of inspecting the plant carefully. There are five main things to look out for: plants that have plenty of new buds and shoots; well-branched, stocky specimens with a neat, overall shape; healthy roots; evidence that the plant has been correctly watered; and plants that are free of pests and diseases. See the column on the right for more information on how to check for these things.

Healthy leaves
The underside of the leaves should be free from pests.

Check the roots
Inspect the roots by tipping the plant out of its pot. Healthy roots of well-established plants hold the soil intact and lots of young roots – which are often creamy white – will be seen. If all the soil drops away, leaving a plant with small roots, this is a sign that the plant is not properly established. A potbound plant has a mass of dark brown roots growing around the sides and through the bottom of the pot, with little soil visible.

Healthy roots
Healthy roots that have filled out in the pot help the plant to get off to a good start in your garden.

Potbound plant
Roots growing through the bottom of the pot are the sign of a potbound plant. These will be harder to establish.

Check for signs of correct watering
Signs of underwatering are severe wilting, soil pulled away from the sides of the pot, and premature flowering. Overwatered plants could have damaged roots. Signs of overwatering are rotting foliage around the crown, grey mould and smelly soil.

Check for pests and diseases
Crowded plants can become leggy and susceptible to pests and diseases. Avoid plants that have aphids on the leaves and the shoot tips. You should also avoid foliage that is distorted or twisted, grey mould on the top growth, any unnatural, mottled yellow foliage, fine webbing beneath the leaves and loss of foliage (see pages 36–37).

Buying by mail order
Unpack the plants as soon they arrive. Contact the nursery at once if you find a problem. Try to plant bare-rooted plants immediately. If this is not possible because of bad weather, place them in pots of soil.

BUYING PLANTS (cont.)

It is easy to be tempted into buying plants without any clear idea of where you are going to put them or whether they will look good together. Try to decide in advance what you want to buy. You may be copying a specific planting scheme, in which case simply take along a list with a note of how many plants of each species you need for your space. If you are not copying a specific planting scheme, consult a plant reference book. If you cannot decide in advance, note down the size of the space you are trying to fill and consult the plant label before buying to check how tall the plant will grow and what its final spread will be.

Choose plants that are suitable for your garden. Note whether your site is sunny or shaded, and what the soil type is (see pages 14–15). If you have doubts about the suitability of a plant, consult the sales staff.

The following chart sets out the best time of year to buy the main types of plants and gives details of the forms in which you will find them.

GUIDE TO BUYING PLANTS

Plant type	When to buy	Description
Shrubs & trees	Available all year. The freshest stock is usually available in autumn or spring.	Shrubs and trees are woody, permanent plants. Younger plants usually establish better and catch up with more expensive, larger specimens. Check the rootball carefully. Look for well-shaped plants with plenty of healthy foliage. Bare-rooted plants from mail-order nurseries are usually sent out from autumn to spring.
Hedging plants	Available all year.	Pot-grown hedging plants are available from garden centres, but they are expensive. If you need a lot of hedging plants, buy bare-rooted plants from mail-order hedging specialists and plant in autumn or spring.
Climbers	Available all year.	Most climbers are permanent plants sold in tall pots and trained to grow up a stake. Some, such as sweet peas, are annuals and can be bought as seed or young plants. If you are buying clematis, try to buy it when it is in flower, as it is often wrongly labelled and can only be correctly identified by its flowers.
Roses	Buy bare-rooted plants in autumn. Container-grown plants should be bought from spring to summer.	Bare-rooted roses are generally inexpensive, but will not be in flower when purchased. Container-grown roses cost more. If you buy a container-grown rose, make sure that it has a full rootball.
Herbaceous perennials	Available all year, but the freshest stock is available in the spring and early summer.	These are non-woody, permanent plants that grow above ground from spring to summer, with the top growth dying back during the winter. A few may be tender and need protecting from frost in some areas. Small pots are available in spring, larger more expensive pots from late spring to summer. Autumn is a good time to plant, but the top growth will have started to die down. Always check the roots and crown before you buy. Bare-rooted plants from mail-order nurseries are usually sent out from autumn to spring.

26

Plant type	When to buy	Description
Annuals	Order from seed catalogues in winter or buy seed from shops or garden centres from winter to spring.	These are plants that flower and seed during the first year. They can be raised from seed or bought as plants (see below).
Bedding plants for summer colour	Buy in spring or early summer.	These are temporary plants that remain in the garden for just one season. Some are tender perennials while others are half-hardy annuals, and they are often used in containers or beds. They can be bought at various stages of development from seedlings to more developed, pot-grown plants. You can buy plants or seeds by mail order or from garden centres. The more advanced the plant is when you buy it, the easier it is to look after. However, remember that you will pay extra for this. Do not plant tender plants until after the last frost in your area.
Bedding plants for spring colour	Buy in autumn or spring.	Similar to bedding plants for summer colour (see above), but these plants are hardy, so they can be planted in the autumn to provide a flowering display in the spring. After they have flowered, remove them to make way for summer bedding.
Bulbs for spring colour	Buy as dry bulbs in autumn and pot-grown plants in spring.	Dry bulbs can be bought loose or prepacked, but loose bulbs are easier to inspect for firmness and damage. Dry bulbs are relatively inexpensive but pot-grown bulbs are becoming increasingly popular as they will provide colour more quickly. Snowdrops are often sold 'in the green' — that is, as plants with green leaves that have already flowered. For conservation reasons, try to buy snowdrops that have not been collected from the wild. Most spring bulbs are permanent. Tulips are the exception, as they may last for only a few years.
Bulbs for summer colour	Available as dry bulbs in spring and pot-grown plants in summer.	Similar to bulbs for spring colour (see above), but many summer-flowering bulbs are not hardy so do not plant them until after the last frosts in your area. To keep them as permanent plants, lift them from the ground and store before the frosts start in the autumn.
Alpines	Available all year. The freshest stock is available in the spring.	These small, neat plants are ideal for rock gardens and are usually sold in small pots. Before buying, check that the soil is not over-wet and that the top of the plant is not rotten.

Sowing Seeds

IF YOU'RE A BEGINNER, sowing plants from seed might sound a little ambitious, but in fact it is remarkably simple. Follow the guidelines outlined on these two pages and you will never look back. You need only a small range of tools and materials (see below). Sowing from seed is also far less expensive than buying established plants – an important consideration if you have a large area to fill.

If you're not sure when to sow, or whether to sow under cover or outdoors, consult the seed packet; most come with clear sowing and raising instructions. However, if the weather is especially cold or wet, or if you have a heavy, clay soil, then it is worth raising seeds under cover even if the packet tells you that you can sow them outdoors.

Seeds in unopened foil packets last for several years, although the seed starts to deteriorate once the packet is opened. However, even an opened packet can be kept until the following year if you store it in an airtight container in a dry, cool place.

Tools and materials for growing seeds

You need only a few simple tools and materials to raise your own plants from seed. The basic items, shown below, are all inexpensive and easy to obtain.

Dibber
Use this small device for making holes in potting compost when preparing to transplant seedlings. You can improvise with the pointed end of a pencil.

Thermometer
Not essential, but useful for monitoring the temperature of your seeds. Many bedding plants germinate most rapidly between 15–18°C (60–65°F).

Potting compost
Use fresh potting compost that is weed-, fungi-, insect- and disease-free. Garden compost or garden soil is not suitable for seeds.

Labels
Label trays with the variety of seed and the date sown. Also include important germination instructions for later reference.

Mister
Use a plastic bottle with an adjustable nozzle to keep seeds moist without dislodging them. It can also be used to apply fungicide.

Vermiculite
These light and absorbent heat-treated particles of mica slowly release water and nutrients to seed starters. Add a thin layer over seeds that are sown on the surface of the potting compost.

Seed starter containers
Grow a single seedling in each cell to enable roots to grow with minimal disturbance. A peat-based soil is essential for small trays.

Propagator
A propagator is like a miniature greenhouse, allowing you to control the seed's environment. They range from ones with simple lids with adjustable vents, to those with a heater and thermostat to provide heat from below.

Flat trays
Flat trays have a larger surface area of compost than round pots, so you can raise more seeds. They also fit into propagators more easily than round pots.

Sowing seed under cover

If you sow seed under cover, in a greenhouse, a propagator or in the house, you will be able to exercise much more control over the growing conditions.

1 Slightly overfill the seed tray with fresh, peat-based compost, breaking up compacted chunks, then level with a soil-firming board. Stand the tray in water until the surface becomes moist.

2 To sow large seeds (shown above), hold them in the palm of one hand and space individual seeds on the soil surface. For small seeds, gently tap the packet to scatter the seeds evenly over the soil .

3 Using a flower pot or a sieve, cover the seeds with a thin layer of potting compost. If your seeds need light to germinate (the seed packet will give you this information), cover them with vermiculite.

4 Label the tray. Place it in a propagator or cover with glass or a clear plastic bag until the seedlings are large enough to handle. If the potting soil dries out, water from below or mist with warm water.

TRANSPLANTING SEEDLINGS

When the first true leaves appear, thin out and transplant seedlings into larger trays, or to other parts of the garden, to give them more space to grow. Handle each seedling by the leaves to avoid crushing the stem. (If a leaf is crushed, the seedling will still survive.)

Make a hole with a dibber or the tip of a pen or pencil, and ease the seedling in. Gently firm the soil around the seedling with your fingers. Water with warm water.

Hardening off

Seedlings raised under cover need to get used to outdoor conditions gradually before they can be planted outside – a process known as 'hardening off', which takes seven to ten days. Place the plants in a closed cold frame – an unheated box with a hinged glass top. Open the lid during daylight hours, opening it wider each day until the plants adjust. Close the lid at night. Keep the seedlings watered. Add half the recommended amount of liquid fertiliser to the water. If you do not have a cold frame, set the plants outside on warm sunny days, increasing the amount of time you leave them outside each day. Bring them in at night. Later in the season, cover with a double layer of fibre-bonded fleece at night.

Sowing seeds outdoors

Many hardy annual and perennial flowers, such as pot marigolds and night-scented stock, germinate so easily that it would be a waste of effort not to sow them outdoors, where you want them to flower; consult the seed packet for details. After sowing, keep the weeds down by hoeing and hand weeding. Thin the plants out when large enough to handle (see below left).

1 First prepare a weed-free seed bed. Rake the soil so that it is level and has a crumbly texture.

2 Mark out the area you are planning to sow with light-coloured sand or vermiculite.

3 Scratch out shallow lines with a stake, varying the angle from patch to patch. The lines should be 15–30 cm (6–12 in) apart depending on the plant. Consult the seed packet for details.

4 Water the soil before you sow if necessary. Sow thinly, taking a pinch of seed between thumb and forefinger. Cover the seeds with soil and firm down the soil.

Planting

THE NEXT FOUR PAGES address the most common types of plants you are likely to encounter and show you, step by step, how to plant them. Before you plant, however, always clear the site of any weeds and add soil improvers if necessary (see pages 16–21).

Spacing is also important: almost all plants will grow to be considerably bigger than they were when you bought them. The plant label should tell you what the final height and spread are likely to be. Planting too close together makes extra work later as the plants can crowd each other out, while planting too far apart leaves space for weeds to colonise. This is less critical for annuals and summer bedding plants that only last for one season, as they do not spread far.

Planting equipment

For successful planting you will want to invest in a few multi-purpose, quality tools. The tools shown below are a good basic starting kit.

Trowel
Use for planting bedding plants and small perennials.

Hand fork
Use for weeding and cultivating the soil around established plants.

Bulb planter
This takes out a core of earth of uniform depth. Use for planting large numbers of bulbs or for planting bulbs in grass.

Spade
Use for digging planting holes for trees and shrubs.

Planting containers

Containers of all sizes are planted in the same way. Make sure water can drain away, so that the plants do not get waterlogged. Containers can dry out quickly, so incorporate water-retaining granules to reduce the amount of watering you need to do.

Although hanging baskets may look more complicated than other types of container, the principles of planting them are exactly the same (see page 62). A wide range of baskets and liners is available, but if you want to plant over the sides of a basket, opt for a traditional wire-mesh basket lined with sphagnum moss.

1 *Choose a container with drainage holes. Place a layer of pebbles or broken ceramic shards in the bottom to encourage drainage.*

2 *Add a layer of a suitable growing medium for your chosen plants. Crumble some slow-release fertiliser granules into the pot.*

3 *Prepare some water-retaining granules according to the instructions on the packet. Inset: Add the granules to the container and mix in to the soil.*

4 *Plant your largest plants first, laying a stake across the top of the pot to check that the plant is level. Add the rest of your plants, working outwards from the centre. Finally, water the container.*

Planting bulbs, tubers and corms

Bulbs, tubers and corms are dormant when you buy them. Plant them as soon as you buy them, or, if this is not possible, store in a cool, dry place. Most bulbs, tubers and corms require a free-draining soil. If the soil is heavy, a shallow layer of fine gravel at the bottom of the hole will help to prevent them from rotting. If you want to keep tubers for several years, remove them and store over winter, then plant the following spring.

Planting bulbs in grass

To achieve a natural effect, plant bulbs randomly but at least one bulb-width apart. Scatter large bulbs by hand and plant with a bulb planter. Plant smaller bulbs by lifting a section of turf.

1 *Mow the grass to make planting easier. Scatter the bulbs randomly over the planting area.*

2 *Make a hole with a bulb planter. Inset: Plant a bulb, pointed end upwards, making sure it touches the hole base.*

3 *Release the core of soil from the bulb planter. Press the turf down gently.*

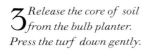

PLANTING DEPTHS FOR BULBS

Plant bulbs so that they are covered with two to three times their height of soil for optimum growth. Always check the instructions on the packet for precise planting details.

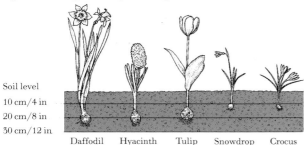

Soil level
10 cm/4 in
20 cm/8 in
30 cm/12 in

Daffodil   Hyacinth   Tulip   Snowdrop   Crocus

Planting water plants

Spring is the best time to add water plants to your pond. Floating plants, such as *Stratiotes aloides*, can simply be thrown into the water, as can oxygenating plants such as *Elodea canadensis*. Push marginal plants into the soft mud at the edge of the pond.

To plant true water plants, follow the instructions below. Any submerged leaves will soon grow to reach the surface of the water.

1 *Line a special plastic water-plant container with hessian and half fill with soil. (The hessian prevents the soil from leaking out.) Inset: Carefully place the water plant in the container and gently firm around the stem .*

2 *Cover the surface of the pot with gravel to prevent the plant from floating to the top of the pond once it has been planted. Gently position the container on the bottom or, in a prefabricated pond, on a shelf at the side of the pond.*

Planting bedding plants

A wide range of bedding plants can be bought from garden centres or by mail order. Harden your plants off in a cold frame for seven to ten days before planting them outside. Do not plant tender plants until the frosts are over in your area.

1 *Allow the plants to soak in a shallow tray of water for about 20 minutes. Potting compost is prone to drying out as the pots are small.*

2 *Space out the plants in the border. Remove them from their pots or packs. Cut bedding strips into sections. Plant and firm the soil around the plants.*

Planting ground-cover plants

Ground-cover plants are either perennials or shrubs and should be planted in the same way (see below and right). Make sure the beds are free from perennial weeds before planting as weeds are very difficult to eradicate once the ground cover has become established.

Often a planting distance is suggested for a particular plant when you buy it. Close spacings provide quick cover, while wider spacings require fewer plants and so prove less expensive. However, remember that you will need to keep the ground between the plants weed free.

If you are using ivy as a ground-cover plant, make U-shaped pegs from 20-cm (8-in) lengths of galvanised wire and use them to pin the stems down to the ground at intervals. Cover the pegs with soil. The stems will root into the ground, giving you quicker cover.

Planting perennials

Perennials are often planted in groups of three or five, to create an impact. Buy several small plants or divide up larger ones. Plant bare-rooted perennials in the same way as bare-rooted shrubs (see right).

1 Set the plants on the soil while they are still in their pots to check the planting distances and positions.

2 Water the plants, allow to drain, then plant at the same level they were in the pot.

3 Firm the plant into the soil so the roots are in contact with the soil. Water again if necessary. If slugs and snails are a problem in your garden, use a product containing aluminium sulphate to control them; traditional slug pellets are known to harm wildlife.

Planting shrubs and hedging plants

When planting hedging plants or several shrubs in a border, be sure to allow them enough space to grow without crowding each other. Shrubs and hedges are easier to plant than trees (see right); there is no need to stake them and it is not normally necessary to install a hose for watering. As they have several stems, it is not critical to protect them from predators such as rabbits, but, if necessary, encircle the shrub with wire mesh.

1 Turn over and weed the site. Set the plants at the correct planting distance. For hedging (shown here), stretch a taut string across the area to be sure you plant in a straight line.

2 Dig a hole for each plant. Check the spacing with a stake that you have cut to the correct planting distance.

3 Firm the ground around the base of each plant with your foot. Water thoroughly, directing the water to the base of the plant.

TIPS FOR PLANTING BARE-ROOTED PLANTS

To protect the roots from drying out before planting, cover them with damp hessian. When you plant, spread the roots out evenly around the plant and make sure there is soil all around the roots. Bare-rooted deciduous plants should be planted in late autumn, winter or early spring – though not when the ground is frozen. Bare-rooted evergreens should be planted in mid-spring.

Planting climbers and climbing roses

Soil at the base of a wall, tree or hedge is likely to be impoverished, so when you are planting a climber or climbing rose always try to dig a hole at least 22.5 cm (9 in) away where the soil is more fertile and moist. If this is not possible, be sure to add plenty of soil improvers to the planting hole and mulch well to get the best out of your soil.

Plant climbers and climbing roses at an angle of about 45 degrees, so that they lean towards the support.

When you are planting climbing roses, always try to choose a fresh site in the garden. Soil that has had roses growing in it for several years can become 'rose sick', so any new rose planted there is unlikely to thrive.

1 *Dig a large hole at least 22.5 cm (9 in) away from the wall, shrub or hedge. If you are planting a clematis, the hole should be about 15 cm (6 in) deeper than the pot in which you bought the plant. Add a soil improver (see pages 17–19) to the planting hole.*

2 *Plant the climber. Firm the soil around the base of the stem and water thoroughly.*

3 *Use a stake to guide the climber to the support. This could be a wooden trellis positioned against a wall or a host plant, such as a strong shrub or a tree. Secure the climber to the stake with string.*

Planting trees

Trees, like shrubs, ground-cover plants, climbers and hedging, are long-term plants and may need a little extra effort to get them established. Make sure the tree is well watered before you plant it and dig a sufficiently large planting hole to take the rootball. Mulching after planting will also help the tree to thrive without competition from other plants and weeds.

1 *Remove a wide circle of turf. Dig a large hole to encourage new roots to spread. Add a handful of bone meal to the topsoil removed from the planting hole.*

2 *Large trees need a stake to anchor them while the roots establish. Drive a stake into the ground at least 60 cm (2 ft) deeper than the bottom of the planting hole. Inset: Lay a hose around the circumference of the planting hole with one end open at the surface so you can pour water directly onto the rootball.*

3 *Remove the tree from its container and position it in the hole. Replace half the soil around the tree to steady it, then protect the tree with a plastic stem guard.*

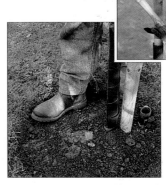

4 *Replace the rest of the soil, firm down, and mulch. Inset: Attach the tree to the stake with a tree tie (a rubber belt with an adjustable buckle). Nail the belt to the stake to secure it.*

Watering

WHEN WATERING YOUR GARDEN, concentrate your efforts on watering the plants that need it most. Make the task as easy as possible by planning ahead and investing in good equipment.

Soak beds or borders and lawns thoroughly once or twice a week. This is better than adding a little water every day. Light watering encourages the roots to grow around the surface of the soil rather than to grow down into the ground. Direct water at the plant's base. Water steadily, letting the soil absorb the water before you add more. If the flow is too fast, water will run off the plant, washing away soil and exposing surface roots.

Watering equipment
These are basic watering items that are essential in most gardens. There are many more items ranging from devices for watering growing bags to sophisticated irrigation systems.

Watering can
Many styles are available in metal or plastic, but those with a long spout and a detachable rose are the most versatile. Some come with a dribble bar attachment. Buy several watering cans in different colours if you need one for mixing chemicals.

Seep hose
These are made from recycled rubber tyres. The sides leak water along the length of the hose. This is an easy way to water newly planted beds or hedging. Lay the hose on the soil surface around the plants or bury it in the ground.

Hose
Essential in all but the smallest garden. The easiest to use are those on a reel or a cassette. Many attachments are available. You can also buy devices for guiding the hose around corners without kinking.

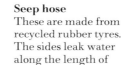

Sprinkler
A hose attachment that sends droplets of water over a large area. Some types send out a static spray pattern; others oscillate or rotate the spray. A sprinkler can be used for watering lawns or beds. It can be wasteful: in hot weather much of the spray evaporates and in wind the spray is blown off target.

Easier watering

To save the time and effort of carrying water yourself, you can set up a watering system that moves water directly to your plants. Once it is set up, all you need to do is turn on the tap. Or, to ensure that your plants are watered regularly, you can install an electronic water timer that can be programmed to turn the water on and off for you at pre-set times. You can buy a complete kit or buy the components separately and design a system to suit your own garden.

There are various brands, but all work on the same principle. A supply tube (the diameter of a standard hose) has lengths of secondary tubing (micro tubing) inserted via adaptors at intervals along its length. The micro tubing, which is about 4 mm ($^3/_{16}$ in) in diameter, takes water from the supply tube directly to each plant. A device that emits water is connected to the end of each length of micro tubing. Some devices cause a steady drip of water; others come out as a spray. Watering systems take time to set up and dismantle at the start and end of the growing season, but they save lots of time during the summer months.

Water barrel

Attach a downspout to your guttering, and direct rain water into a barrel where you can store it to use later for watering plants. Rain water is ideal for acid-loving plants but do not use it on young seedlings. Buy a barrel with a lid, to keep out dirt, and a tap. You may need to raise the water barrel so that a watering can fits easily underneath the tap.

WATERING HANGING BASKETS

Hanging baskets are often positioned above head height, which can make caring for them difficult. Also, because much of the growing matter is exposed, they may need watering up to twice a day in hot weather — although you can add water-retaining granules to the basket to reduce moisture loss from the soil (see page 63).

Watering above head height
To make watering easier, attach a specially designed extender to your watering can or hose. You can also tie a stake to the end of your hose (as shown) to make the hose more rigid.

TIPS FOR WATERING

- *Make watering new plants, planted less than two years ago, a priority as their roots have not developed sufficiently to seek out water deep in the soil.*

- *Containers may need daily watering. Large containers do not dry out as quickly as small ones. Position pots in light shade during the day.*

- *Herbs, mature trees, shrubs and perennials should be able to cope during dry spells without watering. Lawns revive when it rains, so they are not a priority.*

- *Collect rain water in barrels. Use waste water, such as bath water, on older plants. Do not re-use greasy water.*

- *Insert a flower pot or hollow tube into the soil when planting specimen plants. You can pour water straight into the pot or tube to direct water to the plant roots. For beds of smaller plants, lay in a seep hose.*

- *Young seedlings and plants in containers should be watered from below to prevent them from being dislodged.*

- *Reduce evaporation of water from the soil surface by applying a mulch in spring. Watering early in the morning or early evening, when the sun is low in the sky, also helps minimise evaporation.*

Pests and Diseases

PREVENTION OF A PROBLEM is always better than the cure. Good gardening practices, such as regular weeding, clearing garden debris that may harbour pests and diseases, and keeping your plants watered and nourished, will do much to protect the health of your plants and to minimise the likelihood of problems arising. Encouraging natural predators, such as frogs, hedgehogs, birds, hoverflies and ladybirds into your garden will also help deal with many of the most common garden pests (aphids, slugs and snails) in an

ecologically friendly way. The other benefit of using natural predators is that you can avoid the over-use of environmentally harmful chemical controls.

If pests or diseases do occur, always deal with the problem as promptly as possible (see chart, below, for details of how to control some of the most common pests and diseases). Remove affected plant material as soon as you see the first signs of attack. Dispose of diseased material in the dustbin rather than on the compost heap to prevent the problem from spreading.

COMMON PESTS AND DISEASES: HOW TO PREVENT AND CONTROL THEM

Pest or disease	Symptom	Prevention and control
Aphids *Left:* Black fly (black aphid) on golden feverfew (*Tanacetum parthenium*)	Colonies of sap-sucking insects – often green or black. Usually found on young tips. There may also be a sticky honeydew and a black mould. Aphids are widespread and thrive in warm, sheltered conditions.	Encourage natural predators such as hoverflies and ladybirds. If aphids do appear, apply a contact insecticide: a systemic insecticide will work for about two weeks. Organic soap sprays are also available.
Caterpillars *Left:* Caterpillar of large white butterfly (*Pieris brassicae*)	Petals and leaves eaten; caterpillars often seen inside flowers. Caterpillars thrive particularly in weedy, uncultivated ground.	Cover vulnerable plants with fine netting to prevent butterflies from laying their eggs. Pick off small infestations by hand or use a contact insecticide.
Slugs and snails *Left:* Slug on hosta leaf	Irregular holes eaten in the plant. Slime trails near the plant. Slugs and snails thrive in damp, shaded sites.	Put a ring of gravel or sharp sand around the base of young plants to prevent slugs and snails from reaching the stem, or scatter a product containing aluminium sulphate around young plants.
Whitefly *Left:* Whitefly and eggs on underside of leaf	Leaves are pale and sticky. Clouds of tiny white flies take off when the leaves are shaken.	Remove garden debris in the autumn, since whitefly eggs may overwinter on leaves. Plant French marigolds (*Tagetes patula*) near vulnerable plants. If whitefly do appear, use a suitable insecticide. Several applications may be needed.

Pest or disease	Symptom	Prevention and control
Downy mildew *Left:* Downy mildew on pea leaves	Leaves have yellow blotches and beige felt-like patches on the upper surface and greyish or purplish-white patches of fluffy growth on the lower surface. Downy mildew is likely to occur in cool, humid places and when plants are crowded together.	If possible, plant varieties that are sold as being resistant to downy mildew. If downy mildew does occur, destroy affected leaves and spray with a suitable fungicide.
Damping off *Left:* Cress seedlings grown on infected soil (left) and healthy soil (right)	Seedlings collapse at soil level. The problem often starts in small patches of seedlings and then spreads. Damping off tends to occur in cool, moist conditions.	This is a soil- and water-borne fungus; using fresh compost and clean water can prevent the problem, as can spraying with a suitable fungicide. If it does occur, remove and destroy any collapsed seedlings.
Powdery mildew *Left:* Powdery mildew on *Rosa* 'Iceberg' buds and leaves	The upper surface of the leaves and shoots are covered in a white powder. Powdery mildew tends to occur in cool, humid conditions.	To prevent powdery mildew, keep plants well watered and avoid over-crowding. If it does occur, destroy affected leaves and spray with a systemic fungicide.
Rust *Left:* Rust on hypericum leaves	Symptoms vary but may include raised orange or brown spots on the lower leaf surface and stem. Rust tends to occur in humid conditions.	Prevent rust by improving air circulation around plants, and gathering up plant debris and weeds. If it does occur, destroy affected leaves or, if the whole plant is affected, dig up and burn. Spray remaining plants with systemic fungicide.
Viruses *Left:* Yellow stripe virus on *Narcissus* sp. leaves	Flecks or mottling on the leaves or flowers are usually a sign of a virus, although the patterns vary. The plant looks stunted or distorted. Viruses are carried by insect pests such as aphids.	Buy certified virus-free plants if they are available. Prevent viruses by controlling aphid attacks promptly, since aphids carry viruses. Viruses cannot be treated once they occur. Dig up and destroy the whole plant.

TIPS FOR PREVENTING PROBLEMS

• *Check the undersides of leaves and the growing tips of new plants for pests and diseases before you plant them.*

• *If a disease has been a problem in your garden, look for varieties that are resistant to specific diseases.*

• *Clear up plant debris, such as fallen leaves, weeds and old pots. A neat, tidy garden offers fewer hiding places for pests than a weedy, badly tended one.*

• *Inspect young growth on plants regularly and take action promptly if there are any problems.*

• *The warm, humid conditions of a greenhouse are ideal for pests and diseases, so good hygiene and ventilation are especially important in greenhouses.*

• *Avoid over-crowding plants. Space them so that air can circulate between them and you can easily pick off dead foliage.*

• *Destroy infected plants by burning them or discarding them in a dustbin; never put them on the compost heap.*

• *Healthy plants are more likely to survive the onslaught of pests and diseases, so always carry out routine maintenance.*

Caring for Perennials

PERENNIALS DO NOT NEED to be replaced each year like bedding plants or hardy annuals. Once planted, they will come up year after year. How much maintenance they need depends on the species, although all need dead heading and cutting back each autumn (see page 39).

Staking and supporting

Choosing perennials that do not need staking can save time, but most gardeners have a few favourite plants that they are prepared to go to the trouble of supporting in order to show off the flowers. Plants and trees that are over 1.2 m (4 ft) tall need to be staked for the first two years in order to support the plant. Stakes need to be in place by late spring, while the stems are still young and flexible and before the plant flowers. The plant should then grow through the staking system. The stake should not be visible once the tree or plant begins to flower. Supports are usually taken away in late autumn, when the plants are cut back.

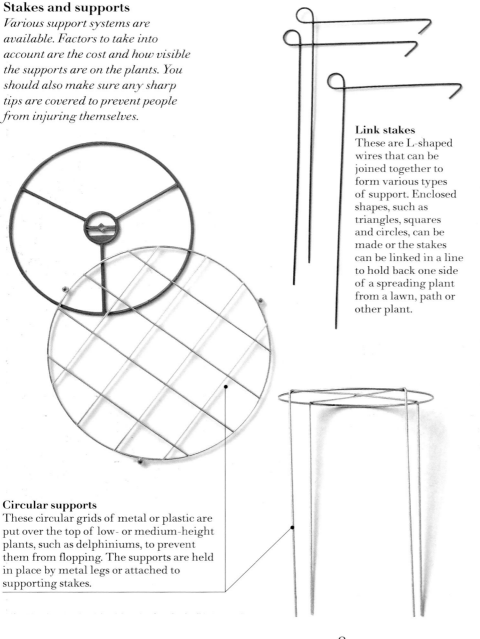

Stakes and supports
Various support systems are available. Factors to take into account are the cost and how visible the supports are on the plants. You should also make sure any sharp tips are covered to prevent people from injuring themselves.

Link stakes
These are L-shaped wires that can be joined together to form various types of support. Enclosed shapes, such as triangles, squares and circles, can be made or the stakes can be linked in a line to hold back one side of a spreading plant from a lawn, path or other plant.

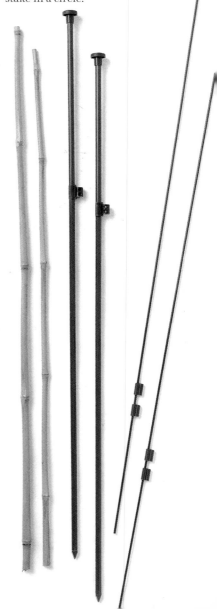

Single stakes
One of the cheapest methods, particularly suitable for tall, large plants. Insert a circle of three or more stakes around the plant. Wrap string or twine around each stake in a circle.

Circular supports
These circular grids of metal or plastic are put over the top of low- or medium-height plants, such as delphiniums, to prevent them from flopping. The supports are held in place by metal legs or attached to supporting stakes.

Staking methods

The method you choose depends on the plant's strength and how you want to display it. Plants with woody stems need more support than soft-stemmed ones.

Stakes and string

1 *Insert 4 stakes into the ground in a circle around the plant, to a depth of 10–15 cm (4–6 in).*

2 *Wind string around each stake. Start near the bottom of the stakes. Repeat higher up as necessary.*

Link stakes

1 *Insert the longest end into the ground, join another stake on at the top, then insert into the ground.*

2 *Continue until a line of stakes has been formed. This will hold back a plant encroaching on a path or lawn.*

Circular supports

1 *Bend the rods into a circle and secure with a connector.*

2 *Adjust the position and size of the ring to suit the plant.*

Dead heading and cutting back

Remove dead flowers promptly. Although most perennials should be cut in late autumn, they can be cut back in spring. Dead growth is ideal for the compost heap.

Plants requiring winter protection need a 15-cm (6-in) layer of insulation such as chipped bark or dead leaves. Remove insulation in spring or the plants may rot.

PROPAGATING PERENNIALS

Propagating is an economical and enjoyable way of increasing your existing plant stock and experimenting with new varieties.

Division

Plant roots can become crowded and deplete the soil. Rejuvenate perennials by dividing the whole plant and replanting the healthiest sections. This process can also be used to propagate more plants.

Divide plants in spring or autumn when the plant is dormant. Lift out large clumps with fibrous roots first to allow you to divide the plant without trampling on neighbouring plants. Smaller sections can be divided by hand. Split dense or woody plant crowns with a sharp spade or knife. Plants with rhizomes (underground stems) are easy to lift up from the soil. Cut into sections, making sure that each section has at least one shoot and some roots. Mature perennials need to be divided only every three to four years.

Cuttings

There are a variety of ways in which to take cuttings, depending on the season and the maturity of the plant, but usually softwood cuttings, taken in late spring or early summer, are the most successful. If this method does not work, use the same technique to take semi-ripe cuttings in late summer.

Rooted geranium cutting
A softwood cutting (see below) was taken in spring.

1 *Cut 7.5 cm (3 in) off a strong, young shoot with a sharp knife. Remove lower leaves and dip stem in hormone rooting powder or liquid.*

2 *Plant the cutting in potting compost and water. Cover the pot with thin plastic wrap and put in a shaded cold frame.*

Pruning

MANY TREES AND SHRUBS do not need regular pruning, just an occasional cutting back to keep them under control. Plants trained into formal shapes, such as wall shrubs or hedges, also need regular pruning to maintain their shape. There are a few exceptions that benefit from annual pruning; check the plant label whenever you buy new plants.

Whatever shrubs you have, always remove dead or diseased branches that can spread to the rest of the plant. You can distinguish dead wood from live wood by scratching the stem with your thumbnail. If green-coloured wood is exposed, then the stem is still alive; if it is brown or white, then the stem is dead.

Knowing whether your shrubs flower best on old wood or on new will help you decide the best time to prune. Old wood is usually darker with a rougher surface, and new wood is lighter and smoother. Once a stem has flowered well, cut it back to allow room for replacement flowering stems to develop the following year. Remember, always feed the plant after pruning to encourage new growth. Mulch in spring after the weather has warmed up.

Pruning tools

Most pruning can be done with secateurs. Large hedges, however, may require shears or a hedgetrimmer. For more mature trees and shrubs, with branches larger than 1 cm (⅜ in) in diameter, you need one or more of the following tools. Take into account the height and accessibility of your trees and shrubs when choosing tools.

Hedge shears
Ideal for new or small hedges, topiary and low-growing shrubs such as heathers. The blades need to be kept sharp and adjusted so that they cut efficiently.

Secateurs
An essential garden tool. Keep the blades sharp; it is worth buying a brand that offers replacement blades. Check that the handles are comfortable and the safety catch is easy to use.

Loppers
Ideal for cutting branches up to 3 cm (1⅛ in) in diameter. The long handles make it easier to reach into prickly or congested shrubs. Some models are heavier than others, so handle a few before buying.

Hedgetrimmer
The longer the blade, the quicker you can cut. Gas-powered models may be best for a large garden. Electric trimmers are less expensive, lighter, and quieter. Battery-powered versions are also worth considering. Choose a model with plenty of safety features.

Pruning saw
A useful tool for branches over 2.5 cm (1 in). The arrow tip makes it easy to cut between branches. Choose a model that can be folded up when not in use.

Bow saw
A fast way to cut thick branches and logs. Replacement blades are available.

Shredder
A shredder is worth considering if your garden produces a lot of tree and shrub prunings. Shredded prunings can be used as mulch or added to a compost heap. This is kinder to the environment than burning them. Shredders are expensive to buy and need to be stored safely. You will need protection from the noise as well as gloves and eye protection. Choose a model that offers safety features and can be moved around easily.

Making the right cut

Make clean cuts with sharp blades. A blunt blade means you have to pull and twist to make a cut, which causes damage to the plant tissue. The angle of the cuts depends on how the buds are arranged on the stem. Most stems have alternate buds (see below). Make a sloping cut just above a bud so that any rain will run away from it. This will reduce the risk of a water-born infection. For opposite buds, cut straight across.

Alternate buds
For a plant that has alternate buds (buds that are placed alternately up the shoot), prune with a diagonal cut just above an outward-facing bud, as shown.

Opposite buds
For a plant that has opposite buds, prune with a straight cut across the stem directly above the buds.

When to prune

Pruning in winter produces vigorous growth the next season as the plant's energy is directed to fewer buds. Pruning in summer removes leaves that produce the plant's food, thereby slowing down growth. Pruning in the later summer or autumn can stimulate fresh growth that may be vulnerable in frosty weather, so it is usually not recommended (although tall, shallow-rooted plants, such as rambling roses, are an exception since they can be damaged by high winds).

Generally, winter or early spring is the time to prune plants that flower in late summer, whereas plants that flower in spring or early summer should be pruned once their flowers have faded. Try to prune at the right time – but if you are in doubt, remember that pruning at the wrong time is unlikely to do irrevocable damage.

Pruning overgrown shrubs

Pruning is essential if your shrubs are overgrown. (This applies to both deciduous and evergreen shrubs.) Stagger the reshaping of overgrown shrubs over a three-year period to minimise shock to the plant. In the first year, cut out one stem in three after the shrub has flowered. (If the shrub flowers after midsummer, do not prune until early the following spring.)

Cut out old or sickly stems or badly placed branches. Leave the shrub alone for a year to produce new growth. In the second and third years, tackle the remaining old growth. You will need loppers and a pruning saw (see opposite) to prune mature shrubs.

☐ Young shoots

✺ Old shoots

Stagger the pruning of overgrown shrubs
Remove one third of the old stems after flowering in the first year. Trim remaining old growth in the next two years.

Pruning deciduous shrubs

Shrubs that flower in late summer usually flower on wood made earlier in the season. Prune in winter or early spring to give plants time to make new wood. Cut back the stems of vigorous plants, such as *Buddleia davidii*, to within two buds of last year's wood. Remove only stems that have flowered and older growth on vigorous shrubs, such as *Hydrangea microphylla*.

Deciduous shrubs that flower in early or mid-spring or early summer should be pruned immediately after flowering to give them as much time as possible to produce flower-bearing wood for the next year. Remove the stems that have just flowered, cutting them back to the previous year's wood. With shrubs that flower when new woody growth has started, be careful not to remove newly grown stems that have not yet flowered.

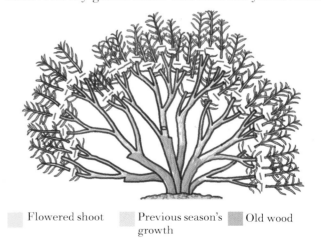

☐ Flowered shoot ☐ Previous season's growth ☐ Old wood

Prune early-flowering deciduous shrubs
Prune just after flowering so that the plant has maximum time to make flower-bearing wood.

Some deciduous shrubs are grown not for their flowers but for some other attractive feature. Dogwoods and willows, for example, are grown for their colourful, bare winter stems. Cut these plants back each year to encourage a flush of fresh, young growth. Some plants, such as lilac, can be grown for their attractive leaves. Cut these back to ground level each spring to create an attractive, leafy summer shrub.

Pruning evergreen shrubs

Most large evergreen shrubs need no regular pruning. If they get straggly, treat them in the same way as any overgrown shrub (see page 41) and reshape them over a three-year period. Some evergreens, such as aucuba and eucalyptus, however, are extremely resilient and respond well to being cut back drastically, so there is no need to stagger their renovation.

There are many small evergreen flowering shrubs, including many useful ground-cover plants and herbs, that need to be clipped annually. Lavender, cotton lavender, periwinkle, marjoram and thyme all fall into this category. Some plants, such as lavender, dislike being cut back too far into old wood, so trim off their flowers and 2.5–5 cm (1–2 in) of the foliage each spring. Cotton lavender can be deadheaded after flowering in summer; in spring, cut far back to within 7.5–15 cm (3–6 in) of the ground, just as the new shoots start to develop, to keep the plant compact. Clip other ground-cover plants to keep them dense and bushy.

Pruning to maintain shape
Pruning shrubs, such as cotton lavender, will encourage new growth and help the plant to keep a regular shape.

Pruning climbing and rambling roses

With climbing roses, training the rose sideways along horizontal supports is more important than actual pruning. Rambler roses produce more growth from the base than climbers, so they can become untidy if not properly trained. Both rambling and climbing roses should be deadheaded regularly throughout the flowering season. Cut back the stems to the next set of leaves beneath the dead flower.

Rambling roses

Mature ramblers should be pruned in late summer after flowering. Cut back any old, diseased or weak shoots to ground level using loppers. Cut side shoots to leave around three healthy buds or shoots. Tie all the young shoots to secure.

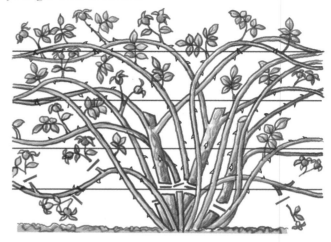

Pruning rambling roses
Cut back stems that have flowered to the supporting stems of the plant in late summer or autumn. Use loppers or a saw to reduce the framework if the plant needs to be thinned out.

Climbing roses

Train these regularly so that you catch them while the growth is still flexible. Remove any dead, diseased, or weak growth in late autumn after flowering or by early spring. Reduce side shoots by 10–15 cm (4–6 in) at the same time. Roses trained along chains or rope between poles, may need to have some of the old shoots cut out to keep the plant under control.

Pruning climbing roses
Prune in late autumn or early spring if they need to be restricted to a particular space. Cut back side shoots to 2–3 buds or 10–15 cm (4–6 in). Cut back the stems to a healthy bud.

Pruning wall shrubs

Shrubs that are trained against walls require annual pruning and training to keep them manageable. Put up a means of support, such as a trellis or horizontal wires (see page 103), and plant the shrub about 23 cm (9 in) from the wall.

Firethorn (Pyracantha)

In the early years tie leading stems to the wires with twine or wire ties. Once the framework has formed, you will need to prune annually. Shorten new side shoots in midsummer so that only two or three leaves remain on each one. If you do not get around to summer pruning, the plant can be tidied up in late winter by clipping with shears. Cut back any extra-long shoots at the same time.

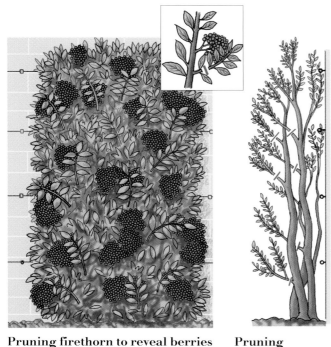

Pruning firethorn to reveal berries
To prevent firethorn berries from being hidden behind new shoots, cut back the new shoots once the flower buds or berries are visible. This will also encourage flowers and berries to grow in subsequent years.

Pruning firethorn to tidy overall shape
Cut off surplus branches that are growing away from the wall.

Pruning climbers

Some varieties of climber are extremely vigorous and can take over the garden if left untended. If pruned regularly, they are ideal for adding interest and height, and can be used to disguise unattractive walls or fences or screening an overlooked part of the garden.

Wisteria

These are very vigorous climbers. After the initial training, which takes three years, prune each summer and winter. In mid to late summer, cut back the extension growths to within five or six leaves or 15 cm (6 in) from the main stem. In winter cut back the same growths again to 2–3 buds or 7.5–10 cm (3–4 in).

Late summer
Trim back long side shoots to within 15 cm (6 in) of the main stem.

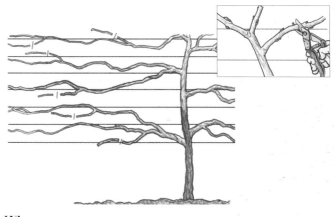

Winter
Cut back side shoots to within 7.5–10 cm (3–4 in) of the main stem.

Honeysuckle

Climbing honeysuckles are divided into two pruning groups depending on when they flower. The first group includes those that flower on the current season's growth, such as the Japanese honeysuckle and its varieties. Cut back the whole plant in early spring. Passion flower can also be pruned by this method.

The second group includes honeysuckles, such as *Lonicera periclymenum* that flower on the previous season's growth. They can be left unpruned, but to tidy them, cut back each flowered shoot to a point where there is a young shoot to replace it.

Clematis

There are three pruning groups depending on flowering time and viguor. Not all need pruning, but group 3 requires regular pruning to flower well.

Group 1

Group 1 comprises evergreen and early, small-flowering species and varieties. Prune after flowering if the plant is untidy. Group 1 clematis include:
Clematis alpina *and cultivars*
Clematis armandii *and cultivars*
Clematis cirrhosa *and cultivars*
Clematis macropetala *and cultivars*
Clematis montana *and cultivars*

Group 2

Group 2 comprises large-flowered species and varieties that flower from early summer. Cut back the healthy stems by one third in early spring, before flowering. Cut to a pair of strong, healthy buds. Group 2 clematis include:
Clematis *'Barbara Jackman'*
Clematis *'Lasurstern'*
Clematis *'Marie Boisselot'*
Clematis *'Nelly Moser'*
Clematis *'Niobe'*
Clematis *'The President'*

Group 3

Group 3 clematis flower during late summer. In early spring, cut away all the previous season's growth to about 75 cm (30 in) above soil level. Group 3 clematis include:
Clematis tangutica *and cultivars*
Clematis viticella *and cultivars*
Clematis *'Hagley Hybrid'*
Clematis *'Jackmanii'*
Clematis *'Perle d'Azur'*
Clematis *'Ville de Lyon'*

Hedges

Hedges need regular pruning, but wait until after birds have left their nests. Most hedges can be trimmed with shears or a hedgetrimmer, but hedges with large leaves should be finished with secateurs. To save time, use secateurs only for the most visible areas.

Keep hedges low and narrow to save time. Most hedges can be lowered if they have grown too large but stagger the work over a couple of seasons. Lay a sheet of polythene along the length of the hedge before you start cutting to speed up gathering fallen clippings.

Tall, formal hedges should taper at the top. This saves cutting time and means that the bottom growth is not shaded, so the hedge should have foliage all over. Low-growing hedging does not need to taper.

PRUNING HEDGES

Hedge	When to cut	Pruning tips
Beech (*Fagus sylvatica*)	Mid summer	Prune with shears to prevent cut leaves from turning brown.
Box, dwarf box (*Buxus sempervirens*)	Mid summer	Can be clipped far back making it a useful subject for topiary.
Lawson's cypress (*Chamaecyparis lawsoniana*)	Mid summer	Do not cut back into old wood; leave 10 cm (4 in) of live foliage.
Leyland cypress (*Cupressocyparis leylandii*)	Mid summer	Do not let it reach more than 2 m (7 ft) high.
Holly (*Ilex*)	Mid summer	Prune with shears to prevent cut leaves from turning brown.
Lavender (*Lavandula*)	Mid summer	Clip lightly with shears after flowering.
Privet (*Ligustrum*)	Late spring to mid summer	Clip each month through the growing season.
Yew (*Taxus baccata*)	Spring or late summer to early autumn	It will regrow even if cut far back into old wood.
Western red cedar (*Thuja plicata*)	Mid summer	It will sometimes regrow but not always if you cut back into old wood.

Pruning to remove problem areas

Even trees and shrubs that do not need regular pruning should always have dead, diseased or problem branches removed as quickly as possible.

Frost damage
Young growing tips of evergreens are often caught by the frost or by cold, dry winds. Cut back to healthy wood once the danger of frost has passed.

Diseased wood
Diseases can gain entry via damaged tissue. Cut back to healthy wood just above a bud. Do not put diseased prunings on a compost heap, always burn them or put in the dustbin.

Damaged wood
Cut back to undamaged wood before the tissue becomes infected.

Crossing branches
Crossing branches make the plant look unattractive and the friction caused by two branches rubbing can damage them. Remove the weakest branch or the one that spoils the shape.

Weak, spindly branches
Cut back weak branches harder than strong, vigorous stems to encourage a more balanced growth.

Suckers
These unwanted shoots grow up from the base of the plant. Scrape back the soil until you find the origin of the sucker, then pull or cut it off close to the main stem.

Variegated plants
Sometimes these produce all-green shoots that are more vigorous than the rest of the plant. If these are not cut out they will take over the whole plant.

SAFETY

- *Wear suitable eye protection, such as goggles and heavy-duty gloves, when pruning. When using an electric hedgetrimmer, work with the cable over your shoulder.*

- *Pruning mature trees requires great care if you must work overhead or from a ladder. In most instances, it is safer to call in an arborist to tackle medium and large trees.*

- *Always close the blades of the secateurs after use and store safely.*

Making a New Border

A NEW FLOWER BED or border can transform your garden. The keys to success are careful planning and site preparation. Before you plant anything, take the opportunity to prepare and condition the ground thoroughly. This may be the only time that you have access to completely bare soil, so it is worth going all out to improve your soil and give your precious new plants the best possible start. This is particularly important for permanent plants, such as trees and shrubs.

Planning your border

First, measure your site and make a drawing of the area on squared paper, using a scale of about one square to 30 cm (12 in). This enables you to plan the dimensions and shape of your border with more confidence. Once you have the basic shape on paper, lay tracing paper over the top and experiment with different shaped borders, such as long thin ones or deep sweeping curved ones. It is often a good idea to add some paving slabs to create a visually firm edge – especially when a border goes around a corner. Think about bed maintenance, too – a paving slab path laid at the back of a deep bed will quickly disappear behind your plants but can make weeding and pruning easier.

Plan before you plant
Once you have settled on a plan, mock it up before you start digging to check that the plan works in practice.

As well as any paving, mark on your plan the position of large plants, such as trees, shrubs, or large herbaceous perennials. Every border should have at least one major plant, often more than one. These plants will provide the basic framework to your planting and you should position them so that they are clearly visible from your home and other parts of the garden.

What works on paper doesn't always work so well in real life, so mock up your plan, and if necessary adjust the posistions of the plants. Lay any paving slabs (see opposite) for edging paths or maintenance access before you begin to dig your new bed.

Preparing the site

Remove the turf from the site and dig the soil to one spade's depth. If necessary, prepare a maintenance path (see opposite). Break up large clods of earth with a fork, and add a multi-purpose fertiliser. Ideally do this in the autumn, for planting the following spring.

1 *Mark out the border with a line of garden stakes and wind twine around them to give you a clear line to follow. Alternatively, you could lay a hose on the ground as a guideline.*
Inset: *If you are cutting a new border out of an existing lawn area, as here, cut out the shape with a half-moon edging tool and then use a spade to lift the turf.*

2 *If you are putting in a maintenance path (see box, opposite), position the slabs. This is to enable you to check the approximate positions before you start digging: there is no need to dig and improve soil that is going to be covered by paving slabs. If neccessary, redistribute the earth beneath the slabs to get a level surface.*

3 *Dig the border with a fork to one spade's depth, putting plenty of compost or manure in the bottom of each successive trench (see page 19).*

Planting the border

Once you have planned out the border, prepared the ground and bought your plants, you can position and plant them. Work from the back of the border to the front to save treading on the soil. Plant the largest first, remembering to dig a generous planting hole and add fertiliser to the roots. Then plant the medium-sized shrubs and perennials and finally the smaller, front-of-the-border perennials.

1 Position the feature plants in their proposed planting positions. If you are happy with these, dig the planting holes, adding fertiliser, and plant them one by one, firming the soil around each plant with your foot. Remember to stake any tall-stemmed trees.

2 Continue to work round the border from the back to the front. It is a good idea when planting container-grown plants to tease out the rootball, as here, before planting, in order to ensure the roots get away to a good start.

TIPS FOR PLANTING A BORDER

• *To create natural-looking clumps of herbaceous perennials, plant groups of three, five or seven plants. Even numbers of plants tend to look more orderly and less natural than odd numbers.*

• *If all the tall plants are at the back of a border, the planting can look over-formal. Stagger the planting line, so that the tallest plants are not all in a row.*

• *As a general rule, plant combinations of contrasting shapes, alternating upright and spiky plants with rounded and bushy ones.*

EDGING PATH

In practice, you would lay a maintenance or edging path at the same time as preparing the site. It is shown separately here, as it is not an essential part of all beds and borders: it is a good idea if your border is wide, as you can gain access to your plants to carry out any garden maintenance, but it is not essential. Without a path you would have to trample on the soil and risk damaging the soil structure and the plants.

Edging paths get relatively little use, so they do not need to be concreted into position. However, make sure the ground is level before you put down any paving slabs – otherwise they may not be stable.

Level the ground and check with a spirit level. Remove any stones and rake smooth. Lay a 2.5-cm (1-in) thick layer of sharp sand as a bed for the slabs. You can brush sand between the slabs to create a grout into which small plants will seed themselves, creating a more natural effect.

1 Level off the soil and lay the sand bed. Position the slabs in place, ensuring each slab is level by laying a spirit level across it, and tap down using a large mallet.

2 Continue to position the slabs until they are all in place and level. Brush sharp sand between the slabs to create a grout.

3 The edging path provides a working area from which to tend the planted border.

The Weekend Gardener's Calendar

THIS CALENDAR SETS out what you need to do throughout the year to keep your garden in good condition. As a weekend gardener, regular maintenance work in the garden – little but often – is the best way to maximise your time. Try to plan for routine tasks each weekend, such as weeding or mowing the lawn. Keep on top of things and you'll be able to complete the boring but essential jobs very quickly – but let things get out of hand and that quiet half hour's pruning will turn into a Herculean afternoon's labour.

The tasks will vary depending on what plants you have chosen to grow. Therefore only very general guidelines are given here, providing a season-by-season, page-at-a-glance reminder of what you need to do and when. For specific information on particular plants, refer to a good plant reference manual and to the maintenance tips that accompany each project in this book.

The exact timing of routine garden maintenance is rarely critical; indeed, it's impossible to give precise timings as conditions vary so much from one part of the country to another. Weather conditions vary, too – not just from one part of the country to another, but also from year to year. Your best key to success is to learn a little about how plants grow and the conditions that they need in order to thrive; once you understand your plants' requirements, you will find it far easier to gauge for yourself whether the time is right to prune a particular shrub, for example. And even if you do prune at what the books tell you is the "wrong" time of year, you are unlikely to do irrevocable damage: you may simply have fewer flowers the following year.

Use this calendar as a prompt – but don't become a slave to it. Instead, relax and enjoy doing what you can when you can: that's what weekends are for.

SPRING

Containers
• Plant new containers – but wait until the danger of frost has passed if you are planning to use frost-tender plants.

• Keep the soil in containers moist, especially in newly planted containers.

• Keep frost-tender container plants inside in a sunny position until the danger of frost has passed, so that they will be well developed when they are ready to go outside. Harden them off gradually (see page 29), leaving them outside for a little longer each day.

• For permanent container plants, discard any winter frost protection and remove dead or unwanted growth from the plants. Scrape off the top 5 cm (2 in) of potting soil and replace it with fresh, incorporating some slow-release fertiliser granules.

• As the weather warms up, watch out for diseases and pests such as aphids (see pages 36–37) and deal with any problems immediately.

• Check hanging basket and window box brackets to make sure that they are still securely fixed and in good condition.

Lawns
• Lay or sow new lawns (see pages 74–77).

• Start mowing established lawns as soon as the grass is visibly growing. Remove any debris from the lawn before you mow using a spring-tined, fan-shaped wire rake. Maintain the grass between 1–5 cm (½–2 in) long.

• Trim the edges of the lawn with long-handled shears every time you mow.

• Remove clippings, since dead grass clippings can build up a thatch of dead material on the surface of the turf.

• Repair any broken lawn edges, bumps or dips (see page 77).

• Remove large, tap-rooted lawn weeds, such as dandelions, using a daisy grubber or narrow trowel or small hand-fork (see page 77). Fill any holes with lump-free soil and a little grass seed and cover the patch with chicken wire to protect the seed and seedlings. Alternatively, rather than handweeding, use a selective weedkiller and fertiliser, following the manufacturer's instructions for dose and application.

Annuals and Bedding Plants
• Sow hardy annuals where they are to flower or in pots or trays indoors (see page 29).

• When the seedlings of autumn-sown hardy annuals are large enough, transplant them to where you want them to flower (see page 29).

• Keep frost-tender and half-hardy bedding plants indoors until the danger of frost is over (see page 31).

• Pinch out the tips of sweet-pea seedlings to create multi-stemmed climbers; pinch out side shoots to create taller ones.

Perennial Plants
• In late spring to early summer, take softwood cuttings from tender perennials such as geraniums (see page 39).

• Cut back and discard any dead growth that was left on perennial plants over the winter.

• Lift and divide large clumps of perennials not divided in autumn (see page 39).

• Position supports for tall perennials while the plants are small (see pages 38–39)

Trees, Shrubs and Climbers

• Trim low hedges, using hand shears rather than an electric trimmer to avoid bruising the leaves.

• Check that the stakes used to support any climbing plants are firm and sound.

• Tie stray stems of climbers.

• Remove any dead, diseased or broken stems.

• In early spring, prune shrubs that flower after mid summer if necessary (see page 41), feeding them with slow-release fertiliser granules after pruning. Small, summer-flowering evergreen shrubs such as lavender and cotton lavender should be pruned each year to keep the plants compact (see page 42).

• In early spring, trim hedges that are planted with summer-flowering climbers such as clematis.

• Cut back shrubs such as dogwood that are grown for their colourful winter stems once their leaves begin to emerge.

• Prune spring-flowering shrubs immediately when flowers fade (see page 41).

• Plant bare-rooted deciduous trees or shrubs before the leaves emerge. Plant bare-rooted evergreen shrubs in mid-spring (see page 32). Container-grown shrubs can be planted at any time during the year, though not when it is frosty or when the soil is very wet (see pages 32–33).

Herb Gardens

• Sow seeds of annual herbs such as parsley.

• Cut out individual straggly stems of large woody herbs such as rosemary and sage.

• Clip small, bushy herbs, such as thyme and marjoram, to keep the plants compact.

Wildflower Gardens

• If you have a spring-flowering meadow, do not mow it during spring. Instead note of where more spring-flowering wild species might be encouraged to grow next year.

• Weed out over-vigorous plants that threaten to shade their neighbours.

Woodland Gardens

• Take care not to disturb nesting birds; avoid pruning or clipping plants that might support bird nests.

Water Gardens

• Remove any plants that have outgrown their planting baskets. Divide them and repot in fresh soil.

• Add more water to the pond if necessary.

• Plant new water plants and marginals in the late spring (see page 31).

• Make sure the soil in the bog garden is moist. When the soil has warmed, in mid-spring, add a layer of compost or manure around the base of the plants as a mulch.

• Use a fan-shaped wire rake to scoop out algae and debris from ponds.

General Maintenance

• Thoroughly weed beds and borders (see pages 20–21). If you do this job well now, before the weather warms up, your plants will grow quickly to swamp out weeds.

• Make sure the ground around the base of your trees, shrubs and climbers is kept clear of weeds and grass.

• Once the soil has warmed, cover exposed, weeded ground with a 2–3-in (5–7.5-cm) layer of mulch (see pages 22–23).

• Mulch around the base of trees, shrubs and climbers in late spring once the soil has warmed up, giving the plants a thorough watering first if the soil is dry.

• Plant the new beds that you prepared in the autumn (see pages 46–47).

• Check that trellises, walls and fences are sound. Repaint if necessary.

• Watch out for infestations of aphids on new growth. Spray with soapy water or remove and dispose of very badly infected stems.

• Water plants – particularly newly planted ones – if the weather is warm and dry.

• Sweep paths and paving with a stiff broom. Apply handfuls of sharp sand to the path before sweeping to help to remove any slime.

• Lift any rocky paving slabs, add coarse sand underneath to correct the rocking and tamp down the slab, checking that it is level with the others.

• Remove any weeds that are growing between paving slabs (see page 21).

SUMMER
Containers

• Finish hardening off frost-tender seedlings and plants (see page 29), then plant.

• Keep all containers well watered (see pages 34–35). If you're going to be away from home for a weekend, move the containers close together in a shaded position and give them a thorough soaking. If you're going to be away from home on a regular basis or for longer than a weekend, then ask a neighbour to water your plants – or consider installing a mechanised watering system.

• Remove dead flowers to encourage new flowers.

• Snip off any dead leaves: they look unsightly and may harbour pests and diseases.

• Remove weeds regularly.

• In early and mid-summer, add liquid fertiliser to the water (use the manufacturer's recommended dosage).

Lawns

• Mow regularly while the grass is growing (unless you are creating a meadow). Keep the grass to a height of about 1–5 cm (½ – 2 in). (You can leave it as long as 5 cm/2 in in hot weather.)

• If you have naturalised bulbs in your lawn, do not mow until the leaves have shrivelled.

• Trim the edges of your lawn with long-handled shears every time you mow.

• If you have left an area of lawn to develop into a spring-flowering meadow, use a strimmer to cut down the grasses and flowers once they have seeded themselves. Leave the cuttings to dry, then rake them up.

• Remove weeds that are shading out grasses using a narrow-bladed trowel or a daisy grubber.

• For a dense, healthy turf with no wild flowers, use a general-purpose lawn feed (see page 75).

Annuals and Bedding Plants

• Snip off dead and tired growth regularly to make way for fresh leaves and flowers.

Perennial Plants

• Watch out for slugs and snails and set traps for them if necessary (see pages 36–37). Large bites taken from leaves and a silvery trail will alert you to the problem.

• In mid-summer, take cuttings of tender perennials, such as pelargoniums, to grow on for next year (see page 39).

• If you have an over-large clump of iris, lift and divide it once the flowers are over.

Trees, Shrubs and Climbers

• Prune late spring- and early summer-flowering shrubs and climbers that flower before mid-summer (see pages 41–44).

• Prune trained trees and shrubs since pruning at this time of year tends to discourage growth, making it easier to keep the shape that you want (see page 43).

• Clip hedges and topiary 1–3 times during the summer months, using sharp shears or secateurs.

• Dead head roses and other shrubs to encourage more flowers to come.

• Tie in climbers as they grow up or along their supports.

• Loosen any ties or tree-stake straps that have become too tight for the tree.

• Shorten the side shoots of young non-flowering wisteria plants to encourage flowering.

Herb Gardens

• Snip off or pinch out flowering stems of herbs as they appear, since herbs are generally thought to taste better before they flower.

• Clip shaped bay trees to keep their growth dense and their shape neat.

• Clip small, bushy herbs, such as thyme and marjoram, to keep them compact.

Wildflower Gardens

• Once spring meadow flowers have faded and seeded, cut them down. Leave cuttings to dry, then add them to the compost heap.

Water Gardens

• Top up the pond water when necessary to maintain the depth of the pond.

• Snip or pull off any water lily leaves that are pushing out of the water.

• Remove pond weed or algae as it appears, scooping it out with a fan-shaped wire rake or twirling it around a stick.

• Keep the soil in the bog garden moist and well weeded.

General Maintenance

• Water plants regularly during hot weather. Water the plants in the shade as the water will evaporate quickly in sunlight and may cause scorching. It is particularly important to water newly planted plants, as their root systems have not yet established, although well established plants will benefit from a thorough soaking, too.

• Weed regularly. If weeds grow through a mulch, pull out and top up the mulch.

• Remove dead flower heads as they appear to encourage more flowers.

• Weed gravel paths and paved areas regularly.

• Add more gravel to paths if necessary.

• Sweep decking paths to keep them clean and non-slippery and remove any weeds.

• Watch for infestations of aphids on new plant growth. Spray with soapy water or remove and dispose of badly infected stems.

AUTUMN
Containers

• Plant pots of spring-flowering bulbs (see page 31 for planting depths) – or use a trowel or bulb planter to plant them in established pots.

• Drain off excess rain water so that your pots don't become waterlogged.

• Lift and remove frost-tender perennials from outdoor containers and pots, and bring indoors to a frost-free place.

Annuals

• Sow hardy annuals for early flowers the following year. Sow them where they are to flower or in pots or trays and keep them in a sheltered place, such as a cold frame, during the winter. Thin out the seedlings when they are large enough to handle.

• Discard annual flowers once they no longer look attractive.

Perennials

• Cut back dead fern fronds. Use dead fronds to insulate vulnerable plants in winter.

• Lift and divide any over-large clumps of perennials.

• Plant winter- and spring-flowering bulbs in bold groups around the garden, especially in places that can be seen from the house (see page 31 for planting depths).

Trees, Shrubs and Climbers

- Autumn is the best time of year to plant new trees and shrubs, while the soil is still warm so that there's time for roots to begin to grow into their new situation before the cold weather sets in.

- Prune rambling roses once flowering is over (see page 42). Other roses, unless they are in an exposed position, are best left until the spring.

Lawns

- Sow lawn seed or lay new turf now, before the winter, or wait until the spring.

- Carry out any repairs to your lawn while the grass is still growing (see page 77).

- Rake up leaves from the lawn (use them to make leaf mould or compost).

- Replace lost air from compacted soil in a lawn by spiking the lawn with a garden fork in boggy areas to introduce air into the soil under the turf. Push the fork in vertically to a depth of 10–15 cm (4–6 in), then withdraw it vertically. Take care to avoid levering the fork, as this will uproot the turf.

- Add a top dressing of equal parts of sieved sand, soil and peat; rake half a bucketful per square metre (yard) over the lawn surface. This will help to nourish the turf and fill out minor bumps and hollows.

- Continue to mow the lawn while the grass is still growing, but raise the height of the blades so that you don't cut the grass any shorter than about 2 cm (¾ in).

- Plant drifts of spring-flowering bulbs in areas of your lawn to create a natural-looking effect (see page 31).

Herb Gardens

- Cut back mint. Lift and divide mint plants that are overcrowded.

- Tidy beds of herbs and mulch using compost or farmyard manure.

Water Gardens

- Remove any frost-tender water plants and store them in buckets of water in a frost-free place.

General Garden Maintenance

- Tidy up beds and borders. Remove unsightly dead growth – but remember that some plants can look attractive as they die off in autumn so don't cut back everything. Leave any new growth at the base of the plant.

- Autumn is the best time to improve the soil in your garden (see pages 16–17).

- Design and create new beds (see pages 46–47).

- Apply a 2–3-in (5–7.5-cm) layer of a coarse mulch, such as bark chippings, to the surface of the soil between the plants and around trees, shrubs and climbers before the cold weather, since this will help to insulate the soil (see pages 22–23).

WINTER

Containers

- Stop watering plants in containers.

- Discard dead plants and store their pots for next year.

- Stand containers in a sheltered position for the winter. If they are left to stand in the rain, freezing rainwater may crack the container and damage the plants' roots. Drain off rain water so that remaining plants are kept relatively dry in cold weather.

- Protect vulnerable plants that you keep permanently in containers by bringing them inside (into an unheated room) or wrapping them in straw (or dead fern fronds) and tying polythene sheeting around the plant.

- Clean containers by scrubbing them in soapy water with a little disinfectant.

Perennials

- Fleshy-rooted plants are more vulnerable to frost damage than fibrous-rooted ones. Perennials with a "crown" of leaves are also at risk, since rain can trickle into the plant and rot it. Protect vulnerable perennials by covering them with straw, dead fern fronds or prunings from evergreens.

Trees, Shrubs and Climbers

- Knock heavy falls of snow off branches since they can snap under the weight and disfigure the plant.

- Prune the side shoots of wisteria back to within about 7.5 cm (3 in) of the main framework of the plant.

- Between winter and early spring, prune late summer-flowering shrubs such as buddleia. As a general principle, prune in winter, when plants are properly dormant, rather than in autumn, since autumn pruning can encourage new growth which then gets frosted.

Lawns

- Avoid walking on lawns during cold, wet weather since you can easily damage the soil structure and therefore soil fertility.

- Clean and sharpen lawn tools; wipe the blades with an oily cloth before storing them in a dry shed or cupboard.

Water Gardens

- Clean the pond pump filter.

- If you have fish in your pond, make sure there is always a hole in the ice during freezing weather.

General Garden Maintenance

- Firm soil down around plants where it has been lifted by frost.

- Make sure that paths and paving are swept regularly and kept free of ice.

- Buy seed catalogues and plan what you are going to plant next year.

CONTAINERS

Potted profusion
This varied collection of pots makes an impressive display of colours and textures against the plain background of the evergreen hedge. The spiny, sword-like clumps of variegated century plants (Agave americana 'Variegata') provide a distinct, almost architectural, structure to this profusion of pink and white geraniums, lilies and other blooms. What better solution is there for a dull front garden than a vibrant blend of foliage and flowers?

Ideas for Using Containers

WHATEVER KIND OF outdoor space you have – large or small, a town flat or a country home – containers of plants can create an almost instant garden. In this respect, containers are ideal for the weekend gardener: quick to plant and relatively easy to maintain. You can find a style to suit any situation, too, from rustic-looking wooden half barrels and terracotta troughs to elegant Versailles tubs that would grace the most sophisticated mansion.

Containers are also a great way of making your gardening more flexible. You can move them around to vary your view. You can grow frost-sensitive plants and bring them inside when the weather turns cold. You can use a different type of soil to the one that is naturally found in your garden – enabling you, for example, to grow acid-loving plants, such as camellias and azaleas, even if your garden soil is alkaline. And you can celebrate each season by replacing spring-flowering bulbs with summer bedding.

The questions on these two pages are designed to help you pinpoint ways in which you can use containers to enhance your garden. Each one is backed up by a step-by-step project that includes suggestions for container plants to use in your own garden.

? *Do you have large expanses of bare paving?*

Visually, containers of plants help to soften an expanse of paving or other hard surface, and add colour and interest where beds cannot be created. ***Right:*** Even this small patio would look bare and uninviting without potted plants to soften edges and break up straight lines. Here, pots of purple pansies with lime-green flowering tobacco plants add a splash of colour, while the clipped box and the ivy cones give the patio a sense of fun. SEE *Grouping Pots, page 56.*

? *Does the entrance to your home look untidy?*

Well-tended containers next to the front door create a wonderful first impression for visitors and make the whole house seem loved and cared for. SEE *Brightening up a Doorway, page 58.*

❓ *Do your walls or window ledges need brightening up?*

Containers are a quick-and-easy way of adding colour and interest. *Left* : Scarlet trailing geraniums and purple flowering lobelia bring vibrant colour to the front of this house throughout the summer. The variegated hebe in the window box and spotted laurel in the troughs provide this planting with attractive foliage.

SEE *Hanging Baskets, page 62;*
Window Dressing, page 64;
Brightening Bare Walls, page 66.

❓ *Is your garden too small for a pond?*

Even if your space is restricted, you can still make an interesting water feature in a container. *Left:* In this trio of barrels, potted ivy, ferns and mosses create a tiny, lush water garden.
SEE *Water Feature for a Small Space, page 68.*

❓ *Is there a view or feature that you want to hide?*

Containers of established plants are ideal for instantly blocking an unwanted view and enhancing your privacy.
SEE *Screening with Containers, page 60.*

Grouping Pots
CONTAINERS FOR PATIOS

CONTAINERS ARE A GREAT WAY OF softening the hard expanse of a patio area and adding colour, but unless it's large and imposing, a single pot can look stark and isolated. You can create a stronger visual effect by arranging several containers together. Moreover, grouping pots means that the display is less exposed than it would be if the pots were arranged singly – and some of the plants will benefit from being slightly more sheltered.

When considering how to group pots, decide whether you want a formal design or a more relaxed style. For a formal, consciously stylish arrangement, choose a matching set of pots and a simple, clearly co-ordinated planting – a row of potted white lilies behind pots of lavender in matching but smaller containers, for example. An informal, more accessible approach would be to vary pot styles, shapes and materials and also the plants you put in them, although some linking theme – flower colour or leaf texture, pot material or glaze, for example – should be apparent to hold the arrangement of pots and plants together visually.

When it comes to choosing plants, a useful rule of thumb is that tall, upright containers need something to trail down them and soften the outline of the pot, while rounded containers generally need an upright and bushy plant as a contrast in shape.

Informal grouping for sun

This trio of pots, two made from glazed terracotta and one left plain, makes an attractive grouping. Although they are different in colour, size and shape, the fact that they are all made from the same material gives them unity. The choice of plants, too, helps to unify the display: lady's mantle appears in two of the pots and, although they are somewhat smaller, the nasturtium and New Zealand burr leaves are sufficiently similar in shape and texture to the lady's mantle for them to work well together. The running bamboo provides much-needed height and a contrast of texture, while the nasturtium flowers give a splash of colour that is echoed by the flowers of the New Zealand burr.

1 Running bamboo
(*Pleioblastus auricomus*)

2 New Zealand burr
(*Acaena microphylla*)

PLANTING ALTERNATIVES

Formal partners for shade

For a shaded patio area, choose plants that thrive in such conditions. The hosta and fern shown below are ideal partners: their leaves contrast in shape and texture, and the mottled green and yellow hosta will reflect what light there is. If space is tight, create a display with height by placing a tall container inside another one; this way the base of the taller pot is softened and it doesn't look so stark. Here, two wooden planters have been put together with a hosta in the taller planter, and a delicate-looking fern at its base.

1 *Hosta fortunei* var. *albopicta*

2 *Polystichum setiferum*

Polystichum setiferum

Hosta fortunei var. *albopicta*

3 Lady's mantle (*Alchemilla mollis*)

4 Nasturtium (*Tropaeolum majus*)

PROJECT PLANNER

TIME SCALE **1 HOUR**

Tools and Materials

Containers • Broken ceramic shards • Trowel • Potting compost • Slow-release fertiliser granules • Water-retaining granules

1 *Clean old pots or buy new ones. Be sure to wash out any old soil. Dry pots thoroughly.*

2 *Experiment with different arrangements of the empty pots to work out how you will group them. If you are using three pots of different shapes and sizes, a triangular arrangement often works well.*

3 *Calculate roughly how many plants you will need for each group and buy them. If you cannot plant them immediately, keep them watered and in the shade.*

4 *Plant the containers (see page 30). Water thoroughly and allow to drain.*

5 *Wash or wipe off any mud on the outside of the container or around the rim.*

6 *Position the containers in the arrangement you have chosen. Make sure that the pots are on level ground.*

MAINTENANCE

• *Keep the pots watered and weeded.*

• *In the autumn, plant a few spring-flowering bulbs, such as crocus, to add interest early in the year.*

• *In spring, scrape away the top 2 cm (1 in) or so of compost and replace it with fresh.*

• *Keep the plants tidy. Snip off any dead foliage or flowers once they've faded. Cut back over-vigorous growth.*

• *Remove the nasturtium in the autumn once it begins to look untidy. Plant fresh nasturtium plants the following spring once the frosts are over.*

Brightening up a Doorway
CONTAINERS FOR A SUNNY SITE

CONTAINERS OF flowering plants next to the front door create a wonderfully welcoming atmosphere for visitors and are the perfect solution for paved areas or steps where you cannot plant directly into the ground. Large containers make a dramatic impression and are easier to care for, since they contain more potting compost and moisture than small ones.

Doorway containers need to look good all year round, so include some permanent plants (ivy, wisteria and cotton lavender are used in this design). After the frosts have passed, introduce summer bedding plants. In the autumn, remove the bedding plants and plant spring- and winter-flowering bulbs. For instructions on how to plant a container, see page 30.

1 Geranium (*Pelargonium* 'Clorinda')

2 *Petunia* 'Super Cascade Lilac'

3 Ivy (*Hedera helix* 'Gracilis')

4 *Wisteria sinensis*

5 Cotton lavender (*Santolina chamaecyparissus*)

6 Night-scented stock (*Matthiola bicornis*)

Sunny lilac and yellow pots

This lilac and yellow planting is suitable for a sunny site. The wisteria will need support and also pruning in summer and winter if it is to flower profusely and be kept to a manageable size. However, its early summer blooms and beautiful foliage make the effort well worthwhile. The geranium and petunias give a continuous show from early summer until the autumn. Cotton lavender, with its grey foliage and yellow flowers, brings a contrast in colour to the other plants, and ivies trail over both pots to soften their edges and help to marry the two very different-looking containers. In the autumn, plant some winter- and spring-flowering bulbs.

PLANTING ALTERNATIVES

Shady glow

Substitute the shade-loving plants listed below for those illustrated (left). A pink and white fuchsia replaces the geranium, with a busy Lizzie providing a splash of lilac. The ivy will thrive in shade and sun. A Japanese aralia replaces the wisteria. Golden-green variegated euonymus replaces cotton lavender and a tobacco plant provides a strong scent.

1 Fuchsia 'Mary Poppins'

2 Busy Lizzie (*Impatiens* 'Super Elfin Pearl')

4 Japanese aralia (*Fatsia japonica*)

5 *Euonymus fortunei* 'Emerald 'n' Gold'

6 Tobacco plant (*Nicotiana alata* 'Lime Green')

PROJECT PLANNER

TIME SCALE **1+ HOURS**

Tools and Materials

Wires and vine eyes • Containers • Gravel • Potting compost • Water-retaining granules • Slow-release fertiliser granules • Trowel

1 *Put up wire supports on the house wall (see page 103) to give the wisteria something to cling to as it grows.*

2 *Buy the plants. If you cannot plant them immediately, store them in a cool place and keep well watered.*

3 *Position the containers. Fill the bottom of each one with gravel and top with 30–45 cm (12–18 in) of potting compost, mixing in water-retaining granules and fertiliser granules following the manufacturer's instructions.*

4 *Plant the wisteria (with its supporting stake) first; undo any ties that are holding the plant to the stake and replace with wire ties or loosely tied soft twine. Set the plant at a slight angle so that it slopes backwards and its cane leads the plant back to the wall. (You can remove the stake after a year or so, once the wisteria is firmly attached to the wire supports.) Plant the remaining plants (see page 30) and water thoroughly.*

MAINTENANCE

• *Deadhead flowers once they are past their best.*

• *Water daily. Six weeks after planting, add liquid feed to the water, following manufacturer's recommendations.*

• *Lift and remove geraniums and petunias in late autumn, before the frosts set in. You can take cuttings of geraniums in the late summer or early autumn. Alternatively, overwinter geraniums in a frost-free place.*

• *Plant winter- and spring-flowering bulbs in place of the geraniums and petunias to keep the containers looking fresh and colourful.*

• *Once the basic shape of the wisteria is established, prune back the side branches to 7.5 cm (3 in) of the main stem each winter. In summer, trim any long, straggly side shoots to about 15 cm (6 in) in length and tie the wisteria to the wires as it grows.*

• *Clip cotton lavender after it has flowered.*

Screening with Containers
TROUGH WITH CLIMBING ROSES

ALMOST EVERY GARDEN has a small area, such as a compost heap or dustbins, that would be better hidden from view. For a quick-and-easy solution, place a trough backed with a trellis in front of the unsightly object, and plant it with climbers and bushy evergreen shrubs. The plants will soon provide a dense screen and make an attractive feature.

If you need to move the screen from time to time – in order to gain access to a drain, for example, or to clear away fallen leaves – screw wheels under the trough so that it can be pushed out of the way when necessary.

For extra summer colour, add bedding plants such as the yellow petunia shown below. In autumn, plant spring-flowering bulbs such as crocuses or dwarf tulips.

Sunny screening

This planter has plenty to distract you from the view beyond – especially in the summer, when you use the garden most. The trellis is adorned with ivy, giving all-year cover, while the rose bears yellow blooms throughout the summer.

2 Yellow climbing rose (*Rosa* 'Golden Showers')

3 Jerusalem sage (*Phlomis fruticosa*)

1 White variegated ivy (*Hedera helix* 'Glacier')

4 *Petunia* 'Yellow Pearl' (yellow multiflora type)

MAINTENANCE

• *Water frequently, twice daily in dry weather.*

• *Six weeks after planting, add a liquid fertiliser to the water once a week until midsummer, following the manufacturer's usage recommendations.*

• *Fix the climbers to the trellis as they grow.*

• *Deadhead the roses as they pass their best to encourage more flowers.*

• *In the autumn, lift and discard the petunias. Remove the top 2.5–5 cm (1–2 in) of compost and replace with fresh compost. Plant winter- and spring-flowering bulbs.*

• *Cut back any dead or unwanted growth of the Jerusalem sage and the climbers in spring.*

PLANTING ALTERNATIVES

Shady site

If your trough is in a lightly shaded position, substitute the following plants for those illustrated. Ivy thrives in sun and shade, but change the rose for a firethorn and enjoy flowers in spring and colour-ful berries in the autumn. Exchange Jerusalem sage for a white-flowering hebe, an evergreen that will tolerate less than ideal light condi-tions. Busy Lizzies replace the petunias at the front of the trough, but do not plant them until the frosts are over.

2 Firethorn (*Pyracantha* 'Orange Glow')

3 Hebe albicans

4 Busy Lizzie (*Impatiens* 'Super Elfin')

PROJECT PLANNER

TIME SCALE 1/2 DAY

Tools and Materials

Planter, at least 30 cm (12 in) deep • 2 posts of 7.5 x 7.5 cm (3 x 3 in) pressure-treated wood about 7.5 cm (3 in) taller than the trellis panel • Screws and screwdriver • 2 decorative post caps • Spirit level • Pencil • Trellis panel about 15 cm (6 in) narrower than the planter • Four 5-cm (2-in) trellis brackets • Four 5-cm (2-in) castors • Wood sealant • Polythene sheet • Broken ceramic shards • Potting compost • Water-retaining granules • Slow-release fertiliser granules • Trowel

1 *Position one post on each side of the back of the planter, checking that you have left enough room for the trellis panel. The posts should extend beyond the bottom of the planter so that they rest just above the ground after the castors have been fixed in place (see Step 5). Attach the posts, using two screws each in order to secure, and fix a decorative post cap to the top of each post.*

2 *Holding the trellis panel in place, use a pencil to mark the position of the brackets near the top and bottom of the side posts.*

3 *Screw the brackets to the trellis and side posts.*

4 *Set the castors in place on the base of the trough and mark the position of the screws. Screw on the castors.*

5 *Apply a coat of plant-friendly wood sealant. This protects the wood and helps to harmonise the colours of the posts, trellis and trough.*

6 *Cut holes in a polythene sheet and line the trough with it. Put in ceramic shards, potting compost, water-retaining granules, and slow-release fertiliser granules.*

7 *Buy the plants. If you cannot plant them immediately, store them in a cool place and keep them well watered.*

8 *Plant the rose and ivy at the back of the trough, entwining the stems through the trellis. Plant the Jerusalem sage and petunias at the front. Water thoroughly.*

Hanging Baskets
SEASONAL COLOUR

Not all planting needs to be at ground level. Extend your garden upwards by means of an eye-catching display of hanging baskets and wall pots (see also pages 66–67).

The critical thing to remember with hanging baskets is that, because they're normally positioned at eye level or higher, the base will be seen as much, if not more, than the top and sides. Bear this in mind when you're planting: no matter how eye-catching the top may be, nothing can ruin the effect more than a dried-out, colourless covering of moss along the sides and bottom.

Don't include too many colours. You can create just as dramatic an effect with just one or two toning shades: delicate blue and white, perhaps; or even, for a shaded alleyway, a monochromatic collection of shade-loving foliage plants such as ferns.

The only special requirements for hanging baskets are regular watering – compost dries out quickly in a small container like this – and a sturdy, securely fixed wall or ceiling bracket. Hanging baskets are quite heavy, particularly just after watering, so any bracket must be strong and secure enough to bear the weight.

Pastel shades for summer

This selection of advancing warm-coloured and receding cool-coloured pastel shades gives an impression of a great depth of planting. The flowers are all of a similar size, so no one element dominates the display.

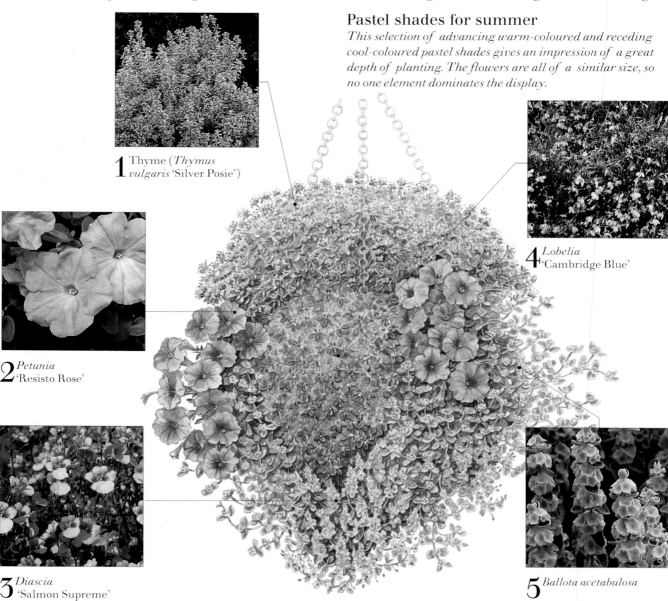

1 Thyme (*Thymus vulgaris* 'Silver Posie')

2 *Petunia* 'Resisto Rose'

3 *Diascia* 'Salmon Supreme'

4 *Lobelia* 'Cambridge Blue'

5 *Ballota acetabulosa*

MAINTENANCE

• *Water the basket regularly, especially in warm dry weather. To make watering easier, keep a step stool nearby or fit a special lance-like attachment to your hose (see page 35).*

• *Snip off any unwanted straggly growth and dead flowers as soon as they appear so that the basket maintains its neat overall shape.*

• *Apply a liquid feed regularly, following the instructions supplied by the feed manufacturer.*

• *Every year, and especially after stormy weather, check that the brackets are still secure.*

PLANTING ALTERNATIVES

Pastel shades for winter

For an attractive winter hanging basket in a pink and white colour scheme, replace the plants shown in the design opposite with the following:

1 Heather (*Erica* sp. – many varieties available)

2 Variegated ivy (*Hedera* sp. – many varieties available)

3 *Cyclamen coum*

4 Snowdrop (*Galanthus nivalis*)

5 White winter-flowering pansy (*Viola* sp. – many varieties available)

PROJECT PLANNER

TIME SCALE 1 HOUR

Tools and Materials

Wall bracket and screws • Drill and appropriate bit • Wire basket • Flower pot • Sphagnum moss • Polythene sheet • Scissors • Potting compost • Slow-release fertiliser granules • Water-retaining granules

1 *Attach a bracket or hook to the wall to hang your basket from and check that it is secure. Buy the plants. If you cannot plant them immediately, store in a cool place and keep well watered.*

3 *Line the moss with a polythene sheet trimmed to fit the basket. Make slits all around the polythene at intervals of about 7.5–10 cm (3–4 in).*

2 *Balance the basket on a flower pot or bucket at a convenient working height. Line the basket with a generous layer of damp sphagnum moss.*

4 *In a bucket, mix fresh potting compost with slow-release fertiliser granules, following the manufacturer's instructions.*

5 *The first plants to go in, around the side and towards the bottom of the basket, are the trailers. Water them first, then gently push their rootballs through the holes in the basket and polythene, past the sphagnum moss.*

6 *Place some water-retaining granules at the bottom of the basket (follow the instructions given on the packet for amounts). As you add more plants and compost, mix in more granules.*

7 *At the top, use an upright, bushy plant in the centre surrounded by spreading plants and more trailers. Top with soil, leaving the finished level 2.5 cm (1 in) below the rim. Hang the chains that are attached to the basket from the hook or bracket that you put on the wall in Step 1.*

Window Dressing
WINDOW BOX FOR SEASONAL COLOUR

WINDOW BOXES are an easy way of brightening up an empty window ledge and making your home look well loved and welcoming. Choose plants of different habits – some upright, some trailing – and plant them close together to give an impression of luxuriant growth. Contrasts of colour are important, too, and the planting below uses a classic combination of scarlet and green to great effect.

Window boxes need regular watering – at least once a day in hot weather. If they are not easily accessible, install an automated watering system (see page 35).

The climate on a window ledge can be extreme – from baking sun to howling winds – so it is wise to replant every season and stick to robust species that can withstand these conditions and give you a long period of colour. Geraniums, petunias, and lobelia are some all-time favourite window-box species.

A plant-filled and well-watered window box can be extremely heavy, so it needs to be securely fixed in place. If you have window ledges for your boxes to sit on, use wedge-shaped blocks of wood under the box to make sure that it is perfectly level. If possible, attach chains to the sides of your box and hang on hooks that you can screw into the outside wall. If you don't have window ledges you can still put up boxes, but they will need wall-mounted brackets to rest on (see opposite).

Strong colours for summer

The scarlet geraniums shown here will flower all summer long with little attention and contrast boldly with the neat, clipped box cones. The ground ivy and helichrysum trail over the edge of the container to provide a contrast in shape with the more upright forms of the box cones and geraniums. The box cones can stay in the window box permanently as long as they are in good condition. They help to give the arrangement structure, and provide a solid green backdrop for the other plants.

1 Geranium (*Pelargonium* 'Madame Fournier')

2 Ground ivy (*Glechoma hederacea* 'Variegata')

3 Box (*Buxus sempervirens*)

4 *Helichrysum petiolare*

MAINTENANCE

- *Water thoroughly — at least once a day in hot weather.*

- *Add a liquid feed to the water six weeks after planting, then once weekly, following the manufacturer's instructions.*

- *Snip off any unwanted growth or dead flowers as they appear. Clip box cones to keep their shape.*

- *Watch out for aphids. Cut out and dispose of badly infected stems.*

- *Take cuttings of frost-tender plants in late summer or autumn (see page 39). Remove them from their container before the frosts set in and overwinter in a frost-free place.*

- *Every year, and especially after stormy weather, check that the brackets are still secure.*

PLANTING ALTERNATIVES

Silvery shades for winter

In the autumn, you may need to replant your window box with frost-hardy subjects. If you are leaving the container in position, plant bulbs in pots so that they can be easily lifted and replaced when their flowers are over. Choose early and late winter-flowering bulbs to keep a continuous display through to spring.

1 Snowdrop
(*Galanthus nivalis*)

2 Winter iris
(*Iris unguicularis*)

4 Silver variegated ivy
(*Hedera helix* 'Heise')

PROJECT PLANNER

TIME SCALE **1/2 DAY**

Tools and Materials

Window box • Two window box brackets • Spirit level • Drill and masonry bit • Screws and screwdriver • Rawl plugs • Liner to fit window box • Broken ceramic shards • Potting compost • Water-retaining granules • Slow-release fertiliser granules • Trowel

1 *Hold the window box in place to determine where you want to attach it. Be sure that the location you choose will give you a good view of the plants while not preventing you from opening the window.*

2 *If you do not have a window ledge, fit brackets to support the window box. Mark the screw holes for each bracket, using a spirit level to check that the bracket is straight.*

3 *Use a masonry bit to make screw holes in the wall. Inset: Push a rawl plug into each screw hole.*

4 *Push the screw through the hole in the bracket and into the centre of the rawl plug and tighten.*

5 *Check that the two brackets are level before tightening the screws. If your spirit level is too short, rest it on a piece of wood.*

6 *Set the window box into position across the bracket. Make sure it is securely in place.*

7 *Insert a window box liner to help preserve the outer box and provide an insulating layer for the plants.*

8 *Buy the plants. If you cannot plant them immediately, store in a cool place and keep well watered.*

9 *Add a layer of broken ceramic shards for drainage. Fill the box with potting compost, mixing in water-retaining granules and slow-release fertiliser granules following the instructions on the packet.*

10 *Insert the plants. Space the box plants evenly and fill in the gaps between them with geraniums and helichrysum. Plant the ground ivy at the front of the window box so that it trails over the edge.*

Brightening Bare Walls
WALL CONTAINERS

A LARGE EXPANSE of bare wall or fence can be turned into an attractive garden feature by adding a collection of wall pots planted with a variety of colourful plants. Use this opportunity to grow plants that are best admired at close quarters, such as those with arching flowers or intriguing markings. Bear in mind that wall pots usually don't contain a great deal of compost, so regular feeding and watering is essential.

Summer subtlety

Kingfisher daisy and wandering sailor are effectively contrasted here by golden feverfew. Convolvulus sabatius *provides a trail of lilac flowers, helping to soften the hard lines of the sides of the pot. All the plants, apart from the feverfew, are frost tender, so wait until the end of the spring frosts before planting.*

1 Kingfisher daisy (*Felicia bergeriana*)

2 Wandering sailor (*Tradescantia fluminensis*)

3 *Convolvulus sabatius*

4 Golden feverfew (*Tanacetum parthenium* 'Aureum')

66

PLANTING ALTERNATIVES

Spring shades

A collection of wall pots containing spring-flowering wood-land plants makes a beautiful feature for the gloomy early months. Lenten roses come in limitless subtle shades and mixtures, but you may not know which colour you have until they flower for the first time. Plant the Lenten roses in a liner so that you can lift them out of the pot once the flowers are over and replace them with new specimens for summer.

2 Purple Lenten rose (*Helleborus* x *hybridus*)

1 White Lenten rose (*Helleborus* x *hybridus*)

3 Ivy (*Hedera helix* 'Eva')

Orange cascade

For a warmer colour scheme, substitute the plants listed below for those illustrated.

1 *Tropaeolum majus* 'Alaska'

3 Black-eyed Susan (*Thunbergia alata*)

4 Snapdragon (*Antirrhinum* 'Coronette') – salmon pink variety

---

PROJECT PLANNER

TIME SCALE 1 HOUR

Tools and Materials

Wall pot • Drill and masonry bit • Rawl plug • Screw and screwdriver • Broken ceramic shards • Potting compost • Slow-release fertiliser granules • Water-retaining granules

1 *Wall pots come in various shapes, sizes, and materials. Choose a style and colour to complement the wall on which it is to be positioned.*

2 *Buy the plants. If you cannot plant them immediately, store them in a cool place and keep well watered.*

3 *Put up the wall pot. Drill a hole in the wall and tap in a rawl plug that is large enough to fit the hole snuggly.*

4 *Position the pot and screw. Tighten, making sure you leave enough of the screw projecting from the wall to support the pot.*

5 *Place broken ceramic shards in the bottom of the pot. Fill with potting compost, mixing in water-retaining and slow-release fertiliser granules following the manufacturer's instructions.*

6 *Plant the pot, following the instructions on page 30. Water thoroughly.*

MAINTENANCE

• *Remove dead flowers and straggly stems as they appear.*

• *Six weeks after planting, add liquid fertiliser to the water, following the manufacturer's instructions.*

• *In the autumn, replace the plants with spring-flowering bulbs. Reuse the ivy if it is in good condition. Discard the kingfisher daisy and replant the feverfew elsewhere. Wandering sailor and convolvulus can be repotted and overwintered somewhere frost free. Both will make new plants from cuttings taken in late summer or early autumn (see page 39).*

Water Feature for a Small Space

POND IN A BARREL

IN ANY GARDEN, a pond – even if it is only a small one – immediately becomes a focal point. Water has the effect of attracting birds and insect life to a garden, and a pond provides an instant 'lift' for any characterless area.

If you don't have the right type of garden to set a pond into the ground, you can create a potted pond in any watertight container – in a large ceramic pot, for example, a stone sink (once the drain hole is tightly plugged), or, as here, a wooden half-barrel. Check that your barrel is suitable for turning into a pond – those designed for planting may have large gaps between the slats. A barrel that once held liquid will be waterproof once it has been thoroughly soaked. Always include an oxygenating species, such as *Elodea canadensis*, to help keep the water fresh. Around the pond you can stand pots of bog plants that look appropriate with a water feature, such as hostas, primulas or ferns.

White water lilies

This wooden half-barrel was made into a miniature pond for a sunny corner of the garden. The white-flowered pygmy water lily and the pale green water lettuce spread over the surface of the water, nestling around the upright dwarf cattail that creates contrast and adds height to the feature.

1 Dwarf cattail (*Typha minima*)

2 Water lettuce (*Pistia stratiotes*)

3 Pygmy water lily (*Nymphaea* 'Pygmaea Alba')

PLANTING ALTERNATIVES

Scarlet cardinal flowers

For a more vibrant colour scheme, substitute the plants listed below for those shown in the illustration. Here, the upright form of the scarlet cardinal flower replaces the pygmy water lily. It is not very hardy, however, and so you may need to transfer it to a bucket and keep it in a frost-free place over winter. The dwarf cattail can remain, since it is small enough for a tiny pond such as this. Parrot's feather is exchanged for water lettuce to provide a more feathery-looking cover at water level.

2 Parrot's feather
(*Myriophyllum aquaticum*)

3 Cardinal flower
(*Lobelia cardinalis*)

Blue water irises

A spiky clump of deep, rich blue Japanese water iris replaces the cattail to provide that all-essential vertical feature of the planting. Parrot's feather spreads over the surface of the water, as in the scarlet-coloured planting above, while fairy moss is substituted for the water lily.

1 Japanese water iris
(*Iris laevigata* 'Midnight')

2 Parrot's feather
(*Myriophyllum aquaticum*)

3 Fairy moss
(*Azolla mexicana*)

PROJECT PLANNER

TIME SCALE 1+ HOURS

Tools and Materials

Wooden barrel (suitable for holding water) • Stiff brush • Hose • Gravel • Brick

1 *Clean the barrel thoroughly with a stiff brush and fill with water. Keep refilling the barrel over a period of 24 hours. Wet wood expands, and this will ensure that the barrel is watertight.*

2 *Place the barrel where you intend to plant it. Place a brick in the centre of the barrel. The major feature of the planting – a water lily – will stand on this. Buy the plants. Keep them in water in the shade until you are ready to put them in the barrel.*

3 *Stand the water plants in their containers in the barrel.*

4 *Spread a layer of washed gravel over the soil of each plant in its container. Place floating water plants on the water's surface.*

MAINTENANCE

• *Remove any floating weed colonising the pond by fishing it out with a kitchen sieve.*

• *Remove blanket weed by inserting a garden cane into it. Twist the cane until the weed starts to entangle and then pull it out.*

• *Cut back any plant that is growing too vigorously. Aim to leave about a quarter of the water's surface uncovered.*

• *Add water as necessary.*

• *Clear out dead plant growth and loose soil in both the autumn and spring to prevent the water from becoming acrid.*

• *In the autumn, lift out the pot of frost-tender water lettuce and place it in a bucket of clean water. Store it in a frost-free place. Replant in the barrel in late spring or early summer, once all danger of frost has passed.*

LAWNS

Glorious grass
*A pristine, weed-free lawn sets off beds, borders
and other garden features beautifully. This
rounded lawn, framed by trellises and climbing
plants, provides a calm oasis of greenery amidst
the extravagant growth all around.*

Ideas for Improving Lawns

ASY TO CREATE and straightforward to maintain, for many people the lawn is the centrepiece of their garden. An impressive sweep of lawn — or even a tiny square of grass — makes a perfect foil for surrounding flower beds and borders.

Remember that a lawn can be far more than an ornamental showpiece: it has many functional uses, too — a means of access from one part of the garden to another; a place to relax and sunbathe with family and friends; a play area for the children, to name a few. The type of grass-seed mixture that you choose depends on how you use your lawn: if one of its main uses is as a football field for the kids, for example, then you will need a hard-wearing type (see page 74).

The questions on these two pages are designed to help you pinpoint ways in which you can improve your existing lawn, or create a new one, in order to enhance your garden. Each one is backed up by a step-by-step project that, where appropriate, includes suggestions for plants to use in your own garden.

? Is there an area of your lawn that gets worn through constant use?

Lay a series of stepping stones across it to protect the grass. This will look attractive and maintenance will be easier and less time-consuming. *Right:* These stepping stones reduce wear and tear on the grass and invite you to explore the rest of the garden.
SEE *Protecting Worn Lawns, page 80.*

? Is your lawn a harsh, geometric shape?

Choosing plants that overhang the edges of the lawn is a good way to soften the shape and create an informal look.
SEE *Softening Lawn Edges, page 78.*

? *Are you making a new lawn from scratch?*

You can choose between laying turves (expensive but quick) or establishing a lawn from seed (much cheaper but slower). *Right:* A well-kept lawn is a credit to your garden and is the perfect setting for your beds and borders.
SEE *Growing a Lawn from Seed, page 74;*
Laying a Lawn from Turf, page 76.

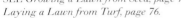

? *Does your lawn slope at an angle?*

Putting in steps will make it easier for you to navigate the lawn – particularly in wet weather, when the grass is slippery. *Above:* Here, lengths of treated wood form shallow steps to create an unusual, rustic-looking pathway.
SEE *Sloping Lawns, page 82.*

Growing a Lawn from Seed

COST-EFFECTIVE SOWING

THE BEST and most beautiful lawns are a real labor of love, but you can grow a good-looking and hard-wearing lawn that you can be proud of with relatively little effort.

If your existing lawn has more bald patches than grass, or if you've inherited a site that has never been grassed over, you'll need to create a new lawn. Decide if you want to grow a lawn from seed or from ready-grown turf (see chart, opposite). If you are sowing from seed, the best time to sow is in autumn, while the soil is still warm, although spring sowing is also acceptable. Do not subject a seed-sown lawn to heavy traffic for at least a year after sowing. Although a lawn grown from seed takes longer to establish itself than a lawn

---

PROJECT PLANNER

TIME SCALE 1/2 DAY

Tools and Materials
Cultivator • Rake • Garden twine
• Garden roller (optional) • Fertiliser
• Lawn Seed • Hay
The time scale given above is for an area measuring approx. 3 m x 3 m (10 ft x 10 ft)

1 *Remove any large stones and deep-rooted weeds from the site. Hire a cultivator and cultivate the soil to a depth of about 5 cm (2 in).*

2 *Next, rake the surface of your soil to remove any existing stones and debris on the plot, and to break up any large lumps of soil.*

3 *Using a rake, push and pull the surface layer of soil. This will further break down any lumps in the soil and smooth out bumps and hollows in your plot.*

4 *Firm down the soil surface by treading it down with your heels.*

5 *Mark out the lawn area using rope or twine. Apply granular fertilizer that contains nitrogen, potassium and phosphorous, and sprinkle the recommended amount evenly over the soil. Inset: Rake in the fertiliser.*

6 *Measure the amount of grass seed recommended on the packet and sprinkle evenly over the soil, working backwards so you don't stand on newly sown areas.*

7 *Spread hay over the seeded area to keep off birds. It will mulch into the lawn. Once the grass is 5–7.5 cm (2–3 in) long, cut it using a rotary mower.*

grown from turf, it is considerably less expensive and a greater variety of seed mixtures is available.

Designing your lawn

The size and shape of your lawn affect the look of your garden. A long, narrow lawn tends to draw the eye down along it, creating a long, narrow appearance, whereas a broad expanse of lawn across the width of the garden makes it seem wider. Use these optical illusions to your advantage when planning the shape of a new lawn, or when altering the shape of an existing one. To make a short garden seem longer, make wide beds or features on each side of the lawn and maximise its short length by tapering it toward one corner. To minimise the length of your garden, divide it crossways to break up the length and create garden areas within the garden.

Wide lawns with narrow flower beds along the edges can be a mistake. If you prefer flower beds bordering a lawn, make sure that the beds are at least 1 m (1 yd) wide – even if it means that your lawn is reduced to a strip rather than an expanse. This makes your flower beds a positive feature in their own right, rather than

little decorations at the edge of your lawn. If your gardening time is too limited to maintain such large areas of planting, then forget about borders altogether and give the whole area over to lawn. Add island beds of specimen trees and shrubs gradually as you feel the need and have the time to look after them.

SEED VS TURF

New lawn from seed
PROS
- Less expensive than turf
- More choice of varieties
- Watering not always essential

CONS
- Soil preparation must be thoroughly done
- You cannot walk on your new lawn for several weeks after sowing

New lawn from turf
PROS
- Gives an instant result
- Soil preparation does not need to be as thorough as for sowing from seed

CONS
- Costly
- Limited choice and variety of turfs
- Watering is usually essential – so you must have access to a water supply and hose

MAINTENANCE

Unless you want to encourage wild flowers to grow, apply a lawn fertiliser and selective weed killer in spring. Use a watering can with a dribble bar attachment to apply liquid formulations in strips, taking care not to overlap the strips.

- *Mow to around 2.5 cm (1 in) or a little higher in dry weather. Vary the mowing pattern to avoid grooves in the lawn.*

- *Cut the lawn edges after mowing using long-handled shears; for awkward grass edges, such as the edge of steps, use single-handed shears. Alternatively, use either a petrol-powered or electric strimmer for both areas.*

In spring, use a fan-shaped spring-tined rake to remove winter debris before you mow for the first time.

- *Always wear strong, thick-soled shoes or boots when mowing. If you're using an electric mower or trimmer, drape the cable over your shoulder to keep it away from the mower blades. Wear goggles when mowing long grass – particularly if it is stony or likely to contain hidden debris.*

In autumn, use a spring-tined rake to remove matted grass and fallen leaves.

- *Top dress the lawn in autumn. Mix equal parts of sharp sand, sieved soil, and peat. Spread half a bucket per square metre (yard) over the lawn surface and rake it in.*

- *In autumn, spike the lawn with a garden fork to improve drainage. Push the fork in to a depth of 10–15 cm (4–6 in), then pull it out vertically.*

Laying a Lawn from Turf

INSTANT COVERAGE

YOU CAN LAY a new lawn from turf at any time of year except during dry, very wet or freezing weather. The advantage of using ready-grown turf, rather than seed, is that it gives you a new lawn almost instantly. You need to avoid walking on new turf for two to three weeks after laying, until it starts to grow – but then you can treat it exactly as you would an established lawn.

Always examine the turf before you buy or accept delivery. Feel the soil under the turf to make sure that it is moist, not dry and crumbly, and unroll a couple of turves and check that the grass is dense and weed free.

Keep newly laid turf damp – otherwise the turves will shrink away from each other leaving large cracks. Water thoroughly and frequently, until the joints between the turves grow together.

PROJECT PLANNER

TIME SCALE 1/2 DAY

Tools and Materials

Rake • Fertilizer • Plank • Knife • Half-moon edger • Rope or twine • Sprinkler
The time scale given above is for an area measuring about 3 m x 3 m (10 ft x 10 ft)

1 *Stack the turf close to your working area. Keep it damp and shaded until you are ready to lay the lawn.*

2 *Clear the site of stones, deep-rooted weeds and other debris. Rake the surface smooth and level several times. If necessary, loosen the top surface with a scuffle hoe. Tread the soil thoroughly all over to compact the surface and eliminate bumps and hollows, then sprinkle on fertiliser (see Step 5 of Growing A Lawn from Seed, page 74) and rake again.*

3 *Working from a side path or plank, unroll and position each turf in the first row. Stagger the next row of turves – to do this, you may have to cut a turf.*

4 *Butt the turves up tightly to one another, then tamp them down.*

5 *Don't position small pieces of turf at the edge of the lawn. Instead, make a gap in the lawn and cut a piece of turf to fit it.*

6 *Again working from a plank or side path, firmly tamp down the entire turfed area using the flat back of your rake.*

7 *Mark out the edge of the lawn using a rope or twine as a guide, then use a half-moon edging tool to cut the turf where necessary.*

8 *Water the turf thoroughly using a lawn sprinkler. Take care not to allow it to dry out until growth is well established.*

LAWN REPAIR

To Repair Bumps and Hollows

1 *First, cut a cross in the turf as shown and peel back the edges.*

1 *Remove a rectangle of turf around the damaged edge and turn it around so that the damaged section is no longer on the edge.*

To Repair Ragged Edges

2 *Tamp down the turf and fill the hole with soil and a little grass seed. This can be done at any time between spring and autumn.*

2 *Using a trowel, add, remove, or redistribute the soil under the turf to even out the bump or hollow.*

To Reseed Bare Patches

1 *Rake the soil to remove dead grass, pull up any weeds, and loosen the surface of the bare patch with a hand fork to create an area of fine soil.*

2 *Carefully scatter the grass seeds over the bare patch.*

3 *Replace the flaps of turf and tamp down using the back of a rake. This can be done at any time between spring and autumn.*

3 *Speed up germination and protect the patch from birds by covering the area with a sheet of pierced clear plastic, pegged down to create a mini greenhouse. (If cats, rabbits, or other animals are a problem, use pegged-down chicken wire to protect the patch.) Remove the plastic covering once the grass seedlings are about 2.5 cm (1 in) high. Water in dry weather.*

Softening Lawn Edges
FRONT-LINE PLANTS

A LONG, STRAIGHT-EDGED lawn can look formal and severe in a garden setting. Use plants to break up the hard lines, make a softer and less regular shape, and give your garden a more informal and natural look.

It is important to choose plants that don't actually spread into or lie on the grass, since they would kill the turf. Instead, choose edging plants that arch over the side of the lawn without getting tangled in the mower. Hardy geraniums (such as *Geranium macrorrhizum*) are an especially useful group of plants for the front of a grass-edged border; they make a low, neat hummock that can easily be nudged out of the way when mowing. Lady's mantle (*Alchemilla mollis*) and London pride (*Saxifraga × urbium*) are also pretty edging plants. To help to give a sense of unity to the whole garden, it is a good idea to make a repeating pattern of plants at the front of the bed or border.

The key to this critical 'front line' between the grass and your garden plants lies in regular maintenance. Trim back the grass at the edge of the lawn every time you mow with single-handed shears to prevent it from invading the bed. While you're at it, you can trim any over-enthusiastic border plants.

Edging in lime yellow, silver and purple

At the front edge of this border, four plants are used in a loosely repeating pattern that helps to give the planting unity. The purple-leaved heuchera and the silver-leaved lamb's ears contrast with the medium-green leaves and lime-green flowers of the lady's mantle and the glossy green of the elephant's ears. The fifth plant, Liriope muscari, *is set back slightly from the front of the border. It forms a tuft of spiky leaves and provides a visual break from the flatter, more horizontal forms of the plants in the front of the border.*

1 *Heuchera micrantha* 'Palace Purple'

2 *Liriope muscari*

3 Elephant's ears (*Bergenia cordifolia*)

MAINTENANCE

- *Water thoroughly in dry weather, especially during the first summer after planting.*

- *Clip back straggly growths that stray onto the lawn.*

- *Clip the lawn edges regularly – ideally every time you mow (see page 75).*

- *Cut back any old flowering stems once they are past their best.*

- *In autumn, or after flowering in spring, lift and divide overgrown clumps of elephant's ears (see page 39). Cut through the fleshy, horizontal underground stems (rhizomes) and replant the pieces.*

- *Replenish the bark-chip mulch in late spring, once the soil warms up.*

PROJECT PLANNER

TIME SCALE 1/2 DAY

Tools and Materials

Fork • Compost or manure • Rake • Trowel • Bark-chip mulch
The time scale above is for a site about 10 m (10 yd) long.

1 *Fork over the front 30 cm (1 ft) of the border soil, and enrich it by adding a bucketful of compost or manure every metre (yard). Tread down the soil and rake it smooth.*

2 *Buy the plants. If you are not able to plant them immediately, keep them watered and in the shade.*

3 *Plant the plants in groups of three or five, about 10–15 cm (4–6 in) from the front of the bed. Repeat the same planting pattern along the length of the bed.*

4 *Water thoroughly. Apply a 5–7.5-cm (2–3-in) layer of bark chippings as a mulch.*

PLANTING ALTERNATIVES

Edging in gold and white

To create a fresher, lighter effect, change the purple-leaved heuchera for green-leaved and white-flowered foam flower and the lamb's ears for white deadnettle. The *Liriope muscari*, elephant's ears, and lady's mantle remain, since they contrast well with the dark green leaves of the foam flower and the white-splashed leaves of the deadnettle.

1 Foam flower (*Tiarella cordifolia*)

4 White deadnettle (*Lamium maculatum* 'Album')

4 Lamb's ears (*Stachys byzantina* 'Silver Carpet')

5 Lady's mantle (*Alchemilla mollis*)

Protecting Worn Lawns
STEPPING-STONE PATH

ALMOST EVERY LAWN has areas that get more wear and tear than others. To protect the lawn, you can put in a stepping-stone path. This will also save you from having to re-seed patches of lawn each year. Make a feature of the path by arranging the paving slabs in a pattern; children will enjoy making a game of hopping along the path.

The easiest method is to cut holes in the turf where each step will be, lift the turf, and replace it with a paving slab. The surrounding turf will hold the slab in place, so there is no need to use cement. You can use irregularly-shaped pieces of flat stone (crazy paving pieces) or regular-shaped manufactured slabs. Choose slabs that are big enough to stand on comfortably.

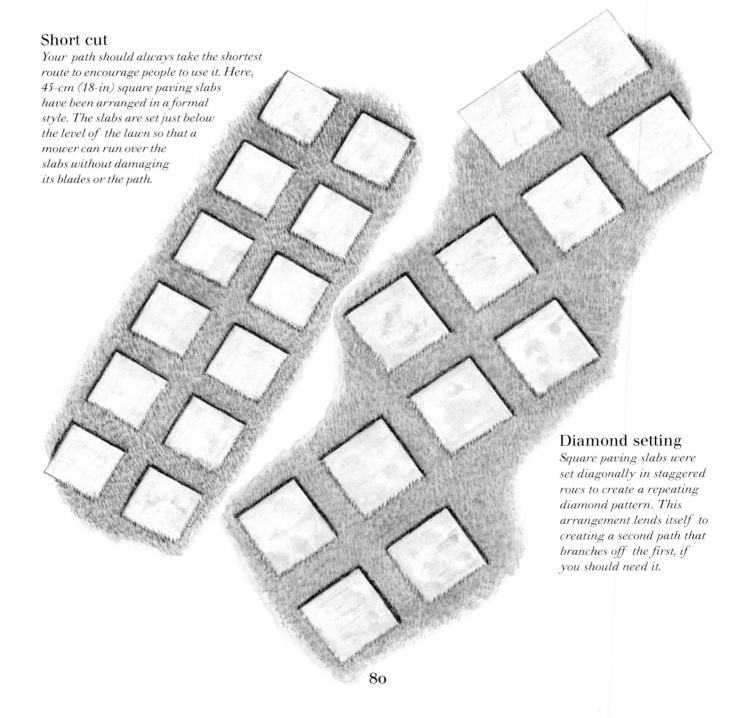

Short cut
Your path should always take the shortest route to encourage people to use it. Here, 45-cm (18-in) square paving slabs have been arranged in a formal style. The slabs are set just below the level of the lawn so that a mower can run over the slabs without damaging its blades or the path.

Diamond setting
Square paving slabs were set diagonally in staggered rows to create a repeating diamond pattern. This arrangement lends itself to creating a second path that branches off the first, if you should need it.

Meadow path

Pressure-treated log slices are ideal for a more natural-looking path, such as in a flowering meadow or an informally-planted shrubbery. Make sure the log slices have been treated with wood preservative to prevent them from rotting. If the route the path is to take is shaded, wrap each slice in chicken wire to create a slip-proof surface before laying them in your lawn.

PROJECT PLANNER

TIME SCALE 1/2 DAY

Tools and Materials
Paving slabs • Garden twine • Half-moon cutter • Spade • Coarse sand • Spirit level • Hard bristle broom

1 *Lay the paving slabs across the lawn. To mark out a straight path, put down a taut line of garden twine and align the slabs with it. Make sure they are evenly spaced. Leave about 15 cm (6 in) of turf between each slab.*

2 *Cut around each slab using a half-moon cutter, cutting deep into the turf.*

3 *Using a spade, carefully lift out the section of turf you have cut.*

4 *Line the space with at least 5 cm (2 in) of coarse sand so that the slab lies just below the level of the rest of the turf.*

5 *Place the slab onto the sand. Check that it is set below the surface of the lawn and that it is level. Finally, sweep the slab clean.*

MAINTENANCE

• *Keep the paving slabs clear of encroaching turf by clipping the edges with single-handed shears.*

• *Use a commercial paving cleaner to remove algae and prevent the paving from becoming slippery.*

• *If a slab becomes loose, lift the slab and add more sand underneath it. Replace the slab and check that it is even using a spirit level.*

Sloping Lawns
INFORMAL STEPS

A GENTLY SLOPING lawn can make a very attractive feature: it conjures up images of rolling countryside and, even if your garden is a small urban one, the smooth sweep of grass creates a tranquil, rural feel.

From a practical point of view, however, a sloping lawn can be difficult to negotiate. In damp weather, when the lawn is likely to become slippery, it can be treacherous under foot. The solution is to inset gentle steps that can become an attractive feature of the lawn in their own right.

Rather than installing permanent steps, opt for the more natural look of informal bark steps shaped to fit your particular slope. They need not be parallel or evenly spaced. The informality of this kind of step adds to the rural feel. Reseed any disturbed grass areas with a meadow-grass seed mixture to encourage some wild flowers to establish themselves.

Soft landings
Make a safe route across a sloping lawn.
Here, wooden risers holding 7.5 cm (3 in)
of chipped bark create a set of
informal country-style steps.

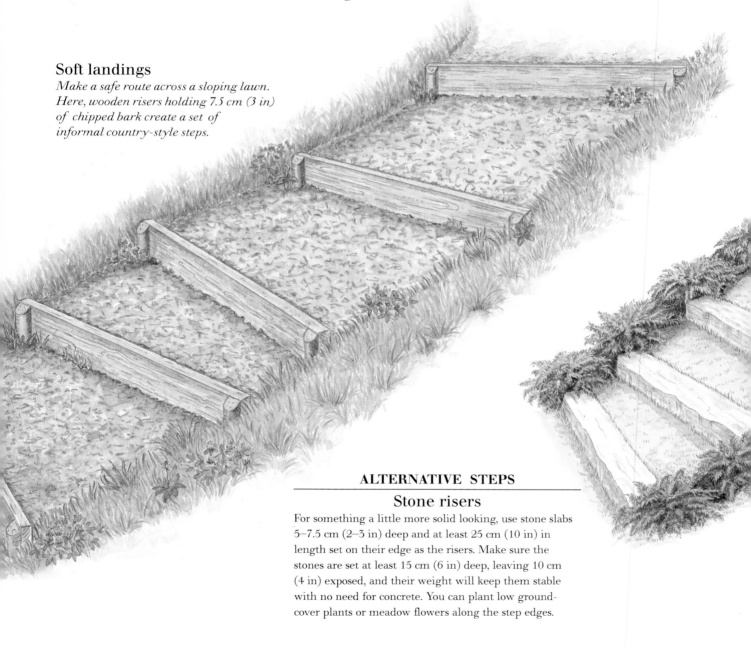

ALTERNATIVE STEPS
Stone risers
For something a little more solid looking, use stone slabs 5–7.5 cm (2–3 in) deep and at least 25 cm (10 in) in length set on their edge as the risers. Make sure the stones are set at least 15 cm (6 in) deep, leaving 10 cm (4 in) exposed, and their weight will keep them stable with no need for concrete. You can plant low ground-cover plants or meadow flowers along the step edges.

MAINTENANCE

• *The edges of the steps, where you removed the turf, may be prone to weeds at first. Until the grass has grown back, check for weeds regularly and remove them as they appear.*

• *After mowing, use a strimmer to keep the edges of the steps tidy.*

• *Replenish the bark chippings as necessary.*

PROJECT PLANNER

TIME SCALE 1/2 DAY

Tools and Materials

Lengths of 10 x 3.8 cm (4 x 1^1/$_2$ in) pressure-treated soft wood • Pressure-treated stakes (2 per step) • Chisel • Spade • Metal piping • Mallet • 7.5-cm (3-in) galvanised nails • Spirit level • Weed-proof membrane • Large bark chippings
The time scale given above is for about 6 bark steps.

1 *Cut riser slats to the required length from 10 x 3.8 cm (4 x 1.5 in) pressure-treated soft wood and lay them across the slope wherever a step is needed. Make the steps descend gradually; each subsequent tread should be no more than 10 cm (4 in) below the previous one.*

2 *Make or buy pressure-treated pointed stakes to hold the risers in position. Bevel one end using a chisel.*

3 *Starting at the bottom of the slope and working uphill so that you can see the slope ahead of you, dig out the first tread to a depth of no more than 10 cm (4 in). Use a spirit level to check that it is level in all directions.*

4 *Make holes for the stakes by driving in a length of piping, marked to the required depth, with a mallet.*

5 *Nail a stake to each end of each riser. Position the stakes in the holes and place a spare piece of wood on top of each riser. Using a mallet, knock in each end of the riser until it is level across the slope.*

6 *Continue in the same way until you have dug out all the treads and positioned the risers. Line each tread with weed-proof membrane and fill it with large bark chippings.*

PATHS AND PAVING

Stony ground
*The soft, muted colours of this brick paving
make a light, neutral background for the
profusion of colourful plants. The formality
of the paving design – alternate steps are laid
out in a pinwheel pattern – is softened by the
plants that overhang the edges.*

Ideas for Improving Paths and Paving

PATIOS AND PAVED areas have an important part to play in your enjoyment of your garden. They're great for entertaining – particularly if the weather has been wet or the dew heavy and you can't walk on the lawn without getting your feet wet. They also provide a wonderful setting for plants – but you need to choose your plants carefully. Paved and concreted surfaces are visually strong, and you need to counteract this by using strong-charactered plants around them – ones with large leaves and dramatic shapes and colours. In fact, paved areas need plants to soften their harsh lines.

Paths have obvious practical uses in enabling you to walk from one part of the garden to another. They can also provide a framework for your planting, dividing the garden into discrete sections. From an aesthetic point of view, they can be used to lead the eye to other features such as a garden ornament or arbour.

The questions on these two pages are designed to help you pinpoint ways in which you can improve your existing paths and paving, or create new ones, in order to enhance your garden. Each one is backed up by a step-by-step project that, where appropriate, includes suggestions for plants to use in your own garden.

? *Do you have a path that is broken or unattractive?*

An easy way to create a new path that is easy to maintain is to dig out most of an existing path and fill the area with gravel or cover it with wooden decking.

Right: This path is made of limestone chippings edged with railroad ties. Orange rock rose, green-flowered hellebores and pink potentilla soften the path edges.

SEE *Non-slip Path, page 94; Quick-and-easy Path, page 96.*

➤·➤·➤·➤·➤·➤·➤·➤·➤·➤·➤·➤·➤·➤

? *Do you have gaps between paving?*

Make a virtue of them by planting in the cracks.

Left: The texture of these slabs contrasts with the lady's mantle and the pebbles between the widely spaced paving.

SEE *Planting between Paving Slabs, page 92.*

◄·◄·◄·◄·◄·◄·◄·◄·◄·◄

? *Do your paved areas have straight edges?*

You can soften the overall shape, and introduce an informal effect, by planting overhanging plants around the edges of your paving.

Left: An attractive cloud of lady's mantle sprawls over the hard edges of this paved path.

SEE *Softening Paving Edges, page 88.*

◄·◄·◄·◄·◄·◄·◄·◄

? *Do you have a large area of dull paving?*

You can brighten up a paved area by removing occasional slabs and planting in the spaces you create.

SEE *Livening up Paving, page 90.*

Softening Paving Edges
BREAKING THE LINE

PATIO AREAS ARE often geometric in shape. Although many people welcome such neat, tidy shapes, they can look bare and stark – not the sort of place you would want to sit and relax in for any length of time.

To soften a paved patio's appearance, allow plants to billow over the edges of the paving to create a gentler overall effect. The best plants to use are ones that have strong enough shapes and shadows to counteract the hardness and flatness of the paving material. Dramatic shapes are better than indistinct ones: fine, feathery foliage such as that of cotton lavender is not as effective as large bold leaves characteristic of hosta.

Patios are often next to the house and in full view, so make sure you have a planting that will provide an attractive show throughout the year. The planting scheme illustrated below uses evergreens to provide a basic framework. To introduce seasonal changes you can add winter- and spring-flowering bulbs and some summer bedding plants.

Evergreens in blue, purple and grey

Although the dramatic clump of purple phormium does not actually overlap the edge of the paving, its bold outline casts leafy shadows that draw attention away from the hard, flat surface. A variegated, white-flowered deadnettle carpets the spaces between the other plants. The spreading blue-grey juniper makes an excellent contrast to the phormium in both its habit and colour. Jerusalem sage is a handsome grey-leaved evergreen that provides a splash of yellow flowers in summer.

1 Jerusalem sage (*Phlomis fruticosa*)

2 Deadnettle (*Lamium maculatum* 'White Nancy')

MAINTENANCE

- Snip off any untidy or dead growth.
- Remove dead flower heads of Jerusalem sage.
- Water regularly in dry weather – especially in the first summer before the plants are well established.

4 *Phormium tenax*

3 Creeping juniper (*Juniperus squamata* 'Blue Carpet')

PROJECT PLANNER

TIME SCALE 1/2 DAY

Tools and Materials

Fork • Manure or garden compost • Rake • Trowel • Bark-chip mulch
The time scale above is for a site about 10 m (10 yd) long.

1 Fork over the front 60 cm (2 ft) of soil bordering the paving. Enrich by adding a bucketful of manure or garden compost every metre (yard). Tread down the soil and rake it smooth.

2 Buy the plants. If you can't plant them immediately, keep them in the shade and water daily.

3 Plant the Jerusalem sage, juniper, and phormium at least 30 cm (1 ft) from the front edge of the bed, staggering their positions slightly so that they are not in a straight line. Plant the deadnettle in front of the phormium and in any big gaps along the front edge.

4 Water thoroughly and apply a 5-cm (2-in) layer of bark-chip mulch over the soil between the plants.

PLANTING ALTERNATIVES

Golden foliage

For a warmer colour scheme, swap the blue-grey creeping juniper for a golden variety. Change the ground-covering deadnettle for yellow-flowered archangel and the phormium for a smaller, but still imposing, daylily with yellow flowers. The yellow flowers of Jerusalem sage work equally well with this golden colour scheme, so it can remain as a source of summer colour.

2 Yellow archangel (*Lamium galeobdolon* 'Variegatum')

3 Ground-cover variegated juniper
(*Juniperus* x *media* 'Carbery Gold')

4 Daylily (*Hemerocallis* 'Marion Vaughn')

Livening up Paving
AROMATIC PATIO CORNER

LIVEN UP YOUR paving and create a conversation-stopping showpiece by replacing occasional stone slabs with unique plantings. Make a repeating pattern of planting spaces to emphasise the corners or edges of your patio or to create a division in the paving – marking off an eating area from a sitting area, for example.

Choose plants that tolerate shallow soil, as they require little watering and are thus easier to care for. Many herbs, desert and rock plants fall into this category. The planting suggestion below, which uses a range of low-growing herbs, is a particularly good choice for a paved area near the house, as the herbs are easily accessible for cooking.

Contrast the texture of the plants with the texture of the paving, alternating squares of soft, cushion-like plants, such as the herbs shown below, with hard, flat, concrete slabs, for example. Colour is important, too: the gold-green and purple plants below work well with the natural beige of the paving slabs.

Herbal chequerboard

Herbs are a great choice for planting in paving since many of them like poor, well-drained soil. They have the added benefit of a delicious aroma, which you can enjoy as you pass by. Here, edged with purple bugle, a small collection of thymes and golden marjoram is arranged in a chequerboard pattern.

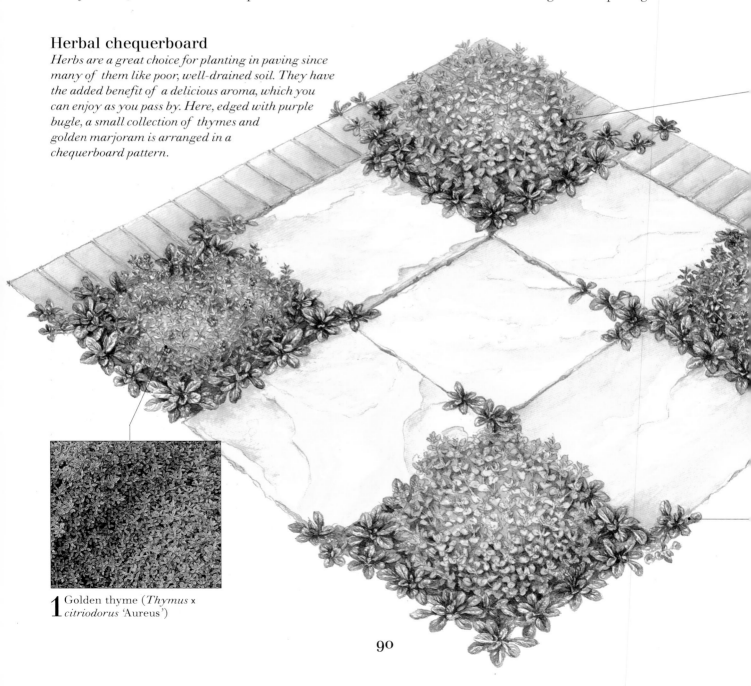

1 Golden thyme (*Thymus* x *citriodorus* 'Aureus')

PLANTING ALTERNATIVES

Rock-plant chequerboard

For an alternative planting scheme, use rock and alpine plants in place of the herbs. Replace the two thymes with thrift (*Armeria maritima*) and the marjoram with alpine aster. This is a simpler design that emphasises the contrasting forms of the thrift and the aster. For edging, replace the bugle with New Zealand burr: its burnished colouring sets off the dark pink thrift and the purple aster. Cover the soil between the plants with a mulch of gravel after planting.

1 and **3** Thrift (*Armeria maritima*)

2 New Zealand burr (*Acaena microphylla*)

4 Alpine aster (*Aster alpinus*)

4 Golden marjoram (*Origanum vulgare* 'Aureum')

3 Thyme (*Thymus vulgaris* 'Silver Posie')

2 Purple variegated bugle (*Ajuga reptans* 'Atropurpurea')

PROJECT PLANNER

TIME SCALE **½ DAY**

Tools and Materials

Mallet • Chisel • Spade • Topsoil • Trowel

The time scale above is for a site about 4 sq m (4 sq yd).

1 *Pry up the paving slabs that you want to remove. If they are bedded in concrete, you will need to break up the mortar joints with a mallet and chisel first. Inset: If the slabs are set in sand, use a spade to lift them up.*

2 *Break up the mortar under the slabs, with the mallet and chisel, and remove it.*

3 *Cover the planting space with topsoil and plant (see page 32). Water thoroughly.*

MAINTENANCE

• *Keep watered and weeded. You may need to weed out over-vigorous bugle stems to prevent them from overwhelming the other plants.*

• *Trim the thymes and marjoram in summer to keep them in shape. You can use the clippings in cooking.*

Planting between Paving Slabs

SELF-SEEDING FLOWERS

PLANTING SELF-SEEDING flowers between paving slabs is a very simple, but eye-catching way of brightening up your paving. Choose plants that enjoy the sparse, often alkaline, soil of paved areas. They will seed themselves, leaving you with little to do beyond occasionally thinning them out if they grow too profusely. Suitable plants include many of the alpines, herbs, annual flowers and short-lived perennials.

This is a particularly useful idea if your paving is old and cracked: instead of going to the expense and disruption of laying new surfaces, make a virtue out of something that many people might consider a defect. Weathered paving has a character and charm that you simply do not find in pristine, newly laid paving and looks particularly good with old-fashioned 'cottage garden' and wild flowers.

Shaded paving

*This attractive planting is ideal for a shaded patio or paved area. The Welsh poppy (*Meconopsis cambrica*) and heartsease (*Viola tricolor*) flower from the late spring through the summer months and the Corsican mint (*Mentha requienii*) provides colour throughout most of the year. The bright yellow poppy combines well with the delicate violet and the rich green foliage of the mint to create a striking display reminiscent of a traditional cottage garden. The mint exudes a wonderful scent when crushed underfoot and its sprawling leaves will reach across the paving, creating interesting shapes within your site.*

1 Heartsease
(*Viola tricolor*)

PLANTING ALTERNATIVES

Sunny paving

For a paved area that receives a lot of sunlight, substitute the plants below for those illustrated. Exchange the shade-loving Corsican mint and the Welsh poppy for a sun-worshipping creeping thyme such as *Thymus serpyllum* 'Goldstream' and the field poppy (*Papaver rhoeas*). Leave the heartsease, as it is happy in either sun or shade and will help to create a colourful show.

2 Creeping thyme (*Thymus serpyllum* 'Goldstream')

3 Field poppy (*Papaver rhoeas*)

2 Welsh poppy
(*Meconopsis cambrica*)

3 Corsican mint
(*Mentha requienii*)

PROJECT PLANNER

TIME SCALE 1+ HOURS

Tools and Materials

Chisel • Mallet • Narrow trowel • Soil-based compost • Fine soil • Chicken wire • Wire pegs or skewers

1 *Clean out the gaps in the paving with the chisel and mallet and remove any loose material with the trowel.*

2 *Fill the cracks with soil-based compost.*

3 *Sow seed thinly in the cracks and cover with fine soil.* Inset: *Cover with chicken wire held in place with wire pegs or skewers until the seedlings are well established to prevent the seeds from being eaten by birds.*

4 *Water the seedlings in dry weather. Thin out the seedlings when they become overcrowded. Replant the excess seedlings elsewhere to help integrate the paved area with the rest of the garden.*

MAINTENANCE

- *Cut the poppies down to ground level once the seedheads are dry.*

- *Shake the contents of the seedheads over the ground to encourage self-seeding.*

- *Deadhead the heartsease (unless you want it to self-sow).*

- *Snip off any straggly mint stems.*

- *Encourage the mint stems to root by pushing them into the paving cracks.*

Non-slip Path
FORMAL GRAVEL FEATURE

AN ELEGANT GRAVEL PATH is perfect for a garden that is formal in style – and it is one of the easiest paths to make. It is also practical: because water drains through the gravel, you can walk on it after rain without worrying about it being slippery.

Some kind of edging needs to be placed along the sides of the path in order to contain the gravel. For this reason, most gravel paths are straight – it is the straight lines that give such paths their formal appearance.

Sketch your design first to make sure that you get the proportions right. Make decorative paths wide enough to stroll along comfortably and balance them with beds of at least the same width. Experiment with different arrangements – paths radiating out in four directions from a central octagonal bed, perhaps, or a single path edging a rectangular lawn.

Gravel and stone chippings come in various sizes and colours, from slate grey to golden brown. The smallest 1.25-cm ($^1/_2$-in) size will be difficult to walk on if it is more than 2.5 cm (1 in) deep. If your path has to be more than 2.5 cm (1 in) deep, lay a bed of 2-cm ($^3/_4$-in) gravel underneath the small chippings.

Golden gravel walk

Intersecting gravel paths form a diagonal cross between triangular flower beds. Trees were positioned to create intriguing views through their branches and bring some height and a little shade to the area. Plants were allowed to overlap the path edging and soften its straight lines.

MAINTENANCE

• *Keep the path weeded: remove any weeds as soon as they emerge. Try not to get any soil on the gravel, since weeds will quickly grow in it.*

• *Add new gravel when necessary and rake smooth.*

PROJECT PLANNER

TIME SCALE 1 DAY

Tools and Materials

Garden line • Tape measure • Spade • Rake • Pointed tannelised pegs, 5 x 5 x 45 cm (2 x 2 x 18 in) • Mallet • Tannelised gravel boards, 12.5 x 2.5 cm (5 x 1 in) • 7.5-cm (3-in) galvanised nails • Weed-proof membrane • Gravel

The time scale given above is for a path 10 m (10 yd) long.

2 *Using a mallet, knock pointed pegs into the ground on the outside edge of the path wherever two boards meet. (This reinforces the join.) The pegs should be level with or just below the boards. Nail the pegs to the boards using 7.5-cm (3-in) galvanised nails.*

1 *Mark out the path, using a garden line and tape measure to make sure that the edges are straight and parallel. Rake the ground and tread it firm and level. Dig a 5-cm (2-in) deep slit at each side of the path. Insert the gravel boards, tapping them down with a mallet so that they are lodged securely.*

3 *Lay weed-proof membrane along the floor of the path. Trim it to fit the path if necessary.*

4 *Pour in the gravel and spread it out evenly over the path. It should be 2.5–5 cm (1–2 in) deep all along the path.*

5 *Rake the gravel smooth. The final level should be about 2.5 cm (1 in) below the top of the gravel board.*

Quick-and-easy Path
DECKING WALKWAY

IF YOU'VE ALWAYS DESIRED a stylish, refined-looking wooden walkway but feared that it would be too difficult or time-consuming to construct yourself, hesitate no more: wooden decking tiles are the answer. Packs of ready-made, pretreated tiles are inexpensive and available at many home and garden stores. Your only requirement is that the ground must be flat: if it is bumpy or sloping, you will need a timber substructure to hold the walkway securely above ground – in which case you may want to hire a contractor to help.

Decking tiles make particularly good paths through flower beds if you need a short cut to another area of the garden. They're also useful as temporary paths to lay across an area that's occasionally muddy.

You can even colour your decking, as woodstains are available in a number of different colours – but make sure you buy one that is suitable for exterior use. The stain should be renewed every few years.

Decking path through the shrubbery
Decking tiles, staggered to create a more interesting shape, are used to create a convenient pathway through a bed of shrubs. Bark chippings scattered alongside the path ensure that the contrast between the decking and the adjoining bed is not too stark.

96

PROJECT PLANNER

TIME SCALE 2 HOURS

Tools and Materials

Garden line • Rake • Spirit level • Decking tiles • Weed-proof membrane • Wire pegs or skewers • Mallet • Pointed tannelised pegs, 5 x 5 x 45 cm (2 x 2 x 18 in) • Large bark chippings
The time scale given above is for a path 10 m (10 yd) long

1 Before you begin, plan the route of the path and mark out its outer edges with a garden line. Rake the path smooth and use a spirit level to check that it is completely level.

2 Set the tiles in position, butting them up against one another to check that they are arranged the way that you want them.

3 Remove the tiles and lay weed-proof membrane along the route of the path, pinning it down with wire pegs or skewers.

4 Lay the tiles in position on top of the weed-proof membrane, butting them up against each other.

5 Using a mallet, knock a tannelised wooden peg in through the weed-proof membrane at each corner of each tile to secure in place.

6 Cover the exposed weed-proof membrane with large bark chippings.

Forming patterns

Experiment with laying the tiles at different angles to form patterns. Here, the tiles are placed at right angles to each other, forming a pattern similar to a basket weave.

MAINTENANCE

• *Keep the path clear of mud, leaves and algae since these will make it slippery.*

• *Remove any weeds that emerge through the slats.*

• *Wash the decking down with a hose and a stiff broom if it gets muddy.*

• *If you use a coloured stain on the tiles, renew it every few years.*

• *Check the tiles once a year for splits or cracks and replace any that are badly damaged.*

WALLS, FENCES AND HEDGES

Beautiful boundaries
Flowering climbers, such as the magnificent white rose, Rosa filipes 'Kiftsgate', make this wall an attractive garden feature. This vibrant splash of colour provides a striking contrast to the plain brickwork of the wall and makes an inviting entrance to the area beyond the gate.

Ideas for Improving Walls, Fences and Hedges

THE EXTERNAL boundaries of your garden – the walls, fences and hedges – provide the basic framework against which all of your plantings are seen. They also have a practical effect on the microclimate of your garden, creating shelter and shade and therefore influencing the types of plants that you can grow. When you choose plants, you need to think not only about factors such as shade, but also about aesthetic considerations – how your plants will blend in or contrast with the boundaries in terms of their colour and texture.

Something that many people overlook is that walls, fences and hedges can also be used as internal divisions – separating a patio area from the rest of the garden, or creating a secluded corner where you can enjoy the afternoon sunshine.

The questions on these two pages are designed to help you pinpoint ways in which you can improve existing boundaries, or create new ones, in order to enhance your garden. Each one is backed up by a step-by-step project that includes suggestions for plants that you might like to use in your own garden.

? *Does your garden feel too open?*

Set up boundaries within the garden to create a separate 'garden room' or a series of 'rooms' and make it more interesting to walk through. *Right:* This garden sanctuary is created by 2.1-m (7-ft) high yew hedging. The petunias and potted marguerite daisies match the striking white statue. SEE *A Garden Divider, page 110; Formal Hedge, page 114.*

? *Does your front-garden fence look dilapidated?*

With a minimum of practical skills, you can create an informal fence that also makes the perfect frame for plants to grow on and around. SEE *Front-garden Boundary, page 118.*

❓ Do buildings enclose or overlook your garden?

Raise the height of boundary walls and fences (be sure to check any local bye-laws) and grow climbers up them to make them look more attractive. *Above*: A trellis, covered in the beautiful *Rosa* 'Handel', increases the height of the low wall and prevents the garden from being overlooked.
SEE *Raising a Wall with Trellis, page 104*

❓ Is your hedge an expanse of single colour?

Plant a flowering hedge or train a succession of flowering climbers through an evergreen hedge to give seasonal variety and colour. *Above*: The colourful splendour of this beautiful garden overflows into the hedges. The clipped, dark-green yew cone is enhanced by the flame-coloured nasturtium.
SEE *Adding Colour to Green Hedges, page 108; Informal Boundary Hedge, page 112.*

❓ Do your bed and border edges look untidy?

Plant a miniature hedge to define the edges.
Left: This miniature box hedge makes a neat edging to the bed and hides the bare rose stems. Alpine daisies and catmint cascade over the wall in front of the hedge.
SEE *Defining Your Beds, page 116.*

❓ Do you have a fence or boundary that is bare and boring?

Use trellis panels to break up a blank wall area and train climbers and wall shrubs through the trellis to soften the edges. If the wall gets the sun, you can create a scented sitting area.
SEE *Enhancing a Bare Wall, page 102; Plants for a Sunny Wall, page 106.*

Enhancing a Bare Wall
LIVING TRELLIS

MANY GARDENS, especially in towns and cities where space is scarce and houses are packed tightly together, are hemmed in by a tall, blank wall. For a conversation-stopping show piece, put up a trellis and train plants over it. This project features espalier-trained firethorns that have been pruned to leave a main vertical stem with several horizontal side stems emerging on each side.

Living wall for a shaded site
Here the firethorn plants have been pruned tightly back to cover their stems with foliage and create a living trellis effect. Their scarlet berries are accentuated in the autumn by the bright red leaves of Virginia creeper. Evergreen euonymous smothers the ground.

One of the problems with this type of situation is that tall walls often shade the soil beneath them from rain and light. The design below uses firethorn and Virginia creeper, both of which thrive in dry, impoverished soil and shade. If you have a sunny wall, try training a fruit tree (an apple, plum, pear or cherry) in the same way.

1 Virginia creeper (*Parthenocissus quinquefolia*)

2 Firethorn (*Pyracantha* 'Mohave')

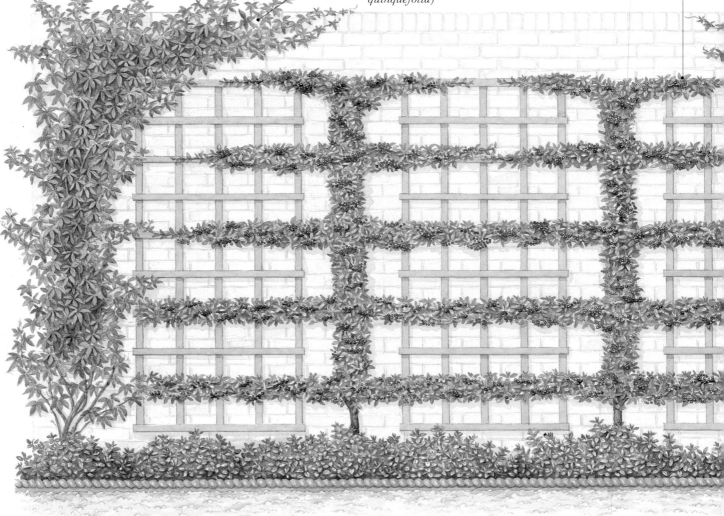

MAINTENANCE

• *Keep the site well weeded and watered and mulch in late spring or autumn.*

• *Prune unwanted growth in summer.*

• *Tie horizontal stems of the firethorn to the trellis as they grow, using plastic-covered wire twists or garden twine. Check the ties occasionally, loosening them if necessary to allow the stems room to grow.*

• *Prune the firethorn in the summer months. Pinch out any shoots that are growing in the wrong place as they emerge. Leave shoots that are growing in the right direction to grow to the required length. Allow these stems to grow side shoots 5–10 cm (2–4 in) in length to clothe the main stem.*

3 Pink-tinged *Euonymous* such as 'Variegata'

PROJECT PLANNER

TIME SCALE ½ DAY

Tools and Materials

Trellis panel • Spirit level • Pencil or chalk • Pretreated 5 x 2.5-cm (2 x 1-in) wooden battens • Screws and screwdriver • Drill with wood and masonry bits • Nails • Rawl plugs • Spade • Compost or manure • Bone meal • Fork • Rake • Tree stake • Wire rings • Secateurs

1 *Position the trellis panel on the wall. Using a spirit level, check that it is straight. Mark its position on the wall with a pencil or chalk.*

2 *Position the battens vertically on the wall in line with the markings. At 45-cm (18-in) intervals, make screw holes in the battens.*

3 *Tap a nail through each batten screw hole into the wall to mark the screw positions. Then drill holes in the wall at each screw point using a masonry bit.*

4 *Insert rawl plugs into the screw holes and screw the battens to the wall. Screw the trellis to the battens, using a spirit level to check that it is straight and level.*

5 *Prepare the ground at the base of the wall, forking in plenty of compost or manure. Plant the firethorn (see page 33) using a tree stake to support the main vertical stem so that it grows straight. You can remove the stake once the plant has reached the required height.*

6 *Spread out the horizontal branches of the firethorn. Remove any that are wrongly placed, cutting them back flush with the main stem. Tie those that are growing in the right direction to the trellis, using wire rings.*

7 *Plant a Virginia creeper at either end of the trellis to soften the edges and to create a frame for the planting. Plant the euonymous in front of the trellis.*

Raising a Wall with Trellis
PLANTS FOR PRIVACY

THERE ARE SEVERAL reasons why you might want to raise the height of a wall or fence – to hide an ugly view, to grow a particular climbing plant and show it off to its full glory or simply to improve your privacy.

Rigid trellis is available from garden centres with slats of differing widths. You can make your own – but use timber that has been pressure treated and is suitable for garden use. Alternatively, you can use folding light-weight diamond-pattern trellis. However, this is quite flimsy, so it is suitable only as a temporary measure. It is sometimes recommended for garden security, since it will not bear the weight of someone climbing over it.

The design below raises an existing 1.3-m (4-ft) wall by placing an 45-cm (18-in) rigid trellis, covered with climbing plants, on top. The trellis lets through some light and air and seems far more neighbour-friendly than a solid fence or wall. The total height of the fence should be roughly at eye level: any wall or fence that is lower than this simply invites people to look over it. A fence that is higher than eye level cuts down the amount of light entering your garden.

A sunny screen of climbers

Here, some attractive, shaped trellis panels were added to a 1.3-m (4-ft) garden wall to create an opportunity to grow climbers and to provide privacy in the summer months. The climbers chosen provide a good spread of interest throughout the spring and summer months.

1 Honeysuckle (*Lonicera periclymenum* 'Serotina')

2 Passionflower (*Passiflora* 'Amethyst')

3 Crimson glory vine
(*Vitis coignetiae*)

PROJECT PLANNER

TIME SCALE **1/2 DAY**

Tools and Materials

Spirit level • Chalk or pencil • 7.5 x 7.5-cm (3 x 3-in) fence posts
• Drill with masonry and standard bits • Tape measure • Rawl plugs
• 10-cm (4-in) screws • Screwdriver • Trellis panels • Trellis brackets
(6 for each trellis panel) • Post caps • Hammer • Manure or compost
• Fork • Rake • Trowel • Bone meal
The time scale given above is for putting up 3–4 trellis panels.

1 *Using a spirit level and chalk or a pencil, mark the position of the fence posts on the wall. Put the posts against the wall. Use a masonry bit to drill holes about 45-cm (18-in) apart through the posts and into the brickwork. Hammer rawl plugs through the posts and into the wall.*

2 *Insert 10-cm (4-in) screws into the rawl plugs in the wall and tighten.*

4 *Attach a decorative post cap to each post. Prepare the bed in front of the wall (see page 46) and plant the climbers (see page 33).*

3 *Hold the trellis panel in position and carefully mark where it should be attached to the posts. Put the panel down. Drill pilot holes and screw the brackets to the posts. Inset: Place the trellis panels in position and screw them to the brackets.*

MAINTENANCE

• *In late spring or autumn, mulch with compost after watering.*

• *Entwine the stems of the climbers through the trellis as they grow.*

• *Prune the climbers as necessary, in spring or autumn (see page 43).*

• *Remove any dead, spindly growth in spring.*

• *Once a year, make sure that the posts and the trellis are still secure.*

• *Keep the plants weeded and watered.*

Plants for a Sunny Wall
SCENTED SEATING AREA

A SUNNY WALL OR fence swathed in climbing plants is a joy to behold. A comfortable bench can transform it into a pleasant sitting area in which you can relax. By planting on each side of the bench you can help to make the area feel enclosed and secret – your own special place.

The best plants for a seating area – especially on a still summer's evening when their perfume lingers in the air – are scented species. Lavender and other herbs that release a heady scent are always popular choices.

If you are planting behind a garden bench or seat, choose subjects that are tall enough to be seen and that don't mind their base being in the shade. Flowering tobacco is used in the planting below. Lilies are another good choice – the many species and varieties available give you a range of heights, from the 1–1.2 m (3–4 ft) regal lily to the 2–2.1 m (6–7 ft) *Lilium henryi*.

The honeysuckle and the climbing rose are supported on wires rather than trellis – the plants quickly scramble along the wires and cover them from view.

Sunny scented arbour

This planting provides a continuous display of flowers from late spring throughout the summer until the frosts. The honeysuckle is the first to flower in late spring. The roses bloom in early summer, but with regular dead heading could still be in flower in the autumn. Lavender blooms in early summer and continues until autumn – although the scent fades with the colour. White flowering tobacco plants peep over the bench – but don't plant them until the frosts are over.

3 Honeysuckle (*Lonicera japonica* 'Halliana')

4 Rose (*Rosa* 'Golden Showers')

2 Flowering tobacco (*Nicotiana sylvestris*)

1 Lavender (*Lavandula angustifolia* 'Hidcote')

MAINTENANCE

• *Water regularly – especially during hot weather.*

• *Remove the rose flowers as they fade, as this will help to prolong the flowering season.*

• *In spring, snip off dead lavender flower heads and sprinkle some granular fertiliser around the base of the lavender plants.*

• *Keep the bed weeded. Mulch with compost or farmyard manure.*

• *Lift and discard the flowering tobacco in early autumn. Plant new flowering tobacco in late spring once the frosts are over.*

PROJECT PLANNER

TIME SCALE **1/2 DAY**

Tools and Materials

Spirit level • Pencil or chalk • Drill and masonry bit • Rawl plugs • Hammer • Screwdriver • 5-cm (2-in) and 7.5-cm (3-in) vine eyes • 2.5-mm (1/10-in) galvanised wire • Wire cutters • Pliers • Plastic-coated wire • Fork • Compost or garden manure • Rake • Wire ties

1 *Decide on the location for the bench, allowing space for a bed at either end. Mark the position of the wires on the wall, spacing the rows about 45–60 cm (18 in–2 ft) apart. Mark the position of the vine eyes, positioning them along each row at intervals of approximately 45 cm (18 in). If possible, avoid putting them in mortar joints. At each end of each row, mark the position for a 5-cm (2-in) vine eye first, with a 7.5-cm (3-in) one 10–15 cm (4–6 in) in from the end of the row.*

2 *Drill holes in the wall at the appropriate points and tap in a rawl plug.*

3 *Screw in a 5-cm (2-in) eye at each end of each row and at the centre, and a 7.5-cm (3-in) eye 10–15 cm (4–6 in) further along the row.*

4 *Using a hammer, bend the 7.5-cm (3-in) vine eyes over so that they are about 45° from the vertical and leaning towards the centre of the row.*

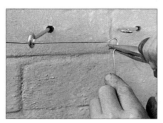

5 *Cut lengths of 2.5-mm (1/10-in) galvanised wire, thread it through the vine eyes, and bend one end of the wire over to form a hook.*

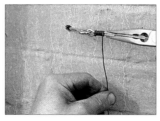

6 *Pinching the bent end of the wire with the pliers to hold it firmly, bind the ends of the galvanised wire with plastic-coated wire.*

7 *Tighten the wire by hammering the angled vine eyes back until they are in a vertical position.*

8 *Prepare the bed at the foot of the wall and at either end of the bench (see page 46).*

9 *Buy the plants. If you can't plant them immediately, stand them in the shade and keep them watered.*

10 *Plant the plants (see pages 30–33). Attach the climber stems to the wires using wire ties.*

Adding Colour to Green Hedges

FLOWERING CLEMATIS HEDGE

IF YOU WOULD LIKE to introduce some variety into an all-green hedge, plant a flowering climber alongside it to lift the sweep of clipped foliage and to create an unusual and attractive garden feature. There are many flowering climbing plants that respond well to being clipped along with your hedge. Annual climbers, such as sweet peas or morning glory, produce an attractive show of summer colour. Alternatively, as here, you can make a permanent feature using a number of perennial climbers that flower at different times.

The clematis group of species, hybrids and varieties — especially the less vigorous ones — are an excellent choice for growing through a hedge. They are strong but not very demanding feeders, so they can tolerate the often impoverished soil at the foot of a hedge. Their flowers and, if you put off clipping the hedge until late autumn, their fluffy seedheads stand out well against most hedging plants, yet their foliage is unobtrusive. The late-flowering Viticella hybrids, such as the dark pink *Clematis* 'Abundance', make an excellent choice for threading through a hedge.

Yellow and purple hedge flowers

If you choose your clematis carefully, you can have something in flower from spring until autumn. Here the silky seedheads of spring-flowering blue Clematis alpina *'Frances Rivis' appear while the other clematis — a yellow* Clematis tangutica *and a purple* Clematis *'Jackmanii Superba' — are flowering. Leave hedge cutting until late in the year to get the best out of the clematis — or do it early in the year before the clematis starts flowering.*

1 *Clematis* 'Jackmanii Superba'

PLANTING ALTERNATIVES

Fiery patchwork hedge

Scarlet and green are opposites on the colour spectrum and, when planted together, make a particularly vivid contrast. The plants listed below work extremely well against a fine-leaved conifer hedge. Flame nasturtium makes a spectacular splash of scarlet during the summer and the crimson glory vine turns yellow and scarlet in the autumn. The large leaves of the crimson glory vine and the golden hop contrast especially well with fine-leaved conifer hedges. Golden hop has wonderful sharp green leaves with twining stems and green, hanging flowers in the autumn.

1 Crimson glory vine (*Vitis coignetiae*)
2 Flame nasturtium (*Tropaeolum speciosum*)
3 Golden hop (*Humulus lupulus* 'Aureus')

PROJECT PLANNER

TIME SCALE 1/2 DAY

Tools and Materials

Hand fork • Watering can or hose • Spade • Manure or garden compost • Bone meal • Mulch
The time scale above is for 10 plants (1 per m/yd).

1 *Buy the plants. If you can't plant immediately, keep them in the shade and water them daily.*

2 *Clear out the ground at the bottom of the hedge. Use a small hand fork to loosen the soil. If necessary, soften the soil with water before planting.*

3 *Carefully remove the stake that supports the clematis.*

4 *Dig a planting hole – clematis are best planted deeper than the level they were planted at in their pot – adding a soil improver to the hole (see page 33).*

5 *Intertwine the clematis stems through the branches of the hedge.*

6 *Water thoroughly and apply a mulch to conserve moisture – the soil at the base of a hedge is often dry and impoverished.*

MAINTENANCE

• *Cut the hedge in early spring, using sharp shears or a powered hedge cutter.*

• *Add a layer of manure or garden compost to the base of the hedge around the clematis plants each spring.*

3 *Clematis tangutica*

2 *Clematis alpina* 'Frances Rivis', shown here in flower in early spring

A Garden Divider
POST-AND-CHAIN ROSE BOUNDARY

To MARK OFF an awkwardly shaped corner of the garden or break up an over-wide expanse of lawn, use a procession of posts linked by chains swathed in climbing roses. A boundary such as this, where you can see between the upright posts, draws the eye to the plants and features that lie beyond and gives a much more open feel than a solid hedge or wall.

This divider makes a particularly successful support for roses, since they benefit from having air circulating through their branches. It provides the ideal opportunity to grow a favourite climbing rose – or even a collection of climbers. Traditionally, thick ropes link the uprights in this sort of design, but here, chain has been used, as it is easier to hook on to the posts.

Pink rose boundary

Here the fabulous shell-pink rambler rose 'Albertine' clambers up the wooden posts and along the black chains. Smother the ground at the foot of the rose with lady's mantle to help disguise the bare stems of the rose and the metal casing at the base of the post.

1 *Rosa 'Albertine'*

MAINTENANCE

- *Remove aphids from young rose growth. Remove infested growth if necessary (see pages 36–37).*

- *Deadhead the roses as they fade.*

- *Trim the lady's mantle in summer to encourage fresh growth.*

- *Prune the roses in autumn (see page 42).*

- *Mulch with compost after pruning.*

2 Lady's mantle
(*Alchemilla mollis*)

PROJECT PLANNER

TIME SCALE 1 DAY

Tools and Materials

Garden twine • Metal rod • Spirit level • Metal post holders • Driving tool • Sledgehammer • 2.5-m (8-ft) pre-treated lumber posts • Screwdriver • 5-cm (2-in) hooks • 2.5–5-cm (1–2-in) chain • Step ladder • Post caps • Garden fork • Compost or manure

1 *Using garden twine, mark where the row of posts will go. Drive a metal rod into the ground, to the same depth as the post holder, as a pilot hole. Check that it is vertical with a spirit level. Repeat every 2.5–3 m (8–10 ft).*

2 *Remove the metal rod and insert a metal post holder into each pilot hole. Knock in the post holders using a sledgehammer.*

3 *Insert the posts into the holders. Knock them in firmly, using the sledgehammer (you may need to stand on a step ladder, getting someone else to hold it steady for you).*

4 *Position the rest of the posts and check that they are level with one another. Screw in the hooks 2.5–5 cm (1–2 in) below the top of each post.*

5 *Place the chain on the hooks and adjust the length of the chain to give the desired loop.*

6 *Fit decorative post caps. Nail the capping plate to the top of the post and screw on the finial.*

7 *Dig in compost or manure around the base of each post, then plant a rose at the base of each post (see page 33). Twine the stems around the posts. Plant lady's mantle at the foot of each rose.*

Informal Boundary Hedge
FLOWERING HEDGE

THERE ARE LOTS of good reasons for planting a hedge to mark a boundary rather than putting up a fence or wall. First, a hedge provides the best wind-break you can have: it allows some wind through, so no turbulence is created and the effect of the wind is reduced. Second, a hedge can screen your garden from the view of passers-by or neighbouring buildings. Last, but by no means least, a hedge is an excellent refuge and food source for wildlife.

If you have enough space, an informal hedge is often the best idea since informal hedges do not need to be clipped as often or as comprehensively as formal, dense hedges do. They also have a slightly rural look – as if your garden is at the edge of the countryside.

Choose a hedging plant that gives you a screen throughout the year. It need not be evergreen but it should be dense and bushy. Also choose something with at least two seasons of interest – flowers followed by berries, for example. Alternatively, plant a mixed hedge with several different species; local wildlife will enjoy this kind of hedge best of all.

Purple flowering hedge
Rosa rugosa makes a dense and attractive hedge all year round, from spring when its crinkled leaves emerge, through its purple-pink flowers in midsummer, and large red hips in the autumn and beyond. It also has prickly stems and is a great deterrent to potential trespassers.

PLANTING ALTERNATIVES

Evergreen, yellow-berried hedge

Firethorns are among the most useful hedging plants –
especially if an impenetrable hedge is required. They are
evergreen plants, with creamy white blossom in spring.
'Saphyr Jaune' makes a dense, disease-free hedge with
bright yellow berries, but there are many other varieties of
firethorn to choose from with red, yellow or orange berries
that last from the autumn through the winter months.

Firethorn (*Pyracantha* 'Saphyr Jaune')

Fast-growing evergreen hedge

Conifers are an extremely popular choice if you want a
fast-growing hedge. However, speed of growth is a double-
edged sword as far as hedges go, since the quicker a plant
grows the more it needs clipping. Many popular conifers
are much too vigorous for hedging, though they are often
sold as suitable hedging plants. Leyland cypress, for example, is much too fast-growing for a hedge – especially in a
small garden – and requires frequent clipping to keep it
within bounds. If you want a fast-growing conifer hedge,
choose the more manageable Lawson's cypress.

Lawson's cypress (*Chamaecyparis lawsoniana*)

Rosa rugosa

PROJECT PLANNER

Tools and Materials

TIME SCALE 1 DAY

Garden line and pegs • Measuring stick
• Fork • Spade • Manure or garden
compost • Bone meal • Secateurs
*The time scale above is for a hedge about
7 m (20 ft) long.*

1 Decide on the location of the hedge. Position cardboard
boxes at the height the hedge will reach when fully
grown. This will show you what the hedge will hide from
view once it is mature. It will also give you an idea of how
much shelter the hedge will give from prevailing wind, and
of how long and dense a shadow it will cast at different
times of day.

2 Mark out the line of the hedge (see page 32) and calculate how many plants you need.

3 Buy the hedging plants. If you buy bare-rooted plants,
soak them for several hours before planting. If you buy
containerised plants and can't plant them immediately, keep
them watered and in the shade.

4 Prepare the site and plant the hedge (see page 32).

5 After planting, water the hedge thoroughly. Apply a
5–7.5-cm (2–3-in) layer of manure or garden compost as
a mulch. If you are planting in warm, dry weather, don't
allow the soil to dry out – especially in the first few weeks
after planting.

6 Trim back the newly planted hedge by one third all the
way around (see page 44). If your site is exposed, use
wind-break netting to protect the hedge for the first season.

MAINTENANCE

• *Keep the hedge bottom free of weeds by regular hoeing.*

• *Water regularly – especially during dry weather in the
first summer.*

• *In spring, once the soil has warmed up, apply a 5–7.5-cm
(2–3-in) layer of garden compost or manure to the soil
around the plants.*

• *Clip the hedge in late summer each year – or, if it
bears fruits in the autumn, in early spring before the birds
start nesting. Use sharp shears or a powered hedgetrimmer.*

Formal Hedge
A GARDEN WITHIN A GARDEN

HEDGES DO NOT ALWAYS mark the external boundary of your garden. A formal clipped hedge is a simple, but extremely effective way of dividing a large garden into smaller, more intimate sections. Plant alleyways of hedges to intrigue visitors and tempt them to walk down them to see what is there; alternatively, as in the design shown below, use the hedge to form a garden within your garden — a natural 'room' where you can sit in seclusion.

A formal hedge makes an ideal backdrop for beds and borders of plants; the plain colour and straight, flat surfaces contrast and set off the irregular shapes and shadows of the plants in front. There are many different types of hedging plants to choose from. Quick-growing conifers and slower-growing beech are just two of the options open to you. Conifers, with finely divided evergreen foliage, make a smooth-textured hedge. However, you should avoid the fast-growing varieties unless you quickly need a wind-break. Beech makes a beautiful fresh green hedge that grows to the height of 1.5 m (5 ft) within 5 years. Although it is not an evergreen, it keeps its dead leaves in winter; they turn a russetty brown that warms up the garden in the coldest months.

To make hedge cutting easier and to make your bed or border plants stand out even more, it is a good idea to lay a path between the hedge and the back of the border. It need not be visible from the front of the border or bed so it can be made from concrete slabs bedded on sharp sand.

Green backdrop
Here a handsome green beech hedge provides a lively but neutral background to a border of shrubs and perennials.

PLANTING ALTERNATIVES

Purple shadows

Instead of bright green, choose a dark, red-leaved beech variety that makes a dramatic contrast behind a bed or border of perennials and shrubs.

Purple beech (*Fagus sylvatica* Atropurpurea Group)

Velvety conifer

The king of conifer hedges is the slow-growing, velvety-looking yew. It may take time to reach the height you want – 5 years or more to reach 5 ft (1.5 m) – but it stays much neater than a fast-growing conifer and does not need as much clipping.

Yew (*Taxus baccata*)

Beech (*Fagus sylvatica*)

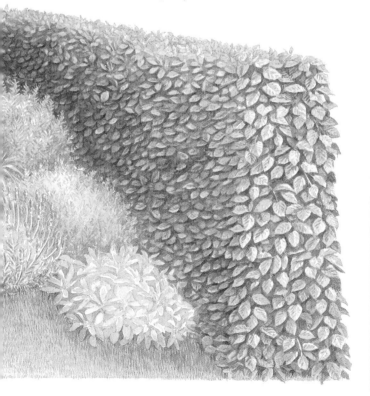

PROJECT PLANNER

TIME SCALE 1 DAY

Tools and Materials

Garden line and pegs • Measuring stick • Watering can or hose • Fork • Spade • Manure or garden compost • Bone meal • Secateurs • Paving slabs • Sharp sand • Spirit level
The time scale above is for a hedge about 7 m (20 ft) long.

1 *Decide on the location of the hedge. Position cardboard boxes at the height the hedge will reach when fully grown. This will show you what the hedge will hide from view once it is mature. It will also give you an idea of how much shelter the hedge will give from prevailing wind, and of how long and dense a shadow it will cast at different times of day.*

2 *Mark the line of the hedge and calculate how many plants you need (see page 32).*

3 *Buy the hedging plants. If you buy bare-rooted plants, soak them for several hours before planting. If you buy containerised plants and can't plant them immediately, keep them watered and in the shade.*

4 *Prepare the site and plant the hedge (see page 32).*

5 *Water thoroughly. Apply a 5–7.5-cm (2–3-in) layer of manure or garden compost to the soil at the bottom of the hedge as a mulch after watering.*

6 *Trim back the newly planted hedge by one third all the way around (see page 44).*

7 *Lay the maintenance-path paving slabs parallel to the hedge. Remove the top 10 cm (4 in) of soil, put down a 5-cm (2-in) layer of sharp sand, then lay down a paving slab. Use a spirit level to check that it is level in every direction before you lay the next slab.*

8 *Create and plant a bed in front of the maintenance path (see page 46).*

MAINTENANCE

• *Keep the hedge bottom free of weeds by regular hoeing.*

• *Water regularly – especially during dry weather in the first summer.*

• *In spring, once the soil has warmed up, apply a 5–7.5-cm (2–3-in) layer of compost or manure to the soil around the plants.*

• *Clip your hedge in late summer each year using sharp shears or a powered hedgetrimmer.*

Defining Your Beds
MINIATURE HEDGING

FOR WELL-DEFINED beds and a stylish-looking garden, edge your beds with dwarf hedging. Uniform edging can transform a random grouping of plants into a coherent unit – similar to framing a picture.

Like regular-sized hedging, miniature hedges can be either formal or informal, depending on the type of hedging plant you choose. For a neat, dark, evergreen line around your beds, box (*Buxus sempervirens* 'Suffruticosa') is very effective. Its tiny leaves give a uniform appearance and its relatively slow growth rate means that clipping is limited to two or three times per summer, ideal for the weekend gardener. For a more relaxed feel, lavender is a colourful, eye-catching way

of setting off a plain, upright planting more than 60 cm (2 ft) high. Choose a compact variety, such as 'Hidcote', which has dark purple flowers.

You can even make a feature that uses miniature hedging plants exclusively, arranging them in a geometric pattern in the same way as traditional 'knot gardens' as in the design below. This is a particularly good idea if you're planting something that will be seen from above – from an upper bedroom window, for example. You can use two, three, or more hedging species with contrasting colours and textures. The only point to consider is the ease of maintenance – make sure you can clip and weed easily or the neatness of the effect will quickly be lost.

Dark green crisscross with lavender

Here a crisscross pattern of box 22.5 cm (9 in) high is framed by a taller 30-cm (1-ft) high hedge of the same plant. A single lavender plant sits in each square, its upright spikiness contrasting dramatically with the horizontal planes of the hedging. The central bay tree ball (potted so that it can be brought indoors in the coldest weather) presents another contrasting form.

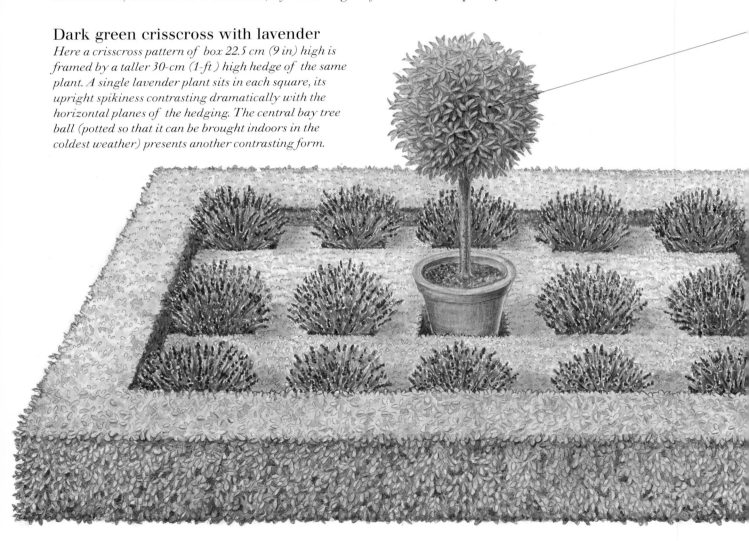

PLANTING ALTERNATIVES

Dark green crisscross with yellow

Use a yellow-flowered lemon verbena, grown as a standard, in place of the bay, and cotton lavender, with its delicate yellow flowers, in place of the lavender.

1 Lemon verbena (*Aloysia triphylla*)

2 Cotton lavender (*Santolina chamaecyparissus*)

1 Bay (*Laurus nobilis*)

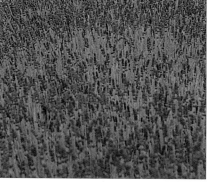

2 Lavender (*Lavandula angustifolia* 'Hidcote')

3 Box (*Buxus sempervirens*)

PROJECT PLANNER

TIME SCALE 1 DAY

Tools and Materials

Pencil and graph paper • Measuring stick • Stakes • Watering can or hose • Spade • Fork • Manure or garden compost • Bone meal • Gravel or bark-chip mulch • Secateurs
The time scale above is for a site about 10 m (10 yd) long.

1 Decide on the pattern you want for your miniature hedging and draw it out on graph paper.

2 Referring to your plan, measure the site with a measuring stick. Mark the line of the hedge with stakes every metre (yard) or more and calculate how many plants you need.

3 Buy the hedging plants. If you buy bare-rooted plants, soak them for several hours before planting. If you buy containerised plants and can't plant them immediately, keep them watered and in the shade.

4 Prepare the site and plant the plants (see page 32). For a miniature hedge, a trench 30 cm (1 ft) wide and 25–30 cm (10–12 in) deep is big enough.

5 Water well and mulch around the base of the trench with gravel or bark.

6 Trim back the sides of the hedging plants by one third after planting, leaving the top intact until the desired height is reached (see page 44).

7 Mulch around the lavender plants with manure or garden compost.

MAINTENANCE

• Keep the bed well watered and weeded.

• In autumn, water the bed well and replenish the mulch.

• Clip the hedge twice each summer.

• Trim lavender in spring and again after the flowers have faded.

• Clip the bay in summer and move it indoors in the autumn before the first frosts.

Front-garden Boundary
PICKET FENCES

A NEAT AND FRESHLY PAINTED front fence sets your house and garden off to its best advantage. Picket fencing is both inexpensive to buy and easy to erect. You can make your own or buy ready-made panels — in which case all you have to do is supply the posts to support the panels and paint the fence your chosen colour. Plant tall flowers, such as lupins, delphiniums, and hollyhocks, along the inside of the fence for a nostalgic cottage-garden look.

Picket fences are available in many different designs. The tops of the slats can be rounded in shape, pointed, intricately carved or pierced. You can have slats that graduate in height, so that the fence looks curved or wavy. You can even change the material and use bamboo canes instead of wooden slats.

The width of the slats and how far apart you space them is up to you. Before you start to assemble the fence, draw your design on graph paper so that you can calculate how many slats you will need.

Picket fences don't last for ever, so check them regularly, clean them, replace any broken or rotten slats, and repaint every 2–3 years to keep them looking fresh.

Unique fencing

Devise your own slat shape and draw the design on graph paper. Get your local timber yard to cut the slats to size, following your pattern. Order more than you need so that you have some spare.

Rounded-top wide slats for a conventional picket fence

Shaped slats for a 'Gothic' style

Slats graduated in length

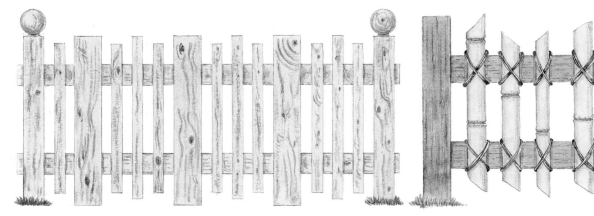

Repeating pattern of variable slat widths and lengths

Bamboo picket with canes

PROJECT PLANNER

TIME SCALE 1 DAY

Tools and Materials

Screwdriver • 5-cm (2-in) screws • Tannelised gate with hinges and catch fittings • Tannelised gate posts • Metal rod • Metal post holders • Post driving tool • Sledgehammer • Spirit level • Slotted fence posts and rails • Garden twine • Fence slats or panels of ready-made picket fence • Nails • Mallet • Exterior wood paint and paint brush
The time scale given above is for a fence about 10 m (10 yd) long.

1 *Screw hinges and catch fittings to gate and posts. Using the rod, make a hole and insert a post holder every 3–4 m (3–4 yds). Hammer posts into holders, covering with the driving tool for protection.*

2 *Position the gate between the gate posts (ask a friend to help you). Shut the gate and check that it is level and that the catch closes correctly.*

3 *Run garden twine along the top of the fence and use this as a guideline for where the top of the slats should be. Slot the fence rails into the fence posts, then check that the fence framework is level.*

4 *Nail the slats to the rails. Ask your helper to push firmly against the rail on the opposite side with a mallet while you hammer in the nail. Put two nails in the top rail and two in the bottom.*

5 *Continue to nail in the slats, checking the levels constantly and making sure they are the correct distance apart. Paint the fence with your chosen finish.*

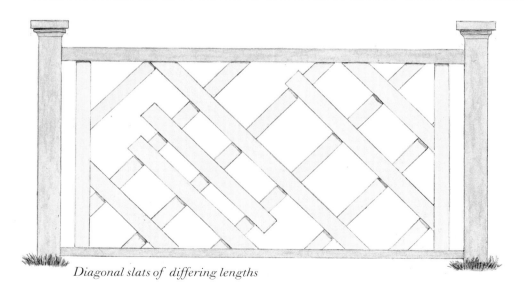

Diagonal slats of differing lengths

MAINTENANCE

• *Check the fence and gate posts every year to make sure they are still firm. If they become wobbly, you may need to reset them in concrete.*

• *Repaint the fence and gate every 2–3 years.*

BEDS AND BORDERS

Glorious colour
From the bushy, yellow daisy flowers of helenium in the foreground to the dramatic spikes of orange crocosmia in the distance, this splendid border of red and gold perennial flowers makes an impressive splash of colour and provides a dramatic focal point to the garden.

Ideas for Sunny Beds and Borders

Beds and borders in sunny situations allow you to grow flowers in abundance. Many of the perennials that form the mainstay of herbaceous borders are sun-loving species. If your garden gets the sun, you will be able to grow these wonderful flowers year after year for their stunning colours and intoxicating fragrance.

However, you must select plants that actually enjoy direct sun: moisture-loving species can survive in sunny spots – but only if you're willing to devote much of your valuable weekend time to watering them. Any good plant manual will give you this information. Study the label accompanying the potted plant before you buy; you'll be making life easier for yourself, since happy plants require less maintenance.

The questions on these two pages are designed to help you pinpoint ways in which you can improve beds and borders. Each one is backed up by a step-by-step project with plants that have been specifically chosen because they thrive in sunny spots.

? *Do you have a sun-baked area where plants often wilt ?*

Not all sun-loving plants thrive in very hot situations. Choose plants that really enjoy sun to reduce the amount of watering required. *Right*: Golden genista lydia, a euphorbia, ornamental onions, grey-leaved sedum, stripy century plant and ground-smothering lamb's ears are all suitable.
SEE *Bed for a Hot, Dry Site, page 124.*

➤·➤

? *Does your garden lack interest at certain times of year?*

Make sure there is always something interesting to look at – spring-flowering bulbs, autumn berries, evergreens and plants with interesting winter bark all help to give year-round visual appeal.
SEE *Planting for Year-round Interest, page 134.*

? *Do you like rich, hot colours?*

Many herbaceous perennials like sunny sites and have hot-coloured flowers (red, gold, orange). They bloom year after year and require relatively little maintenance.
SEE *Emphasising a Sunny Site, page 132.*

? *Does your garden lack a focal point?*

An arbour or archway smothered in blooms makes an eye-catching feature. *Right:* Here, the rambler rose, *Rosa* 'Félicité Perpétue' makes a marvellously colourful spectacle. Rosemary clothes the base of the archway.
SEE *Creating a Focal Point, page 130.*

? *Is there bare earth around new shrubs?*

Bushes and shrubs can take several years to reach their full height and spread. Fill in the gaps with annual flowers that you've grown from seed.
Above: In this border, yellow daisies, orange tickseed and tall white cosmos make a colourful display between the permanent plants.
SEE *Filling Gaps in Borders, page 128.*

? *Do you have a low border where the plants are of similar height?*

Introduce a taller feature, such as a sweet-pea tower, for visual variety.
SEE *Creating Height in a Border, page 126.*

Bed for a Hot, Dry Site
FIERY LANDSCAPE

GIVE YOUR GARDEN the feeling of an oasis in an arid landscape by creating a bed for dry-soil plants. Sheltered, sunny areas lend themselves to re-creating a semi-desert scene, especially if the soil is well drained. Check the soil to make sure that water drains away quickly; you may need to dig in horticultural grit or fine gravel to improve the drainage (see page 19).

Dome the bed slightly so that the soil is higher in the middle and set feature rocks into the slope. Natural semi-desert habitats tend to be barren and rocky. By incorporating rocks in the bed you will create a natural, authentic-looking setting.

After planting, cover the soil with pebbles and gravel to create a natural-looking 'scree' landscape.

8 Mount Etna broom
(*Genista aetnensis*)

Blaze of colour
*The planting in this bed gives
a dramatic appearance.
Fiery hues of red, yellow
and orange predominate,
while contrasts in form,
height and texture give
extra interest.*

1 Myrtle euphorbia
(*Euphorbia myrsinites*)

2 *Yucca gloriosa*

3 Evening primrose (*Oenothera
fruticosa* 'Fireworks')

4 Wood millet (*Milium
effusum* 'Aureum')

124

7 California poppy
(*Eschscholzia californica*)

6 Dwarf juniper (*Juniperus communis* 'Compressa')

5 Cypress spurge
(*Euphorbia cyparissias*)

PROJECT PLANNER

Tools and Materials

TIME SCALE 1 DAY

Fork • Rake • Horticultural grit or fine gravel • Large rocks • Tree stake and ties • Trowel • Pebble or gravel mulch
The time scale above is for a site about 3 x 1.5 m (10 x 5 ft).

1 Mark out the site and prepare the soil (see page 46), adding plenty of horticultural grit or fine gravel if the soil is not sandy to improve drainage.

2 Buy some large rocks (or move them from other areas of the garden) and set them in position. They should be set into the ground so that they look natural.

3 Buy the plants. If you cannot plant them immediately, store them in a cool place and keep well watered.

4 Position the plants around the bed. Once you are happy with their placement, plant them. Plant and stake the Mount Etna broom first, and then plant the yucca, dwarf junipers, and wood millet. Finally, plant the small plants – the evening primroses, California poppies, Cypress spurge, and myrtle euphorbia.

5 Water thoroughly. Cover any exposed soil with pebbles or gravel to act as a mulch and create a natural-looking scree landscape.

MAINTENANCE

• Keep the bed weeded, especially in the first two seasons while plants are establishing themselves. Allow a few clumps of California poppy seedlings to remain.

• Cut back dead, straggly or unwanted growth in autumn.

• Deadhead flowers of all plants once they are past their best to help keep the bed tidy and to encourage a second flush of flowers.

• Plant spring-flowering bulbs such as crocuses or irises in the autumn.

• Replenish the pebble or gravel mulch in late spring to help suppress weed growth.

125

Creating Height in a Border
SWEET-PEA TOWER

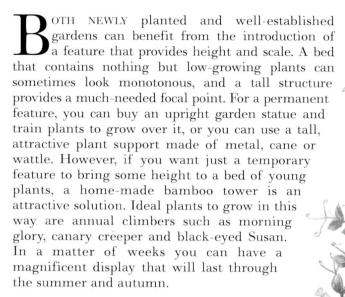

BOTH NEWLY planted and well-established gardens can benefit from the introduction of a feature that provides height and scale. A bed that contains nothing but low-growing plants can sometimes look monotonous, and a tall structure provides a much-needed focal point. For a permanent feature, you can buy an upright garden statue and train plants to grow over it, or you can use a tall, attractive plant support made of metal, cane or wattle. However, if you want just a temporary feature to bring some height to a bed of young plants, a home-made bamboo tower is an attractive solution. Ideal plants to grow in this way are annual climbers such as morning glory, canary creeper and black-eyed Susan. In a matter of weeks you can have a magnificent display that will last through the summer and autumn.

Mixed-colour cascade

Sweet peas are ideal subjects for training up bamboo stakes at the back of a bed. A tall-growing variety will quickly clamber up to create an eye-catching cascade – and the more blooms you pick the more they produce, so you can fill your house with their delicious scent as a bonus.

PLANTING ALTERNATIVES
Single-colour cascade

A number of annual climbers can be grown in the same way as the sweet-pea tower. The plants listed below offer a range of colour schemes.

Morning glory (*Ipomoea rubrocaerulea* 'Heavenly Blue') – blue flowers

Canary creeper (*Tropaeolum peregrinum*) – yellow flowers

Black-eyed Susan (*Thunbergia alata*) – orange flowers

1 Sweet pea (*Lathyrus odoratus* 'Galaxy Mixed')

MAINTENANCE

• *A week or so after the sweet peas are planted, pinch out all but the strongest shoot on each seedling.*

• *Use a wire ring to hold the seedling loosely against the stake. Tendrils will soon grow and cling firmly to the support.*

• *Keep the area free of weeds and water regularly.*

• *Deadhead every few days to keep flowers coming, or pick fresh flowers for the house.*

• *Apply a liquid fertiliser once flowering is established.*

PLANTING ALTERNATIVES

Tasty towers

As an alternative to flowers, there are a number of vegetable crops that can be grown on stakes. All the varieties listed below produce attractive flowers as well as vegetables.

Runner bean (*Phaseolus coccineus* 'Painted Lady') – red and white flowers

Pea (*Pisum sativum* 'Carouby de Maussane') – purple flowers

Pumpkin (*Cucurbita pepo* 'Munchkin') – yellow flowers

PROJECT PLANNER

TIME SCALE 1 HOUR

Tools and Materials

Rake • Eight bamboo stakes, 1.8–2.1 m (6–7 ft) tall • Garden twine, string or raffia • Trowel • Wire rings

1 *Sow sweet peas in a pot or tray indoors in autumn or early spring (see page 29).*

2 *At least two weeks before planting, prepare the ground by turning the earth just as you would if you were creating a new bed (see page 46). Break up any large clumps of soil and rake the surface smooth.*

3 *Arrange the eight bamboo stakes in a circle approximately 1 m (3 ft) in diameter. Insert them firmly into the soil so that they are all the same height.*

4 *Gather the tops of the stakes together in your hand and bind them securely with garden twine, string or raffia.*

5 *Using the same twine, secure the stakes about 1 m (3 ft) from the ground. This will help to stabilise the structure as well as give the growing plants something horizontal to cling on to.*

6 *When the sweet pea seedlings are at least 5 cm (2 in) tall, water them, remove from their containers and gently separate them. Plant a single seedling at the base of each stake.*

Filling Gaps in Borders
PINK AND WHITE PLANTING

IF YOU HAVE GAPS between permanent plants, such as shrubs, why not fill them with a display of colourful summer annuals? As annuals last for only one year, they are not permanent additions to your garden and there is no risk of them crowding out the shrubs. Covering bare ground with plants is also a good way of preventing weeds from growing. You can buy or grow your own annuals, choosing from the range of bedding plants available at garden centres or nurseries. If the choice at your local garden centre is limited, order through seed catalogues.

Although it is time-consuming to grow annuals from seed, it is also satisfying and much less expensive than buying established plants – and it is sometimes easier to find the exact varieties and flower colours that you want. Hardy annuals, such as those shown below, are the easiest plants to grow from seed. Sow them where you want them to flower, then thin out the seedlings when they are large enough to handle to give the others space in which to grow. Half-hardy plants are best raised in trays indoors so that the seedlings are ready to plant outside when the frosty weather is over.

Delicate pink and white

The front of a shrub border can look dull and lifeless even in summer. Here, home-raised hardy annuals are mixed with some bought-in half-hardy balsam plants to create a carpet of white and pink flowers.

PLANTING ALTERNATIVES

Creating a warm glow

For a warm display of predominantly orange and yellow flowers, substitute the plants listed below for those shown in the illustration.

1 Nasturtium
(*Tropaeolum majus* 'Alaska')

3 Poached-egg flower
(*Limnanthes douglasii*)

4 Pot marigold
(*Calendula officinalis*)

1 Balsam (*Impatiens balsamina*)

2 Sweet alyssum (*Lobularia maritima*)

4 Snapdragon (*Antirrhinum* 'White Wonder')

3 Candytuft (*Iberis amara*)

PROJECT PLANNER

TIME SCALE 1 HOUR

Tools and Materials

Fork • Rake • Stick • Sand • Chicken wire • Plant labels • Old kitchen fork

1 Identify the gaps you want to fill. Remove any weeds and fork over the soil. Rake it smooth.

2 If you are growing the hardy annuals from seed, sow the seeds where you want them to flower (see page 29). Label them and protect them from cats and birds with chicken wire. When they are large enough to handle, thin them out using an old kitchen fork. If you are buying the plants, be sure to harden them off before you plant them; leave them outside during the day but bring them indoors at night until all danger of frost has passed.

MAINTENANCE

• After thinning out seedlings to allow enough room for the remaining plants to develop, check the area frequently for weeds, slugs and other pests and remove them as they appear.

• Water frequently, particularly in dry weather.

• Pinch off the tips of snapdragon seedlings to create bushier plants.

• Remove spent flower stems to encourage more flowers to develop.

Creating a Focal Point
SCENTED LILY AND ROSE ARBOUR

A FREE-STANDING ARBOUR or arch swathed in flowers brings several benefits to a garden: it can be used to divide the garden into separate areas, to frame a striking view, or to distract attention from an unattractive one. Beyond these, it provides a focal point – a dramatic, eye-catching feature that makes a strong design statement.

You can make your own arch, but it is far easier to buy one in kit form from a garden centre. There is a wide range to choose from – in wood and metal – and to suit all budgets. Once you have made sure that the arch is well anchored in the ground, you can start to train climbing plants to grow up and around it.

An arch is a particularly effective way of displaying such scented climbers as roses or honeysuckle, since you benefit from wafts of perfume every time you pass through it. Some rose varieties, particularly if they are trained over a wall or solid surface, are prone to mildew in humid conditions. However, growing them over an arch can help prevent this problem, since air is able to circulate freely through the plants' stems.

Fragrant pink and white arch
This arch is smothered in fragrant pink roses, while pots of lilies clothe the base. Geraniums and sweet violets cover the ground and help to minimise weed growth.

1 Pink rambler rose such as *Rosa* 'New Dawn'

2 Madonna lily (*Lilium candidum*)

3 Pink climbing rose such as *Rosa* 'Zéphirine Drouhin'

4 *Geranium* x *magnificum*

5 Sweet violet (*Viola odorata*), shown here in flower in spring

MAINTENANCE

- *Weed regularly.*

- *Water regularly, especially in warm and dry weather.*

- *In spring, sprinkle fertiliser around the base of the rose plants.*

- *Use old tights to tie the stems of the climbing rose to the arch. Wind the plant stems around the arch as they grow.*

- *Deadhead roses as they fade, snipping off their stems to just above a vigorous leaf joint.*

- *Prune* Rosa 'New Dawn' *after it has flowered. Unwind the stems and cut each one that has flowered back to its main stem (see page 42). The other rose used here (*Rosa 'Zéphirine Drouhin'*) is a climber and need not be pruned regularly, though unwanted or dead stems can be removed in spring.*

- *Remove the pots of lilies once their flowers are over and replace them with pots of other flowering plants.*

- *In autumn, remove dead leaves and other debris, and apply a mulch of bark chippings to the soil.*

PLANTING ALTERNATIVES

Golden arch

For a predominantly gold- and cream-coloured planting scheme, substitute the plants listed below for those shown in the illustration.

1 *Rosa* 'Golden Showers'

3 *Rosa* 'Madame Alfred Carrière'

4 Lady's mantle (*Alchemilla mollis*)

5 Heartsease (*Viola tricolor*)

PROJECT PLANNER

TIME SCALE 1 DAY

Tools and Materials

Arch kit • Post holders • Driving tool for post holders • Sledgehammer • Mallet • Spirit level • Fork • Manure • Spade • Bark-chip mulch

1 *Decide where to position your archway. Measure your site roughly so that you can make (or buy) an appropriately sized archway.*

2 *Assemble the sides and top of the archway following the manufacturer's instructions.*

3 *Insert the first metal post holder into the ground. Fit the driving tool over the post holder and use the sledgehammer to knock the holder into position.*

4 *Lay one side panel on the ground to help you check where the second post should be positioned. Drive the second post holder into the ground in the same way as the first one.*

5 *Insert the first side panel into its post holders, knocking it in with a mallet. Lay a crossbar on the ground to help you position the post holders for the second side panel and insert the post holders as in Steps 3 and 4.*

6 *Insert the second side panel into its post holders, as in Step 5. Use a spirit level to check that the tops of the two side panels are level with each other, tapping them with the mallet if necessary.*

7 *Fit the overhead crosspieces into position. Check that they are level. Make any necessary adjustments by tapping them with the mallet.*

8 *Fork over the soil around the archway, incorporating manure so that the ground is well prepared before you plant.*

9 *Plant one rose at each side of the archway. Plant geraniums and sweet violets around the base of the archway for ground cover.*

10 *Water well and cover the soil with a layer of bark chippings.*

11 *Position a container of Madonna lilies on each side of the archway.*

Emphasising a Sunny Site
PERENNIALS IN SCARLET AND GOLD

PERENNIALS ARE the mainstay of the herbaceous border: they flower year after year and, unlike summer bedding plants and many bulbs, which need to be lifted after they have flowered and replaced the next year, they can be left permanently in place – a far easier proposition for the weekend gardener!

Many of the most popular and attractive perennials, including the ones shown below, thrive in full sun, so if you are fortunate enough to have a sunny area in your garden, make the most of it. Choose warm-coloured plants to match the warm temperature – orange, scarlet, gold and bright yellow. Nothing can beat a border of these often colourful and dramatic plants. If you choose your species carefully, you can have a continuous display of flowering plants from late spring until the autumn.

Summer celebration

Enjoy the sunshine and warmth of summer with this scarlet and purple border, shown here in late summer. Bold clumps of red hot pokers, sneezeweed, crocosmia, daylilies and dahlias are set off by plants with a softer form, such as geraniums, lady's mantle and mountain bluet. Spilling over the front of the bed is a miniature hedge of catmint.

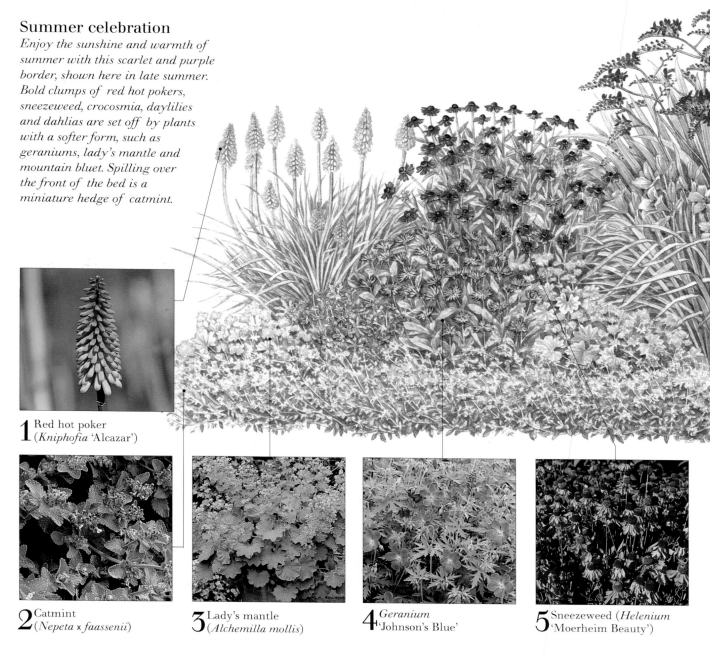

1 Red hot poker (*Kniphofia* 'Alcazar')

2 Catmint (*Nepeta* x *faassenii*)

3 Lady's mantle (*Alchemilla mollis*)

4 *Geranium* 'Johnson's Blue'

5 Sneezeweed (*Helenium* 'Moerheim Beauty')

9 *Crocosmia 'Lucifer'*

8 *Dahlia* 'Bishop of Llandaff', shown here in flower in early summer

PROJECT PLANNER

Tools and Materials

TIME SCALE **1 DAY**

Fork • Rake • Manure • Bone meal • Trowel • 1.2–1.5 m (4–5 ft) canes for dahlias • Mulch
The time scale above is for a site about 4 x 2 m (12 x 6 ft).

1 *Mark out the new bed and prepare the ground thoroughly before planting (see page 46).*

2 *Buy the plants. If you cannot plant them immediately, store in a cool place and keep well watered.*

3 *Position the plants around the bed. Sprinkle a handful of bone meal in the planting hole before backfilling with topsoil. Plant the crocosmia first as it is the central feature of the design, and then the dahlia tubers and their supporting stakes. If you are using ready-grown dahlia plants, don't plant them until all danger of frost is over. Then plant the red hot pokers, sneezeweed, and daylilies. Fill in with geraniums, lady's mantle and mountain bluet. Edge the front of the bed with low-growing catmint.*

4 *Water thoroughly and then cover the spaces between the plants with a layer of mulch, such as bark chippings.*

7 Mountain bluet (*Centaurea montana*)

MAINTENANCE

• For bushy dahlias, pinch out the growing tips of plants when they are about 30–45 cm (12–18 in) tall. For bigger flowers, pinch out some buds, leaving about ten to develop. Feed with granular or liquid fertiliser in early summer.

• In summer, clip back dead flowers and tired leaves to encourage fresh growth and flowers.

• Mulch in the autumn or late spring.

• Weed regularly and water in hot weather.

• Support dahlias and other tall perennials. Insert canes or wire supports around each plant when it is about 30 cm (12 in) tall. Tie the stakes together to provide a framework through which the stems can grow.

• When frosts have killed the dahlia leaves, cut the stems back to 15 cm (6 in). Lift the tubers and leave them to dry in a frost-free shed for 2–3 weeks. Pack them in peat or moss and store in a box over winter.

• Cut back the dead growth of other perennials in the autumn (see page 39).

6 Daylily (*Hemerocallis* 'Stella de Oro')

133

Planting for Year-round Interest
FOUR-SEASON ISLAND BED

IN MANY SITUATIONS it is important for a flower bed or border to look its best throughout the year. Choose plants that have different seasons of interest so that there is always something attractive to look at. Spring-flowering bulbs are a good choice for brightening up the early months of the year before the leaves of other plants emerge. If space is limited, use plants that have more than one season of interest – perhaps a spring-flowering shrub that also has attractive berries in autumn. There are shrubs, such as some dogwoods and willows, that have dramatic, brightly coloured stems in winter and spring if you prune them back each year.

Late-summer splendour

A hazel tree gives height to this island bed. It also has yellow catkins in spring and mid-green leaves in summer turning to yellow in autumn. Ground-cover plants and small bulbs provide a changing focus from season to season.

1 Hazel (*Corylus avellana*)

2 Snowdrop (*Galanthus* sp.) – buy and plant new plants in spring, after flowering but before the leaves die back

3 *Nerine bowdenii* – plant bulbs in the autumn

4 Irish ivy (*Hedera hibernica*)

5 *Berberis thunbergii* 'Atropurpurea Nana'

134

9 Dogwood (*Cornus alba* 'Sibirica'), shown here in winter when its bright red stems are seen to best effect

8 Bistort (*Persicaria bistorta* 'Superba')

PROJECT PLANNER

TIME SCALE 1 DAY

Tools and Materials

- Garden hose or rope • Fork • Spade
- Rake • Bone meal • Manure
- Tree stake and ties • Fine soil
- Bark-chip mulch

The time scale above is for a site about 4 x 2 m (12 x 6 ft).

1 Mark out the shape of the bed with a garden hose or some rope (see page 46).

2 Make the new bed, preparing the ground thoroughly (see page 46).

3 Buy the plants. Store in a cool place and keep well watered until you plant them.

4 Plant and stake the hazel tree (see page 33), and then plant the dogwood, berberis and bistort. Spread the ivy stems over the ground and cover them with soil every 25–30 cm (10–12 in). Plant the cyclamen, snowdrops and winter irises in the autumn, covering the bulbs with fine soil. Plant the nerines in early autumn or spring; the top of the bulb should just break the soil surface.

5 After planting, water thoroughly. Cover any exposed soil with a mulch of bark chippings.

7 *Cyclamen coum* – plant tubers in the autumn

MAINTENANCE

- *Cut back the dogwood to just above ground level each spring. In summer, if it overshadows the iris clump, trim it back.*

- *Weed regularly and mulch in autumn or late spring. Once plants are established, weeding will be greatly reduced, since ground-cover plants are a feature of this design.*

- *Lift and divide the winter iris rhizomes in summer or early autumn (see page 39).*

6 Winter iris (*Iris unguicularis*)

Ideas for Shaded Beds and Borders

FLOWER BEDS AND borders in a shaded situation will never be quite as colourful as those in full sun, but you can still enjoy a rich and varied range of flowers and greenery. Use cool colours — blues, purples, greens — for a tranquil, relaxing feel.

There are also some simple ways of creating the illusion that more light reaches the area than is actually the case: plant pale-coloured flowers to accentuate what little light there is, paint neighbouring walls a light colour, or position a mirror to reflect light outwards. The plants you choose can help, too: small, feathery-leaved plants are better than large, solid-looking species as they give a lighter, less dense overall effect.

The questions on these two pages are designed to help you pinpoint ways in which you can improve shaded beds and borders. Each one is backed up by a step-by-step project with plants that have been specifically chosen because they thrive in shaded spots.

? *Do you have a shaded, water-retentive area of garden?*

The solution is to plant species such as ferns, which thrive in this type of environment. *Right:* This royal fern enjoys the damp, acid conditions in the shade of the trees. SEE *Bed for a Moist, Shaded Site, page 140.*

➤·➤·➤·➤·➤·➤·➤·➤·➤·➤

? *Is a boundary wall or other vertical surface casting too much shade?*

Although high perimeter boundaries give you privacy, they also create shade and deprive plants of light. Reflect light into the area by painting the wall or fence a light colour or by introducing mirrors. ***Right:*** Ferns, climbers and a holly are reflected in the strategically placed mirror, maximising the amount of light that reaches the area.
SEE *Adding Light to a Shaded Corner, page 142.*

? *Do you have a mature tree under which nothing grows well?*

Lack of light is not the only problem: the tree roots may also be taking all the available moisture out of the surrounding soil. You can minimise the problem by planting shade-tolerant species such as small woodland plants.
SEE *Planting Under a Tree, page 138.*

Planting Under a Tree
GROUND COVER FOR DRY SHADE

A TREE, ESPECIALLY a mature one, is possibly the greatest asset a garden can have. Like a living sculpture, it can give your garden a dramatic visual focus. It also brings a feeling of maturity and provides a haven for birds and other wildlife.

Trees are not without their problems, however. Plants growing in their shade can become straggly, and lawns develop bare patches. Trees also extract a lot of water and nutrients from the soil, so neighbouring plants may suffer. Enrich the soil with compost or farmyard manure, add a slow-acting fertiliser, such as bone meal, and mulch to a depth of 7.5–10 cm (3–4 in)

to help retain moisture. If your tree casts very dense shade, you may need to remove lower branches and thin out the canopy. If a branch is safely accessible, remove it yourself with a bow saw; otherwise hire a tree surgeon. Large branches are best removed in late winter or spring, although cherry trees should be pruned in the summer.

Ground-cover plants that thrive in dry shade, such as alyssum or periwinkle, are an excellent solution to the problems caused by trees. They cover bare patches of lawn and provide an attractive carpet of flowers that brings added interest to the area.

Purple shades

Purple is a good choice for shaded situations, since it merges beautifully with shadows. Add a sprinkling of white flowers and variegated leaves to reflect some light. Plant busy Lizzies after the danger of frost has passed. In autumn, add a handful or two of purple, spring-flowering crocus bulbs to fill any gaps.

1 *Heuchera micrantha* 'Palace Purple'

MAINTENANCE

• *Keep the area free of weeds. Once the plants have grown together to form a dense carpet, weeding will be reduced.*

• *Water the bed in hot, dry weather to compensate for the water removed by the tree's roots.*

• *Remove dead growth and mulch in autumn or spring.*

PROJECT PLANNER

TIME SCALE 1+ HOURS

Tools and Materials

Secateurs • Bow saw • Fork • Spade • Rake • Bone meal • Manure • Bark-chip or gravel mulch

1 *If necessary, remove any small and spindly branches growing from the main trunk using a sharp pair of secateurs. Take care not to damage the bark on the tree trunk.*

2 *Remove the bulk of any large branches using a bow saw. Cut the branch from underneath, 7.5–15 cm (3–6 in) from the point where it joins the tree trunk.*

3 *Next, saw from above, 7.5 cm (3 in) further from the trunk. As you saw, the branch will split to the first cut without tearing the uncut branch.*

4 *Neaten the pruned branch, making a clean cut at its base. This is much easier with the main weight of the branch gone.*

5 *There may be a slightly swollen area left near the base of the branch. Leave this on the tree. Do not apply wound paint, since this may encourage disease.*

6 *Gently loosen the soil underneath the tree with a fork, taking care not to damage the roots.*

7 *Enrich the soil by forking in manure and bone meal.*

8 *Buy the plants. If you cannot plant them immediately, store them in a cool place and keep well watered.*

9 *Plant the plants (see page 32) and water thoroughly. Mulch with bark chips or gravel.*

3 Busy Lizzies (*Impatiens*) – white variety

2 Periwinkle (*Vinca minor*)

Bed for a Moist, Shaded Site

WOODLAND FERNERY

IF YOU HAVE A MOIST, shaded corner in your garden, make the most of it by growing plants that thrive in these conditions. Woodland ferns are ideal – and, because many are dramatic-looking, they are visually strong enough to contrast with any areas of hard surfaces, such as rocks, paving and walls.

Ferns more than make up for their lack of flowers by the attractiveness of their leaves, or fronds. Each spring fresh new fronds slowly unfurl and grow into beautiful arching stems of the finest filigree, like the lady fern (*Athyrium filix-femina*). The fronds of others, such as the hart's tongue fern (*Asplenium scolopendrium*), are undivided, handsome and glossy. Many ferns are rampant and so make excellent ground-cover plants for semi-wild areas beneath trees or between shrubs. In autumn, many ferns turn a soft rust colour. Others, such as the soft shield fern (*Polystichum setiferum*), stay green through winter.

Most ferns need a rich, moist soil, although some will tolerate dry conditions and will even grow in shaded crevices in walls. There are a few species that require lime-free soil, but in general ferns are easy-going plants that suffer from few pests or diseases and need little care and attention.

Rocky fernery for acid, neutral or alkaline soil

These ferns, suitable for most ordinary soil types, nestle between large rocks around a shaded paved area. Clumps of small, early spring bulbs growing among the unfurling fern fronds would increase interest early in the season.

1 *Adiantum pedatum*

2 Male fern (*Dryopteris filix-mas*)

3 Shuttlecock fern (*Matteuccia struthiopteris*)

140

PLANTING ALTERNATIVES
Fernery for lime-free soils

If your garden soil is acidic, then you have the opportunity to grow some of the lime-hating ferns, such as the magnificent royal fern (*Osmunda regalis*). To show such a large fern off to its best advantage, reduce the scale of the neighbouring plants. *Cryptogramma crispa* and the hardy maidenhair fern are both relatively small plants. Substitute the ferns listed here for those shown in the illustration below.

2 *Cryptogramma crispa*

3 Royal fern (*Osmunda regalis*)

4 Hardy maidenhair fern (*Adiantum venustum*)

PROJECT PLANNER

TIME SCALE **1 DAY**

Tools and Materials
Fork • Rake • Manure • Large rocks to match the colour of surrounding paving • Trowel• Well-rotted compost • Bone meal • Bark-chip mulch
The time scale above is for a site about 2 x 2 m (6 x 6 ft).

1 *Mark out the shape of the new bed and prepare the soil (see page 46).*

2 *Buy some large rocks or collect them from around the garden. Set them into the soil so that they look natural.*

3 *Buy the plants. Stand them in the shade and keep the soil moist until you plant them.*

4 *Set the plants in position. Plant the large shuttlecock fern first, as this is the most prominent fern in the planting, and then the medium-sized male and soft shield ferns. Then put in the hart's tongue ferns and the adiantums. Plant the little blechnum ferns wherever there are gaps.*

5 *Before refilling the planting holes with soil, fork compost and bone meal in and around the planting holes.*

6 *Water thoroughly and scatter a bark-chip mulch around the base of each fern and over any bare soil.*

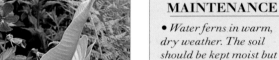

4 Soft shield fern
(*Polystichum setiferum*)

6 Hart's tongue fern
(*Asplenium scolopendrium*)

5 *Blechnum penna-marina*

MAINTENANCE
• *Water ferns in warm, dry weather. The soil should be kept moist but not waterlogged.*

• *Cut back dead fronds in autumn using secateurs. Evergreen fern species should be cut back in spring to make way for new growth.*

• *Weed regularly.*

• *Remove the young fronds of any ferns that are growing in the wrong place to keep your planting neat.*

• *Replenish the bark-chip mulch in late spring after sprinkling a little bone meal around the base of each plant or in autumn before the first frosts.*

Adding Light to a Shaded Corner
MIRROR MIRAGE

MIRRORS ARE AN easy way of reflecting light into a shaded area of the garden. They have the additional benefit of making your garden seem larger and doubling the number of plants growing near by, giving the impression of lush and luxuriant growth. The illusion is even more effective when surrounding walls or fences are painted a light colour. However, even though a mirror will bring more light to your plants, you still need to choose shade-tolerant species, since the extra light may not dramatically alter the overall growing conditions.

In front of the mirror, grow plants that have small, feathery or divided leaves so that you can catch glimpses of the glass and reflections through them. Avoid dense, bushy plants that would produce a solid screen. Train climbers or wall shrubs along the mirror to overlap and disguise its straight edges.

Before you put up a mirror, experiment to find the best place for it. Observe the area throughout the day to discover when and where the light falls. See what view is reflected back, and decide whether the reflection could be made more interesting by positioning a plant, a pot or even a garden statue in front of the mirror.

Light, bright planting for dry, neutral-to-alkaline soil
White paint and mirrors were used here to cheer up a dark house wall. In this planting scheme, tall Japanese anemones (Anemone x hybrida) *and dramatic spires of bear's breeches are reflected in the glass.*

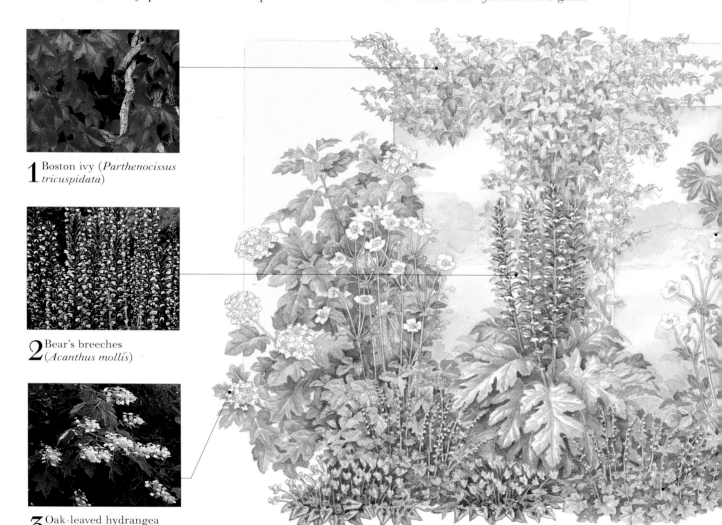

1 Boston ivy (*Parthenocissus tricuspidata*)

2 Bear's breeches (*Acanthus mollis*)

3 Oak-leaved hydrangea (*Hydrangea quercifolia*)

MAINTENANCE

- *Wipe the mirror once a month with a damp cloth.*
- *Remove any leaves or branches that obscure the mirror.*
- *Cut the stems of anemones and bear's breeches flowers back to ground level once flowers are past their best.*
- *The reflective silvering behind the glass will gradually wear away and you may need to replace the mirror.*

4 Japanese anemone (*Anemone* x *hybrida*)

5 Japanese aralia (*Fatsia japonica*)

6 Fringecup (*Tellima grandiflora*)

7 Ivy-leafed cyclamen (*Cyclamen hederifolium*)

PROJECT PLANNER

TIME SCALE 1+ HOURS

Tools and Materials

Pencil • Spirit level • Mirror, predrilled in corners • Drill and masonry bit • Rawl plugs • Rubber washers • Screws and screwdriver

1 Clean the wall or fence on which you are going to position the mirror. Fill any holes, if necessary, and paint the wall a light colour, if desired.

2 Using a spirit level and a pencil, mark the positions of the screw holes on the wall or fence so that they correspond to the holes in the corners of the mirror.

3 Using the appropriate drill bit, drill holes in the wall or fence, and insert one rawl plug into each one. Inset: Position a rubber washer over the first hole and hold it in place.

4 Insert each screw through a rubber washer and into the one you fixed in the wall or fence behind. This washer holds the mirror away from the wall and prevents it from cracking.

5 Prepare the bed (see page 46) and plant.

6 Water thoroughly.

THEMED GARDENS

Sea of tranquillity
In this tranquil, Japanese-style garden, pots of lush ferns, hostas and a purple-leaved Japanese maple frame the shore, while water lilies and reeds decorate the pond.

HERB GARDENS

HERBS HAVE BEEN grown for centuries for their culinary, aromatic, cosmetic and healing properties. Although some are grown for their foliage alone, there are many others that have wonderfully aromatic flowers and leaves, making them a delight to have in the garden.

You can, of course, intersperse herbs with other plants in your beds and borders, but creating a garden specifically for herbs – even if it's on a very small scale – means that the plants are all in one place when you need to use them. It is also aesthetically pleasing: many of the herbs that grow well together look good together, too, as they come from similar habitats in the wild.

The herb gardens in this section feature some of the most popular herbs for culinary and household uses. They also cover a range of situations, from herbs that you can grow indoors on your kitchen windowsill to a raised bed for herbs that like well-drained soil, so you can be sure of finding something that suits your particular requirements.

Herbal haven
Left: This garden is functional as well as visually appealing. Mounds of purple sage and frothy lady's mantle frame the path, leading to a magnificent clump of purple lupins.

Cook's Herb Bed

HERBS FOR YEAR-ROUND COOKING

HAVING A GOOD selection of fresh culinary herbs on hand can transform your cooking – but it is not just their taste that makes growing herbs a good idea: many of the plants are a joy to have in your garden. Rosemary, for example, is a delightful, bluish, grey-leaved plant that can be grown anywhere as a shrub. Thyme makes a useful edging plant, and you can choose whether to clip it into a hedge or leave it to make a softer shape. The feathery texture of dill makes it a beautiful foil to grow in front of brighter plants.

Other useful herbs include mint and basil but both should be grown separately (see pages 150 and 154).

If possible, make sure that your herbs are within easy reach of the kitchen and are growing close together; then, when you need a sprig or two of something to put in the soup, you'll be able to find it easily without having to fight your way through the flower beds. The bed shown below will provide a good range of basic herbs for everyday cooking, but if your family has a favourite herb, be sure to make room for it.

Year-round herb garden

Here, in a sunny position, are the basic necessities for a good bouquet garni (bay, rosemary, thyme and parsley). Other popular herbs – tarragon, sage, dill and chives – complete this versatile herb bed. Pot marigold is not an important herb in cooking, but its bright orange flowers will help brighten up the bed. The whole group is held together visually by a low-growing hedge of clipped thyme.

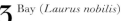

4 Dill (*Anethum graveolens*)

5 Rosemary (*Rosmarinus officinalis*)

3 Bay (*Laurus nobilis*)

2 Chives (*Allium schoenoprasum*)

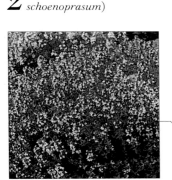

1 Thyme (*Thymus vulgaris*)

PLANTING ALTERNATIVES

Herbs for summer salads

For tasty and unusual summer salads, replace the bay cones with a mound of trimmed dwarf nasturtium. Grow a patch of rocket plants from seed in place of the rosemary, and plant two or three sorrel plants in place of the sage. The tarragon, pot marigold, parsley, chives, dill and thyme remain since all have an important place in summer salads. Use the flowers of the marigold, both the leaves and the flowers of the nasturtium, and the leaves of everything else. Harvest a few leaves from each plant, chop and serve with lettuce.

3 Dwarf nasturtium (*Tropaeolum majus* 'Peach Melba')

5 Rocket (*Eruca vesicaria*)

8 Sorrel (*Rumex acetosa*)

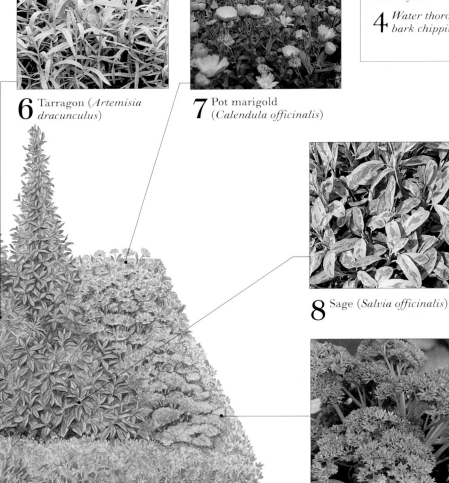

6 Tarragon (*Artemisia dracunculus*)

7 Pot marigold (*Calendula officinalis*)

8 Sage (*Salvia officinalis*)

9 Parsley (*Petroselinum crispum*)

PROJECT PLANNER

TIME SCALE 1 DAY

Tools and Materials

Fork • Rake • Sharp sand (for poorly drained soils only) • Bone meal • Manure or garden compost • Trowel • Watering can or hose • Bark-chip mulch

1 *Measure and mark out the site and prepare the bed for planting (see page 46). If your soil is heavy, add some sharp sand to improve drainage – many herbs dislike wet soil.*

2 *Buy the plants. If you can't plant them immediately, stand them in the shade and keep them watered.*

3 *Plant the clipped bays and the central rosemary first, and then the other herbs, incorporating bone meal and manure or garden compost into the planting holes. Insert the pot marigolds wherever there are any spaces. Edge the bed with thyme.*

4 *Water thoroughly after planting and mulch with bark chippings.*

MAINTENANCE

• *Keep the bed watered and weeded.*

• *Try to stop herbs from flowering since it wastes energy and may adversely affect the plant or the flavour. Snip off the flowering stems of chives at ground level as they are tough and inedible. With woody herbs, such as bay, thyme, rosemary and sage, flowering matters less – although if you want to preserve herbs, it is always best to harvest the leaves before flowering. Allow the pot marigold to flower, but remove the dead heads as they fade.*

• *Prune the thyme hedge in late spring and summer to keep it tidy and to encourage dense growth.*

Bed for Invasive Herbs
MINT BED

MINTS GROW so vigorously that they quickly swamp any other plants in the same bed. This is the last thing you want in a well-ordered herb garden, but mints are such useful plants that it would be a shame to banish them from your garden altogether.

Fortunately, however, there are a number of ways to contain them. You can sink a bottomless bucket into the ground and plant mint inside it so that its roots cannot extend sideways. If you have already planted mint and you want to stop it from spreading, push terracotta or slate tiles into the ground around the clump, overlapping them so there are no gaps between.

Alternatively, as in the design below, make a separate bed and grow different sorts of mint without the risk of them swamping other less vigorous plants. Mints thrive in ordinary garden soil and do not need bright sunshine.

Mint miscellany

This mint border is in a narrow, lightly shaded strip running alongside a paved path. The mints are contained within their own little empire – only the creeping Corsican mint spills over into the paving gaps. The planting is symmetrical, with the tallest mint (the spearmint) standing in the centre of the bed to provide a focal point for the planting. A small, bushy ginger mint on either side provides a contrast in form. Peppermint and apple mint frame the ends of the bed.

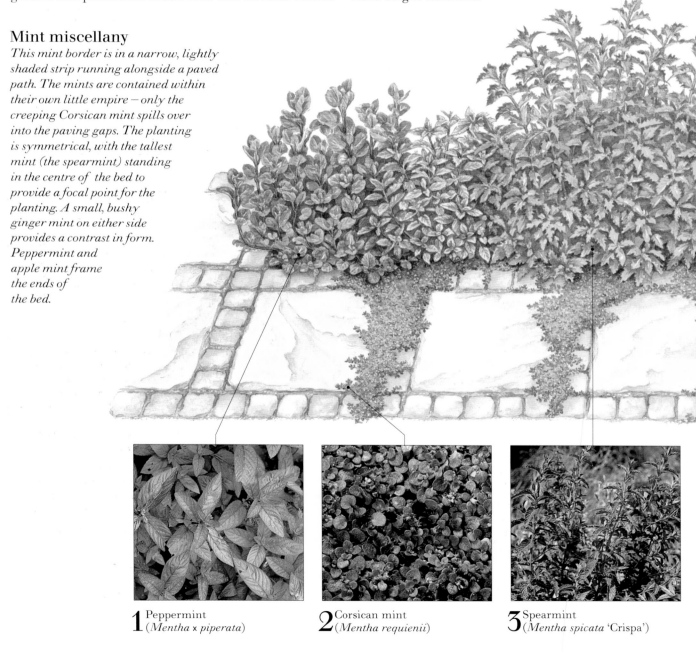

1 Peppermint
(*Mentha x piperata*)

2 Corsican mint
(*Mentha requienii*)

3 Spearmint
(*Mentha spicata* 'Crispa')

150

5 Ginger mint (*Mentha × gracilis*), shown here in flower in summer

PROJECT PLANNER

TIME SCALE 1 HOUR

Tools and Materials

Fork • Spade • Rake • Bone meal • Manure • Trowel • Watering can or hose • Bark-chip mulch

1 *Buy the plants. If you cannot plant them immediately, stand them in the shade and keep them well watered.*

2 *Prepare the bed for planting (see page 46), incorporating bone meal and manure into the soil. Plant the creeping Corsican mint plants in paving gaps or at the edge.*

3 *Set the remaining plants in position on the surface of the bed. When you are satisfied, plant them (see page 32), water thoroughly and apply a 5-cm (2-in) layer of bark chippings over the bare ground as a mulch.*

MAINTENANCE

If one of the mints seems to be growing more strongly than the others, carefully lift it and plant it in a bucket that has holes in the bottom for drainage. The soil level should be 2.5 cm (1 in) below the rim of the bucket. Plant the bucket in the bed. This will prevent the mint from spreading and taking over the whole bed.

• *Harvest regularly. Use the leaves fresh or chop and freeze them with water in ice-cube trays to make mint-flavoured ice cubes which you can use to season stews or sauces.*

• *Cut back the mints to ground level in the autumn.*

• *Lift, divide and replant overcrowded plants in the autumn.*

• *Keep the bed weeded and watered.*

4 Apple mint (*Mentha suaveolens* 'Variegata')

Herbs for Well-drained Soil

RAISED HERB BED

WHETHER YOU WANT to grow herbs for household use, cooking, cosmetics or medicinal purposes, you can create a beautiful herb feature from a raised bed. This will bring height to a large, flat area, such as an expanse of paving or lawn.

A raised bed is particularly suitable for herbs that dislike boggy conditions, since you can supply plenty of drainage beneath the soil. Treat a raised bed as you would any other type of container. Place a 7.5-cm (3-in) layer of drainage material, such as gravel or broken pots, at the bottom of the bed before covering with soil to make sure that water can drain away easily.

Old railway sleepers are used in the illustration below. Alternatively, you could order new ones, cut to size, from good timber merchants. If you use 25-cm (10-in) wide pieces of timber to make the bed, you can sit on the edge and inhale the delicious scent of these aromatic plants.

Choose strongly scented herbs so that you can enjoy their fragrance as you walk past. The curry plant, lavender, thymes and rosemary are all good examples.

Raised herb planter in purple, blue and white

Rosemary, sage and thyme billow over the edges of the bed, while the tall bright blue borage and white sweet rocket provide splashes of light and colour. The borage and sweet rocket will self-seed each year. The other herbs are perennials.

1 Rosemary (*Rosmarinus officinalis*)

2 Borage (*Borago officinalis*)

5 Sweet rocket (*Hesperis matronalis* 'Alba Plena')

4 Silver posie thyme (*Thymus vulgaris* 'Silver Posie')

PROJECT PLANNER

TIME SCALE ½ DAY

Tools and Materials

Old railway sleepers or timber 12.5 x 25 cm (5 x 10 in) cut to required length • Pointed, tannelised pegs, 5 x 5 x 45 cm (2 x 2 x 18 in) • Mallet • 5-cm (2-in) galvanised nails • Hammer • Broken ceramic shards • Topsoil • Trowel • Watering can or hose • Gravel • Rake

1 *Plan the bed and calculate how much timber you need. Order the correct lengths from a timber merchant.*

2 *Position the timber, taking care to stagger the corner joints in order to make the structure stronger.*

3 *Drive wooden pegs into the ground inside the raised bed at each corner, flush with the timbers.*

4 *Nail the wooden pegs to the inside of the raised bed, using galvanised nails.*

5 *Place a 7.5-cm (3-in) layer of broken ceramic shards at the bottom of the bed and cover with topsoil.*

6 *Plant the herbs (see page 32). Water thoroughly. Spread a thin covering of gravel around the bed and rake it level.*

3 Purple sage (*Salvia officinalis* 'Purpurascens')

MAINTENANCE

• *Keep the bed weeded and watered.*

• *In spring or summer, trim back any straggly stems of rosemary, sage and thyme.*

• *Deadhead sweet rocket to encourage more flowers to grow. Allow one or two flowers to go to seed so that you will have plants next year.*

• *Remove the borage and the rocket in the autumn.*

Potted Herbs
POT OF BASIL

Although many culinary herbs can easily be grown outdoors with a minimum of attention from the gardener, some of the most popular and useful ones need a little tender loving care. Basil is one such herb. It originates from the Indian sub-continent, where cold, wet summers are unheard of. In temperate regions, unless the temperature and soil conditions are exactly right, it can succumb to the cold and die. The solution to this problem is to grow it in a container, so that you can bring it inside if the weather becomes very cold.

Basil comes in many different varieties. There's the dark purple-leaved basil, the small-leaved bush basil (the easiest to grow), the crinkly-leaved 'Green Ruffles' and Italian basil, renowned for its flavour. Grow a few to find out which you prefer. However, all basils like moist, well-drained soil, so remember to include plenty of drainage material in the container.

Three in one

The Italian basil in the centre is the tallest of the three basils here, and gives some height to the display. It is also one of the most widely used basils in cooking. Around it are the lower-growing bush and purple-leaved basils. The purple basil provides a dramatic contrast in colour to the other two.

1 Italian basil (*Ocimum basilicum* 'Genovese')

2 Bush basil (*Ocimum basilicum* var. *minimum*)

3 Purple-leaved basil (*Ocimum basilicum* 'Purpurascens')

PROJECT PLANNER

TIME SCALE 1 HOUR

Tools and Materials

Container • Gravel, pebbles or ceramic shards • Potting compost • Water-retaining granules • Slow-release fertiliser granules • Watering can

1 Place a layer of drainage material in the bottom of the container. You can use gravel, pebbles or broken ceramic shards to promote drainage.

2 Fill the container with potting compost , incorporating water-retaining granules and slow-release fertiliser granules in accordance with the manufacturer's instructions.

3 Plant Italian basil in the centre of the pot as it is the tallest. Plant purple-leaved basil at the front and back and bush basil at either side to make the arrangement symmetrical.

4 Water thoroughly. If there is no danger of frost, the pot can be left outside. In cooler weather, keep it indoors in a sunny, draught-free spot.

MAINTENANCE

Pinch out the growing tips of the basil plants regularly to keep them bushy. You can use the pinchings in salads or sandwiches.

• Keep the potting compost damp, but make sure water can drain away from the bottom of the pot.

• In cool weather bring the pot indoors.

Parsley pot

Parsley is another invaluable herb for the cook. It can be grown outdoors, but if you grow it in a pot you can bring it indoors in the autumn and maintain your supply through the winter. Here, French marigolds are grown with the parsley as they are believed to deter pests such as whitefly. They also add a splash of colour to the pot.

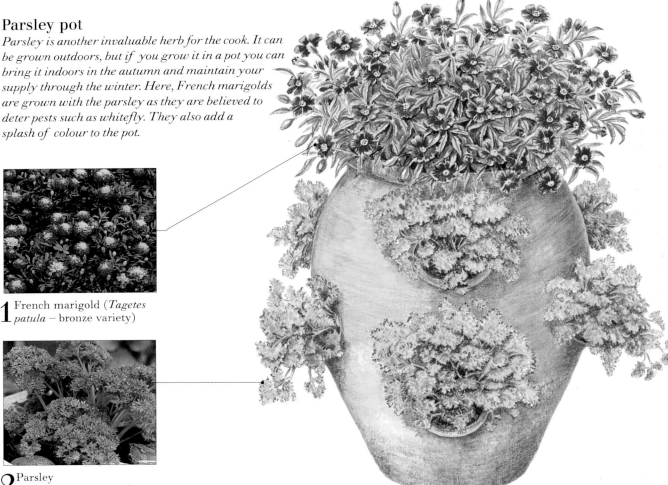

1 French marigold (*Tagetes patula* – bronze variety)

2 Parsley (*Petroselinum crispum*)

Herbs for Household Uses

HERB CORNER

ALTHOUGH WE TEND to think of herbs as something to use in cooking, they have many other uses: they can be used to make pot-pourri or soaps, delicious herbal teas, natural dyes and natural pesticides or insect repellants. There are also a great many herbs that can be used for medicinal purposes – however, you should always seek your doctor's advice before using herbs medicinally.

The household herb bed shown below has plants that fall into all of these categories. One of the reasons why it looks so attractive is that all the plants, except the lavender, belong to the same plant family (the daisy family), and this gives the bed visual coherence. The lavender adds a contrast of colour, form and texture. Instructions on how to harvest and use the herbs are given in the chart opposite.

Household herbs with a silver, blue and yellow theme

Here wormwood and cotton lavender (effective insect repellants) nestle between clumps of lavender (useful for making pot-pourri, soothing headaches and keeping away houseflies and moths). The tall dyer's chamomile gives some height at the back of the bed and can be used as a yellow clothes dye. The flowers of the shorter chamomile make a great relaxing tea after a hard day's gardening.

4 Dyer's chamomile (*Anthemis tinctoria*)

3 Wormwood (*Artemisia* 'Powis Castle')

2 Chamomile (*Chamaemelum nobile*)

1 Cotton lavender (*Santolina chamaecyparissus* 'Lemon Queen')

Harvesting and Using Household Herbs

Chamomile

Use the flowers to make tea. Harvest the flowers when they open in summer. Put half a cup of flower heads into a teapot, cover with a cup of boiling water, and infuse for five minutes, then strain. Other herbs that can be used in this way include mint, fennel and honeysuckle flowers.

Cotton lavender

Use to deter clothes moths. Pick sprigs of leaves and flowers in summer, tie in bunches and hang them up in a warm, dry place until they are brittle. Place a handful of dried leaves and flowers in a small muslin bag. Other herbs that can be used in this way include lavender, wormwood (see below) and alecost.

Dyer's chamomile

Use to dye natural fabrics. Harvest flowers in the summer. Chop them up and place them in a muslin bag. Put the bag in a bowl, pour over hot water and leave to soak overnight. Transfer the bag and water to a pot and boil for about one hour. Remove and discard the bag. Boil the fabric you are dyeing in the liquid for an hour, stirring regularly. Allow to cool. Remove the fabric and rinse until the water runs clear. Do a final rinse in hot, salted water to help fix the colour. Always wash fabric dyed in this way separately from the rest of your wash and in cold water in case the colour runs. Other herbs that can be used in this way include meadowsweet (black dye), sorrel (pink dye) and elder (purple dye).

Lavender

Use to deter houseflies, moths and other insects. Harvest the flowers on long stalks as they open. Dry and use as for cotton lavender. Other herbs that can be used in this way include wormwood (see below) and alecost.

Wormwood

Use to repel clothes moths and other insects. Pick flowers and leaves in summer. Dry and use as for cotton lavender. Other herbs that can be used in the same way include lavender (see above) and alecost.

PROJECT PLANNER

TIME SCALE 1+ HOURS

Tools and Materials

Fork • Rake • Compost or manure • Trowel

1 *Buy the plants. If you are not able to plant immediately, stand them in a shaded place and keep them watered.*

2 *Prepare the bed (see page 46) and plant the plants, starting at the back of the bed and working forwards.*

3 *Water thoroughly, then mulch with bark chippings.*

PLANTING ALTERNATIVES

Household herbs with a gold theme

Replace the cotton lavender with feverfew – an infusion of this has antibacterial properties and can be used to wipe down surfaces in the kitchen or bathroom. Change the chamomile for yarrow, which is a great compost activator and speeds up decomposition dramatically. Instead of dyer's chamomile, plant pyrethrum – the powdered, dried flower heads can be used as an insecticide and are effective against aphids, ants, bed bugs, cockroaches, flies, mosquitoes and spider mites. Replace the lavender with tansy, which deters ants and mice; place a few sprigs of dried tansy under your carpets. Wormwood remains to fill out the centre of the bed.

1 Feverfew (*Tanacetum parthenium* 'Aureum')

2 Yarrow (*Achillea* 'Coronation Gold')

4 Pyrethrum (*Tanacetum coccineum*)

5 Tansy (*Tanacetum vulgare*)

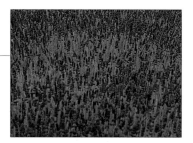

5 Lavender (*Lavandula angustifolia* 'Hidcote')

MAINTENANCE

• *Keep the plants watered and weeded.*

• *Tidy the bed in autumn and apply a layer of compost or farmyard manure.*

WILDFLOWER GARDENS

Y OU CAN MAKE A wonderful contribution to the environment by dedicating even a small part of your garden to local wild flowers. As well as preserving flowers that might be under threat, you will also be encouraging wildlife into your garden in search of food and shelter. An added bonus for the weekend gardener is that wildflower gardens generally require less routine maintenance than more formal planting schemes.

Never dig up flowers from the wild; instead, make a note of what thrives in your local hedgerows and buy seed or plants from your local garden centre or a mail-order catalogue. The wildflower gardens in this section feature plants that are suitable for a number of different habitats, from a hot, dry, prairielike site to a temperate wildflower meadow.

Flowering wilderness
Left: Here, a mixture of hedge parsley, scarlet poppies and blue-stemmed grasses creates an inviting habitat for butterflies, bees and other wildlife.

Wildflower Meadow
SPRING-FLOWERING LAWN

THERE CAN BE FEW more evocative sights than a grassy field dotted with colourful native flowers. Converting part, if not all, of your lawn into a meadow may help to restore the population of some rare plants in your area and encourage birds and other wildlife to visit your garden.

Grow young wildflower plants in bare patches (or seed bare patches) and stop mowing to allow them to colonize. If your lawn is in good condition, you will need to weaken the grasses to allow room for meadow plants to develop. Stop using fertilisers and weedkillers a season before you plan to plant, and mow as normal.

A spring-flowering meadow, such as the one shown below, should be mown for the first time in midsummer, after the flowers have set seed. For a summer-flowering meadow, with species such as ox-eye daisies and harebells, keep the grass down to about 7.5 cm (3 in) until late spring and then allow it to grow so that the wild flowers will develop. Scythe down the grasses and flowers in the autumn and rake up the dried debris.

Meadow magic

A mown path leads to a rustic bench that is surrounded by flowers from early spring until early summer. Drifts of delicate blue, white and pink flowers border the path, with elegant, bright yellow meadow buttercups providing a splash of brighter colour behind the bench. In the background, the leaves of the wild daffodil, which flowers earlier in the year, are dying back.

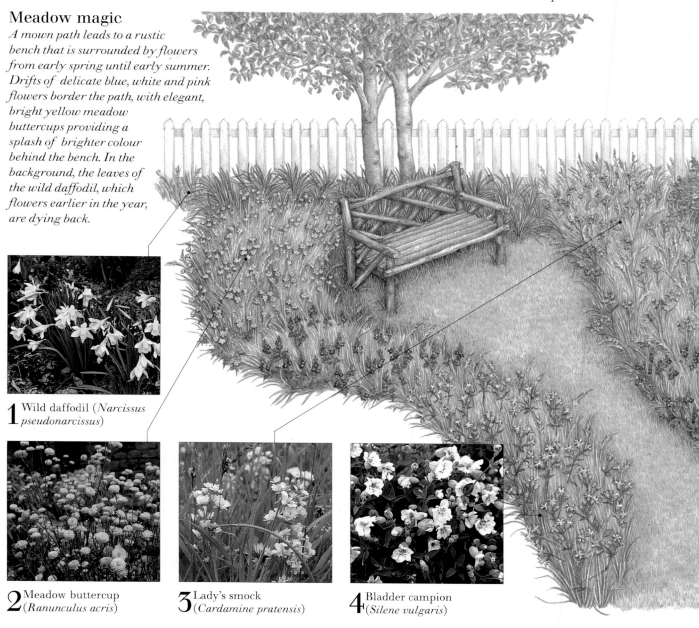

1 Wild daffodil (*Narcissus pseudonarcissus*)

2 Meadow buttercup (*Ranunculus acris*)

3 Lady's smock (*Cardamine pratensis*)

4 Bladder campion (*Silene vulgaris*)

PROJECT PLANNER

TIME SCALE 1/2 DAY

Tools and Materials

Trowel or bulb planter • Hand fork • Watering can with a fine rose spout attachment

1 *At least one season before you plant your meadow, stop using fertilisers and weedkillers of any sort. If your lawn is in good condition, continue mowing, but remove grass clippings since these return grass nutrients to the soil.*

2 *Buy some meadow plants or raise some from seed in pots. Choose local species: visit local wild areas to identify likely candidates for your own garden but never dig up or take seed from plants in the wild.*

3 *Use a trowel or bulb planter to remove a core of turf (see page 31). Place each plant in position, firm it in and water.*

4 *Using a hand fork, loosen the soil surface of any bare patches and sprinkle on wildflower seeds. In dry weather, water with a watering can with a fine rose spout attachment.*

5 Germander speedwell
(*Veronica chamaedrys*)

MAINTENANCE

Cut the grass in mid or late summer using a sickle or a strimmer, then resume regular mowing until the grass stops growing in the late autumn.

Allow the cuttings to dry in the sun before you rake them up.

• *If your lawn develops bare patches, sprinkle a few annual wildflower seeds, such as corncockle or poppies. Loosen the soil surface with a hand fork and sprinkle on the seed. Cover the seeds with chicken wire to prevent birds and animals from getting at them. Remove the chicken wire when the plants are established.*

Wild Flowers to Attract Insects
NECTAR-RICH TROUGH

MANY GARDENERS aim to encourage butterflies, bees and other insects into the garden. Fascinating to watch in their own right, they also attract birds and small mammals.

Butterflies, bees and many other flying insects tend to visit flowers that produce plenty of sweet nectar. The flowers do not have to be wild species; insects find many cultivated plants extremely attractive. Popular shrubs, such as the butterfly bush (*Buddleia davidii*), lavender and marjoram, are all magnets for many species of butterfly.

If your space is limited, plant a container of nectar-rich plants. Position it in a sunny, sheltered spot (butterflies like still air, and a sunny area is always better for flowers than a shaded one). The ideal container is one large enough to create a mini-habitat, which also looks quite rough and natural – an old stone or concrete trough, for example. If you cannot get hold of an old container, paint a new concrete one with a watery solution of manure to encourage mosses and lichens to grow on it and speed up the ageing process.

In the pink

This weathered concrete trough, with its nectar-rich, pink- and purple-flowered plants, will attract butterflies, bees and other insects throughout the summer. The ice plant brings height to the group. Its grey foliage and pink flowers are repeated in the garden pinks in the foreground. Spilling over the front of the trough in front of the cushion of pink-flowered cranesbill is the purple-flowered creeping thyme.

1 Ice plant (*Sedum spectabile* 'Brilliant')

2 Pink (*Dianthus plumarius*)

PLANTING ALTERNATIVES

Yellow and orange theme

Insects are drawn to flowers by their colours as well as by their scent. Change the predominant colour of your planting and you are likely to attract a slightly different range of insects. This orange and yellow scheme will attract hoverflies – their larvae eat greenfly, making them a useful pest control. In place of the ice plant, use yellow-flowered evening primrose. Change the pinks to orange French marigolds, substitute yellow alyssum for the thyme and yellow-flowered gold-moss sedum for the cranesbill.

1 Evening primrose (*Oenothera perennis*)

2 French marigold (*Tagetes patula*)

3 Yellow alyssum (*Aurinaria saxatile*)

4 Gold-moss sedum (*Sedum acre*)

4 Blood-red cranesbill (*Geranium sanguineum* var. *striatum*)

3 Creeping thyme (*Thymus praecox*)

PROJECT PLANNER

TIME SCALE ½ DAY

Tools and Materials

Container • Broken ceramic shards • Potting compost • Slow-release fertiliser granules • Water-retaining granules • Trowel • Watering can or hose • Gravel mulch

1 *Position the container in a sunny place, making sure that any excess water can drain away from the drainage hole. If necessary, stand the pot on blocks of wood to allow water to drain away easily.*

2 *Buy the plants. If you cannot plant them in the container immediately, stand them in a shaded place and keep them watered.*

3 *Plant the container, putting a layer of ceramic shards in the base for drainage and incorporating fertiliser and water-retaining granules into the potting compost in accordance with the manufacturer's instructions (see page 30).*

4 *Water thoroughly and scatter a gravel mulch over the soil.*

MAINTENANCE

• *Keep the trough weeded and watered.*

• *Replenish the gravel as necessary.*

• *Snip off any dead or unwanted growth.*

• *Remove dead flowers once they've faded to encourage more to grow. Ice plant flowers can be left through the winter since they look attractive as they dry out.*

Hot, Dry Wildflower Garden
PRAIRIE GARDEN

IF YOUR GARDEN is sunny, hot and dry in summer and you want a natural-looking planting that requires relatively little maintenance, then a prairie garden is the ideal choice. This type of garden is dominated by grasses and vigorous perennials — hence the idea of the 'prairie', where grasses dominate. They should be planted in widely spaced clumps, incorporating only half the amount of manure or fertiliser that you would normally use when creating a new bed, since a rich soil would encourage weeds. A sprinkling of gravel and a rocky path add to the prairie-like atmosphere. The planting shown below would look wonderful alongside a sun-baked gravel driveway.

Part of the fascination of this type of garden is the way in which it evolves over the years. Unlike most gardens, in which the gardener removes any weeds that compete for space, water and nutrients, in a prairie garden the plants are left virtually to fend for themselves (see Maintenance, opposite). Within a few years, clumps of native grasses and wild flowers will grow up to cover most of the bare ground.

Drift of gold and purple

Here, clumps of strong-growing perennials and grasses, with gold and purple flowers, grow in a bed mulched with gravel. The gravel and the flat rocks set at intervals around the bed echo the natural prairie habitat that these plants would enjoy in the wild.

3 *Eryngium agavifolium*

2 Butterfly weed (*Asclepias tuberosa*)

1 Gay feather (*Liatris spicata*)

MAINTENANCE

• *In the first growing season after planting, keep the plants free of weeds. In subsequent years you can reduce the weeding. Once the plants are well established, you can leave them to fend for themselves, although you should always take out any vigorous weeds, such as ground elder, dandelion, bindweed or couch grass.*

• *In late autumn, once the flowers are over, use a scythe to cut the growth down to ground level. Choose a dry day, so you can rake the debris away easily.*

4 Queen of the prairie
(*Filipendula rubra*)

5 Tufted hair grass
(*Deschampsia caespitosa* 'Golden Veil')

6 *Aster* x *frickartii* 'Mönch'

7 Switch grass
(*Panicum virgatum*)

PROJECT PLANNER

TIME SCALE 1 DAY

Tools and Materials

Fork • Rake • Spade • Rocks • Compost, garden manure or bone meal • Watering can or hose • Gravel or pebbles

1 *Buy the plants. If you can't plant them immediately, put them in a shaded spot and keep them watered.*

2 *Prepare the ground thoroughly (see page 46) and set rocks in position to create a natural-looking path through the 'prairie'.*

3 *Plant the plants, incorporating half the usual amount of bone meal, compost or manure in the planting holes.*

4 *Water thoroughly. Lightly mulch the bed with a layer of gravel or pebbles to give the garden the appearance of a natural-looking, parched, prairie landscape.*

PLANTING ALTERNATIVES

Drift of white and gold

For a dusty, more subtle colour scheme, substitute white and gold flowers for the purple ones. For white flowers, replace the queen of the prairie with heartleaf crambe, which has a huge cloud of tiny white blooms, and one of the clumps of gay feather with white coneflower. To strengthen the gold in the planting, change the other clump of gay feather to *Rudbeckia submentosa*, which has yellow flowers, and the aster to golden rod. The grasses — tufted hair grass, the switch grass, and the butterfly weed — can remain, since their colours and textures blend well with the white- and gold-flowered plants. The *Eryngium agavifolium* can remain, too, as its blue-grey leaves harmonise with the white flowers.

1 White coneflower (*Echinacea purpurea* 'White Swan') and *Rudbeckia submentosa*

4 Heartleaf crambe (*Crambe cordifolia*)

6 Golden rod (*Solidago* 'Goldenmosa')

WOODLAND GARDENS

L EAFY TREES, SHRUBBY undergrowth, and a ground covering of bulbs and shade-loving perennials: these are the conditions that one normally associates with woodland. But even if you don't have mature trees, you can still have a woodland-style garden all of your own. Your garden may have conditions very similar to those in a wooded area: it may be shaded by neighbouring buildings, for example. The same plants thrive in both situations, so you can create the mood and feel of a woodland without the trees!

In this section, you will find a planting scheme for the centre of a woodland area as well as one for the woodland edges. There are also instructions on how to create a natural-looking bark path, edged with spring-flowering bulbs.

Shady spot
Left: This woodland is home to plants that revel in shade. The rounded leaves of the pink-flowered bergenia, the blue-green leaves of the hosta and the fresh fern foliage create an impressive display beneath the trees.

Miniature Woodland

WILDLIFE HAVEN

IMAGINE A COOL, shaded woodland all of your own, where you can sit and escape from the heat of mid-summer. Contrary to what you might expect, you don't need acres of land or even existing mature trees. You can easily create a small-scale woodland from an existing shady shrub border. Just thin out the plants, add a tree or two, and plant some woodland ground cover. Choose small tree species if your space is limited. Silver birch, hawthorn, mountain ash and crab apple are all suitable for small gardens and will attract a wide range of insects and bird life. For larger areas, plant a few oaks among the smaller trees for future generations to enjoy.

Encourage wildlife into your woodland by including features such as bird feeding tables, log piles to provide shelter for insects and small mammals, and nesting boxes for birds and bats. Always position nesting boxes in a shaded place, since they can overheat when the sun shines directly on them. Attach them firmly to a mature tree at least 1.5 m (5 ft) above the ground.

Woodland species for chalk soil

Chalk-tolerant species cover the ground beneath a spreading field maple and a spring-flowering Viburnum plicatum. *The hellebore provides long-lived flowers in early spring, followed by the sweet violets from early to mid-spring, and the variegated deadnettle in summer. In late summer and autumn, the graceful white wands of bugbane sway gently in the breeze. The nesting box will provide a safe haven from cats and other potential predators.*

1 Bugbane (*Cimifuga simplex*), shown here in flower in late summer

2 Stinking hellebore (*Helleborus foetidus*)

6 Field maple
(Acer campestre)

5 Sweet violet
(Viola odorata)

4 *Viburnum plicatum*
'Mariesii'

PROJECT PLANNER

TIME SCALE **1 DAY**

Tools and Materials

Spade • Fork • Rake • Compost or farmyard manure • Tree stake and ties • Trowel • Bark-chip mulch • Ruler • Bird or bat nesting box • 5-cm (2-in) galvanised nails • Hammer

1 *Prepare the area for planting as if you were making a new bed (see page 46).*

2 *Plant the field maple, using a stake to provide it with support in its early stages of growth (see page 33).*

3 *Plant the viburnum and other plants. Water thoroughly and mulch with bark chippings to help create an authentic woodland atmosphere.*

4 *Measure the width of the nesting box to check that it is not too wide for the tree.*

5 *Using a 5-cm (2-in) nail, nail the nesting box to the tree stake (if the tree is young) or to the trunk of the tree (if the tree is more than about 20 cm/8 in in circumference).*

MAINTENANCE

• *Keep the area weeded – especially until the ground-cover plants have become established.*

• *Cut back any unwanted growth to keep plants within bounds.*

• *Replenish bark chippings in late spring.*

• *Gently rake up any leaves that fall from the tree and shrub onto the ground-cover plants.*

3 Deadnettle
(Lamium maculatum)

Woodland-edge Planting

DAPPLED SHADE GARDEN

THE PLANTS THAT do well on the edge of a woodland area are somewhat different to those that thrive in the centre. A truly wooded area is heavily shaded for much of the year and thus requires plants that do well in shade. The woodland edge, on the other hand, has patchy sunlight, or dappled shade, most of the time and perhaps even full sun at some times of day. The soil tends to be fertile and damp, since – unlike the soil in true woodland – it is not completely drained by tree roots or sheltered from rain by a dense overhead canopy of branches.

This means that you can choose from a much wider range of plants. For a natural-style planting use wild plants such as the guelder rose, wild dog rose, foxgloves, ground-hugging primroses, ferns and delicious wild strawberries. For a more cultivated look, shade-tolerant garden plants such as hostas, candelabra primulas and smoky-coloured hellebores are all good choices. Alternatively, as in the illustration below, you can combine wild and garden flowers in the same planting. A mulch of bark helps to keep the weeds down and adds to the woodland atmosphere.

Leafy glade in purple and gold

In this colourful and lush planting scheme shown in early summer, towering purple foxgloves preside over yellow, orange and purple candelabra primulas, while cuckoo pint and Solomon's seal bring a quieter, more subdued feeling. Sweet violets seed themselves around the bed, cropping up here and there to provide a dense ground cover.

1 Solomon's seal
(*Polygonatum* x *hybridum*)

2 Sweet violet
(*Viola odorata*)

3 Cuckoo pint
(*Arum maculatum*)

4 Yellow candelabra primula
(*Primula prolifera*)

9 Foxglove (*Digitalis purpurea*)

8 Shuttlecock fern (*Matteuccia struthiopteris*)

PROJECT PLANNER

TIME SCALE **½ DAY**

Tools and Materials

Fork • Rake • Bone meal • Compost • Trowel • Bark-chip mulch

1 *Prepare the area to be planted as if you were making a new bed (see page 46), enriching it with plenty of well-rotted compost.*

2 *Plant the largest plants first – the shuttlecock fern, lady's fern, Solomon's seal, foxgloves and cuckoo pint. Then plant the primulas. Finally, fill in any gaps in the bed with the sweet violets.*

3 *Scatter a bark-chip mulch between the plants and around the bed.*

7 Orange candelabra primula (*Primula bulleyana*)

6 Lady's fern (*Athyrium filix-femina*)

MAINTENANCE

• *Keep the area weeded and water in dry warm weather.*

• *Watch out for slugs and snails – use traps and deterrents rather than slug pellets that may harm wildlife or pets (see page 36).*

• *Deadhead flowers as they fade.*

• *Cut back and remove dead growth in the autumn before mulching.*

5 Japanese candelabra primula (*Primula japonica* 'Miller's Crimson')

Woodland Pathway
BARK PATH EDGED WITH BULBS

SUNNY SPRING mornings are the perfect time to enjoy a relaxing stroll along a winding woodland path. If you have a few trees, or even a few over-grown shrubs, you can create such a feature on a small scale in your own garden. All you have to do is lay a bark path that gently meanders its way through the undergrowth and winds along between the tree and shrub stems, and plant spring-flowering bulbs along the side of the path to define its edges. A prepared path is better than a dirt track, since it is less likely to turn to a slippery mass of mud in wet weather and weeds can be excluded more easily.

Many beautiful woodland bulbs, including the ones shown in the illustration below, flower in the spring so that they can take advantage of the period of spring warmth and sunlight before the tree canopy shades over the woodland floor. The bulbs will die back and disappear once they have flowered.

Drifts of white, blue and yellow

Informal drifts of wake robins and purple-blue windflowers flop over the edge of a winding bark path, while behind them are waves of Spanish bluebells and sunny yellow erythroniums. Blue and white is a cool colour combination that suits the shade of this tranquil woodland setting, while the small splash of yellow glows in the spring sunshine.

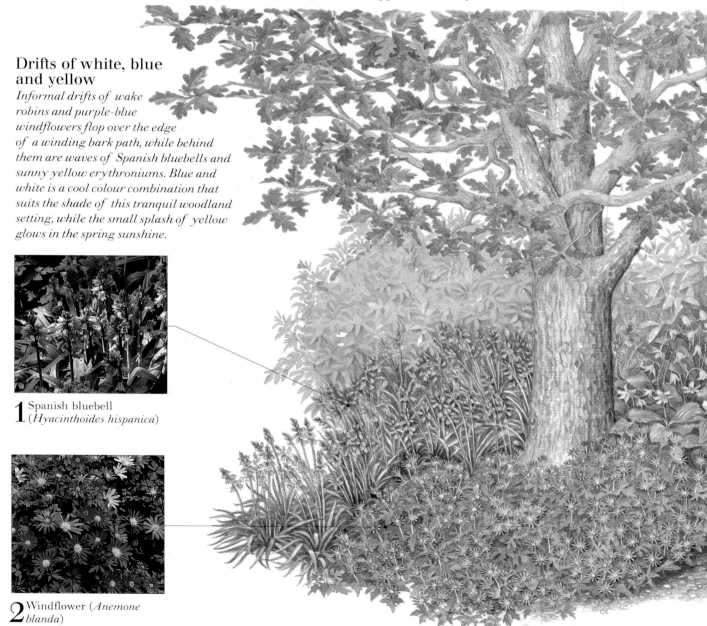

1 Spanish bluebell (*Hyacinthoides hispanica*)

2 Windflower (*Anemone blanda*)

172

4 *Erythronium* '*Pagoda*'

MAINTENANCE

• *Weed and replenish the bark on the path as necessary.*

• *Allow the bulb foliage to die back naturally after flowering.*

• *After the bulbs have flowered, mulch the soil with compost or manure.*

3 Wake robin (*Trillium grandiflorum*)

PROJECT PLANNER

TIME SCALE 1/2 DAY

Tools and Materials

Spade • Mallet • Four pointed, tannelised pegs, 5 x 5 x 45 cm (2 x 2 x 18 in) • Galvanised nails • Two tannelised gravel boards, 12.5 x 2.5 x 100 cm (5 x 1 x 36 in) • Weed-proof membrane • Wire pegs • Large bark chippings • Trowel or bulb planter

The timing given above is for a path about 10 m (10 yd) long

1 *Dig out a trench for the path. It should be about 15 cm (6 in) deep and 1 m (1 yd) wide.*

2 *Using a mallet and peg, make four holes – one at each corner of the start and end of the path.*

3 *Make the path end units. Using galvanised nails, nail a peg to each end of the two gravel boards.*

4 *Push the pegs into the holes made in Step 2. Using a mallet, hammer the board and pegs level with the top of the trench. Lay weed-proof membrane in the bottom of the trench. Push in wire pegs to hold it in place.*

5 *Fill the trench with bark chippings. Rake smooth.*

6 *Using a trowel or bulb planter, plant bulbs along each side of the path (see page 31).*

WATER GARDENS

A WATER GARDEN is one of the most peaceful and tranquil of all types of garden; the soothing sound of trickling water and the gentle buzz of insects make it a wonderful place for the weekend gardener to relax.

Once the water garden is made, taking care of it is not strenuous work. There is almost always some small task to do – fishing out excess pond weed, snipping off unwanted water lily leaves, tending any fish that you have in the pond – but it is the sort of work that you can carry out at your own pace.

The water gardens in this section give you a choice of formal and informal schemes and cover ponds, plants for a boggy area around a pond edge and an easy-to-install decorative pebble fountain.

Peaceful pond
Left: This water garden, surrounded by woodland plants, will attract many passing birds and animals. A small-leaved water lily helps to keep the water clear, and the pink and purple flowers of the candelabra primula and foxgloves provide a burst of colour to this tranquil scene.

Formal Pond

GARDEN GRANDEUR

A FORMAL GARDEN POND, topped by a dazzling white water lily, has a classic, stately elegance that evokes a mood of peace and tranquillity.

Symmetry is the key to any formal design, so before you start digging make a plan of the site. If the pond is to be near the house, make sure that it is parallel to it and not set at an angle. Any surrounding paving should be symmetrical, too.

Ideally, the paving should overhang the pond so that the pond edge is not visible – but to do this, it is best if the slabs are cemented into position. A simpler method is to set the slabs on coarse sand and flush with the edge of the pond or overhanging the pond rim by no more than 12 mm ($^1/_2$ in) – see opposite.

Pond garden in yellow and purple

The appeal of this pond lies in the contrasting shapes – spiky-leaved sweet flag and Japanese water iris, softly rounded kingcups and water lily. Around the edge are sun-loving caraway thyme, heartsease pansies and New Zealand burr, all of which soften the paving.

7 Sweet flag
(*Acorus calamus*)

6 Japanese water iris
(*Iris ensata*)

1 Caraway thyme (*Thymus herba-barona*), shown here in flower in summer

2 Heartsease
(*Viola tricolor*)

3 Kingcup
(*Caltha palustris*)

4 White water lily
(*Nymphaea* 'Virginalis')

176

MAINTENANCE

• *Keep the pond clear of blanket weed and other algae.*

• *Replenish the water in hot, dry weather.*

• *Remove the leaves of any water lilies that are over-crowded and pushing up out of the water.*

• *Remove dead leaves and other debris from the pond in the autumn.*

• *If you have a pump, clean out the filter at least once a year.*

• *Remove over-vigorous growth.*

5 New Zealand burr (*Acaena microphylla*)

PROJECT PLANNER

TIME SCALE 2 DAYS

Tools and Materials

Tape measure • Spirit level • Spade • Sharp sand • Preformed pond liner • Hose and water supply • Rake • Paving slabs • Car body filler • Gravel

1 *Dig out the pond. The rim should sit at least 10 cm (4 in) below the top of the hole. Spread 5–7.5 cm (2–3 in) of sharp sand over the bottom.*

2 *Put the pond in the hole. Using a spirit level, check that it is level in every direction. Fill the pond with water.*

3 *Pack the sides with coarse sand. Push the sand down so that it goes under the pond shelf to support it.*

4 *Remove turf from the edge of the pond to fit the planned paved area. Inset: Spread a 5-cm (2-in) layer of sharp sand around the area to be paved and rake it level.*

5 *Arrange the paving slabs evenly around the pond to make an attractive design that involves no slab cutting.*

6 *Use a spirit level to check that each slab is level and in line with the preceding one. Add or take away sand as necessary to make the slab level and solid.*

7 *Spread car body putty on any visible liner on the edge of the pond and sprinkle gravel on top to hide the liner.*

8 *Plant any gaps in the paving with plants. Mulch with gravel. See page 31 for instructions on how to plant water plants.*

177

Plants for Moist Soil

BOG GARDEN

TALL ELEGANT FLAG irises in blue and yellow, the magnificent gunnera with its giant, umbrella-like leaves, stunning pure white arum lilies: these are just a few of the beautiful plants that you can grow if you have soil that is permanently moist.

In the wild, this sort of situation occurs in a boggy area close to a slow-flowing river. Few of us are lucky enough to have a river flowing through our garden, but you can re-create the same conditions by lining a bed with a perforated plastic sheet and covering it up with damp soil. Make it an irregular shape so that the boggy area looks like a natural, rather than a man-made, feature. Water the bed regularly to keep the soil permanently moist but not waterlogged; a bark or pebble mulch will help to keep the moisture in the soil. If you have a pond, it is even easier: make the surface of the bog garden slightly lower than the water level of the pond so that any overflow will dampen the bog.

Damp, leafy glade

This lightly shaded bog garden is dominated by the spiky leaves and large golden flowers of yellow flag and the smaller arching leaves of the orange-yellow daylily. At ground level, the heart-shaped golden-edged leaves of the two hostas soften the effect of the spiky-leaved plants.
A sea of purple bugle creeps around the edge of the bog and provides a dark, weed-excluding ground cover.

1 Purple variegated bugle (*Ajuga reptans* 'Atropurpurea')

2 *Hosta ventricosa* 'Aureomarginata'

3 Daylily (*Hemerocallis* Stella de Oro')

PROJECT PLANNER

TIME SCALE **2+** HOURS

Tools and Materials

Spade ● Old carpet ● Thick plastic sheet ● Bricks ● Fork ● Soil ● Compost or manure ● Watering can or hose ● Trowel ● Bark-chip or pebble mulch

1 *Dig out your bog garden, giving it a natural, flowing shape. It should be about 30–45 cm (12–18 in) deep in the centre, shelving gently at the sides. Remove any exposed sharp stones.*

2 *Line the hole with a piece of old carpet, trimming it so that the edge extends over the edge of the hole by about 15 cm (6 in).*

3 *Spread the plastic sheet on top of the carpet and weigh it down with bricks, trimming the edges to fit if necessary. Pierce the plastic sheet with a garden fork so that excess water can drain away.*

4 *Fill the liner with good garden soil and fork in some compost or manure. Bring the soil level up to the surrounding ground. Make sure the liner is hidden from view.*

5 *Water the bog garden and leave it to settle for a day or two before planting.*

6 *Plant the plants and mulch with bark chippings or pebbles.*

5 Yellow flag (*Iris pseudacorus*)

4 *Hosta* 'Golden Tiara'

MAINTENANCE

● *Keep the soil moist, but not waterlogged. Check it regularly in hot weather.*

● *Keep the bog garden weeded. Don't let the bugle crowd out the other plants.*

● *Protect plants – particularly the hostas – from slugs and snails (see page 36).*

● *Deadhead the flowers once they are past their best to encourage more flowers to grow.*

● *Clean up and remove dead foliage in the autumn.*

● *Apply a mulch of bark or pebbles in the autumn.*

Water-garden Feature
PEBBLE FOUNTAIN

GURGLING WATER, glistening stones, lush green foliage: even the smallest garden has room for a decorative water feature such as this pebble fountain that comes as an easy-to-install kit.

Steer clear of true bog and water plants, as their roots need to be kept permanently moist. There are plenty of plants, such as hostas, some irises and many ferns, that grow happily in normal soil but enjoy the cool, humid atmosphere created by the fountain.

For a natural look, spread pebbles or shells over the surrounding soil and between the plants. Many stones and shells have beautiful colours when wet; collect unusual ones when you're on holiday.

5 Soft shield fern
(*Polystichum setiferum* Divisilobum Group)

4 Lady's mantle
(*Alchemilla mollis*)

Shady sanctuary
Fern fronds and lady's mantle arch over the pebbles that surround the fountain and, with the Liriope muscari, provide the taller elements of the planting. Foam flower and deadnettle spread over the gaps.

1 Foam flower
(*Tiarella cordifolia*)

PROJECT PLANNER

Tools and Materials

TIME SCALE 2+ HOURS

Spade • Old carpet • Pebble fountain kit (including submersible low-voltage pump, transformer, fountain, liner and lid) • Spirit level • Bricks or stones • Pebbles or shells • Hose • Trowel • Gravel mulch

1 *Choose a level, sheltered site and clear the ground of plants and weeds.*

2 *Dig a hole slightly larger and deeper than the liner. Line the hole with a piece of old carpet to protect the plastic. Insert the liner and check that it is level.*

3 *Position the pump in the centre of the liner and wedge it in position with bricks or stones. Follow the manufacturer's instructions to connect the pump to your power supply.*

5 *Position pebbles or shells so that they hide the liner and the pump cable.*

4 *Put pebbles or shells in the base of the fountain. Fill the liner with water. Test the fountain and then turn it off.*

6 *Plant up the surrounding area and mulch with a layer of gravel.*

3 Liriope muscari, shown here in flower in late summer

2 White deadnettle (*Lamium maculatum* 'White Nancy')

PLANTING ALTERNATIVES

Sunny sizzlers

For a sunny spot, surround the pebble fountain with sun-loving plants. Replace the foam flower with a German iris, the liriope with red hot pokers, and the fern with a yellow-orange flowered daylily. Leave the lady's mantle, since it grows just as happily in sunshine. The white deadnettle is still useful, too, as a crevice-filler.

1 German iris (*Iris germanica*)

3 Red hot poker (*Knifophia* 'Samuel's Sensation')

5 Orange daylily (*Hemerocallis* 'Golden Chimes')

MAINTENANCE

• *Weed the plants surrounding the pebble fountain and water them in hot, dry weather.*

• *Remove any dead or dying flowers or foliage as it appears.*

• *Replenish the gravel mulch in autumn or late spring.*

• *Maintain the pump in accordance with the manufacturer's recommendations.*

Plants for Different Purposes

Here is a useful checklist of plants suitable for particular sites and for particular uses. The main season of interest is given for each plant; where no comment is made, the plant is grown for its attractive foliage. If a plant requires or prefers lime-free (acid) soil conditions, it is marked "A".

If several species and varieties within a particular genus are suitable for the purpose stated, then only the genus has been given. The genus *Hebe*, for example, includes several species and varieties that make suitable evergreen shrubs for containers – and so only the genus is noted in that particular list. Check the plant label or consult a plant encyclopedia to find out whether or not the species or variety you are planning to use is suitable.

If a particular species is listed (for example, the bay tree, *Laurus nobilis*), then this means that only this species – and, if it has them, most of its varieties or cultivars – is suitable. Sometimes a variety is not suitable for the purpose stated – it might be very vigorous or have an ungainly shape, for example – so always check before you buy.

Occasionally, a particular variety is specified on the list – for example, *Glechoma hederacea* 'Variegata'. This is either because it is the only plant commonly available or because it is the only variety of that species that is suitable for the purpose stated.

The lists that follow are based on the plants suggested for the projects in this book, with the addition of a small number of other useful plants.

Evergreen Shrubs for Containers

Potted evergreen shrubs can make an attractive feature for containers. They provide a leafy year-round backdrop to other plants; many are eyecatching enough to form a focal point in their own right.

Evergreen shrubs for containers in a sunny spot

Bay (*Laurus nobilis*)
Box (*Buxus sempervirens*)
Cotton lavender (*Santolina*) – summer flowers
Hebe – summer flowers
Jerusalem sage (*Phlomis fruticosa*) – summer flowers
Lavender (*Lavandula*) – summer flowers
Marjoram (*Origanum*) – summer flowers
New Zealand cabbage palm (*Cordyline australis*)
New Zealand flax (*Phormium tenax*)
Rose (*Rosa*) – summer flowers
Rosemary (*Rosmarinus officinalis*) – spring flowers
Sage (*Salvia officinalis*) – summer flowers

Yucca (*Yucca gloriosa*) – summer flowers
Thyme (*Thymus*) – summer flowers

Evergreen shrubs for containers in a shaded spot

Box (*Buxus sempervirens*)
Camellia (A) – winter or spring flowers
Cotoneaster – spring flowers; autumn berries; some cotoneasters are evergreen
Euonymous (*E. fortunei*)
Japanese aralia (*Fatsia japonica*)
Rhododendron (A) – spring flowers

Perennials for Containers

Although perennials do not have as long a flowering season as bedding plants, there are a few hardy herbaceous perennials that look good and don't mind the cramped conditions of containers.

Perennials for containers in the shade

Bugle (*Ajuga*) – summer

flowers
Deadnettle (*Lamium*) – summer flowers
Elephant's ears (*Bergenia*) – spring flowers
Hellebore (*Helleborus*) – winter and early spring flowers
Heuchera – summer flowers
Hosta
Lady's mantle (*Alchemilla mollis*) – summer flowers
Soft shield fern (*Polystichum setiferum*)

Perennials for containers in the sun

Agapanthus
Catmint (*Nepeta*)
Hardy geranium (*Geranium*)
Iris
Pinks (*Dianthus*)
Sedge (*Carex*)

Herbs for Containers

It's often a good idea to grow herbs in containers positioned conveniently close to the kitchen so that you can reach them easily when you need them for cooking. Many herbs are shallow rooting and like

well-drained soil; growing them in containers is a relatively easy way of recreating their preferred growing conditions.

Herbs for containers in the sun

Bay (*Laurus nobilis*)
Chives (*Allium schoenoprasum*)
Lemon verbena (*Aloysia triphylla*)
Marjoram (*Origanum*)
Sage (*Salvia*)
Tarragon (*Artemisia*)
Thyme (*Thymus*)

Herbs for containers in shade

Basil (*Ocimum*)
Chervil (*Anthriscus cerefolium*)
Lovage (*Levisticum officinale*)
Mint (*Mentha*)
Parsley (*Petroselinum*)

Summer Bedding Plants for Containers

Each spring, many plants are offered by garden centres and

nurseries as temporary bedding plants. These are often specially bred varieties that have a long and prolific flowering season. Many are well suited to growing in containers. Most summer bedding plants grow best in a sunny place. However, there are a few bedding plants that tolerate shade.

Summer bedding plants for containers in the shade

Bedding lobelia (*L. erinus*)
Busy Lizzie (*Impatiens*)
Californian blue bell (*Nemophila*)
Flowering tobacco (*Nicotiana*)
Fuchsia
Monkey flower (*Mimulus*)
Nemesia
Pansy (*Viola* x *wittrockiana*)
Petunia

Summer bedding plants for containers in the sun

Bedding lobelia (*L. erinus*)
Cherry pie (*Heliotropium peruvianum*)
Diascia
Geranium (*Pelargonium*)
Ground ivy (*Glechoma hederacea* 'Variegata')
Helichrysum (*H. petiolare*)
Kingfisher daisy (*Felicia bergeriana*)
Marguerite daisy (*Argyranthemum*)
Marigold (*Tagetes*)
Morning glory (*Convolvulus*)
Nasturtium (*Tropaeolum majus*)
Snapdragon (*Antirrhinum*)
Wandering sailor (*Tradescantia fluminensis*)

Hardy Herbaceous Perennials

In general, hardy herbaceous perennials require a sunny spot with fertile, moist but well-drained soil, and protection from strong winds. Given these conditions, there are many perennials that you can choose from. Tall to medium-height species should be planted towards the back of the bed and medium to low-growing ones towards the front. For shaded sites, shrubs and ground-cover plants are generally better.

Tall to medium-height perennials for sunny summer beds and borders

Aster (*Aster* x *frickartii*)
Bear's breeches (*Acanthus mollis*)
Butterfly weed (*Asclepias tuberosa*)
Daylily (*Hemerocallis*)
Euphorbia
Evening primrose (*Oenothera fruticosa*)
Gay feather (*Liatris spicata*)
Heartleaf crambe (*Crambe cordifolia*)
Japanese anemone (*Anemone* x *hybrida*)
Red hot poker (*Kniphofia*)
Sneezeweed (*Helenium*)
Switch grass (*Panicum virgatum*)
Tufted hair grass (*Deschampsia caespitosa*)

Medium-height to low-growing perennials for sunny summer borders

Catmint (*Nepeta* x *faassenii*) – evergreen
Deadnettle (*Lamium maculatum*) – summer flowers
Elephant's ears (*Bergenia*) – evergreen; spring flowers
Foamflower (*Tiarella cordifolia*) – summer flowers
Geranium – summer flowers
Heuchera (*H. micrantha*)
Ice plant (*Sedum spectabile*) – summer/autumn flowers
Lady's mantle (*Alchemilla mollis*) – summer flowers
Lamb's ears (*Stachys byzantina*) – evergreen
Lirope (*L. muscari*) – autumn flowers
Sweet rocket (*Hesperis matronalis*) – summer flowers
Yellow archangel (*Lamium galeobdolon*) – summer flowers

Weed-excluding Ground-cover Plants

Invaluable to the gardener with limited weeding or mowing time. Use in beds and borders to smother the ground between trees, shrubs and perennials, or to cover an area that's awkward to mow. The plants listed below thrive in both sun and shade and tolerate a wide range of soil conditions.

Bistort (*Persicaria bistorta*) – evergreen; summer flowers
Bugle (*Ajuga reptans*) – summer flowers
Deadnettle (*Lamium maculatum*) – summer flowers
Elephant's ears (*Bergenia*) – evergreen; spring flowers
Foamflower (*Tiarella cordifolia*) – evergreen; summer flowers
Fringecups (*Tellima grandiflora*) – evergreen; summer flowers
Geranium – summer flowers
Heuchera – evergreen; summer flowers
Ivy (*Hedera helix*) – evergreen
Juniper (*J.* x *media*) – evergreen
Juniper (*J. squamata*) – evergreen

Periwinkle (*Vinca minor*) – summer flowers

Self-seeding Annuals

Many plants cast their seed after they have flowered, and some of these will happily mature and flower without any help from the gardener. Among these self-seeding plants, the annuals are the most useful since they don't root deeply and deprive other plants of soil nutrients.

Alyssum (*Lobularia maritima*)
Borage (*Borago officinalis*)
California poppy (*Eschscholzia californica*)
Candytuft (*Iberis amara*)
Field poppy (*Papaver rhoeas*)
Heartsease (*Viola tricolor*)
Pot marigold (*Calendula officinalis*)
Snapdragon (*Antirrhinum majus*)
Welsh poppy (*Meconopsis cambrica*)

Easy-care Shrubs

Shrubs are the backbone of the low-maintenance garden. The shrubs listed below take very little looking after: virtually all you need to do is keep them tidy, weed free, well fed, and watered.

Easy-care shrubs for sun

Barberry (*Berberis*) – spring flowers; autumn berries; some barberries are evergreen
Bay (*Laurus nobilis*) – evergreen
Cotoneaster – spring flowers; autumn berries; some cotoneasters are evergreen
Cotton lavender (*Santolina*) –

evergreen; summer flowers

Dogwood (*Cornus alba*) – winter stems

Hebe – evergreen

Jerusalem sage (*Phlomis fruticosa*) – evergreen; spring flowers

Juniper (*Juniperus*) – evergreen

Lavender (*Lavandula*) – evergreen; summer flowers

Mexican orange (*Choisya ternata*) – evergreen; spring flowers

New Zealand flax (*Phormium tenax*) – evergreen

Rosemary (*Rosmarinus officinalis*) – evergreen; spring flowers

Sage (*Salvia officinalis*) – evergreen; spring flowers

Smoke bush (*Cotinus coggygria*) – summer flowers

Yucca (*Y. filamentosa*) – evergreen; summer flowers

Viburnum – winter or spring flowers; some viburnums have berries in autumn

Easy-care shrubs for shade

Camellia (A) – evergreen; winter or spring flowers

Cotoneaster – spring flowers; autumn berries; some cotoneasters are evergreen

Japanese aralia (*Fatsia japonica*) – evergreen; autumn flowers

Oak-leaved hydrangea (*Hydrangea quercifolia*) – summer flowers

Viburnum – winter or spring flowers; some viburnums have autumn berries; some viburnums are evergreen

Hedging Plants

It's worth taking time to examine your soil conditions first, before you choose what to

plant, to make sure you choose a species that will thrive in your garden. Some hedging plants can tolerate heavy soils; others require well-drained, lighter soils. The ultimate height of hedge that you require also affects your choice: consult a plant reference manual for this information before you buy. To edge a path or border, choose a hedging plant that is easy to keep under 60 cm (2 ft) in height.

Hedging plants that can tolerate heavy soils

Barberry (*Berberis*) – spring flowers; autumn berries; some barberries are evergreen

Beech (*Fagus sylvatica*)

Cherry laurel (*Prunus laurocerasus*) – evergreen

Cotoneaster – spring flowers; autumn berries; some cotoneasters are evergreen

Firethorn (*Pyracantha*) – evergreen; spring flowers; autumn berries

Holly (*Ilex*) – evergreen; winter berries

Potentilla (summer flowers)

Rugosa rose (*Rosa rugosa*)

Tassle bush (*Garrya elliptica*) – evergreen; spring catkins

Hedging plants that require well-drained soils

Camellia – evergreen; winter or spring flowers

Fuchsia – summer flowers

Hebe – evergreen; summer flowers

Shrub rose (*Rosa*) – summer flowers; autumn fruits

Yew (*Taxus baccata*) – evergreen

Dwarf hedging plants

Box (*Buxus sempervirens*) – evergreen

Cotton lavender (*Santolina*) – evergreen; summer flowers

Hyssop (*Hyssopus vulgaris*) – evergreen

Lavender (*Lavandula*) – evergreen; summer flowers

Thyme (*Thymus vulgaris*) – evergreen

Climbing Plants

Some climbers flower well only in sun – although they may prefer to have their roots in shade. Others grow perfectly well in shaded conditions. Many climbing plants and wall shrubs – roses and clematis, for example – are best left to ramble freely over their support. Others can be clipped into shape and trained to make a more formal feature. For this sort of feature, choose climbing plants and wall shrubs that respond well to pruning; they have relatively small leaves that grow densely and so make a uniform pattern of growth.

Climbing plants that require sun (though roots may be shaded)

Actinidia kolomicta – leaves in summer

Clematis – flowers in spring, summer or autumn; seedheads in autumn; some clematis are evergreen

Crimson glory vine (*Vitis coignetiae*) – leaves in autumn

Golden hop (*Humulus lupulus* 'Aureus') – flowers in autumn

Honeysuckle (*Lonicera*) – flowers in spring or summer; some

honeysuckles are evergreen

Morning glory (*Ipomoea rubrocaerulea*) – annual climber

Nasturtium (*Tropaeolum*) – annual climber

Rose (*Rosa*)

Sweet pea (*Lathryus odoratus*) – annual climber

Wisteria – summer flowers

Climbing plants that tolerate shade

Boston ivy (*Parthenocissus*) – leaves in autumn

Climbing hydrangea (*Hydrangea anomala* ssp. *petiolaris*) – summer flowers

Firethorn (*Pyracantha*) – evergreen; spring flowers; autumn berries

Honeysuckle (*Lonicera japonica* 'Halliana') – evergreen; flowers in spring

Ivy (*Hedera helix*) – evergreen

Oriental bittersweet (*Celastrus orbiculatus*)

Russian vine (*Autumnopia baldschuanica*)

Virginia creeper (*Parthenocissus*) – leaves in autumn

Climbing plants and wall shrubs suitable for training

California lilac (*Ceanothus*) – evergreen; spring, summer, or autumn flowers

Euonymous – evergreen

Firethorn (*Pyracantha*) – evergreen; spring flowers; autumn berries

Flowering quince (*Chaenomeles japonica*) – spring flowers

Ivy (*Hedera helix*)

Scented Bedding Plants and Shrubs

Add another dimension to your garden by growing scented plants – particularly near sitting areas, or beside paths, where you will benefit from their fragrance every time you walk past.

Scented bedding plants

Flowering tobacco (*Nicotiana*)
Petunia – some varieties are scented
Stocks (*Matthiola*)
Sweet pea (*Lathyrus odoratus*) – some varieties are scented

Scented shrubs

Daphne – spring or summer flowers; some daphnes are evergreen
Lavender (*Lavandula*) – evergreen; summer flowers
Philadelphus – spring or summer flowers
Viburnum – winter or spring flowers, autumn berries; some viburnums are evergreen
Witch hazel (*Hamamelis*) – winter or spring flowers

Bulbs Suitable for Naturalizing

Grow natural-looking drifts of spring, autumn- or winter-flowering bulbs in your lawn or among trees and shrubs to mark the seasonal changes and add a splash of colour to your garden when relatively few other plants are flowering. The bulbs listed below all multiply to form a growing colony.

Bluebell (*Hyacinthoides*) – spring flowers
Crocus – winter or spring flowers
Cyclamen – autumn or winter flowers
Daffodil (*Narcissus*) – spring flowers
Erythronium – spring flowers
Fritillary (*Fritillaria*) – spring flowers
Glory-of-the-snow (*Chionodoxa*) – spring flowers
Lily-of-the-valley (*Convallaria*) – spring flowers
Scilla – spring flowers
Snowdrop (*Galanthus*) – winter or spring flowers
Wake robin (*Trillium*) – spring flowers
Windflower (*Anemone*) – spring flowers

Spring and Summer Meadow Flowers

The plants listed below thrive in a wide range of conditions, but with a little research you will soon discover your own local wildflower species.

Bladder campion (*Silene vulgaris*) – spring and summer flowers
Cornflower (*Centaurea cyanus*) – summer flowers
Daisy (*Bellis perennis*) – spring and summer flowers
Lady's smock (*Cardamine pratensis*) – spring flowers
Meadow buttercup (*Ranunculus acris*) – spring and summer flowers
Meadow cranesbill (*Geranium pratense*) – summer flowers
Ox-eye daisy (*Leucanthemum vulgare*) – summer flowers
Primrose (*Primula veris*) – spring flowers
Speedwell (*Veronica chamaedrys*) – spring and summer flowers
Yarrow (*Achillea millefolium*) – summer flowers

Trees for Small Gardens

A tree can transform your garden, but the wrong tree can damage your house as some species have wide-spreading root systems that can undermine buildings, wrap around and crack drains, or widen existing fractures in brickwork or concrete. Attractive trees that are not usually the cause of any damage belong to the plant groups listed below. Always check the ultimate height of a tree before you buy it and plant it the same distance away from any building; in that way, you can be reasonably sure that the roots will not damage your building.

Apple (*Malus*) – spring flowers; autumn fruit
Mount Etna broom (*Genista aetnensis*) – summer flowers
Hazel (*Corylus avellana*) – spring flowers
Maple (*Acer*)
Mountain ash (*Sorbus*) – spring flowers; autumn fruit
Pear (*Pyrus*) – spring flowers

Water Plants

Water plants vary in the depth of water that they prefer.

Pond plants that require more than 1 ft (30 cm) of water

Water hawthorn (*Aponogeton distachos*) – summer flowers
Water lily (*Nymphaea*) – summer flowers

Pond plants that thrive in 2–12 in (5–30 cm) of water

Cardinal flower (*Lobelia cardinalis*) – summer flowers
Dwarf cattail (*Typha minima*)
Golden club (*Orontium aquaticum*) – summer flowers
Japanese iris (*Iris laevigata*) – summer flowers
Kingcup (*Caltha palustris*) – summer flowers
Manna grass (*Glyceria maxima*)
Parrot's feather (*Myriophyllum aquaticum*)
Pygmy water lily (*Nymphaea pygmaea*) – summer flowers
Sweet flag (*Acorus calamus*) – summer flowers
Water lettuce (*Pistia stratiotes*)
Yellow flag (*Iris pseudacorus*) – summer flowers

Plants that grow in permanently moist soil

Bugle (*Ajuga*) – summer flowers
Cuckoo pint (*Arum maculatum*) – summer flowers
Daylily (*Hemerocallis*) – summer flowers
Hosta
Primula – summer flowers
Shuttlecock fern (*Matteuccia struthiopteris*)
Solomon's seal (*Polygonatum* x *hybridum*) – summer flowers

Index

Acknowledgements

I would like to thank all those people who have been involved in the production of this book – in particular, Ken Davis, without whom this book would not have been undertaken, for his help and general advice; Liz Dobbs for her contribution to the Gardening Basics section and the step-by-step photography; Phil Binks, Val Burton, Ruth Chivers, Anne de Verteuil, and Wendy Francis for their input on step-by-step photography; Brian Mathew and Janet Swarbrick for checking the plant photographs and nomenclature; Marie Lorimer for the index; to Hozelock Ltd for providing gardening equipment and to Stephen Morgan for supplying plants. Many thanks, too, to Sarah Hoggett, Julia Ward-Hastelow, Alison Lee and Corinne Asghar at Collins & Brown, for their diligence and patience.

Picture Credits

All the photographs in this book were specially taken by Sampson Lloyd, Geoff Dann and Mark Gatehouse for Collins & Brown, except the following:

page 1 Lynne Brotchie/The Garden Picture Library (GPL); page 2 Steven Wooster; page 5 Steven Wooster; page 6 bottom left, Steven Wooster; page 7 top left, top right, Steven Wooster; pages 12–13 Steven Wooster; page 35 John Glover/GPL; page 36 Brian Carter/GPL, Chris Burrows/GPL, Nigel Francis/GPL, JS Sira/GPL; page 37 Holt Studios International (Nigel Cattlin), Holt Studios International (Nigel Cattlin), Neil Holmes/GPL; Neil Holmes/GPL, Holt Studios International (Nigel Cattlin); pages 44–45 Holt Studios International, Brian Carter/GPL; pages 52–53 Steven Wooster; pages 54–55 Steven Wooster; pages 56–57 1 Brian Carter/GPL, 2 Patrick Mason/Collins & Brown, 3 Andrew Lawson, 4 Chris Burrows/GPL; pages 58–59 1 Clive Nichols/Old Rectory, Berkshire, 2 John Glover/GPL, 3 Patrick Mason/Collins & Brown, 4 Chris Smith/Collins & Brown, 5 A-Z Botanical Collection/Neil Joy, 6 Harry Smith Collection; pages 60–61 1 J. S. Sira/GPL, 2 Patrick Mason/Collins & Brown, 3 Neil Holmes/GPL, 4 Harry Smith Collection; pages 62–63 1 Andrew Lawson, 2 Patrick Mason/Collins & Brown, 3 Patrick Mason/Collins & Brown, 4 Harry Smith Collection, 5 Howard Rice/GPL; pages 64–65 1 John Glover/GPL, 2 Harry Smith Collection, 3 Howard Rice, 4 Patrick Mason/Collins & Brown; pages 66–67 1 Harry Smith Collection, 2 Harry Smith Collection, 3 Patrick Mason/Collins & Brown, 4 David Russell/GPL; pages 68–69 1 Patrick Mason/Collins & Brown, 2 Brian Carter/GPL, 3 Harry Smith Collection; pages 70–71 Ron Sutherland/GPL; page 72 Steven Wooster; page 73 Steven Wooster, Neil Campbell-Sharp;

pages 78–79 1 Patrick Mason/Collins & Brown, 2 Clive Nichols Garden Pictures, 3 Clive Nichols Garden Pictures, 4 Patrick Mason/Collins & Brown, 5 Andrew Lawson; pages 84–85 Steven Wooster; pages 86–87 Steven Wooster; pages 88–89 1 Neil Holmes/GPL, 2 Patrick Mason/Collins & Brown, 3 Patrick Mason/Collins & Brown, 4 Clive Nichols Garden Pictures; pages 90–91 1 Jacqui Hurst, 2 Clive Nichols Garden Pictures, 3 Andrew Lawson, 4 Brian Carter/GPL; pages 92–93 1 Howard Rice, 2 Patrick Mason/Collins & Brown, 3 Vaughan Fleming/GPL; pages 98–99 Steven Wooster; pages 100–101 Steven Wooster; pages 102–103 1 Patrick Mason/Collins & Brown, 2 Vaughan Fleming/GPL, 3 Sampson Lloyd/Collins & Brown; pages 104–105 1 Clive Nichols Garden Pictures, 2 Howard Rice/GPL, 3 Patrick Mason/Collins & Brown; pages 106–107 1 Steven Wooster, 2 Andrew Lawson, 3 Neil Holmes/GPL, 4 Patrick Mason/Collins & Brown; pages 108–109 1 Andrew Lawson, 2 Patrick Mason, 3 Patrick Mason/Collins & Brown; pages 110–111 1 Zara McCalmont/GPL, 2 Andrew Lawson; pages 112–113 Patrick Mason/Collins & Brown; pages 114–115 Patrick Mason/Collins & Brown; pages 116–117 1 Andrew Lawson, 2 Steven Wooster, 3 Howard Rice; pages 118–119 Steven Wooster; pages 120–121 Steven Wooster; pages 122–123 Steven Wooster; pages 124–125 1 John Glover/GPL, 2 Robert Estall/GPL, 3 Harry Smith Collection, 4 Andrew Lawson, 5 Andrew Lawson, 6 Patrick Mason/Collins & Brown, 7 Chris Smith/Collins & Brown, 8 Patrick Mason/Collins & Brown; pages 126–127 1 Harry Smith Collection; pages 128–129 1 Harry Smith Collection, 2 Brian Carter/GPL, 3 A-Z Botanical Collection, 4 Harry Smith Collection; pages 130–131 1 Harry Smith Collection, 2 Chris Smith/Collins & Brown, 3 David Askhan/GPL, 4 Howard Rice/GPL, 5 Jacqui Hurst; pages 132–133 1 Patrick Mason/Collins & Brown, 2 Steven Wooster, 3 Andrew Lawson, 4 Howard Rice/GPL, 5 Patrick Mason/Collins & Brown 6 Patrick Mason/Collins & Brown, 7 Densey Clyne/GPL, 8 Chris Smith/Collins & Brown, 9 Patrick Mason/Collins & Brown; pages 134–135 1 Vaughan Fleming/GPL, 2 Andrew Lawson, 3 Clive Nichols/GPL, 4 Photos Horticultural, 5 Patrick Mason/Collins & Brown, 6 Howard Rice, 7 Andrew Lawson, 8 Chris Smith, 9 Clive Nichols; pages 136–137 Steven Wooster, Neil Campbell-Sharp; pages 138–139 1 Patrick Mason/Collins & Brown, 2 Christopher Fairweather/GPL, 3 Chris Burrows/GPL; pages 140–141 1 John Glover/GPL, 2 John Glover/GPL, 3 Andrew Lawson, 4 Steven Wooster, 5 John Glover/GPL, 6 Harry Smith Collection; pages 142–143 1 Clive Nichols/Dinmore Manor, Worcs, 2 Andrew Lawson, 3 Mayer/Le scanff/GPL, 4 Chris

Smith/Collins & Brown, 5 Andrew Lawson, 6 Andrew Lawson, 7 Harry Smith Collection; pages 144–145 Steven Wooster; pages 146–147 Steven Wooster; pages 148–149 1 Jacqui Hurst, 2 Harry Smith Collection, 3 Andrew Lawson, 4 Jerry Pavia/GPL, 5 John Glover/GPL, 6 Harry Smith Collection, 7 Chris Smith/Collins & Brown, 8 Jacqui Hurst/GPL, 9 Juliette Wade/GPL; pages 150–151 1 John Glover/GPL, 2 Vaughan Fleming/GPL, 3 Patrick Mason/Collins & Brown, 4 John Glover/GPL, 5 Photos Horticultural; pages 152–153 1 John Glover/GPL, 2 Juliette Wade/GPL, 3 Patrick Mason/Collins & Brown, 4 Andrew Lawson, 5 Harry Smith Collection; page 154 1 Sampson Lloyd, 2 Photos Horticultural, 3 Joan Dear/GPL; page 155 1 Harry Smith Collection, 2 Juliette Wade/GPL; pages 156–157 1 Harry Smith Collection, 2 Harry Smith Collection, 3 Patrick Mason/Collins & Brown, 4 Patrick Mason/Collins & Brown, 5 Steven Wooster; pages 158–159 Steven Wooster; pages 160–161 1 Didier Willery/GPL, 2 Jacqui Hurst/GPL, 3 Jacqui Hurst/GPL, 4 Michael Howes/GPL, 5 Geoff Dann/GPL; pages 162–163 1 Patrick Mason/Collins & Brown, 2 Jerry Piava/GPL, 3 Patrick Mason, 4 Harry Smith Collection; pages 164–165 1 Patrick Mason/Collins & Brown, 2 Harry Smith Collection, 3 Ron Sutherland/GPL, 4 Clive Boursnell/GPL, 5 Didier Willery/GPL, 6 Chris Smith/Collins & Brown, 7 Harry Smith Collection; pages 166–167 Steven Wooster; pages 168–169 1 Andrew Lawson, 2 Clive Nichols Garden Pictures, 3 Patrick Mason/Collins & Brown, 4 Steven Wooster, 5 Jacqui Hurst, 6 Didier Willery/GPL; pages 170–171 1 Steven Wooster, 2 Jacqui Hurst, 3 Harry Smith Collection, 4 Juliette Wade/GPL, 5 Steven Wooster/GPL, 6 Howard Rice/GPL, 7 Howard Rice/GPL, 8 Mayer/Le scanff/GPL, 9 Steven Wooster; pages 172–173 1 Steven Wooster, 2 Clive Nichols, 3 Steven Wooster, 4 Chris Smith; pages 174–175 Steven Wooster; pages 176–177 1 Jerry Pavia/GPL, 2 Howard Rice, 3 Andrew Lawson, 4 A-Z Botanical Collection/Peter Etchells, 5 Patrick Mason/Collins & Brown, 6 Harry Smith Collection, 7 Harry Smith Collection; pages 178–179 1 Steven Wooster/GPL, 2 Patrick Mason/Collins & Brown, 3 Patrick Mason/Collins & Brown, 4 Steven Wooster, 5 Jacqui Hurst; pages 180–181 1 Joan Dear/GPL, 2 Patrick Mason/Collins & Brown, 3 Clive Nichols Garden Pictures, 4 Andrew Lawson, 5 Steven Wooster

While every effort has been taken to ensure that all pictures have been fully and correctly credited, the publishers would be pleased to hear of any discrepancies or omissions.

040–768–1

THE FILMS OF

FEDERICO FELLINI

- 7 NOV 1991

1989

05

WITHDRAWN
FROM
STOCK

KT-164-978

THE FILMS OF

FEDERICO

BY CLAUDIO G. FAVA AND ALDO VIGANÒ

WITH AN INTRODUCTION BY FELLINI

TRANSLATED BY SHULA CURTO

CITADEL PRESS, SECAUCUS, N.J.

FELLINI

791·43 /314086

First American edition
Copyright © 1981 by Gremese Editore
English translation copyright © 1985 by Citadel Press
All rights reserved

Published by Citadel Press
A division of Lyle Stuart Inc.
120 Enterprise Ave., Secaucus, N.J. 07094

In Canada: Musson Book Company
A division of General Publishing Co. Limited
Don Mills, Ontario
Manufactured in the United States of America by
Halliday Lithograph, West Hanover, Mass.

Book designed by Peter Davis

Library of Congress Cataloging in Publication Data

Fava, Claudio G., 1929-
  The films of Federico Fellini.

  Translation of: I film di Federico Fellini.
  1. Fellini, Federico. I. Viganò, Aldo. II. Title.
PN1998.A3F335713 1984   791.43′0233′0924   84-21466
ISBN 0-8065-0928-7

CONTENTS

ACKNOWLEDGMENTS:

Special thanks are due to Ugo Casiraghi and Aldo Bernardini for their extremely helpful contribution in the preparation of the pictorial section of this book.

Thanks also to Marcello Zago for his generous and valuable assistance in checking and completing the filmographic data relative to each of the films discussed herein.

PHOTOGRAPHS:

According to research carried out by the publisher, the photographs contained in this book are by: Nicola Arresto *(The Nights of Cabiria)*, Domenico Cattarinich *(Satyricon, Toby Dammit)*, Osvaldo Civirani *(The White Sheik)*, Claudio Patriarca *(Toby Dammit)*, Ettore Pesce *(I Vitelloni, Variety Lights)*, A. Piotti *(La Strada)*, Pierluigi *(L Dolce Vita, Amarcord, Casanova, I Vitelloni, Prova d'Orchestra, La Città delle Donne)*, Franco Pinna *(Juliet of the Spirits, Satyricon, The Clowns)*, G.B. Poletto *(Il Bidone, Juliet of the Spirits, Roma)*, Paul Ronald *(The Temptations of Dr. Antonio, 8½)*, Tazio Secchiaroli, *(8½, Toby Dammit, Satyricon)*.

The publisher apologizes for any errors or omissions, and assures they will be corrected in any subsequent editions.

The Films Of

Federico Fellini

"FOR YOUR EYES ONLY"

In order to adapt the Italian edition to the obvious needs of the English translation, I should have logically touched up some parts in the introduction itself, since a publication of this book had been foreseen in the United States. In it there is the account of myself as a long-time, faithful Fellini watcher, and of our belated meeting which came about during the preparation of this book. Actually, I should have rewritten many pages of the original introduction, even if it meant disturbing all logical sense and natural rhythm. But hoping for the American editor to agree with me, I decided to leave everything as it was, adding this short introductory note to the introduction itself (my only fear was that the American reader would get tired and stop reading). To repeat, this is a brief pre-introduction, and its only aim is to introduce the two pages written by Fellini. In them, Fellini by his kindness shows how, in him, the human desire for friendly relationships and the natural journalistic sense for writing certain things at the right moment come together effortlessly.

In this July 1984, Fellini spends his days holed up from morning to evening in his old offices at the "Theater 5" in Cinecittá. Those few rooms gloomily remind one of a thousand other rooms of the same kind in various government and para-government buildings built in Italy under Fascism (and even afterwards, to be honest; in fact, there is a fascist flavor present in Italian public architecture which outlived the change of regimes and generations). Every morning Fellini leaves his home in Margutta street. That is the old street of artists and sculptors, near Piazza del Popolo, in the heart of the most touristic section of Rome. He gets on the "new" subway and gets off near to the last stop, the Cinecittá stop. It is this very same subway whose construction he depicted in some magical sequences in *Roma*. It could be said that in this way he enriched the world of underground excavations "à la Zola," endowing it with realistic and mysterious values at the same time. When I visited Fellini, he talked for a long time about the figure of the engineer in charge of the works. It was a marvelous sketch, fashioned by his words and immediately lost. I should have taped it. In Federico's discourse, the figure of that tenacious maker of subways, that professional digger of city undergrounds, assumed worlds of great magical value. That figure had been his guide to the city's underground, that city which is penetrated with such difficulty, but whose bowels sweetly opened up under the gigantic "mole" penetrating almost as if it were a camera. This subway is ironical, tragic . . . and winking; all of Federico's cinema is like that.

In the two hours I spent with him—two hours taken away from an indistinct and somehow miraculously cast-off preparation for his new film (a world that Federico so skillfully evoked in *8½* to the point of becoming prisoner of it)—everything and nothing happened. As in a pre-script meeting, we were aware of the fact that nothing final would be shot, but that the first ideas would glitter wearily and companionably.

We had lunch at a completely empty, immense restaurant. The owner informed us that in the morning he had met a very nice man, an old olive vendor, I guess. The man was nice, but he had the evil eye, and therefore the owner wasn't in the least surprised that the day's business was nil. Like so many other extras and character actors in Italy, he had worked in *And the Ship Sails On* and other Fellini movies. He and Fellini now talked with quiet wonder about a famous Spanish-speaking writer. He had come to lunch with Federico and had reluctantly shown him a little sketch he had drawn weeks before in Paris, when he didn't know yet that he was supposed to meet Fellini in Italy and the "gazebo," the final touch, hadn't been put in the garden yet. Magic was enveloping us, without drama, but with the same lazy precision in which magic manifests itself in some great scenes in Fellini's cinema, but of course without the neatness and clarity resulting from the final editing. The basic elements, though, were all present, including a mysterious black woman. When she had had to leave the offices at Cinecittá, she came to greet Fellini with the same quiet self-confidence as one who is interpreting an assigned role. The black woman was tall, very beautiful, supple, and spoke Italian with an exotic accent which sounded false, in a way, as if she were dubbed. She left among hugs and kisses, alluding to a mysterious watermelon she had given Fellini years before. He couldn't remember—with some lack of surprise—who the hell she could have been.

Anyway, ours was a long conversation, which at this point I can't possibly report. (Rather, it could be the subject of a short story. A bit cool, a bit ironic, a little poetically astonished tale such as *Magical Visit to Fellini* or *An Exceptional Hour at Cinecittá Without a Story*.)

I went back by subway with Federico's promise that he would send two introductory pages a few days later, written especially for the American edition. I received them directly, and the same day Fellini called me up to know whether they were all right. All right they were, more than fine. Read them yourselves. There you will find all of Federico, his cinema and his way of talking about it—and negating it to himself. His relationship with movie making, the cinema he has created, the movies he has made and will make. There are two brief pages, written with concision and elegance, worthy of the great journalist he would have been had he not turned to cinema. (Actually, we, as spectators, have gained a great deal, but we still regret having lost a columnist.) Do read those pages, and you will find all of what you might find afterwards in the book, but in a more condensed and authentic way.

Federico had wanted to write exclusively for his American readers (and I hope there are some out there), a brief, genial surprise for his public. Here my task is merely to turn these pages over to you, signing them like checks, cutting a fine figure, but knowing that the money, the merit and the value belong to another person.

My friend Claudio Fava prepared this essay on me with much fervor, talent and seriousness, dedicating a couple of years to it. Now he is asking me for a little introduction to the American edition. I can't refuse him; but I'm doing it hesitantly, uncertainly, as if I had been invited to say something as a memorial to myself. This book talks about me, my work and my films. That already makes me feel something between embarrassment and alarm, as if I had learned that in some judge's file there were papers regarding me: reports, monitored phone calls, letters. The first thing that comes to mind to say is that it is not true in the least, that they are fibs, stories that have nothing to do with me, that it isn't true what they are saying about me, it isn't me. In any case, my most yielding attitude would still be to refuse even minimal co-operation to any invitation to help clarify, correct, and explicate. That, I did in part, or tried to do, when Fava, as he was drawing up the first part of the book, loyally and dutifully sought my confirmation of dates and episodes. I derailed him any way I could; the more a thing was likely to have happened, the more I would deny it by proposing a completely different version.

I've always run away from anything that tends to let people identify me, define me, frame me, represent me more or less approximately the way I am. So even when I let go of my films, I do it in quick and clandestine terms, almost unknowingly. They no longer have any interest for me, nor do I want to know where they have ended up, or what they are doing. And when someone—that is, a friend, a critic, or even a person I don't know—wants to talk to me about them in admiring terms, I can't wait to change the subject, seized with a kind of uneasiness, anxiety, and fear which possesses those caught red-handed.

I can't give any rational explanation for this predisposition of mine: perhaps my movies are neither far away nor close by, they are part of me and I don't need yearly checks or controls. When I have to face them on the screen, on television, in a book even if written sympathetically, I am pervaded by a feeling of uneasiness. It is the same feeling that you have when you walk down a street and see a figure looking at you in a store-window or a mirror and with dismay discover it is yourself. It is the simple disconcertion, vexation, ungrateful disappointment that you feel when you succumb to the sentimental curiosity to revisit your high school classroom and try to slide into your old desk.

I am convinced that creative work has its pathological phase too. It is like a disease, and I really don't feel like remembering the days when I had pleurisy or rubella, the medicines I took, the shots I was given, and the number of wrinkles on the doctor's forehead when he frowned.

I realize the danger of appearing ungrateful, presumptuous, affected and even hypocritical. And perhaps it is a bit that way. But I don't care to look back; I need the reassurance that I haven't done anything, that I haven't left any marks. Doubtless it has to do with Catholic conditioning, but in order to work with willingness and live with hope, I absolutely need to believe that everything is still to be accomplished, that the road is still to be traveled. Tomorrow; from tomorrow I will seriously start; don't judge me by the past, for there is no past. From tomorrow I will be a good student, a good citizen, a good husband, I will work seriously, with responsibility, consciousness, whatever. And the preface? That too tomorrow.

Federico Fellini

INTRODUCTION

To review one's life in terms of the cinema is not a very original idea in this day and age. The cinema has virtually ceased to exist as an automatic reference point and is losing that "special" quality it once had. It is now within the reach of everyone, everywhere, everyday. It is up there in the air, like the "manine" in Amarcord, to be captured by the aerials of millions of television sets all over the country.

It is a cinema for daily consumption, with its third-class quality film, full of dots and dashes, reel endings withered as the features of an ancient Uzbek, frames that suddenly whiz forward at breakneck speed like the images in a dream, famous faces lined with rainbow colors as channels overlap, the deep, familiar voices of the dubbing team ringing out in the small hours or mingling with the early morning noises of a family preparing for another day's work. And all around there is the feeling of sharing in some homely ritual, or of living a spineless nightmare.

It is a cinema that pervades our books too, the books that clutter our desks and bedside tables; books for all tastes, books of memoirs, letters, monographs, screenplays, analyses, titles and credits; belated adaptions of some 15-year-old critical fashion or the mumblings of stuffy historians still intent on analyzing the rise and fall of neo-realism; or imaginary "translations" of nonexistent French reviews adapted to suit the local palate. And inevitably it is in things people say, after they have sat at home night after night absorbing films almost intravenously, as in the wildest dreams of a drug addict.

But despite all this, human nature being what it is—essentially narcissistic and self-centered—the lure of simple memoirism is often too great to be ignored, especially for those of us who have passed the half-century mark and are approaching the undignified years of senility, with their frequent retrogressions into adolescence. And even more so for one who has spent the best part of his life in the world of cinema, first as a spectator, then as an active participant. Somewhere along the way, one realizes just how many memories one has gathered and jealously guarded over the years, and which suddenly come flooding back.

It is not surprising, then, that one comes to identify a decisive portion of one's existence with those dark movie theatres and the desultory chatterings of a hidden projector. To the point where one's recollection of a film is not so much the actual story, but rather an actress's face, or an actor's walk, or a feeling that a given setting aroused, or the mood of a film as a whole. No matter if entire episodes have been forgotten, what remains is a vivid impression of the theatre in which the film was shown, of the dull buzz of voices in the foyer, of the gentle draft wafting between the seats, of the subdued play of lights on the screen, mingled with the red glow of the rest-room sign (the only landmark in the theatre as one enters, momentarily blinded in the sudden dark), of distant voices filtering through cracks in the secret doors all theatres seem to have, hidden behind dusty curtains.

And so bygone years come tumbling back, linked haphazardly to film titles, stories, names of directors glimpsed on placards outside the theatre, names which conjured up all manner of romantic reflections and which came to be regarded with the same expectation afforded to a favorite novelist, from whom one demanded endless secrets and unlimited emotion. Even before we became familiar with such literature as Pasinetti's *Filmlexicon*, or *Novissimo Melzi*, or *Cinema*, or became interested in the "letters to the editor" of *Film* and *Hollywood*—before all of this, it was on the movie theatre doors that we first became acquainted with a world destined to mutate in the course of time from a hobby to a deep obligation, from a special event to a day-to-day routine from which there is no escape.

Wide-eyed and spellbound, we read the credits on theatre doors and on the screen, where names and titles which seemed to us so awe-inspiring were displayed: story writers, scriptwriters, directors of photography, set designers (then known by the more voluptuous title of "architect"). I wonder why we were so particularly struck by the impressive name of Nicola Fausto Neroni? And other recurrent appellations, such as Natalie Kalmus, whom we envisaged as some omnipotent scientist, until we discovered that her name was included in the credits of color films merely because of some hereditary right. And in the midst of all these names we soon learned to recognize that of Federico Fellini.

Not that this was difficult. Even though today it might seem as though we are inventing memories, "Federico" was a name we had come to know in *Marc' Aurelio*. It would be impossible for those born after the war to understand precisely what this publication meant to its readers, especially to a small boy who would eagerly rummage through the pile of papers brought home by his father until he found it, and who would then disappear into some private corner and read it all in one sitting. Specifically, a small boy from the north of Italy, who was more familiar with French than with the strange language filling the pages of that magazine. It was a language which was, to all intents and purposes, everyday Italian, yet punctuated by certain mysterious words suggesting a hidden world, a world much larger, more cunning, more active and more luxurious than the one I saw around me.

This then was the world of signorina Memé, of Colonippo Filello, the horrible Genoveffa la Racchia and the poems of Ferrante Alvaro De Torres. And "Federico" was part of it, in his own small but nonetheless fascinating way. His name was tinged with that certain fabulous something that all magazine writers seem to possess in the eyes of their readers—especially those very young readers for whom the words on a printed page have a tantalizing mystery about them.

"Federico" was there with us in those movie houses too, right from the beginning. First as a name in the credits, along with those of other scriptwriters, which I connected with memories of childhood literature. These were my high school and university days. What a thrill it was to watch British and American films for the first time with subtitles (I had never seen subtitles before). And with hidden delight I recall such films as *Open City, Paisan* and *The Bicycle Thief*. Sometimes the theatres were packed (no one stayed at home if there was Fabrizi to see in the role of a priest, or Anna Magnani as a "woman of the people"), and we could relax on those unforgettable Sunday afternoons (no more fear of a sudden air raid alarm), the air heavy with the smell of American cigarettes as the lights went down. Sometimes the theatres were almost empty, but it did not matter.

Casablanca and *The Big Sleep* contrasted with the very different flavor of "movies made in Rome." For many years, then, Federico, our "Federico," was just a small sign flashing by in the credits—much shorter than they are today, there being but a handful of people assigned to the task of preparing these lists. (Perhaps the best remembered is a certain Roberto Chiti, who avidly jotted down every name and title he could find, first by exploring American film credits, other times persuading the projectionist to run the lists through again.)

Around this time Italy was on the threshold of an "economic boom," but as yet we were not aware of the fact. She was a nation weary from the war, but which nonetheless was searching for the courage and strength to fight her way back to prosperity—a strange nation, difficult for a foreigner to understand, and an enigma even to the Italians.

De Santis and Visconti, Rossellini and Germi were hard at work making films, each in his own different way. And Federico too. When was my first real encounter with him? I think it was *Variety Lights.* I still remember the curiosity and pleasure I felt at seeing his name in the place of "director," together with that of Lattuada; and that glimpse of the variety theatre world, with its poverty at once artful and gay, a world we had already tasted on those empty afternoons of student days, I still remember it all. Are they really like that, Federico? I would have liked to have asked—those third-class trains, those tired ballerinas with their homely, dissolute air, those slovenly, pompous comedians, with their artificially pitched, out-of-tune voices, sounding like voices on a badly scratched record? We felt all the provincial sensuality pervading the film, and we noticed reflections of young Fellini the journalist, together with the natural uncertainty of a newcomer to the trade.

Instinctively, one's attention was drawn more to the name of Lattuada, who was already a recognized director. Federico was comfortingly familiar, but little more than a name among the others we were accustomed to seeing rush by in the credits, as we strained our eyes to catch every last word. People were always standing up all around us, with the impatience typical of Italian audiences when it is time for credit to be given. Then again, sometimes we were interrupted halfway through by the projectionist. Sometimes the credits were badly tuned, and always they were accompanied by creaking springs, angry hisses, seats bumping knees.

Strangely enough, my recollection of *The White Sheik* is less clear. We all had to become accustomed to the irony of Fellini's (and Flaiano's) description of the "grandeur" of Italy: a comic strip Italy, a Rome exotically populated by voluptuous, threatening working class women and artless braggarts "à la Sordi." How could we explain to Federico that we had been dominated on the one hand by the press, constantly reminding us to concentrate our attention on a cinema whose aim it was to expound the reality of our country and reawaken public interest in social problems, to desert what they termed "commercial" cinema in favor of films which had a "message" to impart or a "warning" to deliver, and on the other by the irresistible lure of American cinema? Our daily fare in those days was a mixture of melodramatic and crime films, which were accepted condescendingly then and are now idolized by Cineclub fans. The undaunting efforts of these cineasts have brought to light fragments and tattered shreds of films we once devoured eagerly while confidentially exchanging names of famous crime writers such as Chandler and Hammett. (Little did we know then that thirty years later they would be treated with an almost liturgical respect, studied by round tables, analyzed by university professors and mummified at conventions.)

In those early years Fellini ran the risk of fading in our recollections, up to and including *La Strada.* In fact, the international success of *La Strada*, the *emballement* of French audiences for this fanciful Italian, inventor of shabby third-rate circus players, very nearly killed our curiosity and desire to seek further. Had the ironical, fervid writer of early years suddenly become pathetic, poetical?

But our desire to ask questions was reawakened by *Il Bidone*. Even today, this exceptional film is probably underestimated. At this time the Italian cinema still had no "hard-boiled" tradition behind it, though it was often forced maladroitly to invent one, succeeding only in creating grotesque parody. It is not surprising, then, that a story based on three small-time swindlers, portrayed as aimiable, cheerful spongers, did not meet with universal approval. But here again was the old Federico. We feel his astonishment at the cheap, criminal vulgarity of his characters, as he describes this wearisome, fatuous life of immorality. The presence of Broderick Crawford, obtained almost by chance, proved to be decisive. His special "American" way of moving— his heavy stride, his way of looking at his watch worn with the face on the inside of the wrist, the jaded brutality emanating from his every gesture—gave the film an ambiguous quality, a sense of invention and "imitation." The imitation was of something that does not exist, or, rather, of an impalpable heritage of customs and attitudes that the young Federico had captured from American films of the 1930s during those sultry, melancholy Sunday afternoons at the Fulgor theatre in Rimini.

From that moment of experiencing *Il Bidone*, an unspecified moment on an equally sultry and melancholy Sunday afternoon in Genoa, all doubts vanished. Federico was still "Federico," and his way of creating cinema was full of the subtleties and ambiguities of a dispassionate and at the same time bemused talent for telling stories—a strident mixture of episodes, some almost too pathetic, others ruthlessly criminal—difficult to find outside Italy, a blend of cynicism and latent piety, of jest and profound sobriety.

By the 1960s, Fellini was truly Fellini. A name familiar everywhere. Changing customs influenced him not at all. We learned to love French films (being film critic for a daily newspaper, I was able to write the reviews of *The 400 Blows* and *Breathless*. These were the golden years of Godard, and we were enthralled by his films—the petulent haste of his scripts on contemporary and controversial themes, the presence of a cinema of *copains*, his original use of jump cuts and freeze frames. But Federico was Federico.

During the filming of I Vitelloni.

I reviewed his films, but I had no chance to question him about them. Then one day in Genoa, by a strange coincidence, I found myself having to take him to lunch. We went to a fish restaurant at Boccadasse. He was polite, vague and astute, and had about him the distracted air of a businessman obliged to make polite conversation with clients over coffee, an attitude he always assumes when in a "passive" position and compelled to indulge in public relations.

Shortly after that came *La Dolce Vita,* and Fellini became famous the world over. His was one of those names, together with those of certain car, shoe, tie and luggage manufacturers, that make an era, names to which people everywhere reacted automatically. The film created a "scandal" (not that it took much in those days!). Fellini fans found all the old ingredients in this ironical and confused glimpse of a world that did not exist, or that had long since disappeared, or was at least different, but which could be found among the fragile pages of certain magazines and was therefore familiar to thousands of readers.

Fellini's film made this world reality; a world of decadent aristocracy, embarrassed fathers in Rome nightclubs, "literary" gatherings, monstrous friends who play the organ and then commit suicide, destroying their entire families, of false miracles, of passionate, irksome women. And the ineffable Marcello, with his vague, literary aspirations, wandering through Via Veneto with the air of an aimiable playboy in search of a wealthy widow, so typical of journalists of his stamp. It was all so in keeping with the Rome of those days, when it was still a privilege for the city to be the Capital, considering that all around it, especially in the north, was a quietly submissive nation, intent on keeping things going and on paying due tribute accompanied by sighs of envy.

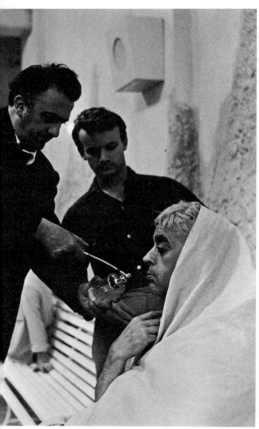

With Mario Pisu, during the filming of 8½.

Twenty-four years have passed since *La Dolce Vita*, during which I have had further occasion to meet and talk with Fellini, and once to watch him on the set of *Prova d'Orchestra*, moving around like some distracted, good-natured architect. His films have appeared at regular intervals and been received in the main with enthusiasm, sometimes with a sort of bored reverence. It has been a period of rapid change. Whatever happened to all that early excitement for the *nouvelle vague,* to that fascination with the torment in Bergman's work, to the crowds that flocked to see the spate of "spaghetti westerns"? Godard gradually became more and more esoteric; now and then we heard rumors of his comeback. And Frankenheimer, what happened to him? Or to the mass hysteria for James Bond, which somewhat puzzled that small group of staunch Ian Fleming readers? And American underground cinema, with its dishevelled directors of strange-sounding Lithuanian and Latvian names, who were often to be seen, camera in hand, roaming the streets of Pesaro, like gurus of the imaginary?

During these twenty-four years, the scene has changed at least five or six times. And as the cinema ages and moves more rapidly than anything else in our society, the world we knew as children is already aeons away, and to modern eyes appears stilted, making us feel decrepit and out-dated. Burt Lancaster's debut in a cult-film like Siodmak's *The Killers* (I still remember the thrill I felt at the film's first screening, the eloquence of the scene where William Conrad and Charles McGraw search for Pete Lunn, alias Ole Anderson, "The Swede") is already an historical event, for young enthusiasts, rather like the American Civil War.

Fellini was part of that past, just as he is part of the present. We have gradually become accustomed to his films, to his eccentricities, almost always pleasing, and to his daydreams, rather like those of a schoolboy puzzling over a Greek exercise and casting furtive glances at the bright spring day beyond the closed windows of the classroom. What excitement there was over *8½*, a "movie on the movie," a type of film that the Italian cinema, unlike the old Hollywood tradition, rarely produces. (Several years later Truffaut made an equally successful attempt with *Day for Night*; this is curious if we consider how different and distant Truffaut is from Fellini, although for many of us he conjures up the same affectionate, friendly interest and camaraderie we feel for Federico.) For many *8½* became a myth, or an automatic point of reference. And today, any attempt to bring autobiography to the screen must inescapably, almost biologically, face comparison with this film. (Look what happened recently to Woody Allen with *Stardust Memories*.)

There is what might be termed an "*8½* feeling," just as there is a "*La Dolce Vita* feeling." The terrible uncertainty besetting the creator of cinema over the personal necessity (advantage, habit, inevitability, obligation and so forth) to make films, is reflected in that feeling of emptiness, of facing a bottomless pit, of fear, of incredulity that comes when it is actually time to begin. What is the message to be this time? And why? It is in some way similar to the dilemma of a writer who, as he completes the words "Part One, Chapter One," suddenly realizes he has lost the urge to go on with his novel, or essay, or play. But

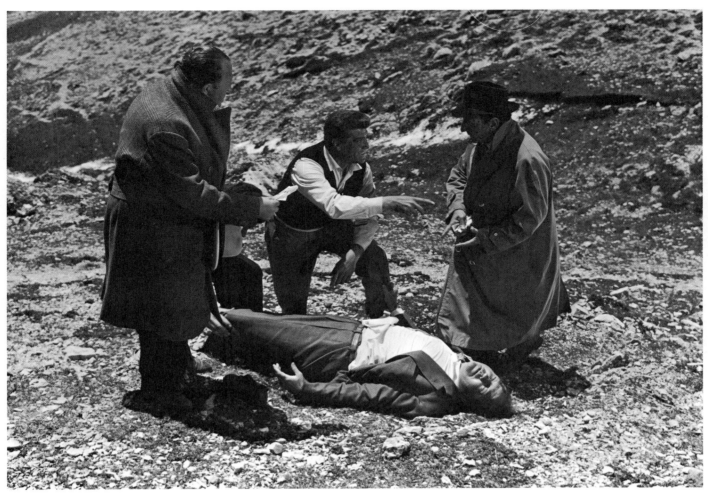

Two scenes from Il Bidone.

Two moments during the filming of 8½.

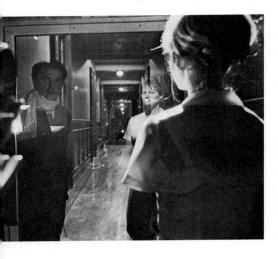

when this happens to a director, it is more intense, and incomparably more far-reaching. Before him is the skeleton of an enormous workshop about to open up, the rickety framework of what is to come, just as it was in the early days of silent films, a place where dreams are made: props, sulky scene-shifters, tired electricians, skeptical cameramen, chairs, ladders, debris, cables and the family tree of the production program about to bear its first, uncertain fruit.

The dilemma of the director rests on a question that every motion picture man, however cynical or enthusiastic he may be, asks himself at least once in his lifetime, and most probably every time he is about to begin a film: What is the point? Is it worth it? Is it worth the trouble, once again, to set up this enormous workshop, this fragile organization tied to a myriad of unpredictable factors? Factors such as the rapport with producers and scriptwriters, finding the right actors and then coaxing them into giving of their best. In different circumstances the same actor can appear as inanimate as a dummy or as eloquent as a poet, giving the impression that he understands everything, can overcome all difficulties, when in reality he knows nothing.

This is one of the miracles of the motion picture world, Fellini's in particular: the miracle of bringing to life the most casual of faces and bodies which, as though by the touch of a magic wand, are suddenly charged with feeling, complicity, hidden meaning. It is as if they had mysteriously inherited the aura possessed by the character of some other film, of which they know nothing, have never seen, or have seen and forgotten. They move within it with the terrified and guilty confusion of a soldier on the battlefield, blindly following orders, knowing nothing of the plan of action of his superiors, nothing of the place in history that the battle will take, nothing at all, intent only on staying alive.

Let's see now, what else was released to Italian screens during the same period as 8½? Terence Young's *Dr. No*, destined to turn Ian Fleming's private myth into a legend of the screen, a legend still alive today. Molinaro's *Arsèn Lupin Contre Arsèn Lupin*; Vancini's *La Banda Casaroli*; *La Commare Secca*, directed by a very young Bertolucci; John Cassavetes' *Shadows*; Olmi's *I Fidanzati*; Visconti's *The Leopard*; Howard Hawk's *Hatari*; Kubrick's *Lolita*; Schlesinger's *A Kind of Loving*; Pietrangeli's *La Parmigiana*; Godard's *My Life to Live*; *Rogopag*, co-directed by Gregoretti, Rossellini, Godard and Pasolini; Risi's *Il Sorpasso*; Ferreri's *Una Storia Moderna: l'Ape Regina;* Melville's *Le Doulos*; Bunuel's *Viridiana*; Wise's *West Side Story*. Each of these films, recalled more or less at random, has left its own special mark in our memories, sometimes fleeting sometimes lasting, sometimes of affection sometimes of disappointment. But in this confrontation of titles we become aware of the unique, almost secret character of Fellini's work. How can there be any comparison with 8½, with its flavor of lace and flounces, thermal waters and clouds of incense, with its carousel of proudly remiss producers and remissly proud actresses, with its haunting background music, unmistakably by Nino Rota?

During the restless years of the 1960s, threshold of an era of contention which was soon to engulf Europe and America alike, Fellini continued to establish his reputation with the bizarre detachment of a solitary decorator, a great inventor of spirits: an ironical, friendly ma-

A pause during the filming of La Dolce Vita.

gician, possessed of a secret predilection for satire, which enables him always to avoid falling into the trap of symbolism.

Two years later came *Juliet of the Spirits*, which I liked as much as many others disliked it, with its dream-like quality evoked by little children, nuns, grandfathers, little old ladies, pompous loose-living females, changing colors. While jotting down these notes, this sort of interview without an interviewee—(I must admit I had my interview in the end. With the solemnity of two plenipotentiaries, Federico and I spent an evening together in a famous north Italian restaurant near Via Veneto. Federico showed me the books he was reading, which included a vintage Isak Dinesen, and he talked away in a lively and enjoyable manner about episodes from the past. He explained that he had suggested Piazza dei Quiriti 8 for Maria Minchi's house in the Rome episode of *Paisan* because he happened to be especially fond of that neighborhood—it was there in fact that he had found his first furnished room—even though the episode was in the end filmed else-

With Marcello Mastroianni, during the filming of 8½.

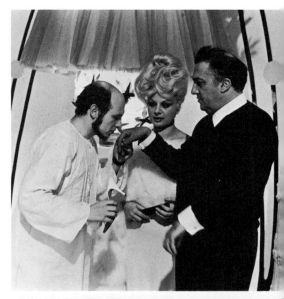

A sketch by Fellini for Juliet of the Spirits.

where. He confided that Rossellini had once tried to persuade him to make a film about numismatics, that Maieroni had at the last minute refused to shoot the scene in which the old comedian is supposed to conduct Leopoldo Trieste in *I Vitelloni* along the sea-front, in the dark, to read a script. Fellini is a born mimic, with the gusto of a true professional, he imitated the round, old-style actor voice of Maieroni and the unmistakable falsetto of Leopoldo Trieste, who is a mutual friend of ours)—as I was saying, while writing these lines, I sought out what I had written about the film at the time, not in a newspaper but in a magazine. I should like to quote myself here, not through any immodesty on my part, but simply because the words I wrote then still seem to have a certain value:

". . . The film has a turgid, almost ambiguous beauty, a superabundance of powerfully delirious images, a turmoil of mannequins, spirits, befeathered females, children, while each shot is adroitly animated by a juxtaposition of figures and shadows. Fellini, having at last shaken off an obsession for ironical realism characteristic of his earlier films, now gives full rein to his deepest instincts, freed by experience of all inhibition. Rather like the spirits revealing to a 'freed' Juliet the fears and fragile ties with the past which once seemed so important, so decisive to her.

"Here then is Fellini's pantheistic sense of nature, his ironico-pagan vision of the world, his delight in recalling the past, lost in the magical shadows of childhood. Guido's memories of school-days in *8½* are the same as those of the young Juliet, who is the central figure in the ingenuously romantic drama of a school play, which is merely a pretext for deeply figurative stylization: nuns in pale blue robes and with hidden faces; young Juliet being raised on a 'flaming' grid towards the ceiling and a dust-covered door behind which God is waiting; the magical, bearded grandfather who stops the play, the grandfather who, years before, ran away with a ballerina. The memory the adult Juliet retains of these episodes is a mixture of reality and fantasy.

" . . . Visually, the film is violent and vividly imaginative, the direction is orthodox, aiming at a quiet and intense style of expression, which develops into images of considerable power—an unexpected backwards travelling shot of Juliet, rather in the style of Resnais, is surprising, but remains an isolated episode. In brief, *Juliet of the Spirits* has considerable 'shock force.' It is pointless to search, as some have done, for any coordinated and conclusive moral value in this film. Fellini's works never have a moral undertone, and this film is no exception; only the spirits of memory and the senses and their 'exorcism' carry weight. As we have said before, Juliet perhaps manages to free herself from the 'recollections of a Catholic upbringing'; but even in this sense, Fellini's position is still one of implicit ambiguity, though it goes without saying that this is his very force and talent. His art is that of sculpting figures, both male (as in the past) and female (as in this film), against a background of friendly, familiar fantasy. Frequently, they are suffering the pains and ties of married life, by which they are nearly always hurt. He is never ideological . . . but always intent on following his own secret train of thought, beyond all logical explanation or demand . . . ; he is not above using fragments of psychoanalysis, sociological con-

notations, but always and only if in someway related to certain personal secrets and artistic exigencies. . . . "

And so followed the other films: *Toby Dammit*, with its singular theme of the "first Catholic western," and old Father Spagna, in whom we find many hidden echoes of Fellini himself. *Satyricon*, a marvelous folly of youth, an Eternal City of yesterday and today crumbling with the same fervid impatience. *Roma*, a magnificent and ferocious glimpse of the contemporary city, a mixture of frantic admiration and idle contempt, the portrait of a lover who grasps the faults of his sweetheart with the ferocity of a maniac. *Amarcord, Prova d'Orchestra* and, finally, *Città delle Donne*, when, for the first time after many years, I had a momentary desire to rebel, to reject his magical potion, his monstrously seductive, but errant memories, those outrageous beds, the pale face of Marcello Mastroianni, called upon yet again to collect the dividends of the past and future on Fellini's behalf. This was the gist of a review I wrote for the newspaper for which I was working at the time. Afterwards I felt guilty, as though I had offended Colonnippo Filello, or Genoveffa la Racchia (characters from the magazine *Marc' Aurelio*).

How many years have passed, and what an extraordinary collection of memories they have left behind. There is, for instance the splendid, magical, solitary almost sly way in which Fellini indulges in his cinema:

Two suggestive photographs of the filming of Prova d'Orchestra.

Consider the ingenuity of the careless, sneaky way in which Ascyltus and Encolpius roam the dissolute Latin society, a sort of post-war Naples reanimated by commemorative plaques and sumptuous patrician villas, a world of arrogantly decadent human beings, which came to us at the time like a message from another planet, while contemporary film festivals were overflowing with Latin-American documentaries. The types of film we had known as children seemed destined to disappear forever, while the new traditions filled us with a feeling of uncertainty. The time was not yet ripe for that "rediscovery of the past" which was to begin in the underground world of the cineclubs, and which today sees young and not so young united in their enthusiasm, sometimes excessive, for "old movies."

Again a quick look at some of the other films of this period. During the first six months of 1970, along with *Fellini-Satyricon*, were such films as Bolognini's *Metello*, Luigi Comencini's *Infanzia, Vocazione e Prime Esperienze di Giacomo Casanova Veneziano*, Bob Fosse's *Sweet Charity* (the film was, in fact, a tribute to Fellini, being inspired by *The Nights of Cabiria*), Gene Kelly's *Hello Dolly!*, Alfred Hitchcock's *Topaz*, Dennis Hopper's *Easy Rider*, Elia Kazan's *The Arrangement*, Dusan Makaveiev's *Innocence Unprotected*, Sam Peckinpah's *The Wild Bunch*, Claude Sautet's *The Things of Life*, Don Siegel's *Death of a Gunfighter*, Visconti's *The Damned*, and Bo Widerberg's *The Adalen Riots*. A mixed group of titles, none of which has anything in common with Fellini. From this comparison we once again feel the splendid ingenuity, the involuntarily autocratic isolation of this director, who continues to use the cinema as his own personal sketchbook, or costly notepad, a television set for his innermost dreams. Once again he proves to be beyond all classification in the motion picture world (soon to be confirmed by *Amarcord,* the ultimate in autobiographical

During the filming of La Città delle Donne.

Giulietta Masina and Fellini during the filming of Juliet of the Spirits.

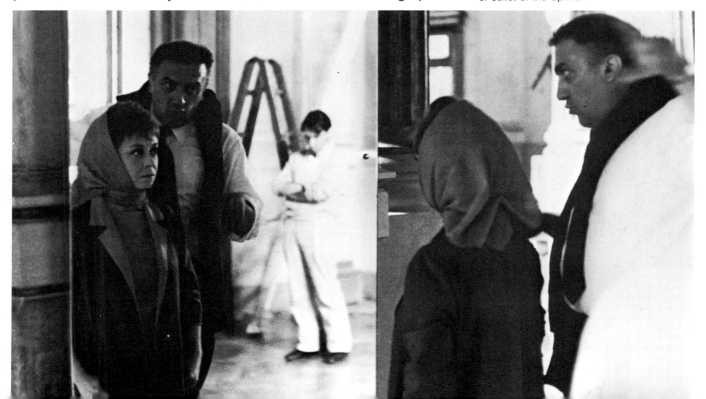

expression). With his talent for combining simple irony and a flourish worthy of a 17th-century fresco painter, Fellini is bound to arouse some exaggerated emotions, but also steadfast allegiance. While outside Italy the reaction is one of amazed admiration and a desperate attempt to "rationalize," mixed with a sort of religious awe with which the northern races, and often the French, too (whose Celtic, Latin and German blood mingles in explosive mythological reactions), regard the derisive splendor of Italian ingenuity.

I have had a one-sided acquaintance with Fellini which has lasted thirty years, with hardly a word having been passed between us, until recently at least, apart from those vague, semi-bureaucratic greetings which famous directors reserve for film critics at previews. And they were always greetings from a distance, made while one was desperately trying not to trip as one made his way up the stairs of those gloomy halls where previews always seem to take place—halls which are normally used for dubbing, dotted with music stands for one to bump into and hidden booths from which issue forth slender tapers of light. There were so many questions never asked; some were forgotten along the way, others I still remember but will never have the courage to voice. (It must be great fun to question Fellini; look at the multitude of interviews he has had to endure, many of which were published recently in *Fare un Film* [*Making a Film*]. Sometimes his replies are splendidly vague, on other occasions surprisingly detailed; he delights in anecdotes which at first glance seem too bizarre to be true, but which on second thought are too bizarre to have been invented. And he shows that rare talent for the sketch, the short story and for choosing just the right adjective at just the right moment, as I point out in my comments to each film.)

Then one day, at last, Fellini telephoned me, just as a friend of mine rang the doorbell. I did not know what to do first, and, in my excitement, dropped the telephone receiver. Fellini congratulated me for what I had written about Mastroianni in a book dedicated to that actor. I felt very flattered. Then he said he was going to address me by the familiar term of *tu* on account of our friendship "which was still to be explored"—a very romantic phrase to be sure (the result was a high-level "diplomatic" tête-à-tête; we exchanged views and reminisced, with a curious sort of reciprocal pleasure; for me it was indeed a pleasure, and I hope that it was for Fellini too).

Still to be explored, but how? By talking, talking, talking, with no set purpose, but with gusto, as one did on the way home from school many years ago.

Well, that is what I have tried to do here.

CLAUDIO G. FAVA

BIOGRAPHY

1926

Federico, aged six, with his younger brother Riccardo.

1920—Federico Fellini was born in Rimini on 20 January, the son of Urbano Fellini, a commercial representative, and Ida Barbiani, the daughter of a well-to-do Roman family of businessmen.

1925-1937—Fellini attended school in Rimini, graduating with a diploma in classical studies.

1937—Fellini went to Florence with a selection of sketches and short stories in the hope of meeting one of the editors of *420*, a weekly satirical-political magazine highly popular at that time. He stayed there six months, free-lancing for *420* and other weeklies published by Società Nerbini, among which was *l'Avventuroso*.

1938—In January Fellini left for Rome with the intention of attending law school there, but as soon as he arrived he began to contact all the weekly, fortnightly and monthly publications printed in Rome at that time, in the hope of publishing a series of short stories, interviews and caricatures and the first two or three chapters of some light novels and adventure stories he had begun to write during high school days. He collaborated on a weekly basis with *Cine Illustrato, Rugantino, La Signorina Grandi Firme, Il Balilla, Cinemagazzino, Settebello, Travasa, Il Piccolo*. He had no steady job and passed each day in one or the other of the editorial offices, while at night he continued to write and sketch, hopping from one rented room to another at the rate of about two or three a month, or passing from a boarding house to a small hotel paid by the hour, from the Excelsior to a bed shared with a friend in some corridor. In just a few months he managed to live in virtually every neighborhood of the city.

He wrote sketches and short plays for the radio, songs for variety theatre, monologues for famous and up-and-coming comedians, advertising slogans, leaflets for the big stores to give out at sale time.

Together with his friend of those bohemian days, the painter Rinaldo Geleng, Fellini also went around daubing shop windows with whitewash and paint in the hope of gaining some publicity, while in the evenings, armed with pastels and paper, he would tour out-of-the-way restaurants, offering to do "look-alike" portraits or "very funny" caricatures of the customers at their meal.

During those footloose months, Fellini met writers, beautiful soubrettes and many actors, among whom was Aldo Fabrizi, who was to become a firm friend. Fabrizi took the young Federico under his massive wing and introduced him into the friendly, carnival atmosphere of the variety theatre. Tommaso Landolfi, Leo Longanesi, Fanfulla the comedian, Alberto Savinio, De Chirico, Nuto Navarrini, Palazzeschi, the Bonos brothers—all became Fellini's good friends.

In the summer of 1938, he joined the staff of *Marc'Aurelio*, a bi-weekly humorous magazine then at the peak of its popularity, and soon became one of its most productive and inventive writers. Together with Ruggero Maccari, he collaborated with the radio variety theatre. Stefano Vanzina (Steno), the first of the *Marc'Aurelio* humorists to branch out to Cinecittà, introduced Fellini into the world of cinema when he asked him to cooperate on the screenplay of the films of Macario: *Lo Vedi Come Sei? Il Pirata Sono Io, Imputato Alzatevi!*

The meeting with Piero Tellini, a well-known story and script writer, soon drew Fellini away from journalism and into scriptwriting for the cinema. He worked with Tellini on the story and screenplay for *Avanti c'è Posto,* for Aldo Fabrizi; then *Campo dei Fiori* and *L'Ultima Carrozzella* again for the same actor; followed by *Chi l'Ha Visto,* with Virgilio Riento, *Quarta Pagina, Documento Zeta 3, Bentornato Signor Gai, Sette Poveri in Automobile, I Predoni del Sahara.* As regards the last film, Fellini had to join the crew in Africa in order to revise the screenplay which had turned out to be a bit vague and inconclusive.

1942—By August, the British 8th Army was relentlessly advancing, forcing the German troops and Italian Army to abandon the African coast. The film crew too was forced to stop work and had to beat a very hasty retreat, almost missing the last regular airline flight out of Tripoli. Fellini made his way once again to Rome, through town and country, where the devastations of war were vividly evident.

Up until that moment, Fellini had managed to avoid call-up, relying on one postponement after another, first as a university student, then thanks to a special permit awarded to journalists—which were generously renewed every three months. Fellini also claimed to suffer from tachycardia and a basedowian eye. But this time when he went to the Celio military hospital he was met by a team of German doctors who declared him fit for active service even before he had had time to strip! He was ordered to join, without further delay, a regiment based in a little village perched high up in the hills of Greece.

No sooner was Fellini out of the hospital than he tore up documents and certificates alike, without so much as a second thought. He travelled day and night to reach the Forlì military zone and, new documents in his pocket, then tried to have another check-up at the military hospital in Bologna. But an air raid, just half an hour before his appointment, destroyed the hospital's records, after which the question of Fellini's call-up was never again mentioned!

1943—On 30 October, Fellini married Giulietta Masina of S. Giorgio di Piano near Bologna. Giulietta was a talented actress. They had met in June, after the characters Cico and Pallina, invented by Federico for *Marc'Aurelio* had gone on the air in a radio program sponsored by the perfume manufacturer "Niba." Giulietta, who had a B.A. degree, had been offered the part of Pallina. Federico had wanted to meet her, and after only a short engagement they were married, as though the event had been pre-established and there was no other possible outcome.

1944—On 4 June Rome was liberated by the Americans. But the enthusiasms aroused by this long-awaited event was soon to give way to a period of anxiety and hardship. The film industry was closed down, while newspapers and radio were in the hands of the P.W.B. Work was hard to find. But Fellini was not without ideas; together with a group of friends from the *Marc'Aurelio*, he opened a shop specializing in caricatures, portraits, photographs, and record-making for U.S., British and Canadian soldiers, soldiers of all races, colors and creeds. It was called The Funny Face Shop.

Still today, Fellini insists that, relatively speaking, he has never made as much money as he did during that period. Two weeks later he opened a second shop, then a third. Within six months Fellini and his friends either owned or controlled nine Funny Face Shops in Rome

Riccardo balilla, *and Federico* avanguardista.

Rimini 1937, Federico the "dandy" (right) with two friends.

Federico (left) with his father and brother in Venice, in September 1937.

Roma 1940. "To my dear mother, Federico."

Rimini 1937. The difficult life of the pre-war vitellone.

alone. Plans were made to open more in Florence, then Milan, keeping pace with the allied troops as they advanced through the country.

One day, writes Angelo Solmi in his book on Fellini, published in 1962 by Rizzoli, Rossellini's face appeared at the window; Rossellini beckoned to Fellini to come outside. He wanted Federico to write the screenplay for a documentary on the life of Don Morosini, who had been shot by the Fascists. Fellini accepted, but without much enthusiasm, and the documentary went on to become *Roma Città Aperta (Open City)*.

1945—The war over and The Funny Face Shops closed down, Fellini went back to the cinema, working again for Rossellini. Together with Amidei he wrote the story and screenplay of *Paisan*, the filming of which he then followed in the role of a rather special assistant director. He did not actually do what an assistant director would normally do; he simply stayed close to the film crew as a friend of Roberto Rossellini's, excitedly watching the creation of what was to become one of the greatest films in the history of cinema.

1946—Fellini met Tullio Pinelli, who soon became a close friend and valuable collaborator. Together, they wrote the screenplay for *Il Delitto di Giovanni Episcopo*, directed by Alberto Lattuada, Duilio Coletti's *Il Passatore*, Lattuada's *Senza Pietà*, in which Giulietta Masina made her first screen appearance, a performance that won her the *Nastro d'Argento* (Silver Ribbon) of the Italian Film Critics for best supporting actress.

Again for Rossellini, Fellini wrote the second episode of the film *L'Amore (Il Miracolo)*, drawing his inspiration, it seems, from a story he had heard at Gambettola during his childhood. Fellini not only wrote the story and the screenplay and was assistant director, but he also played the role of the tramp mistakenly taken by Anna Magnani for St. Joseph. Rossellini had managed to persuade him to bleach his hair, insisting that the character he was to play had to be blond. That same year, with Pinelli, Germi and Mangione, he wrote the screenplay (adapted from Giuseppe Guido's book *Lo Schiavo*) for the film *In Nome della Legge* directed by Pietro Germi.

1949—After writing yet another screenplay with Pinelli for Lattuada's *Il Mulino del Po*, Fellini went back to working with Rossellini on *Francesco Giullare di Dio*, which was based on a project that had initially been broached as far back as the time of the Romagnol episode of *Paisan*, and which was set in a friary.

1950—Again a film for Pietro Germi *Il Cammino della Speranza;* then Comencini's *Persiane Chiuse*, Germi's *Il Brigante di Tacca di Lupo*, Rossellini's *Europa 51* and Germi's *La Città si Difende.* During the spring months Fellini entertained the idea of becoming a glider pilot, but his mother came to hear of it and made her son promise that he would never fly. Fellini kept his promise and gave up the idea.

Fellini joined up with Alberto Lattuada, Giulietta Masina and Carla Del Poggio to form a company which, together with Capitolium, went on to produce *Variety Lights*. The film tells of the adventures, true or imaginary, of the famous tour that Fellini claims to have made with Aldo Fabrizi's Variety Company in the winter of 1939, though everyone else, including Fabrizi, denies ever having made such a tour.

The story was written by Fellini, the screenplay by Fellini and Pinelli, while the film was co-directed by Fellini and Alberto Lattuada. Carla Del Poggio (Lattuada's wife) and Giulietta Masina played the leading female roles, while Peppino De Filippo was the unfortunate, quixotic comedian of the down-at-heel variety group. The film, well received by the critics, was not particularly liked by the general public. It was not until after the world-wide triumph of *La Strada* that *Variety Lights* was given a second chance; it was revaluated even by those critics who had not liked it originally and released to the cinemas a second time with much greater success. But the four partners failed to make a financial profit even this time.

A similar fate was in store for *The White Sheik*, made in 1957, and the first film that Fellini directed alone. The film took its inspiration from some ideas developed by Antonioni on the world of *fumetti* (a sort of photo-novel or cartoon-romance), and offered Fellini the chance to put to good advantage the experience he had acquired when in charge

With Giulietta Masina and Aldo Buzzi, costume designer of Variety Lights.

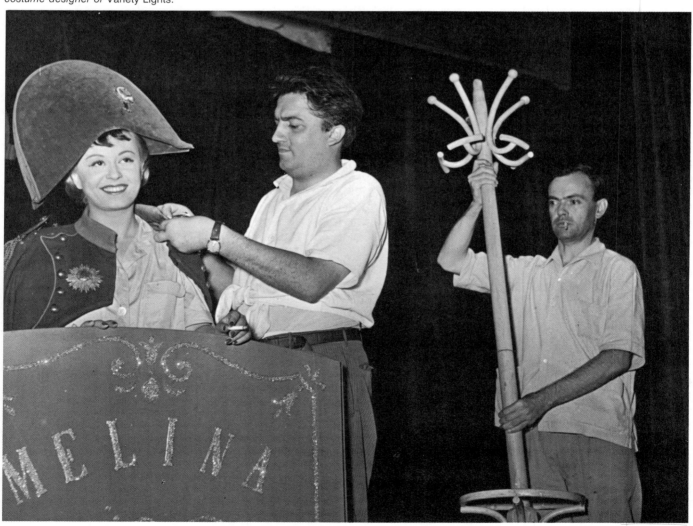

of the post sent in by the readers of *Cine Illustrato.* The screenplay was written by Fellini and Pinelli and Antonioni was approached for director. Antonioni, however, disapproved of the way the story had been set out, and in the end producer Rovere persuaded Fellini to undertake direction of the film himself. After some hesitation Fellini accepted. Alberto Sordi was offered the part of the White Sheik, Leopoldo Trieste that of the bridegroom, while Brunella Bovo was chosen for the role of the young wife infatuated by the mythical hero of a strip cartoon. Giulietta Masina had a small part as a gentle little prostitute, a sort of "spirit of the night," named Cabiria, who comforts the husband abandoned by his young wife during their honeymoon.

The White Sheik was shown at the Venice Film Festival before a matinée audience who seemed to enjoy themselves enormously, even too much perhaps, for the following day the critics dispensed with the film in a few brief and scathing lines, announcing Fellini's debut as a director to be a total failure. Half-heartedly distributed by Fincine, a company that was to go bankrupt a few months later, hampered by the negative publicity received in Venice, the film ran for only a few days before it was taken off by nearly all the theatres in town. It was never even given a second showing. One of the reasons for its failure was that the public took an instant and deep dislike to Alberto Sordi; the distributors claimed that the name of Alberto Sordi kept people away, and so when Fellini again wanted to engage Sordi for his next film, *I Vitelloni*, he met with considerable opposition. And when, after many ups and downs (filming was interrupted four times because producer Lorenzo Pegoraro complained practically every week that there was no money left!), the film was finally completed, the name of Alberto Sordi continued to be a handicap for distribution. In the end it was removed from all posters and from the first fifty copies of the film.

1952—*I Vitelloni* was shown in Venice exactly one year after *The White Sheik*. The audience followed the film with growing enthusiasm, frequently interrupting for a round of applause and giving it a long ovation at the end. For Fellini and his *vitelloni* this was real success.

But how was this famous film born? *I Vitelloni* was made in place of *La Strada*, which producer Pegoraro, one of the few admirers of *The White Sheik*, had refused to do. Pegoraro believed in Fellini—he had seen *The White Sheik* six times—and decided to "capture" him with a contract for two films. Fellini initially proposed his *La Strada* project, on which he was particularly keen, having written it with Tullio Pinelli for his wife, Giulietta Masina. Pegoraro liked the story but did not think that Giulietta Masina was right for the part. This difference of opinion between author and producer led to the cancellation of the first contract. Then there was the second. Fellini, who wanted to be free of the commitment as soon as possible because Pegoraro's refusal of his first project had hurt his feelings, set to work on other stories.

Flaiano too had doubts about *La Strada* and advised Fellini against making it. One afternoon, Federico was chatting with Flaiano about his days in Rimini—those winter evenings at the Caffé Commercio, those melancholy walks on late autumn afternoons, the sea shrouded in mist, those stupid, sometimes violent, jokes with friends, the long wait for summer—when he suddenly had the idea that all these recollections would make good subject matter for a film. Flaiano was enthusiastic. He too came from a seaside town, Pescara, and his recollections were the same, the atmosphere the same, the same ridiculous tomfoolery, the same dreariness, the same boredom. They wrote the story in a couple of weeks and were joined by Tullio Pinelli for the screenplay. Filming began in December and, despite the aforesaid interruptions, was completed the following spring.

1953—As soon as *I Vitelloni* was completed, but prior to its showing in Venice, Federico joined Cesare Zavattini's new project on the theme "love in the city," his contribution being an episode entitled "A Matrimonial Agency." It shows the usual autobiographical intonations, and a certain intolerance for the realistic character of Zavattini's original project. The actors were all from the *Centro Sperimentale di Cinematografia* and the sketch, though well-received by the critics, shared in the film's impopularity with the public when it was released at the end of the year.

In the meantime, Federico had at last found two producers willing to finance *La Strada,* Carlo Ponti and Dino De Laurentiis. After some

The unfortunate bridegroom of The White Sheik.

argument over the cast (Ponti would have preferred Silvana Mangano and Burt Lancaster), filming finally began in December. The crew went on location in Viterbo, Ovindoli, Bagnoregio and a number of small villages in southern Italy, the final shots being filmed in May 1954. On the evening of 7 September, at the Venice Film Festival, *La Strada* was shown in public for the first time. Success was immediate and overwhelming; it won the Venice Silver Lion, international acclaim (the film ran for three years in New York) and a shower of other awards, including an Oscar for the best foreign film.

In Italy, the film had aroused much discordant opinion: the Catholics praised it as a parable of Christian spirituality, while the Marxists judged it an attack against neo-realism and its philosophy. Nearly everyone had something to say: critics, directors, intellectuals, politicians. For months newspapers and magazines carried opposing points of view, which were nearly always more ideological than pertaining to cinema. In all events, Fellini had finally made his mark as a director, and his name was now well-known throughout the world.

1955—For the first time in his life, Fellini agreed to accompany his film *La Strada* to its world première (he never did so again). He and

During the filming of I Vitelloni.

his wife Giulietta received an enthusiastic welcome wherever they went. American directors offered a reception in their honor, congratulations and applause showered in from all directions. Fellini was also awarded a prize, instituted by the American directors specially for the occasion; it was presented to him by a visibly moved John Ford, president of the Screen Guild of Directors. The authorities of a small Dutch community, Nierbëeg, offered him the honorary post of mayor for life. In Paris, London and New York restaurants, cafés, "pizzerie" and nightclubs suddenly sprang up with the name "La Strada." In Switzerland, a cigarette and cigar manufacturer created a new brand of cigar called "Zampanò." The world over, shops were full of dolls looking like Gelsomina. The title *La Strada* was never translated, and even today it would be difficult to find a foreigner who accepts the meaning of the word "strada" in the equivalent of his own language. *La Strada* for all non-Italians came to mean: love, sadness, hope, but above all, that sweet, gently funny clown named Gelsomina.

For several months after the completion of *La Strada*, Fellini seemed set on *Moraldo in Cittá (Moraldo in the City)*, a sort of Roman sequel to the story of the young hero of *I Vitelloni*. This had already been serialized in the magazine *Cinema* from August to December 1954 (numbers 139, 142, 144, 145, 146, 147).

But the project was put aside (to be partially revived later in *Roma*) in favor of a film about three swindlers who spent their time tricking the naïve inhabitants of the Italian provinces, which Pinelli and Flaiano had written with Sordi, Fabrizi and Peppino De Filippo in mind for the three main characters. After the usual tour of producers, Goffredo Lombardo of Titanus finally agreed to finance the film, first allowing Federico and his assistants the time to explore the world of the *bidonisti* (cheats or swindlers). The original idea of a picturesque, free-and-easy film was gradually modified into a much harder, more dramatic story: it centered around one main *bidonista*, for which role Federico first considered Humphrey Bogart, then Pierre Fresnay, finally choosing Broderick Crawford. Filming began in May and ended on 16 July. During August, Federico was hard at work preparing the final copy as the film was billed to close the Venice Film Festival on 10 September. It was given a cool reception by critics and public alike. Although not outrightly slashed, it was accused of slow narrative and structural confusion. After a few cuts, *Il Bidone* went into general release but the takings were modest; ten years later, however, the film was rediscovered by the critics and judged to be one of the most important of Fellini's early career, and a film in which there were already hints of *La Dolce Vita*.

1956—*The Nights of Cabiria*. The story had been in Federico's mind for some time, since 1947 in fact, when he proposed it to Rossellini as an alternative to *Il Miracolo*. Before writing the screenplay, Fellini, Pinelli, and Flaiano explored, as they did for *Il Bidone*, the world they wanted to describe, that of a pathetic little prostitute of the suburbs. Pier Paolo Pasolini was invited by Fellini to revise the dialogue. However, *The Nights of Cabiria* was not immediately chosen as the film to follow the rather unfortunate *Bidone*. According to Solmi, Fellini first examined other projects; among these were two embryonic ideas

Federico Fellini and Giulietta Masina with the Oscar they won for La Strada *in 1955.*

The title La Strada *was never translated. The word* strada *for all non-Italians soon came to mean love, sadness and hope, but above all, that sweet, gentle, funny clown named Gelsomina.*

Franca Marzi, Giulietta Masina and
Amedeo Nazzari in two stills from
The Nights of Cabiria.

which were abandoned almost immediately: the first told of a man with many families who jumped from one to another with whirlwind speed; the second was the story of a nun who, blocked by snow in a mountain convent together with three other nuns, managed to survive with prodigious ingenuity even after all the food had run out. There was also the more substantial idea of adapting for the screen Mario Tobino's *Le Libere Donne di Magliano,* with Montgomery Clift in the leading role.

But at the beginning of the year the final choice fell on *The Nights of Cabiria.* For several months Fellini searched for a producer willing to offer sufficient guarantees. After the customary medley of proposals, discussions, promises and hopes (there were rumors that at least ten producers were involved), Dino De Laurentiis at last gave his consent. Filming began in the summer and took four and a half months to complete. Fellini passed the winter editing the 186,666 feet of film used.

1957—The final copy of *Cabiria* was ready by early March. It was shown at the Cannes Film Festival and was an immediate success (Giulietta Masina won the award for best leading actress), confirmed in the autumn when the film went into general release. This time there was none of the controversy which had greeted *La Strada*, although one or two critics did accuse Fellini of repetition and fragmentary narrative. In the United States the film won another Oscar and the New York Critics' award. In the meantime, Federico was looking for a new story, rumors leaking out of all manner of different projects: a *Barabas* from the book by Pär Lagerkvist and starring Anthony Quinn (later made by Richard Fleischer); a modern version of *Casanova* with Orson Welles; a *Decameron;* a *Don Quixote* with Jacques Tati; an adaption of Flaiano's *Un Marziano a Roma*; and the best proposal, *Viaggio con Anita*, written by Pinelli with Sophia Loren and Gregory Peck in mind (the film was eventually made in 1979 by Mario Monicelli, and includes a tribute to Fellini in the sequence showing the filming of the Trevi Fountain scene of *La Dolce Vita*). The only sure thing during these months, was that Fellini wrote the story and screenplay of *Fortunella,* a film directed by Eduardo De Filippo and starring Giulietta Masina.

1958—Having, for one reason or another, abandoned all of these projects, Fellini had another look at *Moraldo in Città*, the idea being to make some radical changes and bring the story up to date. Instead, he began the lengthy preparation of *La Dolce Vita*. For months, Federico was a frequent visitor to the street cafés of Via Veneto, and the project began to form around these new experiences. By autumn, it was almost ready. The search for a producer ended on 28 October when Federico signed a contract with the company of Riama (Società Rizzoli-Amato). At the beginning of December, Gherardi set to work on the sets and costumes, and selection of the cast continued.

1959—On 16 March, at Cinecittà, the cameras started rolling, though some of the cast still had to be chosen. As regards the leading role, Federico had wanted Marcello Mastroianni from the outset, but he had to resist some strong opposition from those De Laurentiis, for instance, at one point a possible producer who would have preferred Paul Newman or even Burt Lancaster. Choosing the other actors turned out to be even more problematical, names being rumored by the dozens for this and that role. Here we have mentioned only those who were actually contacted by the production team: for the role of Steiner: Henry Fonda, Elio Vittorini the writer, Enrico Maria Salerno; for Maddalena: Silvana Mangano and Madeleine Fischer; for the father: Maurice Chevalier. Right up until May, Luise Rainer seemed certain for the part of Dolores, a nymphomaniac authoress who persuades Mastroianni to write a book in her solitary refuge, but the entire episode was eliminated, being judged too similar to the Steiner episode. Other names mentioned for parts were Edwige Feuillere, Greer Garson, Peter Ustinov and Barbara Stanwick. Filming ended on 27 August, the result being 306,666 feet of film! The first copy, 18,333 feet long, was ready by November and thus began a long succession of private showings for critics and intellectuals. The first hints of controversy were already on the horizon.

1960—The final 16,666-foot-long version of *La Dolce Vita* went into general release in early February. Its success with the public went hand in hand with the growing controversy. When it opened in Milan the film was booed and hissed, and someone even spat at Fellini, who was in the audience. The most recurrent criticisms levelled at the film were "immorality" and a "delight in the indecent." First and foremost among the critics were the clergy and conservative thinkers, though

During the filming of La Dolce Vita: *last minute instructions for the "miracle."*

La Dolce Vita was immediately supported by the more "enlightened" priests. It was strongly attacked by the Catholic Church and frequently declared a source of scandal in Sunday sermons. The matter was even brought before Parliament by a group of MPs and senators, who demanded that the film be withdrawn from general release, but the government refused to take action. Undoubtedly, the avalanche of criticism contributed towards the film's immense success, but on the other hand it often hindered an unbiased analysis. Generally speaking, the accent seems to have been laid rather broadly on "a new type of language," "an important fresco," and adjectives such as "baroque." *La Dolce Vita* began to win national and international awards, including the prized Golden Palm at the Cannes Film Festival.

1961—By now Fellini was recognized as Italy's most famous film director. Reams of paper were filled about his films, which continued to bring crowds to theatres the world over. And he also had sufficient power to create (together with Rizzoli and with the invaluable help of Clemente Fracassi) his own production company: Federiz. While

Two moments during the filming of
La Dolce Vita.

awaiting for more important projects, Federico agreed to film an episode for Zavattini's *Boccaccio 70*, which ended up by including four of the ten sketches originally examined. "The Temptations of Dr. Antonio" was immediately interpreted as a transparent criticism of those who had so vigorously attacked *La Dolce Vita.*

1962—*Boccaccio 70* was presented at a gala performance in Milan on 22 February. It gained a warm but not overwhelming reception. In the meantime, Fellini had found his next big opportunity, *8½*. The project had already been sketched out in October 1960, but without a title, and a real title it was never to have! On the piece of paper where Fellini took notes, in the midst of the usual sketches of voluptuous females, was a large *8½*, indicating that this was Federico's "eighth and a half" film. The title stuck. Lead roles were to be played by Laurence Olivier and Charlie Chaplin "because it's going to be a funny film." By the autumn of 1961 preparations were well under way, and in December the leading role was finally offered to Marcello Mastroianni. In May 1962, following the customary hue and cry over the choice of the rest of the cast, filming began. By October, Fellini was ready to embark on the lengthy process of preparing the final copy.

1963—*8½* went into general release on 15 February, and was acclaimed a triumph by critics and public alike. For his tendency to recall his own life, Fellini was likened to some of the most important writers of the 20th century, especially James Joyce in *Ulysses,* but also Musil,

During the filming of La Dolce Vita *(above)
and* Boccaccio 70 *(below).*

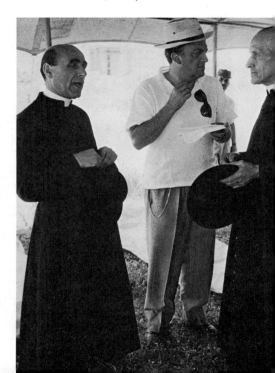

During the filming of 8½.
With Claudio Martufi and Claudia Cardinale.

Pirandello and even Kafka. Afraid that the public would not understand the film, the distributors initially released a certain number of copies in which the dream sequences were represented in sepia color, but the experiment met with disapproval. *8½* won several awards: an Oscar for the best foreign film, first prize at the Moscow Film Festival and seven *Nastri d'Argento* from the Italian Film Critics.

1964-1965—At the height of his success, Federico was hesitant over his next film. But by the close of 1964, the screenplay of *Juliet of the Spirits* was ready. It was to be his first feature film in color. Filming in the Cinecittà studios and the Fregene pine woods went on throughout the spring and summer of 1965. The film went into general release in September; it was praised for its formal values, but the critics were nonetheless puzzled, judging it to be a "baroque" and "feminine" version of the themes brought to the screen in *8½*. The film marked the end of Fellini's working partnership with his friends Tullio Pinelli and Ennio Flaiano. The name of Brunello Rondi also disappeared from the credits, to reappear with *Città delle Donne*.

1966—Fellini spent the entire year working on *Il Viaggio di Mastorna* for which, his partnership with Rizzoli broken and the Federiz company disbanded, he had again contacted De Laurentiis. Preparation of *Mastorna* was slow and in September was blocked completely due to

8½ *(above) and* Juliet of the Spirits *(below, with Sandra Milo).*

Terence Stamp in Toby Dammit.

a split with De Laurentiis. In December, the possibility of direct intervention on the part of the newly formed Italnoleggio relaunched the project.

1967—Discordant rumors continued to circulate on the fate of *Il Viaggio di Mastorna*. Fellini changed his mind about engaging Marcello Mastroianni as the lead actor, and the Americans consequently withdrew from the project. By February, De Laurentiis was back on the scene, trying to save a film that had already cost half a billion lire. For a while Laurence Olivier was considered for the part of Mastorna, then Ugo Tognazzi. But in April the film ran into trouble again when Fellini was rushed to the hospital with a rare and dangerous form of pleurisy. He passed the summer months convalescing in Marzana, using the time to dictate a book on his early life in Rimini (published by Cappelli) and thinking about future plans. *Il Viaggio di Mastorna* was abandoned.

The next proposal came from co-producers Raymond Eger and Alberto Grimaldi for an episode in a film based on the stories of Edgar Allan Poe. They had already approached a number of other internationally famous directors: Joseph Losey, Louis Malle, Orson Welles, Luchino Visconti. In his search for a story, Federico read a collection of short stories by Bernardino Zapponi, *Gobal*. He met and became friends with the author, and unsuccessfully tried to persuade his producers to accept one of the stories for filming. After this, he and Zapponi cooperated in the preparation of the screenplay for *Toby Dammit*, a liberal adaption of Poe's story "Never Bet the Devil Your Head." By September it was finished and they had to decide on the star. Fellini first offered the role to Peter O'Toole, who refused, and the choice finally came down to James Fox and Terence Stamp. Filming began in November with the latter of the two actors, and took 26 days to complete. Two days before filming was due to begin, De Laurentiis had telephoned Fellini asking him if he would direct *Waterloo.*

1968—While at work on the editing of *Toby Dammit,* Federico's thoughts went back to *Mastorna*, the debts of which had been covered by Grimaldi. Out came the old script and it really seemed as though all the obstacles of the past had been left behind once and for all. Re-reading the script after so long, Fellini made no secret of his newfound enthusiasm. He was sure it was the best script he had ever written, that it was by no means out of date, on the contrary, it was more up to date than ever before, and that it would be a film to outshine even the most suggestive of science-fiction films. But yet again it was cancelled, and back into the drawer went the unfortunate script.

Fellini next began to concentrate seriously on the possibility of a *Satyricon*. The idea of adapting Petronius's novel was by no means new to Fellini; he had first considered it back in his *Marc'Aurelio* days when, together with Marchesi and Brancacci, he had contemplated a musical version for Nanda Primavera and Aldo Fabrizi. Certainly, *Satyricon* appeared frequently in Fellini's projects after *I Vitelloni*, and it was no accident that it was a recurrent theme of *La Dolce Vita* reviews. But the subject now acquired a new significance for him, and during the summer months he and Zapponi worked on the screenplay; but before actually starting the filming, Fellini somehow had to rid himself of the "influence" of Mastorna. The opportunity came when he was asked to film a documentary for American television (NBC). The result was: "Fellini: A Director's Notebook" (September-October), built on the ruins of Mastorna and during the search for the cast of *Satyricon*. The editing of "A Director's Notebook" was still underway as the cameras started rolling at Cinecittà (9 November) on *Satyricon*.

1969—In April, "A Director's Notebook" was shown on American television and was a great success. On 23 May the final scenes of *Satyricon* were shot. Initially, Fellini had considered Terence Stamp and Pierre Clementi for the two leading roles of Encolpius and Ascyltus, but at the last minute he instead engaged two completely unknown actors: Martin Potter (Encolpius) who was British, and Hiram Keller (Ascyltus) an American. For the role of Trimalchio, Fellini, to the bitter disappointment of a host of actors who thought they had an undeniable right to the part, chose a famous Roman restaurant owner, known to everyone by the nickname "Il Moro."

At the Venice Film Festival the film was given a mixed reception. Some said it was Fellini's best film ever, while others were openly puzzled and disconcerted, failing perhaps to see in its dream-like sequences the pagan world of tradition. In one country, however, the film was an overwhelming success: Japan, where *Satyricon* remained in release for four years. Kurosawa who, during the filming of *Satyricon*, had been in touch with both Fellini and Bergman over a joint project for an episode-based film, sent a letter to Fellini expressing his total support of *Satyricon*.

1970—Following the success of "A Director's Notebook," Fellini began to receive other proposals for television work. With his customary verve, he examined several: a portrait of Mao Tse Tung, an American factory, the Pope, my town . . . the choice finally falling on "the clowns, the ambassadors of my profession." Co-produced by the Italian, French and German television networks, the film took the summer months to make and was shown on Italian screens on Christmas Day. During the course of the year, Fellini agreed to appear as himself in Paul Mazursky's film *Alex in Wonderland*, in which he has a brief conversation with the hero, a young American director (the film has evident

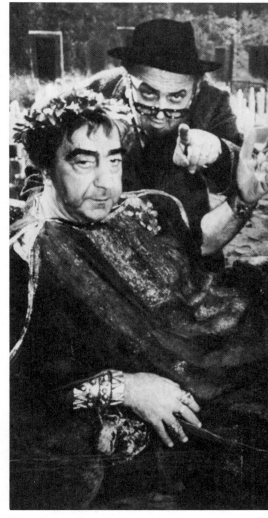

With "Il Moro," chosen for the part of Trimalchio in Satyricon.

autobiographic undertones) who is going through a difficult moment after a first successful film, and who is a fervent admirer of *8½*.

1971-1972—Fellini returned to the big screen and during the summer and autumn of 1971 was at work on the filming of *Roma*, which both renews the themes of *Moraldo in Città* and is a "syncretic portrait of all big cities, but which nonetheless has that undefinable quality, that certain mysterious something that makes Rome unique" (Fellini). Filming was accompanied by that atmosphere of curiosity and confusion that had become quite normal for Fellini's films. As a matter of fact, Fellini admits that he enjoys confusing the issue and insists that his work is always the result of total improvisation: "The dimensions have not yet been established and that is partly why I am obliged to film a bit at a time," but he seems quite happy with the conditions in which he works ("I am free of all restrictions. The only limit imposed on me is that of money. When all the money is gone, then the film is finished"). In March 1972, *Roma* was released to Italian cinemas, to be received by critics and audiences with the usual chorus of praise and reservation.

1973—This was the year of *Amarcord*. Fellini's account of his early days in Rimini, recreated entirely in the Cinecittà studio, was an enormous success everywhere. The film collected award after award and brought Fellini the fifth Oscar of his career. In Italy the film was released during the Christmas period, and magazines had a delightful time trying to relate the characters of the film to persons known to Fellini during his youth. He began to receive growing attention from critics the world over, and the international publishing world enthusiastically accepted

Under the "big top" of the Orfei Circus, for the filming of The Clowns.

proposals for monographs and essays dedicated to him.

1974-1975—During this period Fellini was less active. For months there was almost total silence from him, then in the spring of 1975, news began to leak out of *Casanova*. Fellini's remarks regarding his hero seemed to lay the accent on a sort of love-hate relationship. Anyway, it was the most expensive film of his career: eight million dollars, sixty sets, seven Cinecittà studios occupied by a troupe of 170 persons for 26 weeks. Filming was interrupted for two months, from December 1975 to March 1976, when producer Grimaldi declared that he had run into financial difficulty. The press even reported the theft of a number of reels of scenes just filmed. But Fellini tackled all the problems calmly: "I am the most economical, most rapid of directors, and I don't indulge in whims, but I have certain expressive necessities which I cannot ignore. If a painter needs a certain shade of red, he won't put up with just any red," said Fellini at the time. Regarding the theft of the reels, he remarked: "In their place I shall have an enormous placard appear on the screen, bearing the words: scenes stolen!" In November 1976 the cameras rolled to a halt and one month later *Casanova* was released to Italian cinemas.

Roma, *1972.*

1977-1978—Federico turned his thoughts to the story that was to become *La Città delle Donne*. By December 1978 it was practically ready, but while searching for a producer, Fellini returned to television and in no time at all completed *Prova d'Orchestra*. Fellini was both amused and puzzled by the violent reaction provoked in political and intellectual circles—and in the film world too—by what he referred to as "a simple and direct allegory" which has no hint of "intellectual

Amarcord, *1973.*

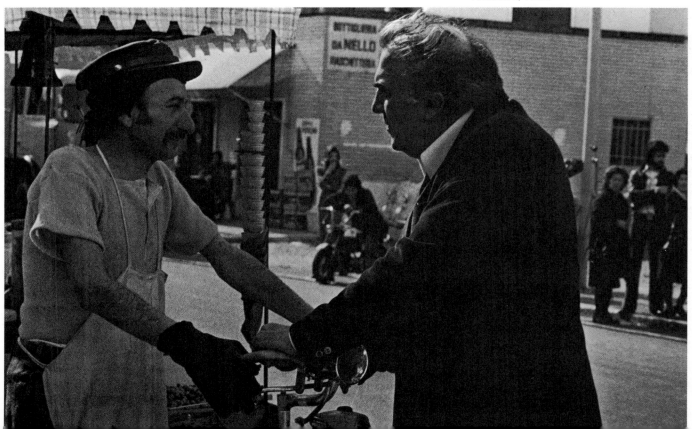

sophistry" but rather "the universality of a discussion of ideas which belong to all of us" (as he wrote in *La Republica*, 23 February 1979).

1979—In accordance with the production contract, *Prova d'Orchestra* was first released to the cinema and then shown on television. In the meantime, Fellini was at work on *La Città delle Donne*. But just before filming was about to begin, the sad death of Nino Rota, perhaps the most congenial and invaluable of Fellini's collaborators, occurred. Filming began in April, and was heavy going, hindered by all manner of unfortunate incidents; during the seventh week the actor Ettore Manni died. The producers forced Fellini to stop filming for a couple of months in order to reorganize his plans. By the end of October the team was back at work, and the last scene was shot on 29 November.

1980—Preceded by a vast number of previews and private showings, *La Città delle Donne* finally went into general release at the end of March, distributed by Gaumont. During the course of the year, Fellini accepted a proposal from the Einaudi publishing company to edit a selection of statements and interviews made during the course of his career. The book was entitled *Fare un Film (Making a Film)*.

1981—Fellini is currently preparing a film on the assassination of Francesco Ferdinand, Archduke of Austria, in Sarajevo, from a story written in collaboration with Tonino Guerra.

Other projects on Fellini's schedule include a series of stories on the Italian political and social situation to be shown on Italian television, and a series of stories based on Greek myths is being considered for CBS, in collaboration with Gaumont. Fellini has never directed either theatre or opera despite many proposals. There is, it seems, another project that is especially dear to him, but as usual he refuses to speak about it, yet.

This biography was edited and completed by Fellini himself. As the reader will have noticed, Fellini has included a number of episodes and particulars which have never before been published. We have altered none of the additions and corrections made by Fellini, even the most unexpected ones. As regards the cinema specifically, the director's contribution has brought to light his collaboration, of which no trace existed, in the writing of the screenplay for Mario Mattòli's *Imputato Alzatevi!* and in two other films: *Bentornato Signor Gai* (together with Pino Tellini) and *Sette Poveri in Automobile*, of which there was no mention in earlier records of Fellini's work. The former was never actually filmed, it seems, while the latter is probably *Cinque Poveri in Automobile*, directed in 1952 by Mario Mattòli. Nor was there any previous evidence of Fellini's collaboration in the screenplay of *I Predoni del Sahara*. Fellini points out that the title of the film, which was never completed, changed several times during filming, from *I Cavalieri del Deserto* to *Gli Ultimi Tuareg* and even *Le Avventure del Capitano Bottego*.

A.V.

Casanova, *1976*.

THE FILMS

VARIETY LIGHTS

LUCI DEL VARIETÀ   ITALY   1950

Produced by Federico Fellini and Alberto Lattuada for Capitolium Film. Directors: Federico Fellini and Alberto Lattuada. Screenplay: Federico Fellini, Ennio Flaiano, Alberto Lattuada, Tullio Pinelli, from a story by Federico Fellini. Photography: Otello Martelli. Camera operator: Luciano Trasatti. Music: Felice Lattuada. Art director: Aldo Buzzi. Costumes: Aldo Buzzi. Editor: Mario Bonotti. Assistant director: Angelo D'Alessandro. Production manager: Bianca Lattuada. Distribution in Italy: Fincine. Running time: 100 minutes.

CAST:

Carla del Poggio (Liliana "Lilly" Antonelli), Peppino De Filippo (Checco Dalmonte), Giulietta Masina (Melina Amour), Folco Lulli (Adelmo Conti, the lover), Franca Valeri (the Hungarian designer), Carlo Romano (Enzo La Rosa, the lawyer), John Kitzmuller (Johnny, the trumpet player), Silvio Bagolini (Bruno Antonini, the journalist), Dante Maggio (Remo, the comedian), Alberto Bonucci and Vittorio Caprioli (the duet), Giulio Cali (Edison Will, the swami), Checco Durante (theatre owner), Joe Fallotta (Bill), Giacomo Furia (Duke), Renato Malavasi (hotel-keeper), Fanny Marchiò (soubrette), Gina Mascetti (Valeria Del Sole), Vania Orico (gypsy singer), Enrico Piergentili (Melina's father), Marco Tulli (spectator), Alberto Lattuada (theatre attendant).

SYNOPSIS

Liliana is a pretty young girl from a provincial town who dreams of becoming a famous star of the theatre. She runs away from home and joins up with a group of variety show performers, led by the "international comedian," Checco Delmonte, and his fiancée, Melina Amour, who does impersonations. Checco soon falls under the spell of Liliana's innocent charm and decides to help her. That very same evening Liliana makes her debut in a small provincial theatre, receiving an enthusiastic response from the audience at the end of her number, during which she loses her skirt!

Some days later, Liliana and the rest of the performers are invited to the house of a wealthy lawyer, Enzo, who happens to have taken a liking to the girl. During the night, Enzo tries to enter Liliana's room, but he is stopped by Checco. A violent quarrel ensues and the performers are turned out of the house and forced to walk all the way back into town, where they finally arrive cold and tired.

Checco and Liliana decide to leave the company and set off for the big city, where they hope to

The players on their way to the party offered by the wealthy lawyer; they have that air of cynical and naïve indifference typical of the variety theatre world.

Together at the café (Dante Maggio, Carla Del Poggio, Peppino De Filippo, Giulietta Masina).

find something better. But because of Checco's jealousy, Liliana loses her only opportunity to join a real variety show.

Having borrowed money from Melina, Checco decides to form another, bigger company of his own, and so he begins to hire new acts (a black trumpet player, a Hungarian set designer, a target-shooter), but just before the opening performance, Liliana abandons the show to sign a contract with the same theatrical producer who had shown so much interest in her shapely legs before. While Liliana finally realizes her dream on the big stage, Checco, now penniless, returns to his old friends and to Melina, who has forgiven him. Into the third-class carriage in which the performers are travelling to their next engagement walks another pretty young girl. Checco raises his head from Melina's shoulder and adjusts his tie. The story is about to begin again.

NOTES

Fellini's debut in filmmaking has the same familiar, almost magical, quality that is the keynote of his entire public and private life. Fellini was already well-known as a screenwriter when Lattuada asked him to co-direct *Variety Lights.* Both Fellini's and Lat-

tuada's wives Giulietta Masina and Carla Del Poggio, had roles in the films (see Lattuada's comments in the Film Reviews). We cannot help wondering what Fellini must have felt, on the set for the first time, when Lattuada shouted, "Action." The adventure was about to begin. "Federico" disappeared, his place to be taken by "Mr. Fellini."

In the years and decades to come, bespectacled young intellectuals, journalists from all over the world, garrulous and implacable like Geraldine Chaplin in *Nashville,* were to bombard Fellini with questions such as: "What does the cinema mean to you?"; "How do you make cinema?"; "What do you think of the cinema?"; "Do you go to the cinema?" (The answer to the last question is simple; he never goes! But then with Fellini we are never quite sure if he is telling us the truth.) It all began on the set of *Variety Lights,* as in a dream without illusions and without a rude awakening, there among the rough Roman voices of the film crew; it must have been exciting and ironically amusing to see the words he had written suddenly come to life, generate movement, witty remarks; the actors really moved, the "takes" were real too.

At this point we are reminded of Fellini's comments in *Fare un film:* ". . . At the time I thought I was not cut out to be a director. I had no de-

sire to be a tyrant, I was not particularly persevering, or meticulous and lots of other things besides, but above all I lacked authority. Not one of the qualities I thought necessary is inherent in my nature. As a child I was introvert, sensitive, very vulnerable and a loner and, whatever people might think, I am still very shy. How could you possibly reconcile all this with the boots, megaphone and roaring voice that are the traditional weapons of the cinema? Directing a film is as hard a job as Christopher Columbus had in persuading his crew to go on. All around you are faces with the unspoken question: 'We're not going to work late again, are we?' If you don't show a bit of authority, they would good naturedly push you off the set." In a few well-chosen words, Fellini has summed up his relationship with the cinema and filmmaking. In Italy, that is. (It would be hard to imagine Fellini in the Hollywood of the 1950s, which probably differed little from the Hollywood of pre-war years, battling with American film crews accustomed to rigid discipline and an exacting timetable.)

Anyone who has actually seen Fellini at work on the set, will realize that his is a quiet, gentle authority, combined with a mildly dictatorial ability to handle technicians and actors alike (thought often they are not actors at all, but people picked out from the crowd because of some special physical attribute or expression). He imparts orders with the air of a reverend uncle giving Greek lessons, with philosophical grace but few illusions, to a slightly retarded nephew; or with the air of a benevolent curate at work in his studio, amidst old, familiar books, photographs of the seminary, yellowing prints, empty tobacco tins. This is how Fellini moves among his crew, chatting in that gentle yet slightly arrogant voice of his with its unmistakable "Romagnolo" accent, almost totally unchanged despite forty years of working with the rough Roman tongue. And so, with the confidence of an accountant dictating tax statements to his faithful secretary, in thirty years Fellini has obviously learned all there is to know.

Moreover, the fact that he had his

first experience with an established director like Lattuada (who had directed such films as *La danza delle Lancette,* together with Baffico, then alone: *Giacomo L'Idealista, La Freccia nel Fianco, Il Bandito, Il Delitto di Giovanni Episcopo, Senza Pietà, Il Mulino del Po;* he was a qualified architect, had founded, together with friends, the Milan Cineteca Italiana, and was also a good writer) gave Fellini's debut a rather special character. The dreamy, colloquial, baroque sensuality of the man from Romagna allies well with the apparently lucid and in reality explosively controlled sensuality of the man from Lombardy; both are meticulous, though this is disguised as improvisation with Fellini, while with Lattuada it is a a direct consequence of his technical and technological background.

The very theme of the film—a company of itinerant actors touring the variety theatres of provincial Italy—was something of a discovery for both, a pointer to the future. Through the years, Lattuada's heroines have become more and more like the potential stars of a variety theatre act—smooth-skinned, gently-curved young girls, provocative and sharp-witted at the same time. Fellini, too, never misses an opportunity to recapture the atmosphere of the music hall; for instance, the company in *Vitelloni,* with its homosexual comedian and jaded dancers; or the raucous variety theatre scene from *Roma,* which has become a classic of its kind. It all began with *Variety Lights.* The credits included names that were to be associated with Fellini's films for many years to come, and the cast surged with faces familiar at that time, even among the supporting players: John Kitzmuller, Dante Maggio, Caprioli and Bonucci, Calì, Bagnolini, Checco Durante, Fanny Marchiò.   ***(c.g.f.)***

Checco Dalmonte finds out just how embarrassing his young protégée's desire to enjoy herself can be.

REVIEWS

"Working with Fellini in the filming of Variety Lights *was without doubt one of the happiest periods of my life and career. We had been 'hatching' the film together for some time and we thoroughly enjoyed making it, although I must admit we were really rather irresponsible and went way over all the estimates. But it was our money, and we were using it to make a film we wanted to make, it also meant that we were able to avoid all the customary production problems. . . .*

Alberto Lattuada, BIANCO E NERO, Roma, XXII, 2–3 February-March 1961.

". . . Briefly, this is what happened. We were about to start making the film when I suddenly had the idea of forming what might be termed a sort of 'family' group. I engaged my wife Carla Del Poggio, Giulietta Masina, my father for the music score, my sister for production manager and I thought to myself: Now we have to face the distribution block, our best bet is to form a closely-knit group, plus a few other young people, so that we create a kind of avalanche and see

The embarrassing moment when the waiter comes to take Checco's order (Carla Del Poggio and Peppino De Filippo.)

if we can't break through some- how. So what happened? Some- where along the line, I said to Fel- lini, an extraordinarily talented young man who was my assistant director: 'As our wives are working side by side, and you are working so close to me, and as we've writ- ten two or three films together, why don't you sign as co-director?' And that was how his name appeared in the credits, after mine, though. . . ."

Alberto Lattuada (interview with Brunello Rondi), BIANCO E NERO, Roma, XXII, 6 June 1961.

". . . Developed from a story by Federico Fellini, Variety Lights takes its inspiration from the world of the variety theatre. With intelli- gence and just the right measure of bitter humor, the film shows us the true face of small-time vaude- ville, describing the daily heroics of its comedians, dancers, imperson- ators and all the other characters in some way involved in this type of entertainment. . . . Despite one or two rather slow-moving epi- sodes (for instance, the one in which Franca Valeri appears), the film in general moves at a com- fortable pace and in an atmosphere which is at the same time poignant and full of psychological under- tones. . . ."

t.c. (Tullio Cicciarelli), IL LAVORO NUOVO, Genoa, 7 December 1950.

". . . It is strange that this film, being directed by an accomplished scriptwriter (among other things, Fellini had worked on the screen- plays of Open City and Paisan), seems to lack a real script and gives the impression of having been put together on the spur of the moment the day before shoot- ing was about to begin. The story is disjointed and many of its epi- sodes appear lacking in substance. Some of them (such as the singer's fainting fit) are almost melodra- matic. But other sequences (the comedians' chomping jaws as they satiate their hunger at dinner; the man in the audience who catcalls the quick-change artist, but does not dare do it again when the actor appears as Garibaldi, because Garibaldi means something in a working-class environment) bear witness to an acute and lively imagination. The film is agreeable and amusing to watch, despite its disparity; what a pity that its char- acters have an all too familiar air of pathos about them, and that the least well-defined is indeed that of the heroine. . . .

Lan. (Arturo Lanocita), CORRIERE DELLA SERA, Milan, 13 January 1951.

"That Alberto Lattuada decided against a producer who could have financed the film, was the most im- portant factor in the making of Va- riety Lights (1950). Alberto Lattu- ada, story-writer and co-director Federico Fellini, directory of pho- tography Otello Martelli and lead actor Peppini De Filippo have pro- duced this film for themselves, creating a veritable cinema coop- erative. That the film is only partly successful, does not in any way detract from the importance of the initiative. Variety Lights' greatest fault is its persistence in trying to achieve a comical effect from the pathos centered on the character of Checco. . . . This does not mean that Peppino De Filippo is not up to his role, quite the opposite; but his Checco fails to produce that touch of humanity necessary to help us forget that he is really only a caricature. . . ."

m.c. (Carlo Marcello Rietmann), IL SECOLO XIX , Genoa, 8 December 1950.

". . . In this film Fellini . . . is bor- dering on pure symbolism. In other words, the travels of this group of itinerant actors, the portrayal of this type of "variety" entertainment, this sample of deformed humanity, the gloomy, provincial back- ground, so typical of Italy, have given Fellini the chance to create a series of vibrantly emblematic images; sometimes they develop into brief allegorical episodes which alone epitomize the deso- lation characteristic of Fellini's new-style cinema. For instance, the way in which the figures are ar- ranged on the stage, sometimes almost 'crucified' in the light, the importance given to the back- ground, the skill, mingled with a certain delight in the uncomely, with which the character of the soubrette is portrayed—those ges- tures and attitudes which go be- yond the grotesque to become al- most horrifying. Other gestures have a transcendental quality; for instance, the two dancers crossing themselves before they go on stage, while others, in direct con- trast are absurd; take, for example, the entire episode of the old fakir, with its grotesque and fabulous (in

Liliana has at last become a ''soubrette'': sparkling head-dress and a costume daringly scanty for those days (Carla Del Poggio).

the sense that it no longer belongs to reality) 'close-up' of the old man's mouth as he eats glass. . . ."

Brunello Rondi, Il Cinema di Fellini, Edizioni di BIANCO E NERO, *Rome, 1965.*

". . . In this film we find all the traditional myths of Fellini's work together with the basis for his future films: the loneliness of his characters and the absurdity of their situation are portrayed in an unusual setting, the main elements of which are a sense of the 'spectacle' and movement. The baroque quality becomes more evident in the suffocating and provocative atmosphere of the small provincial theatre where Clara [sic] performs her act. The episode in which the company is invited to the house of the lawyer who has taken a fancy to Clara [sic] has all the earmarks of the dance scenes from I Vitelloni and Il Bidone, and the wedding scene from La Strada.

"Also recognizable in later films is the way in which the dramatic element is built up here. The idea being to first dissolve the individual problem in the frenzied movement of the crowd, then to isolate it bit by bit so that in the end it has all of the inner loneliness it had before. This is a favorite technique of Fellini's. In Variety Lights we see the host, Clara [sic] and Peppino leave the crowd, thus focusing the drama more and more upon themselves; then the actors are turned out of the house after a violent quarrel and, as in other films, dawn finds them out in the open, tired and cold and with a renewed feeling of bitter loneliness. In this particular scene we already see imagination and reality opposed as in The White Sheik and later words. . . ."

Geneviève Agel, Les Chemins de Fellini, EDITIONS DU CERF, *Paris, 1965.*

THE WHITE SHEIK

LO SCEICCO BIANCO

Produced by Luigi Rovere for PDC-OFI. Director: Federico Fellini. Screenplay: Federico Fellini, Tullio Pinelli, Ennio Flaiano, from a story by Federico Fellini and Tullio Pinelli, based on an idea by Michealangelo Antonioni. Photography: Arturo Gallea. Camera operator: Antonio Belviso. Music: Nino Rota. Conductor: Fernando Previtali. Art Director: Raffaello Tolfo. Editor: Rolando Bebedetti. Assistant director: Stefano Ubezio. Sound: Armando Grilli, Walfredo Traversari. Makeup: Franco Titi. Continuity: Moraldo Rossi. Production manager: Enzo Provenzale. Production secretary: Renato Panetuzzi. Distribution in Italy: PDC. Running time: 85 minutes.

CAST

Alberto Sordi (Fernando Rivoli, ''The White Sheik''), Brunella Bovo (Wanda Cavalli), Leopoldo Trieste (Ivan Cavalli), Giulietta Masina (Cabiria), Lilia Landi (Felga), Ernesto Almirante (director of ''White Sheik'' strip), Fanny Marchiò (Marilena Vellardi), Gina Mascetti (''White Sheik's'' wife), Enzo Maggio (hotel concierge), Ettore M. Margadonna (Ivan's uncle), Jole Silvani, Anna Primula, Nino Billi, Armando Libianchi, Ugo Attanasio, Elettra Zago, Giulio Moreschi, Piero Antonucci, Aroldino the comedian, Giorgio Savioni, Antonio Acqua, Carlo Mazzoni, Rino Leandri, Guglielmo Leoncini.

SYNOPSIS

It is Holy Year, and two young newlyweds from a provincial town, Wanda and Ivan, are spending their honeymoon in Rome. They have a full program of sights to see, relatives to visit, monuments to admire. While Ivan, a typical petit bourgeois husband and the antithesis of spontaneity and emotion, is concerned only with his own conventional efficiency, Wanda embodies a rather naïve attempt to break out of the provincial form and her conventional marriage into a world of fantasy and illusion. She steals away from the hotel at the first opportunity to go in search of her hero, the White Sheik of a fotoromanzo. She first goes to the editorial office of Blue Romance, as the magazine is called, where she learns that the Sheik is "filming" on the beach at Fregene. Wanda, carried away by the lure of this romantic world, leaves Rome together with the troupe.

In the meantime, Ivan has realized that his bride is missing and goes looking for her all over the city. After a succession of ridiculous adventures, Wanda slowly begins to see that the true characters of her picture story, especially the Sheik, are very different from those of her dreams. Ivan meanwhile continues his search, having to invent all manner of excuses to hide his wife's disappearance from his relatives and to keep up appearances.

Wanda, bitterly disappointed by her adventure into this world of illusions, makes a feeble attempt to commit suicide by jumping into the Tiber, but the water level is sufficient only to dampen her spirits! She is saved and taken back to her hotel and her husband, but he defers all explanation until some other time as they have to rush off to St. Peter's Square, where the relatives are waiting to go with them to visit the Pope.

An Italy brought up on fumetti, *an Italy which became acquainted with the world of words and pictures through a sumptuous and shabby liturgy of incredible adventures, goes hand in hand in* The White Sheik *with a respectably conventional petit bourgeois Italy: above, Brunello Bovo gazes ecstatically at photographs of her "sheik."*

Alberto Sordi, in one of the first of his remarkable characterizations, battles with the tin-foil and papier mâché of his trade.

NOTES

Over the years, *The White Sheik* has become something of a minor cult film. It was received favorably, but not without a certain reserve, as the words of critic Arturo Lanocita show: "... a film full of comic moments, of an easy, slightly banal humor, but which is nonetheless only partly successful...; its main fault lies in its rhythm, which is singularly slow...." Four years later, Geneviève Agel wrote, with Gallic devotion: "... a lyrical poem about life. The height of baroque expression... it is without doubt Fellini's most *dégagé* film..."

In actual fact, it was the first time Fellini had made a film of his own; in it he describes something he knows in depth, just as he knows the variety theatre—that is to say, the world of the photo-novel or cartoon-romance, especially as it was in those days, before it became study material for university professors. All the problems involved in making a film had to be solved here once and for all. An account of the story behind the making of *The White Sheik* is given in the book *Fare un Film,* but I would just like to point out here that the film's origins stem from a screenplay proposed for Antonioni, who had just finished a documentary on *fumetti* entitled *L'Amorosa Menzogna.* As he discussed it with Pinelli, Fellini began to imagine the character of the young bride, the honeymoon, her escape into a world of illusions in search of her hero; gradually a story full of ironical humor, quite different from the original intention, began to take shape in his mind. Harried by a succession of complications, Fellini finally gave in to the urgings of producer Luigi Rovere and agreed to direct the film himself. As Fellini admits, the first day of filming seemed to embody all the catastrophic doubts I mentioned earlier in relation to *Variety Lights.*

The result was a film which provoked both perplexity and praise, but which had, to some extent, stepped out of line with current trends: too slow, too much talking, too much day-dreaming, too ironical, etc. Moreover, there was Sordi, who had yet to gain favor in the eyes of the public and the critics; Sordi, with his large pliable face, his troubled expression, his essentially Romanesque irony, the self-destructive vein evident in all his better-known characters. All these factors have helped to make *The White Sheik* a unique testimony to a past era, but it also anticipated the future: the score was by Nino Rota and one of the actors was Leopoldo Trieste, who was to become one of Fellini's closest friends. Trieste was at that time a promising young comedy writer who was just beginning to make a name for himself as a scriptwriter (*Preludio d'Amore, Gioventù Perduta, Il Cielo è Rosso,* etc.). The role of the young bridegroom, Ivan Cavalli, was to start him on a series of bizarre adventures as an actor, and which have shown him to be one of the most extraordinary character actors of Italian cinema.

(c.g.f.)

"The story of The White Sheik, *having first been considered as film material by Antonioni and Lattuada, finally, and rightly, ended up in the hands of Federico Fellini, who had originally devised the main threads. Fellini was undoubtedly the best qualified to make the film, and for two reasons: firstly, his experience as a gag writer, and consequently his familiarity with the secrets and intrigues of the world he was about to bring to the screen; secondly, his gift for sarcastic comment and delight in satirizing tradition.... "After seeing* The White Sheik, *it is more easy to recognize the part played by Fellini in* Variety Lights.... *The similarity between the two films is evident, both as regards the design of certain characters ... and certain elements of fantasy. For instance, the nocturnal sequence in* The White Sheik, *animated by the presence of the two picturesque peripatetics, is almost a repetition of the night scene in* Variety Lights, *which focuses on an assortment of wayfarers, and in particular on the black trumpet player. These almost too similar episodes take me to a very marked tendency in Fellini's work: his search for fantasy within the reality of everyday life.... But this is countered by another, more dominant, element in this film: the element of realistic farce which, in Fellini's work, has a startling clarity, a fervor rigidly controlled at all times by an undercurrent of truth. The result is unusual and stimulating, but derives more from the failure to establish a basic mood or tone, rather than from any direct intention. Fellini should find this tone in future works, if he is to avoid the discontinuity we find here....*

Giulio Cesare Castello, CINEMA V, 99-100, Milan, 15-31 December 1952.

"... This is a film full of comic moments of an easy, slightly banal humor, but which is nonetheless only partly successful, seeking effect in secondary themes rather than in the main design. The screenplay is excellent ... but the plot is weak. If Fellini's intention was to scrutinize the mind of a fanciful young girl, then he has done it superficially. This is why the most successful part of the film, or at least the most amusing, is the abandoned husband's anxiety and not the girl's disappearance.... As regards the film's structure, its main fault lies in its rhythm, which is singularly slow, as if the director had suddenly found himself in difficulty, or the actors even, who seem almost to have been left too much to their own devices...."

Arturo Lanocita, CORRIERE DELLA SERA, Milan, 7 September 1952.

"... The first part of the film, the part which, through a series of realistic sketches denoting sound directing technique, delight in detail and the ability to render it with maximum effect, creates the premise for the 'action,' is both agreeable and amusing.... Where the film falls down is when it tries to emphasize an episode or environment which is just not strong enough to keep afloat...."

Vice, IL LAVORO NUOVO, Genoa, 5 June 1953.

"The story of the film The White Sheik *might have happened like this. Federico Fellini, story-writer and director, had for some time been considering the strange and tragic adventure of a newlywed*

The "sheik's" wife shows the verbal and physical violence typical of the Roman woman of the Italian cinema of that period (Brunella Bovo, Alberto Sordi and Gina Mascetti).

A summer cocktail with the "sheik" (Alberto Sordi and Brunella Bovo).

couple on their honeymoon who become lost in their trifling dreams and provincial prejudices. The result could have been a vicious satire, and perhaps this was the author's original intention. Then, during filming, Fellini took pity on the sad characters he was portraying and began to feel excessive affection for them. Perhaps without realizing it, he began to express this newfound sentiment, dampening the action, softening images, prolonging shots until each character appears not only funny, ridiculous and stupid as before, but also very human, a creature in need of love. This, of course, is mere conjecture, but it does, I think, explain the "exasperating slowness" of which the critics spoke at the Venice Film Festival, in order to explain their summary and perhaps unjust remarks. . . .

"But there is considerable discord between the brutality of the subject matter and the loving kindness with which Fellini has brought it to the screen. This is why the dia-

logue sometimes seems to move more rapidly than the images, and why the spectator has the impression that beneath the visible surface there is a more caustic, more real, more vigorous story to be told. And this is why one of the best episodes of the film is Ivan's night encounter with the two prostitutes: compassion has its rightful place, it is the mainspring of the action, and not to be hidden, as it is elsewhere, under a patina of irony. But Fellini's real shortcoming, which nobody seems to have recognized, was to have shown too little faith in the power of the comical action—fast moving, decisive and violent—to express the tragical or pathetic side of life. But a film like The White Sheik cannot be dismissed so easily. . . . It is a good film, perhaps an excellent film, and in all events one to be 'understood.' And here we are back where we started, back to that the basic goodness of heart which is Fellini's special quality and which has slowed down the rhythm of his

story, but which is also the most significant of the film's positive features. This is best explained in one of the scenes, when Ivan, after several adventures, returns to his hotel, twenty-four hours after the disappearance of his bride. In the lobby is an unidentified woman, who is obviously a stranger to any feelings of sympathy or unselfish love. She does not utter a word, but the look she gives the unfortunate bridegroom is full of the affectionate understanding we so often find from the most unexpected sources during the course of our daily lives.

"In short, The White Sheik is a vein of sarcastic, but at the same time comforting, humor, flowing among the lies on which we live, the dreams we nurture and which are sometimes called 'fumetti,' the paradoxes life sometimes throws in our path, the characteristic military step of the Bersaglieri, the songs about Rome and the papal audiences. . . . "

Vittorio Bonicelli, TEMPO, Milan, 11 October 1952.

" . . . When discussing a favorite film, it is very difficult to separate the importance we afford to its supposed significance from the importance of the pleasure we receive from it. When, in Preston Sturge's Sullivan's Travels, the prisoners are seen to laugh, this was said by some to illustrate that comedy films were like a drug, designed to distract one's attention. I know for sure that Sturges merely wanted to show that laughter is the ultimate weapon of any slave, and that one will never be a total prisoner as long as one can laugh. In my opinion, The White Sheik, with its indefinable air of the burlesque and the horror it frequently evokes, should be interpreted in the same manner. The film's 'happy ending,' with the errant bride reunited with her family, the solemn march towards St. Peter's to receive the Pope's blessing, has two possible interpretations, but we would have to be quite insensitive to satire not to see the delightfully horrific reserve behind that march towards 'happiness.' I would not go so far as to say that the young Brunella Bovo, on the arm of her pensive husband, is going off to meet a new White Sheik, who will tell new and equally imaginative stories, in other words the Pope himself, although the rich humor of such an ending does not escape me. . . . "

Pierre Kast, CAHIERS DU CINÉMA, *53, Paris, December 1955.*

" . . . The White Sheik *is like a lyrical poem about life. The height of baroque expression, the action is rampant, the feeling one of confusion, with characters and situations pushed to the limit. It is without doubt Fellini's most dégagé film; this does not mean that it lacks depth, but its rapid action, its variegated plot, leave little room for immediate meditation. . . . The story is tragicomic, but the tragedy does not appear until after we have had time to enjoy the film's baroque qualities. . . . "*

Geneviève Agel, LES CHEMINS DE FELLINI, *Editions du Cerf, Paris, 1956.*

"The originality of expression in The White Sheik lies in a sense of

During filming, Fellini "invented" the character of a quaintly sweet, naïve, good-naturedly aggressive little prostitute, Cabiria, which seemed to be tailor-made for the actress (Giulietta Masina).

anxiety with no outlet, which is reflected in the 'malice' with which the camera films, here and there lingering ruthlessly to fix an impression in our minds, then soliciting, in satirical tones, certain gestures and actions from these simple characters as they struggle vainly to fulfill their provincial dreams. The story is about middle class people who cannot accept reality, and who instead follow the banal and empty myths of life with an almost touching enthusiasm: from the military band of the Bersaglieri—symbolizing the rhetoric of patriotism—to the world of the 'fumetti'; from the horse-drawn carriage ride through the streets of Rome, to the futile suicide attempt over a question of honor, to the long awaited Papal audience.

"Fellini gives Mr. and Mrs. Cavalli all they have ever dreamed of; but it is a diabolical present, a trap with a thousand enticing doors by which to enter, but no way out, and a trap that is inexorably sprung. The world of false myths brought to light expands out of all proportion, becoming in the end both paradox and paroxysm. The characters are too blind, too limited, to see that someone is pushing them, encouraging them to unmask themselves publicly. Someone who, thanks to a cruel, almost fairytale expedient, offers Wanda her Sheik, just as she had always imagined him in her dreams. She dances to the sentimental music of a popular song in the arms of a symbol dressed in hired costume. Someone who, on the edge of the pinewood bordering the Fregene beach, organizes a dance which, by way of a geometrical alternation of close-ups and long-shots, expressively illustrates the psychological harmony between the individuals and their environment. The wind mercilessly deranges everything in sight, almost stripping people of their clothes and heightening their ungainliness. An unnatural wind, that no weather forecast could possibly have anticipated, because it is the product of a story-book gimmick, the derisive yet amusing epitome of the general style of the film. Under pressure from all directions, newlyweds, relatives and actors alike are forced to reveal their innermost selves. They are stripped of their clothes and their appearances by an unknown personage. . . .

"According to the critics, The White Sheik is the most objective of all Fellini's films, the least tied to the poetry of retrospection, where the director has no relation to his film, nor does he identify with one of its characters. This observation is correct if referred to the flesh and blood characters moving visibly across the screen. But in The White Sheik, the main character never appears directly, but remains invisible, cynically weaving the threads of the story, creating biting undercurrents, intervening sarcastically to transfigure everyone way beyond any intentional attempt at realism, or any reasonable criticism of custom. . . . "

Lino Del Fra, BIANCO E NERO, XVIII, n. 6, June 1957.

The gawkishness of an entire generation obstinately loyal to its petty dreams and prejudices is summed up in the Cavallis (Brunella Bovo and Leopoldo Trieste).

Fanny Marchiò and Brunella Bovo.

I VITELLONI

I VITELLONI

ITALY/FRANCE   1953

Produced by Lorenzo Pegoraro for PEG Films (Rome) and Cité Films (Paris). Director: Federico Fellini. Screenplay: Federico Fellini, Ennio Flaiano, based on a story by Federico Fellini, Ennio Flaiano, from an idea by Tullio Pinelli. Photography: Otello Martelli, Luciano Trasatti, Carlo Carlini. Camera operators: Roberto Girardi, Franco Villa. Music: Nino Rota. Conductor: Franco Ferrara. Art director: Mario Chiari. Costumes: M. Marinari Bomarzi. Editor: Rolando Benedetti. Production manager: Luigi Giacosi. Production supervisor: Danilo Fallani. Production secretary: Ugo Benvenuti. Distribution in Italy: ENIC. Running time: 103 minutes.

CAST

Franco Interlenghi (Moraldo), Alberto Sordi (Alberto), Franco Fabrizi (Fausto), Leopoldo Trieste (Leopoldo), Riccardo Fellini (Riccardo), Eleonora Ruffo (Sandra), Jean Brochard (Fausto's father), Claude Farell (Alberto's sister), Carlo Romano (Michele, Fausto's employer), Lida Baarova (Giulia, Michele's wife), Enrico Viarisio and Paola Borboni (parents of Moraldo and Sandra), Arlette Sauvage (dark lady in theatre), Vira Silenti (Cinesina, Leopoldo's· date), Maja Nipora (soubrette), Achille Majeroni (comedian), Silvio Bagolini (the fool), Giovanna Galli, Franca Gandolfi, Gondrano Trucchi, Guido Martufi, Milvia Chianelli, Gustavo De Nardo, Graziella De Roc.

SYNOPSIS

The scene is a small provincial town on the Romagna coast. Summer is once again drawing to a close. A violent downpour interrupts the beauty pageant at which Riccardo has finally had the chance to try his talent as a singer.

In the hustle and bustle that follows, word gets out that Sandra, Moraldo's sister, is expecting Fausto's baby. The two families have no choice but to accept a forced marriage. The town falls back into the provincial monotony of the winter months.

Though they are no longer youths, Fausto's friends, supported by their families, spend their days doing nothing, passing from one café to another and playing the same childish pranks they have been playing for years. They are the "vitelloni," which in the slang of Rimini means overgrown adolescents. Alberto is the most pathetic, a weak, effeminate individual; Leopoldo is a would-be poet; while Riccardo is poorly developed and simply a very pleasant fellow with a melodious voice. The youngest and most sensitive of the group is Moraldo, who longs to find the courage to escape from this provincial boredom to the big city.

Fausto, "guide and spiritual leader" of the group, is back from his honeymoon, and is forced to take a job selling religious articles in the shop of a friend of his father-in-law's. Vain and superficial, he soon begins flirting with his employer's wife, but he is discovered and fired. Sandra runs away from home with the baby. Moraldo and Fausto are helped by their friends in their search for her. They finally find her in the house of Fausto's father, who gives his son a sound beating.

The "vitelloni" return to their customary life-style; Fausto continues to flirt with other girls, Leopoldo has a bitter experience with an aged homosexual actor, while Alberto, returning .home from a masked carnival ball, to which he has been dressed as a woman, finds that his sister is about to run away with a married man. Moraldo alone manages in the end to find the willpower to break away from his sordid past. He tells nobody, and as the train pulls away from the

The myth of the variety theatre, with its arrogant, naïvely aggressive dancers, its homosexual comedian, is one of the oldest most recurrent themes of Fellinian mythology (Maja Nipora, Franca Gandolfi and Achille Majeroni).

station bound for Rome, Moraldo, in his imagination, sees his old friends: they are all at home in bed, their attitudes in sleep clearly stating that for them nothing has changed, nor will it ever.

NOTES

With the title of this film Fellini invented (or rather made famous, which is virtually the same thing) a neologism that is still alive and used today. He again engaged Sordi, despite tough opposition. (Fellini recalls that when he finally managed to find a distributor, he was forced at first to omit Sordi's name from all advertisements: "It puts people off—they insisted—the public don't like him, he's 'antipatico'"). But above all, he finally showed himself to be what he really was, and still is: a master story-teller with a gift for ironical description.

The critics declared the film an intelligent second attempt by a young director with a bright future ahead of him, and Fellini himself an artist who stood out from the other young men of post-war Italian cinema; they spoke also of a further bizarre example of this young man's amused and caustic way of commenting on life. Despite the praise and applause *I Vitelloni* received at the Venice Film Festival, it seems that most people at the time failed to appreciate the film's true genius: the author's extraordinary ability, as he portrays this indolent and hollow provincial town, to harmonize the autobiographic vein underlying and linking each episode with a fundamental intention to create pure fiction. Moreover, the film was to have a lasting effect on several of the actors, Sordi first and foremost, while Franco Fabrizi drew from it a cliché he was to repeat constantly in the years to come.

Fellini's account of the difficulties he had to overcome in order to persuade the distributors to accept his film provides a worthy postscript to Moraldo's dreams: "Nobody wanted to distribute it"—he explains—"we went around almost begging them to take it on. Some of the showings we sat through were appalling. When the showings were over, people would avoid my gaze, while sympathetically shaking producer Pegoraro's hand, as if to comfort him after some terrible disaster." And yet after only a few years the film came to be considered as a minor classic. I remember just after the Cannes Film Festival in 1957 watching a showing of the film in a local cineclub. André Bazin gave a subtle illustration of the film, while the audience listened with the menacing diffidence typical of such occasions. Dubbed into French, *I Vitelloni* was immediately less effective, as are all dubbed films whatever their origin, but it was still an exceptional film. I

A grey and melancholy sea echoes the restless, idle loneliness of the vitelloni.

Alberto's carnival ball, a mixture of naïve and cunning surliness (Alberto Sordi). ➤

The traditional iconography of the middle-class wedding of the 1950s (left to right: Riccardo Fellini, Franco Interlenghi, Eleonora Ruffo, Leopoldo Trieste, Franco Fabrizi, Paola Borboni, Enrico Viarisio, Jean Brochard).

A meeting with the beautiful stranger "seduced" in the cinema, a typical vitellone *dream (Arlette Sauvage and Franco Fabrizi).*

realized then that after only a few years it was becoming a small myth, something to be revered, something that shed light on a certain part of Italian culture and who knows what else. Probably Cannes (at least in the 1950s) was just as full of *vitelloni*, bearing some similarity to Fellini's *vitelloni* of Romagna, despite their very different backgrounds. I do not remember if this was mentioned in the discussion that followed.

(c.g.f.)

REVIEWS

" . . . *A film of a certain importance. Above all because it has many intelligent moments; then because of its sound portrayal of provincial life; lastly because it is the second film of a young director who evidently has considerable talent. . . . The Italian film industry now has another director, and one who puts his own personal ideas before any of the customary traditions of the trade. . . . Fellini's is a fresh approach. It is much to his credit that his work is uncomplicated and original; he allows himself to be governed by his feelings and by sentiments trivial at first glance. In these moments he is a true artist, his work vibrant and full of meaning. . . . Some of the episodes are less successful . . . but this glimpse of life in a small, provincial, seaside town, from one summer season to the next, is in the main lively, well defined and enjoyable. Had the film succeeded in amalgamating the episodes into an organic whole, the result would have been unforgettable. As it stands, it is still one of the best Italian films of recent years, and makes us eager to savor Fellini's next creation.*"

m.g. (Mario Gromo), LA STAMPA, Turin, 9 October 1953.

" . . . *It is the atmosphere that counts most in this unusual film, an intensely human and poetical atmosphere, which is quite estranged from the provincialism of the setting. . . . It is quite beyond*

A lively family reunion for vitellone Moraldo (left to right, Eleonora Ruffo, Franco Fabrizi, Franco Interlenghi, Paola Borboni and Enrico Viarisio).

One of the classical shots from the film: the vitelloni in their pretentiously luxurious car (left to right: Franco Fabrizi, Alberto Sordi, half hidden, Leopoldo Trieste and Riccardo Fellini).

discussion that Fellini has something to say, and that he will say it with an acute sense of observation, and that here is someone quite apart from the other young directors of post-war Italian cinema. Fellini has a magical touch, and

has come very close to giving us a film which runs smoothly and surely from the first to last shot. . . ."

Francesco Càllari, GAZZETTA DEL LUNEDÌ, Genoa, 31 August 1953.

An unsuccessful attempt to sell the statue of the angel (Franco Fabrizi, Franco Interlenghi and Silvio Bagolini).

Moraldo and young Romagnol railwayman (Franco Interlenghi and Guido Martufi).

"... The applause received by I Vitelloni at the Venice Film Festival has determined the personal success of its young director, Federico Fellini, even before the film has had a chance to do so.... It should be recognized, however, that the route by which he has achieved this result was by no means an easy one. I Vitelloni does not have a particularly solid structure, the story is discontinuous, seeking unity through the complex symbiosis of episodes and details. ... The narrative, built up around strong emotions and powerful situations, lacks solid organic unity, and at times this undermines the story's creative force, resulting in an imbalance of tone and pace and a certain sense of tedium. But such shortcomings are amply atoned for by the film's sincerity and authenticity. Fellini has been accused of a reluctance to dramatize, but this seems to us a highly commendable quality, and an integral part of his personality as a writer and artist...."

Ermanno Contini, IL SECOLO XIX, *Genoa, 28 August 1953.*

"... I Vitelloni *is like a sketch, its outlines being suggested but not defined. Rather, Fellini defines an atmosphere. The film gives a graphic and authentic picture of certain aimless evenings, the streets populated by groups of idle youths, shouting, bothering the passers-by, sometimes showing themselves for what they really are: overgrown adolescents, sometimes pretending to be 'misunderstood.' The film is a series of annotations, hints, allusions, and it has no unity.... And even if we were not aware of his past activity ... it is obvious right from the opening shots that Fellini is a humorist. A melancholic humorist, however contradictory this may sound. He smiles, but bitterly. Clearly, the lazy, turbulent world he describes gives him the same unpleasant feeling that he transmits to us; a world of wasted time and wasted lives. He understands this world, and studies it. I would not say that he actually scoffs at it; in-*stead he pities it. With an ironical touch, he seeks to show the contrast between the way his characters see themselves and the way they really are. The film has certain weaknesses, however: some episodes are long-drawn-out, sometimes there are gaps in the action.... But whether or not the film appeals to a goût rafiné, whether or not the public like it, whether or not one or two episodes are to be judged of dubious taste (such as the one with the homosexual actor), it is still one of the best to come from Italy in recent years...."

Arturo Lanocita, CORRERE DELLA SERA, *Milan, 28 August 1953.*

"... After The White Sheik, I Vitelloni *confirms Fellini's talent for satiring culture and custom. First the world of fumetti and its fans, now the stagnant, mediocre provinces and the typical inhabitant: the idle youth with few standards and a lot of illusions, who lives off others, spends his time getting into trouble, and who talks about making a break, but would not know what to do if he made it, and in any case is too lazy to do anything about it....* I Vitelloni *is as interesting and enjoyable as* The White Sheik, *but it shows greater maturity of style and narrative, the harder to achieve the more the story is deliberately broken down into a series of psychological annotations and sensations, without a true structure, and with several topics to follow at the same time.... Strangely enough, the story writers..., believing it would give the narrative greater unity and substance, have resorted to elements typical of the serial, to expedients which seem hardly credible, and so forth.... I do not wish to seem pedantic over a film which, basically, I admire. But I think Fellini, who was a very attentive scriptwriter, should take care to avoid such errors. Perhaps, with this rather unusual and not very commercial film, he had to concede something to the producers, accustomed to dealing with more 'traditional' stories. Nonetheless,* I Vitelloni *proves that Fellini is the Italian film industry's most talented satirist, and an acute observer and psychologist of human behavior. Like any good moralist, he knows how to give his story a meaning, to provide more than just simple 'divertissement.'...*"

Giulio Cesare Castello, CINEMA VI, *116, Milan, 31 August 1953.*

The terrible distress of the ingenuous Sandra (Eleonora Ruffo).

" . . . By virtue of the quality of the narrative, and the balance and control of the film as a whole, I Vitelloni is neither commercial, nor does it have those provocative traits which normally permit a work of art to be consecrated and defined. With a surprising and effective sense of cinema, Fellini endows his characters with a life both simple and real. His caricatures could have been savage, instead they have a guileless charm. . . . "

André Martin, CAHIERS DU CINÉMA, 35, Paris, May 1954.

"A presumably irritating problem in post-war Italy—that of the lazy, parasitic sons of good middle-class families—is explored by Federico Fellini with a sense of its tragi-comic character. . . . If director Fellini makes it seem a little more urgent than it is, you may charge that off to his volatile disposition and a desire to make a stinging film.

"For he does certainly take a vigorous whiplash to the breed of over-grown and oversexed young men who hang around their local poolrooms and shun work as though it were a foul disease. He ridicules them with all the candor of his sharp neo-realist style, revealing their self-admiration to be sadly immature and absurd. And without going into reasons for the slack state of these young men, he indicates that they are piteous and merit some sympathy too.

"The weakness of this picture is that it reaches a weak, conventional end. The bawdy hero forsakes his infidelities when his wife runs away from him, and the philosophical brother pulls himself together and leaves town to find a job. It seems as though Signor Fellini simply got tired and called it off.

"But when the drama is spinning, it is lively and interesting, and everybody in it does a commendable job. . . . As usual, Signor Fellini uses music to comic and poignant effect. The dialogue that he and Ennio Flaiano have written is obviously more lively than the English subtitles that translate it."

Bosley Crowther, THE NEW YORK TIMES, October 24, 1956.

LOVE IN THE CITY

AMORE IN CITTÀ   ITALY   1953

Episode: *Agenzia Matrimoniale* (*A Matrimonial Agency*) produced by Cesare Zavattini, Renato Ghione, Marco Ferreri for Faro Films. Director: Federico Fellini. Screenplay: Federico Fellini, Tullio Pinelli, from a story by Federico Fellini. Photography: Gianni Di Venanzo. Music: Mario Nascimbene. Art Director: Gianni Polidori. Set decorator: Giovanni Checchi. Assistant director: Luigi Vanzi. Editor: Eraldo da Roma. Distribution in Italy: DCN. Running time: c. 20 minutes.

CAST

Antonio Cifariello (the journalist), and other non-professional actors.

Other episodes of the film are: *L'amore che Si Paga* by Carlo Lizzani, *Paradiso per Quattro Ore* by Dino Risi, *Tentato Suicidio* by Michelangelo Antonioni, *Storia di Caterina* by Francesco Maselli and Cesare Zavattini, *Gli Italiani Si Voltano* by Alberto Lattuada.

SYNOPSIS

A young journalist, by nature skeptical and indifferent, is engaged to carry out a survey on marriage agencies. In order to give his article more "spice," he pretends to be a client in search of a wife for a rich childhood friend who suffers from epileptic fits and has to live in the country because, on nights when there is a full moon, he turns into a werewolf. To the journalist's great surprise, the agency finds him a young girl, apparently willing to marry his friend. She is gentle natured, tender and innocent and in the end completely upsets the journalist's skeptical apathy.

NOTES

This is certainly one of Fellini's lesser known films, being as it is an episode in a collective work which, though of no little interest, circulated only briefly when it first came out; it now has the occasional showing on certain cable TV stations. The more reflective reviews (for instance Brunello Rondi's, in actual fact written some years later and therefore, possibly, from a different point of view to those appearing at the time of release) emphasize the irony with which Fellini, by no means a documentary film maker in the traditional sense of the word, has imbued his episode. Writes Rondi: "This colorless journalist. . . . is, in a way, a caricature of the documentary film maker. . . ." And when we look back at *L'Amore in Città,* and other "fragments" of Fellini's work, we cannot help thinking what a pity it is that he did not make more of them. Fellini is like an Elzevirian, driven by a vivid imagination to contemplating impossible projects. Just think, a career studded with innumerable sketches, each of which is by nature romantic. But Fellini almost achieves this with *La Dolce Vita.* However, more about that later.

(c.g.f.)

REVIEWS

". . . In the third episode of **Amore in Città***, Fellini examines the activities of a marriage agency; he paints a clear picture from a rather bitter story with a moral ending. . . ."*

t.c. (Tullio Cicciarelli), IL LAVORO NUOVO, *Genoa, 29 November 1953.*

" . . . Being a film comprised of different episodes, one is bound to make comparisons; personally, I preferred those by Fellini, Risi and Lattuada. . . . Fellini has applied moderation, Risi a lively wit, but the most amusing is the last one, by Lattuada. . . . "

Lan. (Arturo Lanocita), CORRIERE DELLA SERA, *Milan, 28 November 1953.*

"However much a film comprised of episodes might seem to indicate a lagging imagination on the part of the Italian film industry, this par-

Fellini is not particularly fond of making documentaries, preferring as he does to "manipulate" reality with his imagination. This particular effort was quite successful, however.

Writes Brunello Rondi: ".... Fellini secretly intended this episode to appear in contrast with the 'Zavattinian' tone of the rest of the film" (above and below, Antonio Cifariello).

ticular film does carry some signs of revival; shall we say it indicates tiredness rather than exhaustion, a momentary pause rather than chronic indolence. In Agenzia Matrimoniale we have the impression that the episode really occurred, but how remote are Fellini's 'reality' and 'realism.' He never remains within the situation he is describing, but always seems to be running ahead of it, abnormally. Agenzia Matrimoniale is an exaggeration, aimed to surprise.... The hyperbole is used to shock and to release violent feelings."

Saverio Vòllaro, RASSEGNA DEL FILM III, *20, Turin, January-May 1954.*

"... Of the two episodes (the other is Storia di Caterina) Fellini's Agenzia Matrimoniale is the most successful: it opens on an amusing note, moves swiftly, and gradually becomes pathetic, but as to whether it probes as deeply as producer Zavattini would have liked is a question for debate. Fellini relates that the adventure he describes here actually happened to him, during the research on the film. I do not doubt it, but the tone of the narrative is fanciful (in the best and most realistic sense of the word), and underlying it is a creative process through which the raw material of the subject is 'refined,' becoming in the end pure fantasy. And this is confirmed by the fact that the actors are not actually the people who experienced the adventure.... "

Giulio Cesare Castello, CINEMA VI, *123, Milan, 15 December 1953.*

"... It is clear that Fellini secretly intended this episode to appear in contrast with the 'Zavattinian' tone of the rest of the film. This colorless, in truth rather foolish young man, who goes around profaning reality is, in a way, a caricature of the documentary film maker.... The reality and the human dimension of the situation are so great that in the end the hero is swept away by them. "

Brunello Rondi, IL CINEMA DI FELLINI, *Edizioni di Bianco e Nero, Rome, 1965, pages 126-127.*

LA STRADA

LA STRADA — ITALY 1954

Produced by Carlo Ponti and Dino De Laurentiis. Director: Federico Fellini. Screenplay: Federico Fellini, Tullio Pinelli, Ennio Flaiano, from a story by Federico Fellini and Tullio Pinelli. Dialogue: Ennio Flaiano. Photography: Otello Martelli. Camera Operator: Roberto Girardi. Music: Nino Rota. Conductor: Franco Ferraro. Art Director: Mario Ravasco. Costumes: Margherita Marinari. Editor: Leo Catozzo. Assistant editor: Lina Caterini. Sound: A. Calpini. Assistant directors: Moraldo Rossi, Paolo Nuzzi. Makeup: Erigio Trani. Continuity: Narciso Vicari. Production manager: Luigi Giacosi. Distribution in Italy: Paramount. Running time: 94 minutes.

CAST

Giulietta Masina *(Gelsomina Di Costanzo)*, Anthony Quinn *(Zampanò)*, Richard Basehart *(il Matto)*, Aldo Silvani *(the circus owner)*, Marcella Rovere *(the widow)*, Livia Venturini *(the nun)*, Mario Passante, Yami Kamedeva, Anna Primula.

SYNOPSIS

Zampanò the gypsy, a primitive and violent man by nature, journeys from town to town doing his sword-swallowing, strongman, fire-eating act in local piazze and country fairs. In one village he meets a poor peasant woman burdened by too many children. For ten thousand lire he buys from her the naïve, ignorant but sensitive Gelsomina to help him in his act. Gelsomina becomes his mistress, but to Zampanò she is just another of his objects. He ill-treats her, is unfaithful to her, but when she tries to run away, he immediately goes after her. They then join up with an equestrian circus where they meet il Matto (the Fool), an itinerant tightrope-walker. Gelsomina is fascinated by his kindness, and this irks Zampanò. In the end the two men come to blows and il Matto is killed. Zampanò probably did not mean to kill him, but in any case he throws the body under a train. The incident seems to drive Gelsomina out of her senses; day and night she is haunted by the sight of the dying man. At last, fed up with Gelsomina and her moody silence, Zampanò sneaks away from his sleeping companion. He continues his vagrant life, living in fear of being arrested for il Matto's death. Some years later, he learns by chance of Gelsomina's death. As he stands before the sea, he suddenly becomes aware of his desperate loneliness and bursts into uncontrollable tears.

NOTES

Without doubt, *La Strada* was the film which finally established Fellini's name abroad. Parisians even queued up to see *Là Stradà* (to make it sound more French!). It provoked such adjectives as: "poetical," "typically Italian," "fantastic," "irrational" and "moving," as is to be expected of any worthwhile Italian product. The making of the film is every bit as interesting as the finished work (it seems to me that this is always the case with Fellini, especially as it is Fellini himself who relates these behind-the-scenes adventures; it is like listening to a third film, with its own dialogue and drama, stubborn producers, feeble-minded distributors, and a host of secondary, but nonetheless exciting circumstances). It is described by Fellini in the following terms:

" . . . In the beginning the film was just a confused sensation, a note of music suspended in the air which gave me a feeling of indefinable melancholy, a pervasive sense of guilt hanging over me like a shadow; it was vague and consuming at the same time, full of memories and omens. The feeling persistently suggested two people on a journey, two people thrown together by destiny without

The clown, a typical Fellinian myth, already peers out from behind Zampanò's crude mask (Giulietta Masina and Anthony Quinn).

The duo in the making: Zampanò explains the secrets of the art of trumpet playing (Anthony Quinn and Giulietta Masina).

knowing why. The story began to fall into place without difficulty—the characters came to life spontaneously, suggesting others as they did so, almost as though the film had been ready for some time and had been waiting for someone to find it.

"How *did* I find it? In the first place I think it was Giulietta. I had been thinking of creating a film for her for some time. She seemed to me to be an actress born to express the astonishment, dismay, frenzied gaiety and comical gloom of a clown. . . . And that was how I imagined Gelsomina, a clown, and beside her, in contrast, a dark, towering shadow, Zampanò. Then of course, the road, the circus with its confusion of colors, its heartrending music and fairy tale atmosphere. . . . When I approached Pinelli with a still rather vague outline of the film, he went blank with astonishment. Having regained his composure, he told me that during his summer holidays, while out riding on his estate in the Tuscan countryside, he too had built up a story around a group of wanderers, travelling the dusty roads from one village to another; a picturesque tale of gypsies and itinerant acrobats. We talked excitedly for the entire afternoon. It was as though Gelsomina and Zampanò were telling us the saga of their wanderings, their lives and the people they had encountered along the way."

This clearly implies that the film is essentially a gigantic, organized reverie with its own natural poetry evoked by the dusty road, the big top standing alone in the menacingly still countryside. It is the picaresque side of Fellini which finds full scope for expression here. And it is precisely this element which captivated the French critics and audiences most of all. Take, for instance, the words of Dominique Aubier: "A film like *La Strada* belongs to the mythological class, a class intended to captivate the critics rather more perhaps than the general public. . . . To create such a film, the author must have had, not only a considerable gift for expression, but also a deep understanding of certain spiritual problems. . . . The film in fact deals with the sacred, by this I do not mean the religious or to do with religion. . . ."

The strongman: teeth of granite, bare chest, leather belt studded with tin bosses . . . (Anthony Quinn). (Below) The wandering players chat inside the Big Top: puzzled but poetical (Richard Basehart, Aldo Silvani and Anthony Quinn).

And so the ironic, fervid, dreamy, sardonic Federico became known in Italy, and above all abroad, for his magical evocations of the splendid and ferocious naïveté of peasant life. And in a country like France, where the poetry of the *gens de voyage* has always been revered, *La Strada* could not but cause a sensation.

(c.g.f.)

REVIEWS

" . . . Fellini's latest film has the air of an unfinished poem, but one deliberately unfinished for fear that its essence be lost in the callousness of critical definition, or in the ambiguity of classification. La Strada cannot be classified, nor does it sustain the weight of rational discussion and comparison (when the film was shown at the Venice Film Festival, many critics saw in it suggestions of Chaplin); the film should either be accepted as it is, with its strange fragility and certain rather too colorful, almost artificial moments, or totally rejected. If we try to analyze Fellini's film, its fragmentary quality becomes immediately evident, and we are obliged to treat each fragment, each personal comment, each secret confession separate-

ly . . . . One fact remains, however, La Strada is the fruit of some rare emotion, perhaps dangerous for Fellini even, so distant is it from The White Sheik and I Vitelloni. La Strada is pure poetry. . . ."

Tullio Cicciarelli, IL LAVORO NUOVO, Genoa, 2 October 1954.

" . . . After an excellent beginning, the style of the film remains harmonious for some time, up until the moment when the two main characters are separated for the first time, at which point the tone becomes increasingly artificial and literary, the pace increasingly fragmentary and incoherent. According to the author, the two main characters' utter failure to communicate is accentuated, on the road, by the absolute predominance of madness, violence and bestiality. The first part of the film is pervaded by this atmosphere of desperate pessimism, punctuated by moments of deep emotion, and an absolute purity of style. The characters are instilled with a profound humanity while the story, unfolding in a climate of suffering, is allusive, lyrical and narrated at a well-controlled pace. . . .

"Unfortunately, the film fails to maintain this level, becoming

A film created for the dreamy simplicity of Gelsomina (Giulietta Masina).

gradually more artificial and literary, while the narrative loses its former dramatic key, becoming sketchy with a certain taste for the anecdote. The rhythm becomes fragmentary, the film in general tedious . . . , superficial and didactic . . . , in vain it seeks to draw from external elements the dramatic quality which should instead spring from the essence of its characters. . . . "

Nino Ghelli, BIANCO E NERO XV, 8, Rome, August 1954.

" . . . La Strada is a surprising and mysterious film; the spectator is both subdued and disturbed by it, although he finds it hard to understand just why this should be, especially where Fellini has created his story more with the force of sentiment than with the clarity of the intellect. He conceived Gelsomina a long time ago, before The White Sheik, before I Vitelloni, and he gradually began to unravel her story with the clairvoyant licence of a fanatic. Fellini has not, I think, managed to tell us everything about Gelsomina, but this reticence has something noble about it, and this we realize and respect. However, Gelsomina is the only character who seems vaguely un-

The brutality of Zampanò and the gentle, childish sweetness of Gelsomina (Anthony Quinn and Giulietta Masina).

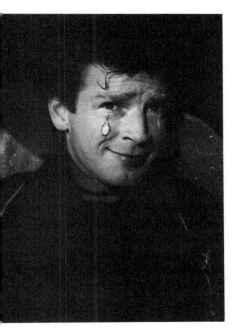

A tear on a cheek: painted onto the face of ''Il Matto,'' it recalls the very character of the film, a mixture of realistic observation and fairy-tale invention (Richard Basehart).

real. Zampanò is one of the most powerful, solid and dramatic heroes of contemporary cinema. The style is one of the purest and most lucid of neo-realism (the characters are light, intense and warm, and they are quickly defined in scenes such as the wedding breakfast, or when Gelsomina is led off by the host of children to visit the sick boy). I think it unjust to say that Fellini has created a film about escape from reality. We would do better to examine Fellini's nature, his love of the extremely 'innocent' being, in a Dostoevskian sense. . . . "

Vittorio Bonicelli, TEMPO; Milan, 7 October 1954.

" . . . Fellini is a master story-teller; the narrative of this film is light and harmonious, drawing its essence, resilience, uniformity and purpose from small details, subtle annotations and soft tones which slip naturally into the humble plot of a story apparently void of action. But how much meaning, how much ferment enrich this apparent simplicity! It is all there, though not always clearly evident, not always interpreted with full poetical and human eloquence; but it is suggested with considerable delicacy

and sustained by a subtle emotive force. . . . "

Ermanno Contini, IL SECOLO XIX, Genoa, 8 September 1954.

" . . . La Strada gives the impression of being a rough copy which merely hints at the main points of the story. . . . Fellini has been sincerely, tenderly affectionate with Zampanò and Gelsomina, but by his refusal to compromise, he has perhaps enveloped his elegy in a kind of grey obscurity, so that the force of each episode is dimmed, the characters hard to distinguish. . . . Fellini seems to have preferred shadow where marked contrast would have been more effective. The story is romantically picturesque, and does, in fact, contain the elements of a strongly colorful saga; but Fellini has avoided them. . . . "

Arturo Lanocita, CORRIERE DELLA SERA, Milan, 8 September 1954.

"A film like La Strada belongs to the mythological class, a class intended to captivate the critics rather more perhaps than the general public. Federico Fellini attains a summit rarely reached by other film directors: style at the service of the artist's mythological universe. This example once more proves that the cinema has less need of technicians—there are too many already—than of creative intelligence. . . . To create such a film, the author must have had, not only a considerable gift for expression, but also a deep understanding of certain spiritual problems.

"The film in fact deals with the sacred; by this I do not mean the religious or to do with religion. I mean that primitive need specific to man which pushes us into metaphysical activities, whether in the form of religion or in the form of art. And Fellini shows us this in its pure state in Gelsomina. In one of the first scenes of the film, Gelsomina has two faces, one sad, one happy, the latter she turns towards the sea with a solitary, irreproachable smile of satisfaction. 'I like being an artist!' she declares shortly after. According to Nietzsche, art is the only metaphysical activity of this world. And this seems to be Fellini's view too, whether he is aware of it or not.

"Not that this is surprising. Mediterranean tradition has never forgotten the ancient discovery made by the Greeks. Music, song, poetry have always been revered by this small pagan world which sleeps

The poetry of the gens de voyage and of the terrain vague: no wonder the film caused a sensation in France (Giulietta Masina and Anthony Quinn).

peacefully beneath the massive ornaments of the Faith. And Fellini is Italian. Even Saint Francis was surrounded by pagan beliefs. Centuries of spiritual activity, despite the social changes that have taken place, continue to inspire mankind. Fellini shows that this is true of even the poorest, most frustrated of creatures, notwithstanding the highly organized world in which they live. Cervantes too realized that the most metaphysical human beings are the starving. Today, art corresponds and responds better to this psychological need of human nature. Fellini's passion is centered round the circus and music, as an analysis of the story clearly illustrates. . . ."

Dominique Aubier, CAHIERS DU CINÉMA, *49, Paris, July 1955.*

Signor Fellini has not handled his story in merely tragic or heavily dramatic fashion. In Giulietta Masina (Mrs. Fellini in private life) he has an extremely versatile performer who mirrors the simple passions and anxieties of the childlike girl with rare and acute perception. She is expert at pantomime, funny as the tow-headed, doe-eyed and trusting foil and sentient enough to portray in wordless tension her fear of the man she basically loves. Anthony Quinn is excellent as the growling, monosyllabic and apparently ruthless strong man, whose tastes are primitive and immediate. But his characterization is sensitively developed so that his innate loneliness shows through the chinks of his rough exterior. . . . Signor Fellini has used his small cast, and, equally importantly, his camera, with the unmistakable touch of an artist. His vignettes fill his movie with beauty, sadness, humor and understanding."

A.H. Weiler, THE NEW YORK TIMES, *July 17, 1956.*

"The Theme of Federico Fellini's spiritual fable is that everyone has a purpose in the universe. It is acted out by three symbolic characters. . . . Though the background of the film is neo-realist poverty, it is transformed by the romanticism of the conception. [Masina's] performance has been compared variously to Chaplin, Harry Langdon, Stan Laurel, Barrault and Marceau, and the comparisons are just— maybe too just. Basehart's performance of the fool, which is not like the work of other performers, is possibly more exciting. Even if one rejects the concepts of this movie, its mood and the details of scenes stay with one; a year or two later, a gesture or a situation suddenly brings it all back."

Pauline Kael, 5001 NIGHTS AT THE MOVIES, *Holt, Rinehart and Winston, 1982.*

IL BIDONE

IL BIDONE

Produced for Titanus (Rome)/SGC (Paris). Director: Federico Fellini. Screenplay: Federico Fellini, Ennio Flaiano, Tullio Pinelli, from an idea by Federico Fellini. Photography: Otello Martelli. Camera operator: Roberto Gerardi. Assistant camera operator: Arturo Zavattini. Music: Nino Rota. Conductor: Franco Ferrara. Art direction and costumes: Dario Cecchi. Editor: Mario Serandrei, Giuseppe Vari. Sound: Giovanni Rossi. Assistant directors: Moraldo Rossi, Narciso Vicario, Dominique Delouche, Paolo Nuzzi. Artistic collaboration: Brunello Rondi. Makeup: Eligio Trani. Continuity: Nada Delle Piane. Wigs: Fiamma Rocchetti. Set decorator: Massimiliano Capriccioli. Production manager: Giuseppe Colizzi. Production supervisor: Antonio Negri. Production secretary: Manolo Bolognini. Administration secretary: Ezio Rodi. Distribution in Italy: Titanus. Running time: 104 minutes.

CAST

Broderick Crawford (Augusto), Richard Basehart (Picasso), Franco Fabrizi (Roberto), Giulietta Masina (Iris), Giacomo Gabrielli (Baron Vargas), Alberto De Amicis (Rinaldo), Sue Ellen Blake (Susanna), Lorella De Luca (Patrizia), Mara Werlen (la danseuse), Irene Cefaro (Marisa, the girl at Rinaldo's party), Xenia Walderi, Mario Passante, Riccardo Garrone, Paul Grenter, Emilio Manfredi, Lucetta Muratori, Sara Simoni, Maria Zanoli, Ettore Bevilacqua, Ada Colangeli, Amedeo Trilli, Tiziano Cortini, Gino Buzzanca, Rosanna Fabrizi, Barbara Varenna, Yami Kamedeva, Gustavo De Nardo, Gianna Corbelli, Tullio Tomadoni, Grazia Carini, Giuliana Manoni.

Broderick Crawford is dubbed by Arnoldo Foà, Richard Basehart by Enrico Maria Salerno.

SYNOPSIS

Augusto, Picasso and Roberto are three specialists in the art of swindling. Dressed as priests, they extort money from simple, gullible peasants under the pretext of saying mass for the souls of their dead relatives. For their second swindle they go to take the census of a shantytown posing as housing commissioners. Then they trick petrol pump attendants by selling them patched-up overcoats for new. They meet up again at a New Year's Eve party during which Iris, Picasso's wife, discovers the truth about her husband.

One day Augusto, walking through the streets of Rome, bumps unexpectedly into his daughter, Patrizia. She is now a university student with a promising, honest future ahead of her. His fatherly love is reawakened. He takes her to lunch and then to the cinema, but here he is unfortunately recognized by a former accomplice he once swindled. He is arrested.

On leaving prison, he joins up again with his old gang and they try the priest swindle in another area. But when Augusto, disguised as a priest, is called upon to comfort a young crippled girl about the same age as his daughter, he is filled with remorse and would like to give back the money he has extorted from the girl's poor parents. But his companions are not of the same opinion, and they come to blows. As he tries to escape, Augusto falls into a ravine and breaks his spine. His companions take the money and leave him to his fate. Augusto comes to know a whole desert of suffering, solitude, hunger and thirst before he realizes the full measure of his spiritual waste-

The cheap enjoyment of the bidonisti *(Richard Basehart, Franco Fabrizi, Broderick Crawford).*

land and finally dies a lonely death.

NOTES

This film is admirably summed up in the words of Pietro Bianchi: " . . . it is a cocktail of ribald gaiety worthy of *Satyricon* and of the desperation and bitterness expressed so well in the unforgettable Zampanò." While Vittorio Bonicelli, one of the most important film critics of the 1950s, notes with considerable insight that the film "goes one step further" in comparison with *La Strada*. In fact, there remains little of that literary indulgence characteristic of the earlier film, yet the "tragedy of human loneliness . . . is carried to its extreme consequence." Even François Truffaut who, during his youth and before he became a director (which he dreamed of becoming, and was therefore impatient and severe in his judgment) was a highly controversial person, admits that "he could have watched Broderick Crawford die for hours." In my opinion, *Il Bidone* is one of the most fascinating, most complex, most underestimated and most skillfully derisive of Fellini's early works.

The film is a portrait of three petty criminals, fundamentally non-violent because they lack the courage to be so, three shabby, sly *bidonisti*. Fellini is less baroque here, but he confirms his talent for observing minute detail, for portraying the more insignificant characters of this world, the outsiders, whose story is interesting nevertheless because it is unorthodox.

Fellini's swindlers are like *vitelloni* of petty crime, overgrown adolescents who dream of bringing off the really big "job." They are small-time criminals who are at the same time cruel and cowardly, predator and clown, with a depraved touch of artistic genius shown in their use of makeup, masquerade and disguise. Angelo Solmi, in his *Storia di Federico Fellini* (Milan, Rizzoli, 1962), divulges that Fellini first began to work on the story in 1954, following the success of *La Strada*, when everyone was pressing him for a sequel, such as the *Return of Gelsomina*. The question of "the sequel" has always been a typical Fellini problem, but

then it has been a problem for authors the world over. There were people who would like to have seen a sequel to *I Vitelloni*; indeed, was not the famous *Moraldo in Città*, rarely far from Fellini's mind but never actually brought to the screen, a continuation of the adventures of *vitellone* Moraldo?

While filming *La Strada*, Fellini had been able to observe the tortured, semi-legal, sometimes overtly illegal, world of people "of the road," which was never far from the world of swindlers and braggarts.

One evening, at a restaurant in Ovindoli, a two-bit hawker had told Fellini his life story. Slowly, the idea began to form in Fellini's mind of a film about a group of such characters, criminal *vitelloni*, starring Sordi, Fabrizi and Peppino De Filippo. (Looking back on it, it could have been a great film, a sort of Italian-style comedy à la Fellini.) But as more and more *bidonisti* were found and interviewed, it became clear that theirs was a seamy, cruel, ruthless world, populated by callous go-getters who were not content to trifle with crime, but aimed for the "big time," and to

The simple, naïve country folk and the greedy, cunning bidonisti, *in a typical scene from the film, which marvellously shows Fellini's special talent for ruthless irony (Richard Basehart, Franco Fabrizi, Broderick Crawford).*

get it were prepared to fight among themselves "to the death." In the end Fellini decided to build his story around one main *bidonista*, flanked by two minor characters, and to follow him through his sordid adventures to his inevitable decline and death. For this role, Fellini had first thought of Bogart, then of Fresnay. In the end he had to "make do" with Broderick Crawford, who was apparently unknown to Fellini at that time, despite the fame he had already acquired as star of Robert Rossen's *All the King's Men*.

Still today, this seems to me an exceptionally lucky choice. Crawford endowed the film not only with that mark of professionalism typical of American cinema, but also an astute cynicism, a disenchanted cunning, which make Augusto a cruelly pathetic character.

And I think that Gilbert Salachas is right when he says that fundamentally Zampanò is one of Augusto's ancestors, "an ancestor from the stone age" to be precise, and that "in appearances more dignified, Augusto is born of the same obscurity." The merit is mostly Fellini's, for he has managed to create around Augusto a world of petty swindling and fraud which, however base, is not completely without "poetry" (for example, Augusto's classical swindle where he is dressed as a priest, and which finally brings about his downfall). But some of the merit must go to the actor who, though working in an environment quite different from that of Hollywood, still manages to give a fine performance. This has not always been the case, especially in the past, when an American actor has had to work in the more fragile, more "artificial" world of European cinema.

(c.g.f.)

Picasso's trusting wife and the jaded cynicism of Augusto (Giulietta Masina and Broderick Crawford).

REVIEWS

" . . . *However we might wish to judge this film, it undeniably represents a step forward in Fellini's career, and a necessary step at that. As regards style, there is little trace of the literary clichés characteristic of* La Strada. . . . *As regards subject matter, the problem of human loneliness, which has always obsessed Fellini, is taken here to its extreme and at the same time most natural consequences; the swindler's crime without passion ends in emptiness, in obscurity. . . .* "

Vittorio Bonicelli, TEMPO, *Milan, 15 October 1955.*

" . . . *We have the feeling here that Fellini had little faith in the ability of his audience to understand and assimilate his work. His insistence on certain scenes shows that he was afraid of not having explained himself clearly, and this has led to persistent, rather irksome, repeti-* *tion. The remedy is simple: some cuts should be made (as in fact they were after the film had been shown in Venice and before it went into general release). Less easy to remedy are certain other qualities of the film which seem to denote flagging imagination on the part of the director. . . . Basically, though there are of course differences, the main theme of* Il Bidone *is the same as that of* La Strada *and* I Vitelloni: *human solitude. Fellini's predilection for certain suggestive sequences, such as nocturnal wanderings through the darkened streets of a town, is as evident in* Il Bidone *as it is in his other films, from* Variety Lights *to* The White

Sheik, *from* I Vitelloni *to* La Strada. *Moreover, the heroes have the same psychological makeup. . . . "*

Arturo Lanocita, CORRIERE DELLA SERA, *Milan, 11 September 1955.*

" . . . The crepuscolarismo *of Fellini, the recurrent themes of his philosophy and symbolism, his occasional step into reality (only in part nourished by realistic elements and attitudes), once again hints of insincerity. The film seems almost prefabricated, containing exactly the same components as earlier films, earlier sequences: the crying baby or the horse from* La Strada, *the nocturnal wanderings, the fête; and Picasso speaks*

and acts like Il Matto, while Iris his wife strongly resembles Gelsomina. . . . "

Guido Aristarco, CINEMA NUOVO IV, *67, Milan, 25 September 1955.*

" . . . The film has two basic faults: the first lies in its general tone, the second in its dramatic force. It seems as though the author had been torn between two alternatives: whether to relate the story on a humorous note . . . , or whether to give it a tragic key . . . . This accounts for the clear imbalance between the first part of the film, in which the bidonisti *remind us of the* vitelloni, *and the second,*

where the incomprehension and loneliness of the heroes are much closer to La Strada. *This problem automatically leads to the second: the dramatic content of the film is slow in developing, and the human condition of its characters is poorly defined. . . . "*

Nino Ghelli, BIANCO E NERO XVI, *9-10, Rome, September-October 1955.*

" . . . The episodic and descriptive structure of the film; certain stylistic incongruencies and a certain prolixity; its reluctance to externalize the innermost conflicts of its heroes; its insistence on superficial details and secondary episodes,

The calculated dignity of the false priest: Broderick Crawford's special talent was particularly suited to this role.

make the story slow-moving and elusive, undermining the emotional force of each situation. Nonetheless, the film maintains throughout an unexpected dignity and purity, carrying the unmistakable hallmark of an original, self-assured personality. . . . "

Ermanno Contini, IL SECOLO XIX, Genoa, 11 September 1955.

Il Bidone, even more so than its parent, La Strada, is a cocktail of ribald gaiety worthy of Satyricon and of the desperation and bitterness expressed so well in the unforgettable Zampanò. We must add, however, that not always do these two ingredients mingle successfully: there is an occasional lack of inspiration, a certain slowing down of the narrative rhythm and a little too much repetition. It does not have the arcane poetry of La Strada, which arose from a majestically indifferent landscape, and from the slow transition of the seasons quite independently from the sufferings and the loneliness of man. On the other hand, Il Bidone is more complex, with a more elaborate orchestration. The Fellinian theme of someone having to account for his deeds to some transcendental being is more evident; there is less of the metaphysical and more of the purely human."

Pietro Bianchi, ''Federico Fellini (1955),'' in MAESTRI DEL CINEMA, Garzanti, Milan, 1972.

'' . . . Once again, if we were to establish a stylistic and spiritual precedent for Fellini, we would find ourselves with Kafka. The itinerary of the jaded old bidonista complies with the Kafkian mechanism of trial and punishment in a world of tired, indifferent men. It is not surprising that Il Bidone bothers the dogmatists, who are unable to place it in perspective.''

Tullio Kezich, SIPARIO X, 115, Milan, November 1955.

'' . . . The film is built around a succession of slow and fast-moving episodes. It combines sequences where the rhythm is de-

The bidonista *is arrested: handcuffed, Broderick Crawford suddenly looks American, despite his extraordinary ability to adapt to his environment, but the grey-green uniforms of the policemen, long since gone from the scene, are typical of a certain period of Italian life.*

liberately slowed down with moments of hysterical paroxysm. . . . The style is, therefore, at once viscous and eruptive. . . . "

Henri Agel, ETUDES, Paris, December 1957.

" . . . I find all Fellini's films irritating: The White Sheik because it is petty, A Matrimonial Agency because of its feigned sensitivity, I Vitelloni because of its limitations, La Strada because of its laborious and literary punctiliousness. Il Bidone combines the qualities of these four films to the extent that Fellini's faults, which are always the

same: lack of substance, gross symbolism, technical errors, become secondary, are miles away in the depth of field, masked and diluted by the sublime features and imposing stature of Broderick Crawford. Il Bidone begins rudely and ends solemnly. At a film festival, this explosive mixture might not be appreciated by an audience impatient to leave the theatre almost before they sit down. But I had all the time in the world, and could have watched Broderick Crawford dying for hours."

François Truffaut, CAHIERS DU CINÉMA, 51, Paris, October 1955.

" . . . Zampanò (La Strada) could be considered an ancestor of Augusto (Il Bidone), an ancestor from the stone age, a hybrid whose animal makeup is only barely akin to the human condition. The weight of his physical structure, the opaqueness of his mind, give him the flacid, passive and stupid attitude typical of those who rarely feel the stirrings of a conscience. Beneath his apparent dignity, Augusto is just the same. Like the uncouth Zampanò, he appears to be unmoved by the world around him; he is unapproachable, his mind elsewhere. He is like a sort of vitellone with no redeeming features, not even a hint of simple foolishness, a sclerotic vitellone with no hope left at all. . . .

"Here, beside the wretched human beings afflicted by an intellectual, moral and spiritual emptiness, we find a new kind of Fellinian bestiary: the farandole of the simple-minded and the fool. . . . Il Matto is an acrobat, Picasso a swindler. It makes no difference, these two comedians are brothers. Picasso understands the power of a smile, the necessary (though not sufficient) condition of the 'messenger/agitator,' someone who upsets the natural order of things. At a certain point in the film, this cheerful young swindler leaves his accomplices to go off who knows where in search of new excitement. But Patrizia, Augusto's daughter, is there to take his place. A studious,

timid, gentle, well-balanced young girl, she too belongs to the clan of 'spoilsports.' Less so perhaps than the sensible Susanna, human incarnation of the three theological virtues. Susanna is the cripple who crosses old Augusto's path. There she is, incredibly happy and gay, primitively optimistic, transparent as a diamond, unable to conceal the enthusiasm and trust which light up her face. The absolute, for which Fellini's nocturnal heroes paradoxically seek, is reached without effort by this young peasant. She possesses Grace, in both a profane and sacred sense. . . . "

Gilbert Salachas, FEDERICO FELLINI, Seghers, Paris, 1963, pages 51-52.

Even those who disliked the film had to admit that the final scene of Augusto's death was exceptional, and the one in which the talents of Crawford and Fellini achieved greatest harmony.

NIGHTS OF CABIRIA

LE NOTTI DI CABIRIA   ITALY/FRANCE   1957

Produced by Dino De Laurentiis (Rome) and Les Films Marceau (Paris). Director: Federico Fellini. Screenplay: Federico Fellini, Ennio Flaiano, Tullio Pinelli, from an idea by Federico Fellini. Additional dialogue: Pier Paolo Pasolini. Artistic consultant: Brunello Rondi. Photography: Aldo Tonti. Music: Nino Rota. Conductor: Franco Ferrara. Art direction and costumes: Piero Gherardi. Editor: Leo Catozzo. Assistant editor: Adriana Olasio. Sound: Roy Mangano. Assistant directors: Moraldo Rossi, Dominique Delouche. Makeup: Eligio Trani. Production manager: Luigi De Laurentiis. Distribution in Italy: Paramount. Running time: 110 minutes.

CAST

Giulietta Masina (Cabiria), François Périer (Oscar D'Onofrio), Franca Marzi (Wanda), Dorian Gray (Jessy), Amedeo Nazzari (Alberto Lazzari, the actor), Aldo Silvani (the hypnotist), Mario Passante (the cripple), Pina Gualandri (Matilda, Cabiria's enemy), Polidor (the monk), Ennio Girolami, Christian Tassou, Jean Molier, Riccardo Fellini, Maria Luisa Rolando, Amedeo Girard, Loretta Capitoli, Mimmo Poli, Giovanna Gattinoni.

SYNOPSIS

Cabiria is a little prostitute whose simple, candid soul is rooted in hope, despite the unfortunate life she has had. A friend tried to kill her in order to steal her money; her nighttime companions make fun of her; a famous actor humiliates her after having given her false hopes. During an hysterical religious ceremony dedicated to the Divine Love, Cabiria prays for a miracle, that something will happen to change her life. Shortly after, a hypnotist predicts the idyllic future she has always dreamed of.

The prediction seems to be coming true when she meets Oscar, a timid, hard-working, serious man. Oscar begins to date Cabiria regularly and very soon he asks her to marry him.

Cabiria, happy and unsuspecting, entrusts her fiancé with her savings. But again she has a bitter disappointment. Oscar turns out to be nothing better than a seducer after her money, and he would even kill her to get it. Once again, Cabiria has run the risk of coming to a sad end because of her gullibility. Now desperate, she roams the woods with no destination and no purpose. But she meets a group of young people laughing and joking happily together. Suddenly she stops crying, a smile begins to form on her face and hope reawakens in her heart.

NOTES

The original idea for this film had been in Fellini's mind as far back as the days when he was only a scriptwriter. He had created it for Anna Magnani, at a time when the actress's name was linked with Rossellini. Fel-

Cabiria is Gelsomina visiting the world of vice: the striped blouse, the bit of fur are the pathetic signs of her desire to be sinful at all costs (Giulietta Masina and, in the car, Franca Marzi).

lini suggested two possible stories: the first was that of a prostitute who is picked up by a famous actor, then forced to hide in the bathroom of his apartment while he quarrels with his mistress; the second story told of an ignorant peasant girl who is made pregnant by a vagabond she believes to be Saint Joseph, so that when the baby is born she believes him to be divine. Anna Magnani was enthusiastic about the second story (which became Rossellini's *Amore*, and in which Fellini himself made an admirable appearance as an actor alongside Anna Magnani), but strongly disapproved of the first. (Fellini confesses that, after having listened to the story with growing indignation, the actress suddenly exploded: "Federì, can you honestly see someone like me allowing herself to get locked in the john by some bastard actor?" which accurately sums up the idea Magnani had of herself as an actress; in fact, she almost always played characters who were a mixture of pathos, pride and aggressiveness typical of a working-class Roman woman, who sees the world as a battlefield, full of people who are out to cheat you).

During the years to come, Fellini continued to nurture the idea of a fairy-tale prostitute; he unobtrusively introduced her in *The White Sheik*, giving her the name of Cabiria and entrusting the role to his wife, Giulietta Masina. She was one of the two prostitutes to whom Cavalli the accountant, played by Leopoldo Trieste, tells his sorrows to in a Roman piazza after his wife has run away. Cabiria had not even been included in the original screenplay, confesses Fellini. She suddenly came to life in the director's mind and gained such stature that, years later, he decided to ded-

The mystical moment of the procession to the shrine of the Divine Love: Wanda and Cabiria are deeply moved (Franca Marzi and Giulietta Masina).

icate an entire film to her.

Fellini felt that Cabiria's scornful but innocent laughter, wild excitement, silent grimaces of mockery or sympathy were so poetically pathetic and funny as to give this odd little character potentially the same force as Gelsomina had in *La Strada*. Fellini was further encouraged in his ambition when, during the filming of *Il Bidone* on the outskirts of Rome, he had a chance meeting with an eccentric old woman who was living in an illegally built house in constant terror of being turned out. The woman's tale, a mixture of personal experience and prevarication, provided the final touch to the makeup of Cabiria, although she was to go through many more changes before actually reaching the screen. But then even Fellini admits that he has never made an ''easy'' film; he has always had trouble with producers either disappearing at the last minute, or wanting to make some radical changes, or being short of money. The career of a famous director, and of minor directors for that matter, is often studded with episodes such as the chance meeting with the eccentric old woman, and this is one of the many curiosities of the trade. Angelo Solmi's biography of Fellini is rich in curious and amusing little incidents; for instance, Fellini's meeting with Goffredo Lombardo of Titanus (the distributors). According to an eyewitness, the conversation went something like this: ''It's a dangerous film. . . . Let's be frank. . . . You've made a film about queers [he was obviously referring to *I Vitelloni* and the character of Natali], then one about gypsies, another about petty crooks. You wanted to make one about lunatics, and now you come up with a prostitute! I just wonder what the next film is going to deal with!'' ''Producers,'' Fellini muttered irritably. After having approached ten others, Fellini finally came to an agreement with De Laurentiis and the film was made. The screenplay was entrusted to Ennio Flaiano and Tullio Pinelli, while a closer look at the credits reveals the name of Pier Paolo Pasolini, who wrote the dialogue for the Divine Love episode and made sure that the lines spoken by the prostitutes were

They have tried to drown her, but Cabiria will survive (Giulietta Masina).

in pure Roman dialect. According to Solmi, he had also suggested an additional sequence which was not in the original screenplay (Cabiria and a group of thieves speeding through the night in a car); however, it was not included in the final film.

According to the credits, director of photography was Aldo Tonti, but apparently, during the last three weeks of filming, Martelli stepped in in Tonti's place, as Tonti had another engagement. Work had, in fact, been halted for some fifty days, after the star had been involved in an accident on the set. The film was presented at the 1957 Cannes Film Festival and Giulietta Masina was voted best actress.

(c.g.f.)

REVIEWS

'' . . . This film . . . is certainly the best of all his [Fellini's] films so far and one of the most interesting of post-war Italian cinema. This poor creature's desperate desire for love is expressed both poetically and realistically. For instance, the scene where she informs her friend of her coming marriage, or the one with the hypnotist, or the procession to the shrine of the Divine

Love, or the lunch at the lake. The heroine is placed in all manner of environments, each depicted with striking simplicity. . . . Each image, the broad, sorrowful rhythm, reflects the heroine's mood, her innermost feelings. The director's feelings, thoughts and moral judgment are expressed in form, never once becoming rhetorical or didactic. . . . ''

Luigi Chiarini, PANORAMA DEL CINEMA CONTEMPORANEO, *Edizioni di Bianco e Nero, Rome, 1957, pages 145-147.*

'' . . . Much has been said about 'recurrent moments' in Fellini's work and we see it again in this film. We do not, of course, think that this denotes a lack of inspiration . . . ; but is more an illustration of the poetical characteristics of Fellini's personality. Those desolate beaches, nocturnal flights, lonely people searching within their souls for something they cannot find, the amazement of children faced with something unfamiliar to them, the tenderness of simple folk when in contact with nature, these are the elements from which Fellini creates poetry. For instance, the opening beach scene . . . , the quarrel on the Pas-

seggiata Archeologica, the scenes in the nightclub and at the actor's house, the procession at night, the visit to the shrine of the Divine Love, Cabiria's dream on the theatre stage, the secrets she shares with Wanda, the gentle music of the brief closing scene. These are admirable examples of the art of cinema, in which a wealth of ideas is given full expression. . . . "

Nazareno Taddei, LETTURE XII, *6, Milan, June 1957.*

" . . . The Nights of Cabiria, *thanks to its delicate equilibrium, arising from the director's deep understanding of his main character and of technique, is Fellini's most mature and successful film so far, full of poetry and with few questionable moments; it cannot fail to make an impression. . . . "*

Lino Del Fra, BIANCO E NERO XVIII, *6, Rome, June 1957.*

The famous actor Alberto Lazzari allows himself a moment of drunken amusement. Cabiria is very flattered and thinks the visit to the nightclub fantastic (above and below, Amedeo Nazzari and Giulietta Masina).

" . . . *The poetical, erratic Cabiria could not be expressed in any way other than the cinema, and by no director other than Fellini. Only a true artist would have the ability to avoid falling into a double trap: firstly, that of over-poeticizing, which would have distorted his picture of the heroine, and secondly, of creating too trivial a reality, which would have made the character intolerable. . . . "*

Pietro Bianchi, IL GIORNO, *Milan, 12 May 1957.*

" . . . *The episodes, whether brief or long, follow one another without any liaison, except perhaps the classical fondu which serves only to underline the time elapsing between them. The only exception: when the paralyzed old man falls to the ground; this is followed immediately by a close-up of the same character gluttonously eating on the grass. The sudden opposition of a scene of religious par-*

oxysm followed by a prosaic epilogue, underlines a rapid return to reality after the mass hysteria of a group of people fallen into a state of collective hypnosis. This is Fellini's only lapse into the spectacular. The editing too tends to break up each scene into numerous, brief sequences. The movements of the camera are generally functional; they follow or fix the characters' actions with the maximum economy. The camera seems to disarrange each scene by using angle-shots. Screenplay and editing are dynamic: the camera never lingers on a given image, with shots following one after the other in rapid succession. . . . "

Pierre Thuillier and Gilbert Salachas, TÉLÉCINÉ, 72, Paris 1958.

" . . . If there are tensions and climaxes in the films of Fellini which leave nothing to be desired as regards drama or tragedy, it is because, in the absence of traditional dramatic causality, the incidents in his films develop effects of analogy and echo. Fellini's hero never reaches the final crisis (which destroys him and saves him) by a progressive dramatic linking, but because the circumstances somehow or other affect him, build up inside him, like the vibrant energy in a resonating body. He does not evolve, he is transformed, overturning finally like an iceberg whose center of buoyancy has shifted imperceptibly.

"By way of conclusion, and to compress the disturbing perfection of The Nights of Cabiria into a single phrase, I would like to analyze the final shot of the film, which strikes me, when everything else is taken into account, as the most powerful shot in the whole of Fellini's work. Cabiria, stripped of everything—her money, her love, her faith—emptied now of herself, stands on a road without hope. A group of boys and girls swarm into the scene singing and dancing as they go, and from the depths of her nothingness, Cabiria slowly returns to life; she starts to smile again, soon she is dancing too. It is easy

to imagine how artificial and symbolic this ending could have been, casting aside as it does all the objections of verisimilitude, if Fellini had not succeeded in projecting his film onto a higher plane by a single detail of direction, a stroke of real genius that forces us suddenly to identify with his heroine.

"Chaplin's name is often mentioned in connection with La Strada, but I have never thought the comparison between Gelsomina and Charlie (which I find hard to take in itself) very convincing. The first shot which is not only up to Chaplin's level, but the true equal of his best inventions, is the final shot of The Nights of Cabiria, when Giulietta Masina turns towards the camera and her glance meets ours. As far as I know, Chaplin is the only man in the history of cinema who made successful systematic use of this gesture, which the books about filmmaking are unanimous in condemning. Nor would it be in place if, when she looked us in the eye, Cabiria seemed to be bearing some ultimate truth. But the finishing touch to this directorial stroke of genius is this, that Cabiria's glance falls several times on the camera without ever quite coming

Cabiria is still ignorant of her fiancé's true character and she continues to dream of a fairy-tale romance; very soon she will discover that he is really a coldblooded crook (above and below, Francois Périer and Giulietta Masina in two shots from the same sequence).

to rest on it. The lights go up on this marvel of ambiguity. Cabiria is doubtless still the heroine of the adventures which she has been living out before us, somewhere behind that screen, but here she is now inviting us too, with her glance, to follow her on the road to which she is about to return. The invitation is chaste, discreet and indefinite enough that we can pretend to think she means to be looking at somebody else. At the same time, though, it is definite and direct enough, too, to remove us quite finally from our role of spectator."

André Bazin, CAHIERS DU CINÉMA, 76, *Paris, November 1957.*

"Miss Masina gives a remarkable performance, capturing shades of pain and happiness that are rarely approached on the screen. Her pathos is almost unbearable. . . . If the film falls short of greatness, it may be because the parts are more brilliant than the whole. In scene after scene, exciting images and ideas leap out at anyone who admires the film art. It is Fellini's theme that may leave you in despair. . . . Though the director probably intended his tale to be hopeful, you can find fault with the point that he has made, but not with the way he has made it."

William K. Zinsser, NEW YORK HERALD TRIBUNE, *October 27, 1957.*

"Possibly Federico Fellini's finest film, and a work in which Giulietta Masina earns the praise she received for La Strada . . . . Though the film seems free and almost unplanned, each apparent irrelevance falls into place."

Pauline Kael, 5001 NIGHTS AT THE MOVIES, *Holt, Rinehart and Winston, 1982.*

Cabiria's entreaties: even in the moments of greatest despair the character hides an indestructible optimism. This is one of the secrets of the early Fellini, who was always hovering between irony and mysticism (Giulietta Masina).

LA DOLCE VITA

LA DOLCE VITA   ITALY/FRANCE 1960

Produced by Giuseppe Amato and Angelo Rizzoli for Riama Film, Roma/Pathé Consortium Cinema–Gray Film, Paris. Director: Federico Fellini. Screenplay: Federico Fellini, Tullio Pinelli, Ennio Flaiano, with the collaboration of Brunello Rondi. From a story by Federico Fellini, Tullio Pinelli, Ennio Flaiano, based on an idea by Federico Fellini. Photography (Totalscope): Otello Martelli. Camera operator: Ennio Guarnieri. Music: Nino Rota. Conductor: Franco Ferrara. Singers: "I Campinino," Adriano Celentano. Art director: Piero Gherardi. Assistant directors: Giorgio Giovannini, Lucia Mirisola, Vito Ansalone. Costumes: Piero Gherardi. Editor: Leo Catozzo. Assistant editors: Adriana and Wanda Olasio. Assistant directors: Guidarino Guidi, Paolo Nuzzi, Dominique Delouche, Giancarlo Romani, Gianfranco Mingozzi, Lilli Veenman. Artistic collaboration: Brunello Rondi. Sound: Agostino Moretti. Continuity: Isa Mari. Makeup: Otello Fava. Hair styles: Renata Magnanti. Executive producer: Franco Magli. Production managers: Manlio M. Moretti, Nello Meniconi. Production supervisor: Alessandro Von Norman. Production secretaries: Mario Basile, Mario De Biasi, Osvaldo De Micheli. Distribution in Italy: Cineriz. Running time: 178 minutes.

CAST

Marcello Mastroianni (Marcello Rubini), Walter Santesso (Paparazzo), Giulio Paradisi (2nd photographer), Enzo Cerusico (3rd photographer), Enzo Doria (4th photographer), Anouk Aimée (Maddalena), Cesare Miceli Picardi (irritable man in nightclub), Donatella Esparmer (woman with irritable man), Maria Pia Serafini (2nd woman with irritable man), Adriana Moneta (prostitute), Anna Maria Salerno (2nd prostitute), Oscar Ghiglia (1st pimp), Gino Marturano (2nd pimp), Yvonne Fourneaux (Emma), Thomas Torres (journalist at hospital), Carlo Mariotti (male nurse), Leonardo Botta (doctor), Anita Ekberg (Sylvia), Harriet White (Edna, Sylvia's secretary), Carlo Di Maggio (Totò Scalise, Sylvia's producer), Francesco Luzi (radio commentator), Francesco Consalvo (Scalise's assistant), Guglielmo Leoncini (Scalise's secretary), Sandy von Norman (interpreter at Sylvia's press conference), Lex Barker (Robert), Tiziano Cortini (newsreel camera operator), Henry Thody, Donatella Della Nora, Maité Morand, Donato Castellaneta, John Francis Lane, Concetta Ragusa, François Dieudonné, Mario Mallamo, Nadia Balabine, Umberto Felici, Maurizio Guelfi (journalists at Sylvia's press conference), Adriano Celentano (rock'n'roll singer), Gondrano Trucchi (waiter at Caracalla's), Gio Staiano (young effeminate man), Archie Savage (black dancer), Alain Dijon (Frankie Stout), Paolo Labia (servant at Maddalena's house), Giacomo Garbielli (Maddalena's father), Alain Cuny (Steiner), Gianfranco Mingozzi (young priest), Valeria Ciangottini (Paola), Alfredo Rizzo (television director), Alex Messoyedoff (miracle priest), Rina Fran-

The dramatic, almost excessive, loneliness of Emma (Yvonne Fournaux).

chetti *(mother of the miracle children)*, Aurelio Nardi *(uncle of the miracle children)*, Marianna Leibl *(woman with Yvonne at the miracle)*, Giovanna and Massimo *(miracle children)*, Renée Longarini *(Mrs. Steiner)*, Iris Tree, Leonida Repaci, Anna Salvatore, Letizia Spadini, Margherita Russo, Winie Vagliani, Desmond O'Grady *(guests at Steiner house)*, Nello Meniconi *(angry man on Via Veneto)*, Massimo Busetti *(Pierrone)*, Annibale Ninchi *(Marcello's father)*, Vittorio Manfrino *(maître d' at the Kit Kat)*, Polidor *(clown with balloons)*, Magali Noël *(Fanny the chorus girl)*, Lilly Granado *(Lucy)*, Gloria Jones *(Gloria)*, Nico Otzak *(Nico)*, Prince Vadim Wolkonsky *(Prince Mascalchi, owner of castle)*, Giulio Questi *(don Giulio Mascalchi)*, Prince don Eugenio Ruspoli di Poggio Suasa *(don Eugenio Mascalchi)*, Count Ivenda Dobrzensky *(don Giovanni Mascalchi)*, Audrey McDonald *(Sonia)*, Juan Antequera *(Spanish politician)*, Rosemary Rennel Rodd *(English medium)*, Fernando Brofferio *(Maddalena's lover)*, Donna Doris Pignatelli, Princess of Monteroduni *(woman with white cloak)*, Ida Galli *(the debutante)*, Mario De Grenet *(tired boy with dogs)*, Franco Rossellini *(the hand-some rider)*, Maria Marigliano *(Massimilla)*, Loretta Ramaciotti *(possessed woman at the séance)*, Cristina dei conti Paolozzi *(laughing girl)*, Countess Elisabetta Cini *(sleeping dutchess)*, Maria Teresa Wolodimeroff *(tired woman)*, Count Carlo Kechler *(man with watch)*, Count Bruno Serego Alighieri *(boy with mink)*, Nani Colombo *(woman looking in the mirror)*, Giulio Girola *(police commissioner in charge of mass death investigation)*, Giuseppe Addobbati *(doctor)*, Paolo Fadda *(vice police commissioner)*, Vando Tres *(area police commissioner)*, Franco Giacobini *(journalist on the telephone)*, Giuliana Lo Jodice *(maid at Steiner house)*, Federika André *(lodger at Steiner house)*, Giancarlo Romani *(carabiniere)*, Nadia Gray *(Nadia)*, Mino Doro *(Nadia's lover)*, Antonio Jacono *(Domino)*, Carlo Musto *(Carlo)*, Tito Buzzo *(muscleman)*, Sandra Lee *(Spoleto dancer)*, Jacques Sernas *(matinee idol)*, Leontine von Stein *(matinee idol's mistress)*, Leo Coleman *(black dancer)*, Laura Betti *(Laura, the blond actress/singer)*, Daniela Calvino *(Daniela)*, Christine Denise *(woman eating chicken)*, Riccardo Garrone *(Riccardo, master of the house)*, Decimo Cristiani *(boy who does not speak)*, Umberto Orsini *(boy who helps Nadia to undress)*, Sandra Tes *(the girl who sits beside him)*, Renato Mambor *(tall young man)*, Mario Conocchia *(man with bra on his head)*, Enrico Glori *(Nadia's admirer)*, Lucia Vasilicò *(young girl confessing)*, Franca Pasutt *(girl covered in feathers)*.

Alain Cuny is dubbed by Romolo Valli, Anouk Aimée by Lilla Brignone, Yvonne Fourneaux by Gabriella Genta.

SYNOPSIS

Marcello Rubini is a journalist who writes for a scandal magazine, though he entertains hopes of one day becoming a serious writer. For seven nights and seven days he becomes the guide in a journey through the "sweet life" of Rome. We meet him first in a helicopter as he follows the statue of Christ the Laborer, which is suspended by cable from a second helicopter over the Roman ruins. That evening, in a nightclub, Marcello meets Maddalena, a young heiress who is constantly in search of new sensations and with whom he ends up making love in some prostitute's bed.

On his return home at dawn Marcello finds that his mistress, Emma, has tried to commit suicide in a fit of jealousy. He takes her to the hospital, but must leave her immediately to reach Ciampino airport in time for the arrival of Sylvia, a famous film star. After a press conference, a trip to St. Peter's dome and a visit to Caracalla's nightclub, Marcello decides to follow Sylvia all night in the hope of finding a favorable moment which, in fact, never comes. After a plunge in the Trevi fountain, the two go back to Sylvia's hotel where they are insulted and roughed up by the actress's fiancé.

Marcello next meets an intellectual friend of his, Steiner, whose comfortable life with his wife and two children seems to Marcello ideal. The journalist's next assignment brings him into contact with an episode of collective fanaticism provoked by two children who pre-

The fascinating beauty of Via Veneto recreated in the film studio, the open sports car, father and a photographer friend . . . (Annibale Ninchi, Marcello Mastroianni and Walter Santesso).

Marcello, distant, desirous and indifferent before this representation of ''Catholic'' Rome of the early 1960s (Marcello Mastroianni and Anita Ekberg).

tend to have seen the Virgin Mary in a field near to Terni. On another occasion, Marcello receives a visit from his father and together they go to an old-style nightclub.

Almost by chance, Marcello then joins an aristocrats' party being held in a castle; here he declares his love for Maddalena, but ends up in bed with another, older woman. Next day, Marcello learns that his friend Steiner has committed suicide after having first killed his two children. We catch up with Marcello again in a villa at Fregene, where a sordid orgy is going on.

At dawn, everyone goes onto the beach to watch a monstrous fish being caught. Here, Marcello is greeted by an innocent-looking young girl whom he had met in a restaurant, but he neither recognizes her, nor hears what she says.

NOTES

Twenty-four years after the making of this film, it is difficult not to be influenced by the potpourri of comments and criticism prompted by La Dolce Vita when it first appeared. The film was symbolic of an entire era of Italian cinema and gave rise to a host of neologisms (like ''vitelloni''). The words ''dolce vita,'' pronounced with the accent on the adjective rather than the noun, became part of everyday language, meaning an unspecific feeling of physical enjoyment; the two words later came to refer to a polo-

necked sweater, like the one worn by Ivenda Dobrzensky at the aristocrats' party in the castle).

The selection of reviews, though reflecting the general reaction to the film, is of course very limited. It is virtually impossible today to explain the effect of La Dolce Vita twenty-four years ago: the controversy, curiosity, disappointment and enthusiasm it provoked. Each one of us has, I think, his own recollection of this famous film; I personally dedicated to it a whole page of the newspaper for which I was working, which was even more unusual then than it would be today. I can still recall how fascinated I was by the immense scenario created by Fellini for Marcello, at grips with the statue of Christ, unruly photographers (incidentally, the term "paparazzo," the surname of the character played by Walter Santesso, came to mean a certain type of bothersome photographer and is still used today), decadent aristocrats obstinately congregating together in their decadent castles, mystical apparitions, intellectual gatherings, fearful meetings with his father at the nightclub and so forth.

The making of the film was marked by the usual minuet of proposals and refusals with producers before an agreement was finally reached with Angelo Rizzoli. Tullio Kezich's account of the making of *La Dolce Vita* reveals Fellini's tenacious, enticing, cheerfully stoic efforts to complete what was, and still is, an extraordinary undertaking: his attempt to place on film a sensation, a series of impressions, shadows and rapid glimpses of people which vanish almost before they have a chance to become reality.

The film evokes Italy of the 1950s, with its naïve *joie de vivre* its unrefined vivacity, its love of good clothes, the evenings spent driving around town or sitting under the bright lights of some elegant street café. This era was already on the wane when Fellini made his film (the Via Veneto set reconstructed in the studios is a lighthearted memorial to this dying era). And his portrayal of it had such vitality and intensity that it amazed even those who already had complete faith in Fellini's talent.

The final result differed little from the original screenplay written by Fellini, Flaiano and Pinelli, with the collaboration of Brunello Rondi. Only two of the original episodes were omitted (one concerning a writer named Dolores who protects Marcello, and another about a boat trip during which a young girl is burned to death), to be replaced by two new ones created by Fellini himself and unquestionably among the most poignant of the entire film: the "miracle" and the aristocrats' party. As had been the case on more than one occasion during those early years, Fellini took his inspiration from *Moraldo in Città* (which, together with the *Ritorno of G. Mastorna*, is the most famous of Fellini's unmade films). But the mood of the 1950s (in 1958, when

Marcello feels for Steiner the same admiration he feels for all "organic" intellectuals, while he considers himself to be a superficial person (Marcello Mastroianni and Alain Cuny).

the film first began to take shape, there was much talk about the Via Veneto "Café Society," of actors and actresses being harried by photographers, of parties and intellectual gatherings, of the euphoria of a society which, though banal and frivolous, was nonetheless curiously alive) gradually gained the upper hand, so that the final result centered around a journalist, Marcello Rubini, who was both serious minded and fun loving. He is one of Fellini's most approachable characters and one of Marcello Mastroianni's most convincing roles (from the outset the role was created for Mastroianni).

Filming began on 16 March 1959 at Cinecittà and was completed on 27 August of the same year at Passo Corese (near Rome); almost six months of filming produced 92,000 metres of film which were cut to 5,000 in the final version. The film went into general release in February 1960 and, as we said before, created a sensation which today seems to belong to another world; almost as

though a century had gone by and not just two decades. During the première in Milan, Fellini was insulted by a group of people, and a woman even spat in his face. The matter was later discussed in Parliament, where a certain faction actually advised that it be withdrawn, or at least censored. Luckily, no action was taken; but these incidents do give some idea of the exaggerated reaction provoked by a film which was to be a bone of contention for many years to come.

(c.g.f.)

REVIEWS

*" . . . In our opinion, **La Dolce Vita** is the confirmation of a spiritual journey and, at the same time, the completion of that journey. Because of the freedom of its construction and the amplitude of its subject, the film does allow itself a few concessions: it is occasionally dispersive and repetitive, but less so than past films. And these*

pauses carry little weight, indeed they often have their own special poetry.... Having concluded his second anthology with The Nights of Cabiria, *Fellini has now commenced a third, and he has done so with energy and enthusiasm, the insight of a great narrator, selecting his material with discretion. Brutal analysis, shared emotions, visionary impetus combine in this terrible and fascinating polyptych of a modern Babylon.... The fact that, while passing judgment he also expresses a deep feeling for the humanity of his characters, even the most abject among them—and by this I mean that by putting himself in their place, he understands the reason for their being what they are—is another sign of the vitality, force and compassion that his film possesses to a high degree."*

Morando Morandini, SCHERMI III, 20, Milan, January-February 1960.

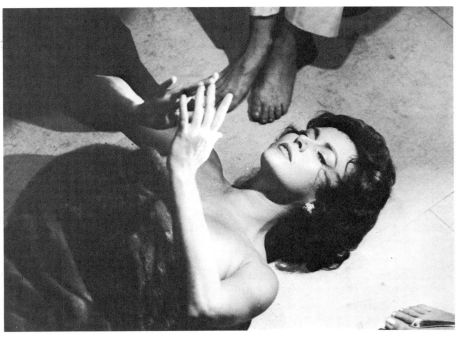

The dreamy abstraction of an "orgy," 1960s style (Nadia Gray).

The miracle takes place in the open, in the presence of believers, the police and a sailor who presents arms.

"... La Dolce Vita *is above all the film of a crisis, the crisis of the director's Christian beliefs; gone is hope, gone is faith; the film ends as it began. ...* La Dolce Vita *is like waiting for the dawn of an unknown day, a journey into the night, while reason sleeps, through a corrupt and putrescent civilization, where everything is collapsing, whether it concerns authentic values or false myths, age-old traditions or newly formed convictions. ..."*

Vittorio Spinazzola, NUOVA GENERA-ZIONE, Milan, 21 February 1960.

"... *The narrative shows a rich variety of resources creating a spectacular impression, of leitmotivs recurring in a symbolic manner (the photographers' assault), and an unexpected degree of liberty in the way in which the camera is used, making it seem more and more like the human eye. The screenplay offers images which, though taken from everyday life, become extraordinarily fantastical in quality. ... The metaphysic and spiritual symbolism is, however, a little obscure. ..."*

Vito Pandolfi, FILM 1961, Feltrinelli, Milan, 1961, p. 21.

"... La Dolce Vita, *one of the most remarkable and in its own way tragic films of recent years, is a saga of all the falsehood, mystification and corruption of our times; it is the funeral march of a society, on the surface still young and healthy but which, as in Medieval paintings, is really dancing with Death and does not know it. It is the 'human comedy' of a crisis which, like Goya's paintings or the works of Kafka, is making 'monsters' out of men who are too blind to see it happening. ... Controversy, symbolism, allegory, accusation? No. Fellini purposely avoided programmatic, rhetoric or moralistic intonations, preferring instead to simply describe the 'monsters' of today to his contemporaries. ... And he had done this with a dramatic force, an impetus and an originality of language which, despite the weakness of certain episodes, make* La Dolce Vita *one of today's most 'modern' films. ..."*

Gian Luigi Rondi, IL TEMPO, Rome, 5 February 1960.

"... *From the point of view of style,* La Dolce Vita *is very interesting. Highly expressive throughout, Fellini seems to change the tone according to the subject matter of each episode, ranging from expressionist caricature to pure neo-realism. In general, the tendency to caricature is greater the more severe the film's moral judgment, though this is never totally contemptuous, there being always a touch of complacence and participation, such as in the final orgy scene or the episode of the aristocrats' party, the latter being particularly effective for its descriptive acuteness and narrative rhythm. ..."*

Alberto Moravia, L'ESPRESSO, Rome, 14 February 1960.

"... *What* La Dolce Vita *lacks is the structure of a masterpiece. In fact, the film has no proper structure, it is a succession of moments of cinema, some more convincing than others. ... In the face of criticism,* La Dolce Vita *disintegrates, leaving behind little more than a sequence of "events" with no common denominator linking them into a meaningful whole. ..."*

Jacques Doniol-Valcroze, FRANCE OBSERVATEUR, Paris, 19 May 1960.

"... *Fellini's greatest failing here is that he shows a singular lack of ideas in the making of this film. There are some skillful sequences ... but there are no ideas. It is a cinematographic song, with the occasional recitative to break the monotony, but it does not belong to the cinema. ..."*

Jean Domarchi, CAHIERS DU CIN-ÉMA, 108, Paris, June 1960.

"... *Rarely have the many facets of the art of cinema (images, dialogue, music, actors' performances, shooting angle, depth of field, etc.) been so harmoniously combined, so powerfully used. ... Nonetheless, this technical perfection does not try to dominate, it is not that of a virtuoso. ... The purest, most audacious cinema is [in* La Dolce Vita*] at the service of one of the deepest, most original visions of our time. The two main trends of the Italian school—the tendency to free the cinema from the romanticism of Zavattini, and the tendency to express, in a way ever closer to the truth, what lies beyond the reality of Rossellini—are combined in this film. ..."*

René Cortade, ARTS, Paris, 18 May 1960.

"... *Fellini's* La Dolce Vita *is too important to be discussed as we would normally discuss a film. Though not as great as Chaplin, Eisenstein or Mizoguchi, Fellini is unquestionably an 'author' rather than a 'director.' The film is, therefore, his and his alone, it belongs to neither the actors nor the tech-*

At last, Valeria Ciangottini's great occasion; she is a mysterious, lily-like, gently optimistic creature.

nicians: nothing in it is fortuitous. . . . The camera moves and fixes in such a way as to create a sort of diaphragm around each object, thus making its entry into and relationship with the world around appear as irrational and magical as possible. Almost always, as each new episode begins, the camera is moving, its movements never being simple. Frequently, however, these sinuously and parenthetically subordinate movements of the camera are brutally punctuated by a very simple, almost documentary shot, like a quotation from everyday language. . . . For instance, the arrival of the film star at Ciampino airport. . . . "

Pier Paolo Pasolini, FILMCRITICA XI, *94, Rome, February 1960.*

"The film is a landmark of cinematic social comment. . . . What is Fellini's message? It is certainly not irreligious, although it is as succinctly critical of a certain specious religiosity as of the moral chaos that rots most of the film's char-

acters. On the surface he seems to be dealing negatively with everything, but this is so only if one forgets to consider the possible position from which he can view things in this light. Far from being indelicate, he is peculiarly tactful. Curiously enough, the very vividness of Fellini's imagery in these early scenes may lead one to revel in the ecstasy of the visual moment so completely as to lose sight of certain seemingly incidental elements that are actually key points in the drive toward the ultimate tragedy. It is one of the few films that make one think wistfully of the literary handiness of glancing back at a passage in a book already read. It is therefore one of the few films that one feels can be seen with increasing enjoyment a second or third time."

Paul V. Backley, NEW YORK HERALD TRIBUNE, *April 20, 1961.*

"This sensational representation of certain aspects of life in contemporary Rome, as revealed in the clamorous experience of a free-

wheeling newspaper man, is a brilliantly graphic estimation of a whole swath of society in sad decay and, eventually, a withering commentary upon the tragedy of the over-civilized. . . . Signor Fellini is nothing if not fertile, fierce and urbane in calculating the social scene around him and packing it onto the screen. He has an uncanny eye for finding the offbeat and grotesque incident, the gross and bizarre occurrence that exposes a glaring irony. He has, too, a splendid sense of balance and a deliciously sardonic wit that not only guided his cameras but also affected the writing of his script. As a consequence there are scores of piercing ideas that pop out in the picture's nigh three hours and leave one shocked, amused, revolted and possibly stunned and bewildered at the end. . . . In sum, it is an awesome picture, licentious in content but moral and vastly sophisticated in its attitude and what it says."

Bosley Crowther, THE NEW YORK TIMES, *April 20, 1961.*

One of the film's most emotionally tense moments: Marcello takes his father to the nightclub (Annibale Ninchi, Marcello Mastroianni and Walter Santesso).

BOCCACCIO 70

Episode: *Le Tentazioni del Dottor Antonio* (*The Temptations of Doctor Antonio*).

Produced by Carlo Ponti and Antonio Cervi for Concordia Compagnia Cinematografica–Cineriz, Rome/Francinex–Gray Films, Paris. Director: Federico Fellini. Screenplay: Federico Fellini, Tullio Pinelli, Ennio Flaiano, with the collaboration of Brunello Rondi and Goffredo Parise. Based on a story by Federico Fellini. Photography:(Technicolor): Otello Martelli. Camera operator: Arturo Zavattini. Music: Nino Rota. Art director: Piero Zuffi. Editor: Leo Catozzo. Distribution in Italy: Cineriz. Running time: 60 minutes.

CAST

Peppino De Filippo (*Dr. Antonio Mazzuolo*), Anita Ekberg (*Anita, the girl in the poster*), Antonio Acqua (*Commendatore La Pappa*), Eleonora Nagy (*Cupid*), Donatella Della Nora (*Antonio's sister*), Dante Maggio, Giacomo Furia, Alfredo Rizzo, Alberto Sorrentino, Monique Berger, Polidor, Mario Passante, Silvio Bagolini, Achille Majeroni, Enrico Ribulsi, Gesa Meiken, Gondrano Trucchi, Ciccio Bardi, Giulio Paradisi.

Other episodes of the film are: *Renzo e Luciana* by Mario Monicelli, *Il Lavoro* by Luchino Visconti, *La Riffa* by Vittorio De Sica. The film was coordinated by Cesare Zavattini.

SYNOPSIS

Dr. Antonio is an intransigent defender of morality. He harangues the Boy Scouts, makes a point of disturbing young couples in search of privacy and tears up the covers of scandal magazines on display at newsstands. One day, right beneath the windows of his house, an enormous advertisement is put up, depicting a buxom blonde who smilingly invites the public to drink more milk. After several unsuccessful attempts to have the poster removed, Dr. Antonio launches his own offensive by throwing bottles of ink over the photograph. The authorities intervene covering the poster up with sheets of white paper. But a downpour washes away paper and ink and the incriminating opulence of the poster girl is back on display. In his obsession, Dr. Antonio imagines the gigantic figure coming to life and, small and frightened, in his dreams he gives in to her amourous enticements. Next morning, the moralist is found delirious on top of the poster. From the roof of the ambulance taking Dr. Antonio to the hospital, Cupid winks to the world.

NOTES

This particular Fellini episode—possibly because it was combined with three quite different ones: the "Milanese" realism of Monicelli; the worldly irony of Visconti; the sensuality typical of bawdy story from the north as seen through the eyes of a Roman, De Sica—was not very popular. Many reviews were scathing and contemptuous, while others were highly favorable. As often happens with Fellini, many critics failed to see that here, in this brief episode, were shades of the director's youthful sympathies, of his experience as a journalist with a humorous magazine, and his talent for sketching and caricature, especially of film characters, which allows him to give full rein to that very special sense of humor he had instilled in the caricatures he drew of allied soldiers at The Funny Face Shop. The immense form of "Anitona," which suddenly comes to life and descends from the huge milk advertisement, is an idea which might seem somewhat banal today, but which, in 1962, had a certain malicious flavor about it to which Fellini must have been particularly attracted.

(c.g.f.)

REVIEWS

*" . . . With **The Temptations of Dr. Antonio**, Fellini has allowed himself a holiday! He decided to enjoy himself and knew how to, by dealing with one of the more grotesque aspects of certain moralistic crusades. He has solicited a fine performance from Peppino De Filippo and has skillfully guided Anita Ekberg into using all of her natural talent. Around them, he has placed a small group of people characterized to the utmost. In this he has been particularly successful . . . , confirming the extent of his inventive power and the eloquence of his sarcasm. But it is no more than a smile. . . ."*

Giovanni Grazzini, CORRIERE DELLA SERA, *Milan, 24 February 1962.*

" . . . Fellini narrates his story to a dance rhythm, to a leit-motiv with a propagandistic ring to it. The story has two parts: the first takes us up to the moment when the poster is erected; the second describes what goes on in the sick mind of the moralist as he daydreams about Anita. . . . The first part is by no means overshadowed by the second, on the contrary, the latter appears less harmonious. Fellini seems less at home describing Dr. Antonio's imaginary flight. In the second part, he only half manages to lay bare the inner structure of his character. . . ."

Aldo d'Angelo, FILM SELEZIONE III, *10, Rome, March–April 1962.*

Dr. Antonio Mazzuolo has no intention of tolerating this provocation (Peppino De Filippo and, in the poster, Anita Ekberg).

"... Fellini's film, based on the excellent idea of relating a comedy of manners, turns out to be vulgar and singularly boring. A complete disaster. It has the lot! An immoderate female, faked miracles, priests, religion and sex, sacrilege blessed by the Vatican, occultism of the poor and so forth. Moreover, in his use of color, to which he makes recourse for the first time, Fellini shows a typical lack of good taste...."

Jean Douchet, CAHIERS DU CINEMA, *132, Paris, June 1962.*

"... The author of La Dolce Vita has really surprised us here, and favorably too. Gone are the mysticism, the favorite clichés, the decadent and falsely autobiographical dross. Fellini has retraced his steps back to the timid, respectable bookkeeper of The White Sheik, *back to his origins in fact.... The fabulous and the monstrous join forces against the four horsemen of a modern Apocalypse: hypocrisy in the first place, followed by obtuseness, intolerance and falsehood."*

I.p. (Lorenzo Pellizzari), CINEMA NUOVO XI, *157, Milan, May–June 1962.*

"... Fellini's episode is clearly meant to be polemical.... He is defending his Dolce Vita *with an obvious and continual reference to this earlier film. And he does so by attacking the enemy position.... His indictment is ruthless, malicious and holds nothing back.... Here and there, as was perhaps inevitable, this desire to add new concatenations to his tirade, carries Fellini off course, although he does manage, with a few crafty and* intelligent surrealist twists, to get away with quite a lot...."

t.c. (Tommaso Chiaretti), CINEMA 60 II, *21–22, Rome, March–April 1962.*

"The prize [is] Miss Loren in all her peasant blend of insolence and melting sentimentality ... certainly there is a lot of fun in the picture as a whole. It makes you suppose the directors and their casts were relaxing with their shoes off. You can relax with them but you are never unaware of the inappropriate lavishness of means, the too ostentatious use of color, the tendency to make every point with the subtlety of a bowling ball crashing into the pins, and you end by sighing at the spectacle of a work choking on its own lymph."

Paul V. Beckley, THE NEW YORK HERALD TRIBUNE, *June 27, 1962.*

"*The display of Miss Loren's figure is excessive to the point of tedium, and the portrayals of her various grunting suitors are more callow than comical. How Carlo Ponti, her husband and the producer of this film, could have allowed her and Signor De Sica to revert to such an artless crudity after their powerful creation of Two Women is an incidental mystery. As a consequence [the film] ends like a bum dirty joke and leaves one reflecting ruefully on Signor Fellini's witty spoof.*"

Bosley Crowther, THE NEW YORK TIMES, *January 24, 1962.*

A flight of stairs and an usher to greet the solitary moralist (Peppino De Filippo).

(Bottom) Peppino De Filippo (left) encased in a derisively erotic suit of armor, and Anita Ekberg (right), a milky monument to eroticism in advertising.

8 1/2

OTTO E MEZZO

Produced by Angelo Rizzoli and Federico Fellini for Cineriz (Rome) and Francinex (Paris). Director: Federico Fellini. Screenplay: Federico Fellini, Tullio Pinelli, Ennio Flaiano, Brunello Rondi, based on a story by Federico Fellini and Ennio Flaiano. Photography: Gianni Di Venanzo. Camera operator: Pasquale De Santis. Music: Nino Rota. Art direction and costumes: Piero Gherardi. Assistant art directors: Luciano Riccieri, Vito Anzalone, Orietta Nasalli Rocca. Editor: Leo Catozzo. Assistant editor: Adriana Olasio. Assistant directors: Guidarino Guidi, Giulio Paradisi, Francesco Aluigi. Artistic collaboration: Brunello Rondi. Continuity: Mirella Comacchio. Makeup: Otello Fava. Hair styles: Renata Magnanti. Production manager: Nello Meniconi.

Production supervisor: Mario Basili. Production secretary: Albino Morandin. Distribution in Italy: Cineriz. Running time: 114 minutes.

CAST

Marcello Mastroianni (*Guido Anselmi*), Anouk Aimée (*Luisa, Guido's wife*), Sandra Milo (*Carla*), Claudia Cardinale (*Claudia*), Rossella Falk (*Rossella*), Barbara Steele (*Gloria*), Guido Alberti (*Pace, the producer*), Madeleine Lebeau (*French actress*), Jean Rougeul (*Daumier, the critic*), Caterina Boratto (*beautiful, unidentified woman at the spa*), Annibale Ninchi (*Guido's father*), Giuditta Rissone (*Guido's mother*), Edra Gale (*la Saraghina*), Mario Conocchia (*production manager*), Cesarino Miceli Picardi (*production supervisor*), Tito Masini (*cardinal*), Mario Pisu (*Mezzabotta*), Yvonne Casadei (*Jacqueline Bonbon, the soubrette*), Ian Dallas (*master of ceremonies*), Georgia Simmons (*Guido's grandmother*), Edy Vessel (*Edy, the model*), Annie Gorassini (*Pace's girlfriend*), Rossella Como, Francesco Rigamonti, Matilde Calnam (*Luisa's friends*), Gilda Dahlberg (*American journalist's wife and magazine writer*), Olimpia Cavalli (*Olimpia*), Hazel Rogers (*black woman in harem*), Bruno Agostini (*production secretary*), E. Cini (*a cardinal*), Mario Tedeschi (*Father Superior*), Elisabetta Catalano (*Luisa's sister*), Sebastiano De Leandro (*a priest*), Frazier Rippy (*advance man for the cardinal*), Roberta Valli (*child*), Eva Gioia, Dina

Ballerinas, feathers, white gowns and cardinals: a synthesis of the dream world of 8½.

De Santis (*production supervisor's girls*), Roby Nicolosi (*doctor at the spa*), Polidor (*a clown*), Neil Robinson (*French actress's agent*), Mino Doro (*Claudia's agent*), Mario Tarchetti (*Claudia's press officer*), Eugene Walter (*American journalist*), Mary Indovino (*telepathist's partner*), John Stacy (*accountant*), Mark Heron (*Enrico, Luisa's satellite*), Alfredo De Lafeld (*cardinal's secretary*), Marisa Colomber, Maria Raimondi (*Guido's aunts*), Nadine Sanders (*hostess*), Riccardo Guglielmi (*Guido as a boy*), Marco Gemini (*Guido as a schoolboy*), Guido Calì.

SYNOPSIS

Guido Anselmi is a famous director who is undergoing a cure at a health resort. He is troubled by recurrent nightmares, memories of childhood and a sense of guilt deriving from a Catholic upbringing. He is preparing a new film, and is consequently surrounded by people who are in some way involved in his work: the producer, constantly worried about losing the money he has invested; a pedantic, intellectual critic; actors and would-be actors; not to mention the customary army of faithful collaborators. Then there are the people from his private life: his voluptuous but rather scatterbrained, mistress; his wife, from whom he is growing daily more apart; an old friend with his young and sophisticated girl-friend, who mingle with the strange, out-of-this-world clientele at the baths; society ladies, priests and cardinals, and an angelic nurse.

Guido is going through a crisis. The images of the screen-tests done for the film merge with those of his nocturnal nightmares. We see him as he meets his dead parents at the cemetery, we watch him, clad in school uniform, run to join his companions at the dance of the buxom Saraghina, and we witness his fantastic vision of a harem in which he whips wife and concubines into mutual accord. Rumors that the film will never be finished grow more insistent and so the producer decides to call a

A symbol of Fellini's cinema: cotton-wool snow for an artificial night, in an expression of "studio-made" cinema (Marcello Mastroianni).

press conference on the set. Guido is bombarded by questions. He dreams of committing suicide. But, just as he is on the point of announcing his decision to abandon the film, the scene is filled with all the characters from his life. In the middle of this procession, Guido suddenly picks up a megaphone and begins to give orders. Filming is about to begin. Or is it. . .?

NOTES

" . . . Powerfully creative meditation on the inability to create . . ." says Christian Metz (see reviews) of *8½,* which was originally given the title

(created by Flaiano) *La Bella Confusione.* As always, Fellini started off with a host of ideas, all tied to a central theme, none of which was absolutely clear in his mind. Basically, there was to be a central character (a writer? a professional man of some kind? a theatrical producer?) forced to interrupt his everyday routine because of a mild illness. He is advised to take a rest and so goes to a health resort at Chianciano. He has a wife, a mistress and interests everywhere, making his life a hectic rush, but without which he would probably be completely lost because he feels he has no roots anywhere. His life-style has gradually become a sort of terrifying delirium, without sense or pur-

The colorful taste of a man who delights in exploring the backwoods of his memory (Marco Gemini in the role of Guido the schoolboy).

pose. But what is the point of his trying to pull himself out of it? Would it perhaps not be better merely to become part of this bizarre and fantastic dance and to throw all one's energy into trying to keep in step?

These were the opening phrases, more or less, of a long letter that Fellini wrote to Brunello Rondi (whose name figures among the writers of the screenplay, while the story is attributed to Fellini and Flaiano only). This letter appears in *Fare un Film* and was also published in Camilla Cederna's lively introduction to the book on *8½*. In the letter Fellini, who had himself spent some time at Chianciano followed by a few days at Fregene with Flaiano to jot down ideas, had already created many of the characters who were to appear in the film and many of the main themes too: loneliness, uncertainty, silent fear over the duties one has to perform.

We find the doctor who visits Guido, his mistress (writes Fellini: " . . . naturally she is voluptuous, pale-skinned and not very bright. Placid, good-natured, the ideal mistress because she creates no problems, but rather she is meek and submissive. She is married and speaks of her husband with affection, she would even like Guido to give him a hand. Anselmi's relationship with her is based on a sort of bland sense of physical well-being, rather like a baby taking milk from its bottle and then falling asleep satiated and exhausted. She talks a lot, but is not irksome, for she has a gentle voice and requires no more than an occasional smile to keep her happy. . ." The role seemed tailor-made for Sandra Milo), and the girl at the health resort (" . . . what about Claudia Cardinale, beautiful, young, but already mature at heart, an offer of authenticity which the hero no longer

knows how to accept. . .?"). There is the friend in trouble (" . . . he is a sixty-year-old intellectual . . . he is staying at Chianciano with the young girl for whom he has left his wife after forty years of marriage. . . ." The role was played by Mario Pisu). There is the telepathic couple, and then the bishop (" . . . I am still not too clear about the bishop . . . but I think that one evening he and the hero should meet and talk, although I haven't yet decided what they should say to one another. . ."). There is Guido's wife, played by Anouk Aimée (" . . . a very important character of the film. Theirs is a relationship both tortured and tender at the same time. They both believe that peace of mind lies in separation, but as soon as they are apart, they cannot wait to be back together again. They discuss separation, but without conviction, like two convicts planning a break that they know to be impossible. . .''). There is Saraghina ('' . . . an overpowering but splendid creature who represents the hero's first traumatic vision of sex. . .''). And the harem scene, of which Fellini says ('' . . . the inevitable harem-house, with all his women, even his wife: one is sewing, another is cooking while two others are watching TV'').

Bit by bit, we discover that the letter contains virtually the whole film, except the final idea, which is so obvious that it is astounding: the idea of the cinema, of making the hero a film director, terrified by the reality of actually having to make a film, to bring his ideas to life before the camera, to discuss matters with his producer, to make plans with his technicians, and then the moment of truth, the moment when filming really must begin, as though everyone were ''really'' sure of what they were about to do. . . .

We all have our favorite films, and our favorite Fellini films. My own personal feelings about *8½* have not, I think, changed since the first time I saw the film. I was invited to Milan for the preview. I left Genoa with a group of colleagues early in the morning, walked to the theatre, saw the film—Fellini put in a brief appearance then disappeared, with that mysterious air he always seems to have on such occasions—then there was the journey home. The next day I published a long article on the film which was, I remember, full of praise, though this is nearly always the case with Fellini's works, for which I seem to have an inexplicable weakness, as indeed I have for the work of a number of other directors—Ford and Truffaut, Sautet and Schoendoerffer, Phil Karlson and Howard Hawks, Richard Fleischer and Anthony Mann, Sam Peckinpah and Antonio Pietrangeli, Richard Brooks and Helmut Kautner—such a mixed bunch that some might argue: ''How can you like them all, different as they are one from the other?'' But I do. The title of my article read: ''A Producer's Crisis,'' which referred, of course, to the producer in the film, but the distributors were rather worried that people might think I had meant Fellini himself. I suppose they should be excused for being so indignant; they were only thinking about their

The director as a suppliant and tamer (Marcello Mastroianni).

film and the film distribution business was different in the early 1960s, as was the film business and perhaps the world in general.

Mine was the same response as I had to all Fellini's films: a feeling of satisfied pleasure at being in on the game, even on those occasions where Fellini's ''magic'' was less convincing; the delight of seeing the cinema used to interpret the cinema, with all its customary harassed pro-

ducers, angry intellectuals, bare-chested technicians running around the place with mischievous, self-satisfied expressions on their faces, just like someone who has just told a bawdy joke. And accompanying all was the music of Nino Rota which, in the case of *8½*, was to become particularly famous.

Rota (1911–1979) wrote the music for all Fellini's films from *The White Sheik* to *Prova d'Orchestra*. He

113

The "bishop" was a character Fellini wanted in the film at all costs, though he was not sure at first what his bishop was going to do or say (Marcello Mastroianni and Tito Masini).

started in the film business in 1933 and wrote the score for many famous films besides Fellini's: in early postwar years he worked for Castellani (*Mio Figlio Professore; E' Primavera; Sotto il Sole di Roma*), for Monicelli (*Un Eroe dei Nostri Tempi; La Grande Guerra*), for Lattuada (*Mafioso; Senza Pietà*), for Visconti (*Le Notti Bianche; Rocco e i Suoi Fratelli; Il Gattopardo*), for Soldati (*Fuga in Francia; Le Miserie del Signor Travet*), just to mention a few. But his closest ties were undoubtedly with Fellini, and much of his music, from the very first note, recalls the very image of Fellini and the bizarre characters of his world.

(c.g.f.)

REVIEWS

" . . . 8½ *embodies many of the themes of Fellini's earlier films. That of communication or rather the power to communicate, which was at the heart of* La Strada; *Luisa treats her husband ironically as 'the prophet who wants to speak to the multitude,' whereas in reality he is incapable of telling the truth. Religion and faith expressed as a moral and social phenomenon, as an educational system which he has always challenged: but the critic accuses Guido of involuntar-*ily *becoming a party to all he desires to denounce; in any event, there is no apparent religious anxiety in* 8½. *Childhood, adolescence . . . , the boredom and dreariness of provincial life: Guido bumps into a young girl he had met at the Cinema-Teatro Apollo in Bologna, and she reminds us of the sad young dancers of* Variety Lights *and* I Vitelloni. *Desperation, death, suicide: to some degree, these are present in all of Fellini's films. . . . Last of all, an obsession over purity: the arrival on the scene of Claudia, symbol of purity, who reminds us of the young cripple whose simple faith disarmed the corrupt old bidonista, or the girl who appears at the end of* La Dolce Vita. *Nonetheless, there is something new in* 8½ : *exuberance, self-assurance, joie de vivre, despite the verbal interruptions and superficial anxiety. . . .*"

Marcel Martin, CINÉMA 63, *78, Paris, July–August 1963.*

" . . . *His earlier film (*La Dolce Vita*) was comprised of a series of pictures following one after the other as though by an association of ideas, the hero passing from one to the other according to the ever declining parabola of his personal destiny, first as an accomplice, then as a victim of the malicious* world *he had unwisely entered. The interrelationship between the hero's personal story and the description of the environment guaranteed the film's vitality, though it did not totally guarantee its structural solidity.* 8½ *is similarly built around a series of 'frescoes,' but it is dedicated to personal existence and not to social life. Far from benefiting from this, the portrayal of the hero is often undermined; the film, though seemingly better integrated, tends instead to be dispersive, and powerfully effective episodes are interspersed with sequences of little meaning. The director's only chance of amalgamating these fragments is to create a surprise: he quickly discards the disquieting paraphernalia he has just displayed, and strikes up a lively worry-dispelling ring-a-ring-a-roses.*"

Vittorio Spinazzola, FILM 1964, *Feltrinelli, Milan 1964, p. 36.*

" . . . *Fellini's hero is an erotomaniac, a sadist, a masochist, a mythomaniac, an adulterer, a cheat, a fickle man, afraid of life and in need of maternal love. In some respects he resembles Leopold Bloom, the hero of Joyce's* Ulysses, *and we have the impression that Fellini has read and contem-*

The master of ceremonies, a mysterious character, part religious, part cunning, and an essential protagonist of the film, charged with an ambiguous magnetism (Ian Dallas and Marcello Mastroianni).

The mother, sad and threatening (Giuditta Rissone).

plated this book. The film is introverted, a sort of private monologue interspersed with occasional glimpses of reality. The neurosis of impotence is illustrated by Fellini with a surprising degree of clinical precision, which is more than likely involuntary at times.... Fellini's dreams are always surprising and, in a figurative sense, original, but his memories are pervaded by a deeper, more delicate sentiment. This is why the two episodes concerning the hero's childhood at the old country house in Romagna, and his meeting with the woman on the beach in Rimini, are the best of the film, and among the best of all Fellini's works...."

Alberto Moravia, L'ESPRESSO, Rome, 17 February 1963.

"... *The parabola drawn by Fellini could leave an indifferent impression, if removed from context ...*, but the beauty of the film lies in its 'confusion' ... a mixture of error and truth, reality and dream, stylistic and human values, and in the complete harmony between Fellini's cinematographic language and Guido's rambling imagination. It is impossible to distinguish the director of fiction from the director of fact, and so Fellini's faults coincide with Guido's spiritual doubts. The osmosis between art and life is amazing. It will be difficult to repeat this achievement. ... The film outlines an infinite number of issues (and controversies), they are all well-known and it would be pointless to list them here, as it would the human traits portrayed. It is rare to find such genius in the cinema. Every environment, every character, every situation has its own precise meaning in 8½. ..."*

Giovanni Grazzini, CORRIERE DELLA SERA, Milan, 16 February 1963.

"... *My admiration for Fellini is not without limits. For instance, I did not enjoy La Strada, but I did I Vitelloni. But I think we must all admit that 8½, leaving aside for the moment all prejudice and reserve, is prodigious. Fantastic liberality, a total absence of precaution and hypocrisy, absolutely dispassionate sincerity, artistic and financial courage, these are the characteristics of this incredible undertaking. ... Intellectually and aesthetically 8½ is a lyrical, moving and forceful attempt to achieve unity,* beyond contradiction and internal and external obstacles. From this state of eternal anxiety a work of art is born, from this baroque folly is created a beautifully balanced piece of architecture, in a passionate denial of convention and traditional values, in a neo-Franciscan search for some sort of equilibrium. I liked neither La Strada, nor Cabiria. Here, Fellini re-examines all that he had to say in I Vitelloni and The White Sheik, and I do not think that it is because he has a taste for self-quotation, but rather as though he were sharpening his own knife against himself. In this way, he overcomes his anxieties, and those indeed of every cinema man, shocked by the state of inferiority and subjection in which the art of film-making moves. ..."*

Pierra Kast, CAHIERS DU CINÉMA, 145, Paris, July 1963.

"... *Fellini's words, his most burning thoughts are fed into a microphone which multiplies over and over again this mea culpa, while a host of loudspeakers amplify, multiply and recompose the sound in an atmosphere similar to that of an equestrian circus. ... In the midst of all these good intentions and terrible torment is the feeling that Fellini is really only pretending, knowing full well that his audience is not prepared for simple self-examination, preferring instead manifestations of spiritual histrionics. ..."*

Mino Argentieri, RINASCITA, Rome, 16 February 1963.

"... *If 8½ differs from other films that are doubled in on themselves, it is not only because this 'doubling in' is more systematic or more central, but also and above all because it functions differently. For 8½, one should be careful to realize, is a film that is doubly doubled, and when one speaks of it as having a mirror construction (construction en abŷme), it is really a double mirror construction one should be talking about. It is not only a film about the cinema, it is a film about a film that is presumably about the*

A childhood paradise, rustic, immense and dialectical.

cinema; it is not only a film about a director, but a film about a director who is reflecting himself onto his film. . . . It is therefore not enough to speak of a 'film within the film' : 8½ is the film of 8½ being made; the 'film in the film' is, in this case, the film itself. . . . This triple-action construction gives the ending of the film, which has been variously interpreted, its true meaning. The version Fellini finally retained contains not one but three successive denouements. . . . And though one is right to underline the paradoxical and startling thing about 8½—that is, a powerfully creative meditation on the inability to create—the fact remains that this theme takes us back, beyond any possible affectation on Fellini's part, to a situation more fundamental and less paradoxical than it is occasionally said to be. Out of all the confusion we have witnessed in the film, an admirably constructed film, and one that is as little confused as possible, will, it is true, be born. . . ."

Christian Metz, SEMIOLOGIA DEL CINEMA, *Garzanti, Milan 1972, pages 306–311.*

" . . . 8½ is firm proof that La Dolce Vita was, and still is, the highest point of Fellini's creative parabola. Here his style is less constrained and he allows himself a few refinements; the 'liberal' construction of the story . . . allows the director a wide margin for invention and the impromptu style of certain episodes, true or false as they may be, is palpable and highly enjoyable. But 8½ says nothing more, adds nothing to what Fellini has tried to say before in La Dolce Vita. And it is also less autobiographical than the earlier work. . . ."

Corrado Terzi, AVANTI!, *Milan, 16 February 1963.*

"Here is a piece of entertainment that will really make you sit up straight and think, a movie endowed with the challenge of a fascinating intellectual game. It has no more plot than a horse race, no more order than a pinball machine, and it bounces around on several levels of consciousness, dreams and memories as it details a man's rather casual analysis of himself. But it sets up a labyrinthine ego for the daring and thoughtful to explore, and it harbors some elegant treasures of wit and satire along the way. . . . If Mr. Fellini has not produced another masterpiece—another all-powerful exposure of

A confidential chat between two men of the trade (Mario Conocchia and Guido Alberti).

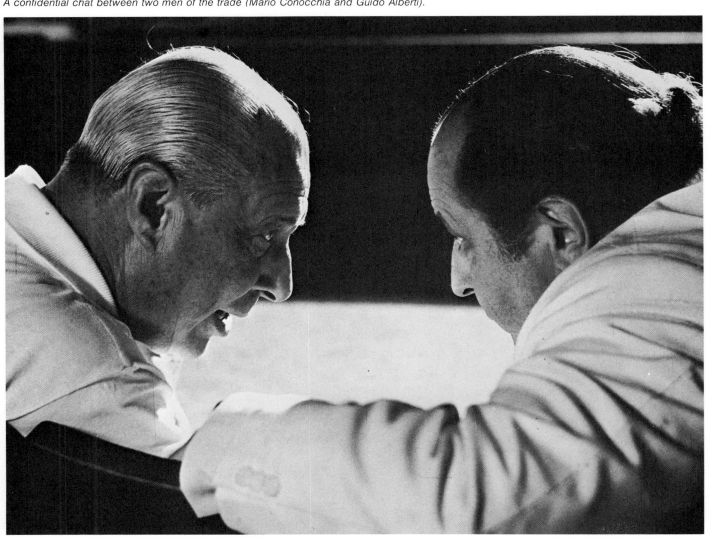

Italy's ironic sweet life—he has made a stimulating contemplation of what might be called, with equal irony, a sweet guy."

Bosley Crowther, THE NEW YORK TIMES, *June 26,1963.*

"Not only does [the film] constitute a kind of review and summary of Fellini's picture-making, it also must provide a look at his own mode of living, thinking and feeling, insofar as these truths can be presented in a meaningful film. It is said that [the film] has been more popular in Italy than La Dolce Vita. One may doubt that it will appeal quite so directly to the American public, or as strongly. This is a subtler, more imaginative, less sensational piece of work. There

will be more people here who consider it confused and confusing. And when they do understand what it is about, the simultaneous creation of a work of art, a philosophy of living together in happiness, and the imposition of each upon the other, they will not be as pleased as if they had attended the exposition of an international scandal."

Archer Winsten, THE NEW YORK POST, *June 26,1963.*

"It is an 'in' movie, a strangely cold and uninvolving one for the non-devout. Dazzled by the technique and the mind in control of it, we watch and listen with fascination, captives for the duration. And at the end we are instantly freed by the sudden realization that the

heart has not been touched nor the spirit moved. . . . For the devout, the cultists who are intimates of Fellini's personal and professional history, the film is obviously a total revelation of the master. For those of us who are but admirers of his work, it is as if we are eavesdropping on the psychoanalysis of a comparative stranger—and hearing nothing that makes us care very much about him."

NEW YORK HERALD TRIBUNE, *June 26,1963*

A typical Fellinian scene: a priest in the shadows, tiled walls, steam and an indefinable mysticism.

JULIET OF THE SPIRITS

GIULIETTA DEGLI SPIRITI   ITALY/FRANCE   1965

Produced by Angelo Rizzoli for Federiz (Roma) and Francoriz (Paris). Director: Federico Fellini. Screenplay: Federico Fellini, Tullio Pinelli, Ennio Flaiano, with the collaboration of Brunello Rondi. Based on a story by Federico Fellini, Tullio Pinelli, from an idea by Federico Fellini. Photography (Technicolor): Gianni Di Venanzo. Camera operator: Pasquale De Santis. Music: Nino Rota. Conductor: Carlo Savina. Art direction and costumes: Piero Gherardi. Assistant art directors: Luciano Ricceri, E. Benazzi Taglietti, Giantito Burchiellaro. Assistant costumers: Bruna Parmesan, Alda Marussig. Editor: Ruggero Mas:roianni. Set decorator: Vito Anzalone. Assistant set decorator: Franco Cuppini. Assistant directors: Francesco Aluigi, Liliana Betti, Rosalba Zavoli. Sound: Mario Faraoni, Mario Morici. Makeup: Otello Fava, Eligio Trani. Continuity: Eschilo Tarquini. Hair styles: Renata Magnanti, Marisa Fraticelli. Assistant editor: Adriana Olasio. Production managers: Mario Basili, Alessandro Von Norman. Production supervisor: Walter Benelli. Production secretaries: Renato Fié, Ennio Onorati. Distribution in Italy: Cineriz. Running time: 129 minutes.

Cunningly indulgent, luxuriously bedecked females haunt the film like shining apparitions (Sandra Milo and Giulietta Masina).

The entire film is like a dream, passing from an apparition to a scene of domestic bliss, from an ugly quarrel to a gentle dream (above, Sandra Milo).

CAST

Giulietta Masina (*Giulietta Boldrini*), Mario Pisu (*Giorgio, her husband*), Sandra Milo (*Susy/Iris/Fanny*), Valentina Cortese (*Valentina*), Caterina Boratto (*Giulietta's mother*), Lou Gilbert (*Giulietta's grandfather*), Sylvia Koscina (*Sylvia, Giulietta's sister*), Luisa della Noce (*Adele, Giulietta's other sister*), José de Villalonga (*José*), Valeska Gert (*Bhishma, the fortuneteller*), Silvana Jachino (*Dolores*), Fred Williams (*Arab prince*), Milena Vukotic (*Giulietta's maid*), Fredrich Lebedur (*headmaster*), Anne Francine (*psychoanalyst*), Elena Fondra (*Elena*), Elisabetta Gray (*another of Giulietta's maids*), Genius (*homosexual medium*), Dany Paris (*desperate friend*), Alberto Plebani (*Lynx-Eyes*), Yvonne Casadei, Dina De Santis, Hildegard Golez (*Susy's maids*), Mario Canocchia (*the family lawyer*), Cesarino Miceli Picardi (*Giorgio's friend*), Felice Fulchignoni (*Dr. Raffaele*), Lia Pistis (*friend on the beach*), Alba Cancellieri (*Giulietta as a child*), Walter Harrison, Asoka and Sujata Rubener (*Bhishma's assistants*), Bill Edwards, Elena Cumani (*visitors at Bhishma's*), Gianni Bertoncin (*bearded man*), Federico Valli, Grillo Rufino, Remo Risalti (*Lynx-Eyes' employees*), Giorgio Ardisson, Nadir Moretti, Alba Rosa, Bob Edwards (*models of Dolores the sculptress*), Alberto Cevenini (*priestess' attendant*), Seyna Seyn (*Susy's masseuse*), Anita Sanders, Wanani, Jacques Herlin (*guests at Susy's party*), Robert Walders (*false bearded corpse*), Maria Tedeschi (*psychoanalyst's patient*), Raffaele Guida (*Susy's oriental lover*), Alicia Brandet (*dancer on television*), Mary Arden (*actress on television*), Sabrina Gigli, Rossella Di Sepio (*Giulietta's nieces*), Irina Alexeieva (*Susy's grandmother*), Alessandra Mannoukine (*Susy's mother*), Gilberto Galvan (*Susy's chaffeur*), Eduardo Torricella (*Russian teacher*), Massimo Sarchielli (*Valentina's lover*), Jacqueline Gerard, Guido Alberti, Mino Doro.

SYNOPSIS

Giulietta, a married woman of Roman upper middle class society, spends her summers at her villa in Fregene. She has been educated by nuns and has fond memories of her grandfather who ran away with a dancer. Giorgio, her husband, is a brilliant public relations man. On the occasion of their wedding anniversary, Giuletta organizes a party at the villa during which a séance is held and spirits evoked: Iris, the saintly one who promises a "Christian love for everyone," but later betrays this promise by turning into a profligate neighbor, Susy; and Olaf, the heathen who embarrasses Giulietta with his coarse remarks. In insulting her, Olaf reawakens the identity crisis from which Giulietta has been suffering. This crisis becomes even more acute when she begins to suspect that her husband is unfaithful to her. Giulietta's mother is concerned only with her physical appearance; her sisters are empty-headed and superficial. She has no one in whom she can confide. She first consults an oriental fortune-teller, but this fails dismally; equally unsuccessful are the advances of a friend of Giorgio's, and the decision to have her husband followed in order to confirm her suspicions.

Giulietta's crisis is deeply rooted, growing from a conflict between the dictations of a Catholic upbringing and the temptations of a life with no inhibitions. The latter is exemplified by her neighbor, Susy, who invites Giulietta to her villa, which has been transformed into a sort of sex paradise. Giulietta at first tries to resist the temptation; then, tormented by the evidence gathered by the detective hired to follow Giorgio, she dolls herself up and joins Susy's orgy. But, plagued by guilt, once again she flees.

Giulietta is on the verge of a breakdown. The memory of a school play in which she played the part of a saint martyred on a grid mingles with the ghosts of lust. But she does not give in. She goes to a psychiatrist, she tries to talk to her husband's mistress, and she finds the courage to let Giorgio

An eloquent flow of colorful, glossy images, masterfully recreated by Gianni Di Venanzo, a director of photography whose highly personal style has left a lasting impression on Italian cinema.

walk out of her life. Alone in her huge house, Giulietta battles against the temptations, the inhibitions and the spirits which assail her. She wins. Dressed in white, she walks away into the wind blowing off the sea.

NOTES

Although many people did not enjoy this film, to devout Fellini fans it has all the typical mannerisms of this director: that cautious, childishly excited way of his of moving through a world of dreams, splendidly illuminated here by the photography of Gianni Di Venanzo (who was one of the great directors of photography of Italian cinema), in whose hands colors shine like glossy covers, acute as those of a trichromatic print. *Juliet*

Giulietta Masina.

of the Spirits* is probably Fellini's most "personal" film, where all his customary themes become pure abstraction, the manifestation of a desire to build dreams: around beautiful mistresses, gardens mantled with impeccable lawns, gentle maids, mysterious Spanish friends (the most significant of this colorful assembly is not Sandra Milo, nor Valentina Cortese, nor Caterina Boratto, but José-Luis de Villalonga, a writer of no little importance, a grandee of Spain in exile, launched into films by the French as a "luxury extra," and "a man who emanates charm," as somebody once described him).

Fellini himself has made some very interesting comments on *Juliet of the Spirits,* but they are so lengthy and complex that any attempt to summarize would only alter their meaning. They are to be found in

Fare un Film—which has gathered its information from twelve different publications—and in Tullio Kezich's interview, which appeared initially in the book on the making of *Juliet,* and was later included in *Fare un Film.* Fellini confirms that the film was created "around Giulietta and for Giulietta" and that he first began to develop the idea during the filming of *La Strada,* when they came across the diary of a nun. Later, Fellini conceived the idea of building the story around Eileen Garret, the medium, but the difficulties involved in writing the biography of a clairvoyant eventually persuaded him to abandon this project too. Next he was attracted by the idea of Giulietta playing different characters in the same film: an avaricious, overbearing woman, a fortuneteller, a millionairess, etc. In the end, after many tries (with his usual collaborators Pinelli, Flaiano and Rondi), Fellini came up with Juliet and her spirits, her dreams, her vision of the school play: gorgeous pictures from a Fellinian mythology which, strangely, is not always accepted, though for opposing reasons—too magical, too feline, too bright, too subdued, too many symbols of childhood (children, nuns, clowns, musicians, dreams), too mystical, too atheistic, too evasive, too explicit, too much everything. Luckily, although Fellini has always taken note of what is said of him, he has always managed to make light of it and has continued to go his own way.

(c.g.f.)

REVIEWS

Juliet of the Spirits is a sort of insipid parody of 8½, a film dominated by the unbearably negative patience of Giulietta Masina, a potpourri of trite situations, a Reader's Digest of Italian middle class culture; it is disconcertingly banal and mediocre. . . . It is total repetition . . . ; it is no longer a question of self-analysis as in 8½, but rather one of psychoanalysis of a character who is so distant and yet so near as might be a woman (especially if the biographical link is dominant and the woman is your wife), and what is more, using instruments that are imperfect and dangerous. . . . Added to all this, in a decidedly spectacular perspective, are all the customary stunts of the Fellinian circus, the church and the brothel, jugglers and living wonders, all bunched together in a carousel that rings false from start to finish, and which repeats, without any noticeable variations and therefore without any possibility for surprise, the themes of the preceding film."

Goffredo Fofi, QUADERNI PIACENTINI IV, 26, Piacenza, November–December 1965, now in CAPIRE CON IL CINEMA, Feltrinelli, Milan 1977, p. 65.

" . . . In recent years, Fellini's imagination has been enriched by a taste for what is generally known as the baroque: an ornamental frenzy, or decorative beatitude. When, as in this film, Fellini exercises his imagination on the situations of a reality envisaged as a psychadelic explosion of lines and colors, then the narrative balance between introspection and representation is upset; the ambiguity between fantasy and objective reality is the pretext for a grand display of illusionism; the juggler draws us into a universe from which we return dazed but unscathed. Juliet's marital crisis is suffocated by the luxuriance of the setting, by the vehemence or delicacy of the colors, by the bizarre magnificence of the costumes; though there is an occasional hint of humanity [in] those moments of sharp realism (her last meeting with the detective, the visit to Gabriella's house, Juliet's final parting from her husband) where the emotion is aroused without artifice. More often than not, however, a cascade of frills, bows and embellishments confuses us, distracting our attention from the heroine's drama. . . ."

Giovanni Grazzini, CORRIERE DELLA SERA, Milan, 23 October 1965.

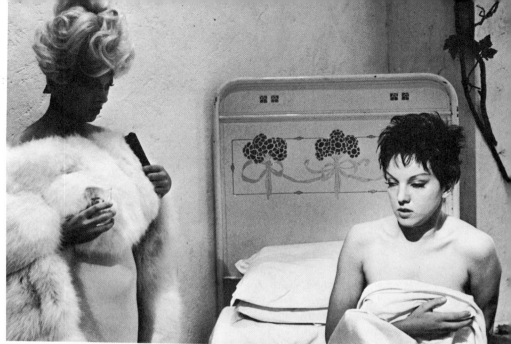

(Above) A female universe full of affectation (Sandra Milo and Dany Paris).

(Below) The malicious, gossipy world of the housemaids (on the right, Milena Vukotic).

" . . . *Juliet of the Spirits* is the film of a 'master artist'; if it is in part a failure, it is within the context of this artist's poetry that this failure lies. It is not the result of a compromise. . . . He develops the theme, but he does not express it. The theme is Juliet's victory over her spirits. The film is instead the spirits' revenge on Juliet. . . ."

Ugo Casiraghi, L'UNITA, Milan, 23 October 1965.

" . . . Paradoxically, Juliet of the Spirits might be termed a film to 'browse through' rather than to watch. The best way to appreciate it, would be to reduce it to some one thousand shots, to be examined one by one, rather like the photographs in an album. . . . One has the suspicion that Fellini was conditioned—and held in check—by the colors, not just by Juliet. . . ."

Morando Morandini, L'OSSERVATORE POLITICO LETTERARIO, Milan, 12 December 1965.

"... One has the impression that this film has been made rather like a sandwich, the unbuttered crusts of which are atoned for by the richness of the filling! On the one hand, Giulietta Masina, with her sad, stereotyped smile throughout, on the other the 'supercarnival', a typical Fellini weapon. There is no relationship between the two ingredients, except perhaps the director's dictatorship. ..."

Henri Chapier, COMBAT, Paris, 22 October 1965.

"... This change of style, from the objectified dialogue of La Dolce Vita and the substantially subjective one of 8½, resulting from a quest for a new style of language, has, in reality, determined a modification of choices, observations and ideas even though the basic themes remain the same. ... Less successful is the change from a subjectivism expressed in the first person, to one expressed in the third person. ... Paradoxically, the best parts of the film, that is to say the most enjoyable to watch, are also the worst in that they develop outside the main character and for no special reason. Once again Fellini has failed to create a precise condition: the realism is intentional, without effecting the 'things,' persons and objects that surround us."

Eduardo Bruno, FILMCRITICA XVI, 161, Rome, 1965.

"... The style of the film is baroque, redundant, even congested; on occasions, for instance at Susy's party, we even have a slight sense of nausea. It is easy to admire the unending succession of inventions, the ability to create a universe of absurdities, the ever more precise definition of a poetical vision. Equally evident, however, is a certain opacity which, at times, seems to take over, a sense of anxiety, the sort of feeling a man might have when, halfway through a journey, he suddenly has the sensation that he will never reach his destination."

Tullio Kezich, PANORAMA, Milan, 30 October 1965.

"... Juliet of the Spirits is the latest caravan to be added to the Fellini-Barnum circus. ... Briefly, reality and the supernatural, past and present are collated on the same plane, that of Fellinian baroque, where personal conventions have the same importance as the conventions of reality. ..."

Jean-Louis Bory, ARTS, Paris, 20–26, October 1965.

"The story is beautifully photographed and imaginatively pictured on the screen, but it has been allowed to run too long. The tempo of the action is slow, which is befitting the dream-like quality of the story, but because of this, it should have been tightened to keep it from dragging at the end. Giulietta Masina has a way of striking a sympathetic chord in the hearts of her audience and she manages to hold it throughout the filming. She is no longer the gamin of La Strada and Nights of Cabiria but is an older, simple, trusting, childless woman entirely dependent on her husband's love, when she is suddenly

The grandfather, the ballerina, the airplane: a composition which was to become famous (Lou Gilbert and Sandra Milo).

faced with his desertion. . . . Fellini has used color in a bold and fascinating manner to express the woman's spirit world. Its figures are, apparently, the expressions of her fears and desires. . . . As an imaginative piece of work, [the film] is extraordinarily interesting but may not be every moviegoer's cup of espresso as Fellini's appeal is more cerebral than emotional."

Kate Cameron, NEW YORK DAILY NEWS, *November 4, 1965.*

"Signor Fellini has reared back and truly passed a cinematographic miracle in this gaudy, surrealistic rendering of the fantasies of a wealthy, bourgeois wife when her mind is aroused by the suspicion that her husband is cheating on her. . . . It isn't necessary that you fit the pieces too snugly to enjoy the film. Mr. Fellini is not trying to resolve a mystery. He is trying primarily to give you an exciting experience on the screen, generated by a bold conglomeration of visual and aural stimuli. And that he does, with becoming accretions of humor and poignancy."

Bosley Crowther, THE NEW YORK TIMES, *November 4, 1965.*

Feathers, soft cushions, dreamy youths for Juliet's imagination (Fred Williams and Sandra Milo).

Toby Dammit

Episode: Toby Dammit/*Il ne Faut Jamais Parier la Tête avec le Diable*) Produced by Alberto Grimaldi and Raymond Eger for PEA, Rome and Les Films Marceau–Cocinor, Paris. Director: Federico Fellini. Screenplay: Federico Fellini, Bernardino Zapponi, liberally adapted from "Never Bet the Devil Your Head" by Edgar Allan Poe. Photography (Technicolor-Eastmancolor): Giuseppe Rotunno. Music: Nino Rota. Art direction and costumes: Piero Tosi. Editor: Ruggero Mastroianni. Camera operator: Giuseppe Maccari. Optical effects: Joseph Natanson. Song: "Ruby," words by Mitchell Parish, music by Heinz Roemheld. Singer: Ray Charles. Set decorator: Carlo Leva. Assistant directors: Eschilo Tarquini, Francesco Aluigi, Liliana Betti. Assistant editors: Adriana and Wanda Olasio. Production manager: Tommaso Sagone. Distribution in Italy: PEA. Running time: 37 minutes.

CAST

Terence Stamp (*Toby Dammit*), Salvo Randone (*Father Spagna, the priest*), Antonia Pietrosi (*actress*), Polidor (*old actor*), Anne Tonietti (*television commentator*), Fabrizio Angeli (*first director*), Ernesto Colli (*second director*), Aleardo Ward (*first interviewer*), Paul Cooper (*second interviewer*), Marisa Traversi, Rick Boyd, Mimmo Poli (*guests at the party*), Marina Yaru (*the child*), Brigitte (*the tall girl*).

The other episodes in the film are: *Metzengerstein* by Roger Vadim, *William Wilson* by Louis Malle.

SYNOPSIS

Toby Dammit is a young English actor consumed by alcohol and drugs. He flies to Rome to play the

The part of the old actor is played, in fact, by an old actor, who appears in Fellini's film as a sort of symbol: Polidor, real name Fernand Guillaume, star of the silent days with the stage names of Polidor and Tontolini, also appeared in The Nights of Cabiria, La Dolce Vita *and* The Temptations of Dr. Antonio.

Terence Stamp in the role of Toby Dammit, a young English actor consumed by alcohol and drugs, who goes to Rome to star in the "first Catholic western." Initially, Richard Burton, Marlon Brando and above all Peter O'Toole had been considered for the part.

lead role in the "first Catholic western." He is surrounded by photographers, journalists, producers and representatives of the Church mobilized especially for the occasion. Dragged from party to party, to fashion shows, to prize givings, Toby Dammit makes no effort to hide his gloomy indifference. His eyes light up for an instant only when a mysterious child throws him a ball as a sign that she wants him to play with her.

Boredom returns. At a certain point, the actor, who has publicly announced on television that he believes only in the devil, has a fit of temper. He insults the people around him, rushes out of the room and jumps into the sports car given to him as a present by the producers. At breakneck speed, he drives through Rome and reaches the outskirts. Night falls. Toby Dammit ignores the signs warning motorists that a bridge has collapsed

further along the road. He is following the mysterious child. He tries to jump the gap where the bridge was but fails to see a steel cable stretching across it, which neatly beheads him. The child runs to pick up the head as it rolls into a field, as though it were her ball.

NOTES

For the first time, the familiar names of Pinelli and Flaiano (and Brunello Rondi) are missing from the credits, their place to be taken by a new name: Bernardino Zapponi, who was to assist Fellini in many of his more recent films. In my opinion, the critics did not give this "changing of the guard" sufficient attention. And although a Fellini film is essentially a film by Fellini, regardless of who is assisting him in the writing of the story and the screenplay, it is equally true that the suggestions offered by Pinelli (who had a long history as a comedy

writer) and Flaiano (who was a brilliant essayist and moralist, as widely appreciated after his death as during his lifetime) were unique and never to be equalled. In all events, they mark a whole era in Fellini's career and in the history of Italian post-war cinema in general.

Toby Dammit was finally filmed, after the customary succession of productive vicissitudes, in an interval during which Fellini had once again tried to develop the by now mythical Viaggio di G. Mastorna, an idea he never seems able to put out of his mind completely. Initially, it was producer Raymond Egar who suggested a film comprised of some seven episodes, all inspired by Edgar Allen Poe stories, and each the work of a different director. Besides the three that actually remained, there were to be episodes by Joseph Losey ("Il Contratto"), Claude Chabrol ("The System of Doctor Tar and Professor Feather"), Orson Welles (a single

(Above) Toby Dammit has his palm read.

(Below) The mysterious features of Salvo Randone, one of Italy's greatest actors, in the role of Father Spagna.

". . . Poe's abstract northern ghosts are restored to us here after an encounter with the concrete, Mediterranean obsessions of Fellini . . ." wrote Jacques Aumont (Terence Stamp).

story drawn from "The Masque of the Red Death" and "The Cask of Amontillado"), Luchino Visconti (an episode combining "Maelzel's Chess Player" and "The Tell-Tale Heart").

The ups and downs which finally resulted in the initial project's being abandoned are described by Liliana Betti in the chapter dedicated to Fellini's episode in her book on *Tre Passi nel Delirio.* She tells of how Fellini first met Zapponi. Fellini (who was initially asked to direct "The Tell-Tale Heart") was not interested in the project at all. At about this same time, Zapponi had published a selection of short stories entitled *Gobal.* Fellini had taken a fancy to one of them: *"C'é Una Volta nella Mia Vita"* and had, in the meantime, discovered that Zapponi lived right opposite his new office. In search of a producer, Fellini eventually turned to the French (a large portion of Liliana Betti's account describes Fellini's interminable quarrels and reconciliations with Dino De Laurentiis over the famous *Mastorna,* but they are too complex to mention

here), only to learn that the copyright of Zapponi's story had already been bought by another Italian director. So Fellini proposed another of Zapponi's stories: *"L'Autista,"* but the French were not interested and would agree only to an Edgar Allen Poe story. Fellini finally gave in and chose one of Poe's most sinister and conventional stories, "The Premature Burial," transforming it, with his vivid imagination, into a sort of savage farce. But again he was refused. His next suggestion was: "Never Bet the Devil Your Head," and this time the proposal was accepted. He set to work on the screenplay with the result that, after two months of conjecture, doubt, disappointment and success, all that was left of Poe's original story was a title, a bridge and a bet.

Thus began the final phase, though not without its share of setbacks. Fellini had built his story around the figure of Peter O'Toole, but after all manner of discussions and negotiations (Richard Burton and Marlon Brando were also consid-

ered), the part went to Terence Stamp. Two days before filming was scheduled to begin, De Laurentiis telephoned Fellini offering him a film which no one would have thought in Fellini's line at all: *Waterloo.* Fellini was surprised, fascinated and interested, but of course, he had to say no.

Toby Dammit took just twenty-six days to film. Liliana Betti reveals that, one evening, at dinner with Nino Rota, after the film had been completed, Fellini spoke of Poe with considerable enthusiasm, but had to admit that he had read "Never Bet the Devil Your Head" for the first time only the day before!

(c.g.f.)

REVIEWS

" . . . [Of the three episodes] **Toby Dammit** *is the one which diverges most from the original Poe story; it is totally immersed in the Fellini world, from* **La Dolce Vita** *to* **Juliet**

of the Spirits. *We find here the dissipation of La Dolce Vita, the masks of Juliet, the procession of 8½ and more besides. . . . Weak as subject matter for a film, almost without substance, Toby Dammit is full of memories, nostalgia and the illusions dear to Fellini, with his out-of-this-world actresses, and aged Polidor, now little more than a mask. The film is all technique, the mists and glimmers of 8½, the colors of Juliet, giving way here to the problem of illumination, skillfully handled by Rotunno's photography: floodlights, lamps, headlights. Technique, sets and lighting are all-important. This formal exhibitionism, this technical virtuosity, is at times an end in itself. . . ."*

Mario Verdon, BIANCO E NERO XXIX, 11–12, Rome, November–December 1968.

" . . . Two elements, the macabre and the fantastic, characterize this particular episode, and though each is derived from a traditional Fellini theme, this time they are employed to create tragedy. Autobiographic as always, Fellini must evidently have been feeling the effects of his recent illness. His tone becomes gloomy, his gallery of monsters has a sinister air. His narrative structure, his characters, even Nino Rota's music score are no longer used as signs of a reality which can be changed for the better through compassion and hope . . . , but as a single, atrocious substance of a life that is no longer worth living, because it is totally void of freedom. . . ."

Giovanni Grazzini, CORRIERE DELLA SERA, Milan, 18 May 1968.

" . . . Poe's abstract northern ghosts are restored to us here after an encounter with the concrete, Mediterranean obsessions of Fellini who, for the first time, has managed to give us a realistic rendering of that 'pestilent and mystic vapor, dull, sluggish, faintly discernible and leaden-hued' which enshrouds the House of Usher and pervades all of Poe's

works. . . . The entire film is infused with a sense of the unreal, especially in the case of the two main characters (the hero and the devil, the only two whose monstrosity is totally inhuman), which transforms the earthly depravity of the protagonists and the typically Fellinian situations of the story into some terrifying and diabolical vision; this is emphasized by the haziness of each shot. Contrary to many other films where an atmosphere of fantasy and illusion is summarily achieved by the use of smoke devices, here it is the torment of the subject matter which requires and justifies 'hazy' shots. This is excellent cinema, which takes full advantage of all the possibilities offered by imagery . . . , editing . . . , and sound. Any excess is purely functional, designed to draw the essence from Poe's story."

Jacques Aumont, CAHIERS DU CINÉMA, 203, Paris, August 1968.

" . . . Fellini observes through the eyes of his characters; first he is a priest, then a Catholic scriptwriter, now a ruthless reporter, or he satirizes Totò, a blind, tottering comedian on the arm of a voluptuous blond actress. The Rome of Fellini-Poe portrays all this as though through a cloud of vapors, as though dreamed in a long-ago nightmare, unreal though punctuated by moments of verisimilitude. . . ."

e.b. (Eduardo Bruno), FILMCRITICA XIX, 193, Rome, December 1968.

The child with the ball (Marina Yaru) was called, in a sketch of Fellini's for the film, the "devil-child."

FELLINI: A DIRECTOR'S NOTEBOOK

Produced by Peter Goldfarb for NBC-TV. Director Federico Fellini. Screenplay: Federico Fellini, Bernardino Zapponi. Photography: Pasquale De Santis. Music: Nino Rota. Editor: Ruggero Mastroianni. Assistant editor: Adriana Olasio. Continuity: Norma Giacchero. Assistant directors: Maurizio Mein, Liliana Betti. Series unit manager: Joseph Nash. Dialogue: Christopher Cruise. English dialogue: Eugene Walter. Running time: 60 minutes.

CAST

Federico Fellini, Giulietta Masina, Marcello Mastroianni, Caterina Boratto, Marina Boratto, David Maumsell, Genius the medium, Cesarino, Gasparino, Bernardino Zapponi, Lina Alberti (all appearing as themselves) and numerous non-professional actors.

REVIEWS

"Burlington Industries, an American chemical company, had, at one stage, requested and obtained authorization to finance (obviously for publicity reasons) a TV 'special' within the framework of a cultural program produced by NBC. The 'special' was to be a long interview with Federico Fellini on his world of poetry, his abandoned projects (Il Viaggio di G. Mastorna), his latest film (Satyricon).... When the financers finally received the sixty-minute interview, 'Fellini: A Director's Notebook' they found that it contained all the traditional Fellini ingredients (prostitutes, voluptuous women, homosexuals, clowns, etc.) and consequently withdrew from the project. So as not to lose the program altogether, NBC had to take on the financial burden as well.... And what had originally been intended as a long interview

had, in the making, developed into a 'television film,' directed and signed by Federico Fellini. Faced with the necessity to meditate on himself ... and on his poetical and moral world, Fellini ... had virtually taken over the reins and come up with a splendid self-portrait; it had few autobiographical notes, few revelations and little gossip (less so perhaps than the financers would have' liked), but it was more revealing than any interview could possibly have been.... 'Fellini's Notebook' contains episodes of rare beauty, for instance: a visit to the abandoned set for Mastorna, and a look at some of the props and set designs in a warehouse; the search for old Roman faces for Satyricon; a visit to the freaky night

people who inhabit the Colosseum; a day in the life of the director who, in his offices, receives old and new acquaintances and aspiring actors and extras for his next film. Throughout, Fellini never tries to objectify himself; the object he presents for our attention is instead his own special world. Thus we discover ... that this succession of jaded faces, weary bodies, dull glances, furiously vital enthusiasm, surrealist visions, sex, solitude, irony and tenderness which makes up Fellini's world, is in effect the way, and the only way, in which he envisages reality...."

Lino Micciché, AVANTI!, Rome, 7 May 1969, now in CINEMA ITALIANO DEGLI ANNI '70, Marsilio Editori, Venice 1980, pages 35–37.

Fellini's Satyricon

FELLINI-SATYRICON   ITALY/FRANCE   1969

Produced by Alberti Grimaldi for PEA, Rome/Les Productions Artistes Associés, Paris. Director: Federico Fellini. Screenplay: Federico Fellini, Bernardino Zapponi, freely adapted from the work by Petronius Arbiter. Photography (Technicolor-Panavision): Giuseppe Rotunno. Camera Operator: Giuseppe Maccari. Optical effects: Joseph Natanson. Music: Nino Rota, with the collaboration of Ilhan Mimaroglu, Tod Docksader, Andrew Rudin. Art direction: Danilo Donati, Luigi Scaccianoce, with scenery sketches by Federico Fellini. Set decorations and costumes: Danilo Donati. Assistant art directors: Dante Ferreti, Carlo Agate. Assistant costumers: Franco Antonelli, Renzo Bronchi, Dafne Cirrocchi. Painting consultant: Nino Scordia. Head of painting department: Italo Tomassi. Architect: Giorgio Giovannini. Editor: Ruggero Mastroianni. Assistant editor: Adriana Olasio. Continuity: Enzo Ocone. Continuity secretary: Norma Giacchero. Assistant directors: Maurizio Mein, Liliana Betti, Lia Consalvo. Makeup: Rino Carboni. Hair styles: Lùciano Vito. Latin language consultant: Luca Canali. Production manager: Roberto Cocco. Production supervisors: Lamberto Pippia, Gilberto Scarpellini, Fernando Rossi. Production secretary: Michele Pesce. Distribution in Italy: PEA. Running time: 138 minutes.

CAST

Martin Potter (*Encolpius*), Hiram Keller (*Ascyltus*), Max Born (*Giton*), Salvo Randone (*Eumolpus*), Mario Romagnoli, "Il Moro" (*Trimalchio*), Magali Noël (*Fortunata*), Capucine (*Tryphaena*), Alain Cuny (*Lichas*), Fanfulla (*Vernacchio*), Danika La Loggia (*Scintilla*), Giuseppe Sanvitale (*Habinnas*), Genius (*Parvenue, the Freedman*), Lucia Bosé (*matron*), Joseph Wheeler (*suicide*), Hylette Adolphe (*slave girl*), Tanya Lopert (*emperor*), Gordon Mitchell (*thief*), Luigi Montefiori (*Minotaur*), Marcello

Magali Nöel, in the part of Fortunata, and Mario Romagnoli, ''Il Moro,'' as Trimalchio, in a shot which eloquently sums up the jaded, ironical tone of the entire film.

Fellini could hardly miss an occasion to offer us this magnificently retrospective hunchback and the slippery hill swarming with gladiators

De Falco (*Proconsul*), Elisa Mainardi (*Ariadne*), Donyale Luna (*Oenothea*), Carlo Giordana (*captain*), Pasquale Baldassarre (*hermaphrodite*), Lina Alberti (*golden idol*).

SYNOPSIS

Encolpius and Ascyltus are two young Romans, both enamored of the lewd and inconstant Giton. Encolpius, in his search for the ephebe who has been abducted by Ascyltus, learns at the baths that the boy has been sold to Vernacchio, the actor. He goes to the theatre, where Vernacchio is performing a licentious play, and reclaims his lover. The two of them take refuge in a palace which turns out to be a den of iniquity. Here they are joined by Ascyltus, whom Giton says he prefers to Encolpius. Encolpius decides to commit suicide, but an earthquake destroys the palace before he can do so.

The danger over, Encolpius meets Eumolpus, the ancient poet, who accompanies him to the house of Trimalchio, a wealthy freeman. A sumptuous and vulgar party is being held, during which Eumolpo is beaten up and Trimalchio conducts his guests to see his tomb. Encolpius is made a slave on the ship of Lichas, a sort of pirate in the service of the emperor. Here he again meets Giton and Ascyltus. Giton is forced to copulate with a child while Encolpius, beaten by Lichas in a duel, is forced to become Lichas' spouse. Rebel soldiers kill the emperor and Lichas is beheaded. Encolpius and Ascyltus end up in the villa of an aristocratic couple who have just committed suicide by slashing their veins. Here they rape a young slave girl.

Their adventures continue. After they have done their best to placate the passions of a nymphomaniac, they kidnap, in a temple, an hermaphrodite reputed to have divinatory powers, but "it" dies during the journey. Encolpius, captured by soldiers, is forced to fight the Minotaur. Among the spectators are Ascyltus and Eumolpus. Encolpius is beaten and has to prove his vi-

Lichas' extraordinary boat (Alain Cuny).

rility with Ariadne. He fails and is laughed at by everybody. In order to cure him of his impotence, Eumolpus leads him to the Garden of Delights, but the remedies applied by the adept young girls prove totally ineffective. It is not until he is taken to Oenothea that his sexual prowess is restored.

Encolpius' happiness is overshadowed by the unexpected death of Ascyltus. So he decides to join the ship of Encolpius, who has in the meantime died leaving as his heirs those willing to eat his corpse. Encolpius refuses to participate in this gruesome feast, but he sails with the ship towards Africa.

NOTES

Dario Zanelli, film critic of the newspaper *Resto del Carlino* and editor of the book *Fellini Satyricon* explains that Fellini first began to toy with the idea of making a film from the work by Petronius Arbiter in the summer of 1967. Fellini, who was just recovering from a bad attack of pleurisy and a strange experience with hallucinatory drugs, conducted under medical surveillance, was particularly enthusiastic about the hippy move-ment (which was at that time at the height of its popularity and seemed to be bearing heaven knows what manner of naïve message). Fellini soon reached an agreement with Alberto Grimaldi of PEA (the distributors) according to which he was to start making *Satyricon* just as soon as he had finished the legendary *Viaggio di G. Mastorna* (after so many years of hearing about it, this is the one film we would really like to see brought to the screen).

The two years that elapsed before the film was released (September 1969) were marked by the customary milestones: contracts, agreements, changes, alterations in the screenplay, filming (from November 1968 to May 1969), editing, mixing, printing and so forth. Plus all the old problems and a new one besides: competition, in the shape of another *Satyricon* produced by Bini, directed by Gian Luigi Polidoro, with screenplay by Rodolfo Sonego and starring Tina Aumont, Don Backy, Mario Carotenuto, Franco Fabrizi, and Ugo Tognazzi. Under the circumstances, the title of Fellini's film was changed to *Fellini-Satyricon.* But not before the director had invented and discarded other such titles as *The Satirical Romance,* after the title given to Petronius's book in the eighteenth cen-tury, and *Myths and Legends o[f] Ancient Rome,* which ironically sug[ge]sts some erudite symposium. The producers on their part had come u[p] with such titles as *Fellinicon* and *Heroticon,* which sound vaguely like parodies of some more serious film[s].

The film was meticulously pre pared. Both Fellini and Zapponi read widely on the subject and consulted several famous Latin scholars among whom was Ettore Paratore. Another expert, Luca Canali, forme[r] assistant to Paratore and lecturer a[t] Pisa University, became the film's official consultant. Fellini had at one point considered adopting Latin for al[l] the dialogue, but as this would have been incomprehensible to the vas[t] majority, he had to abandon the idea. Nonetheless, fragments of Latin were left in, which, for anyone who can still remember a smattering of the lan guage from school-days, are a source of considerable amusement.

For all those who love Fellini, the film is full of delightful moments. Rome is at once dissipated, splendid, jaded, ambiguous, inhabited by al[l] manner of strange beings, from the very rich to the very poor, from slaves to masters, from prostitutes to sexua[l] perverts; the sensation being that o[f] a vast and luxurious parody mingled with a vision of a past which is both existent and nonexistent at the same time. Robert Benayoun sums up this sensation admirably, when he says " . . . we go beyond autobiography here, though we do not abandon it. The childhood rediscovered in *8½,* the maturity crisis underlined in *Juliet of the Spirits* are conditions into which Fellini projects himself, recapturing youth through Marcello Mastroianni, maturing in the figure of Mario Pisu (Giulietta's husband). Here, in *Satyricon,* he no longer feels the need to be reincarnated in some physica[l] form. He has spectacularly established contact between the nostalgic funambulist Fellini of early films and the gentler, almost senile Fellini of the 1960s.''

Especially evident in this film is Fellini's magical, almost savage delight in human features. (All accounts of the preparation of Fellini's films contain a passage on his search for ''faces,'' explaining how he and his assistants spend hours scrutinizing albums full of photographs of possible extras, walk-ons and actors which Fellini, with his acute sense of observation, rapidly and succinctly assesses. Generally, he has a clear idea of what he is looking for, and will not rest until he finds it—for instance, he had always imagined Trimalchio as a sort of gloomy, apathetic Onassis: a mummy, in fact, and the part eventually went to Mario Romagnoli, nicknamed "Il Moro," owner of the famous restaurant of the same name.) There are two other points of interest mentioned by Zanelli. Fellini's first encounter with *Satyricon* dates back to the days of the *Marc'Aurelio*, when Marcello Marchesi one day brought to the office a much-modified edition of the book. Fellini and Mario Brancacci read it and toyed with the idea of adapting it for a stage show. They worked on it solidly for two nights, fending off exhaustion with stimulants, but that was as far as the project went.

The second encounter occurred during the heyday of The Funny Face Shops. One day, a publisher came to the shop in search of a drawing for the front cover of a new edition of *Satyricon*. In the end he preferred the sketch drawn by De Seta (another illustrator of that period and partner of Fellini's). It was not until after the filming of *I Vitelloni* that Fellini first had occasion to read an unabridged version of Petronius's story and seriously began to entertain the idea of someday making it into a film. Generally speaking, these vague ideas of Fellini's are long-lived—and productive.

(c.g.f.)

REVIEWS

" . . . *Fellini's Rome bears absolutely no relationship to the Rome we learned about in school books. It is a place outside historical time, an area of the unconscious in which the episodes related by Petronius are relived among the ghosts of Fellini. . . . His Satyricon is a journey through a fairytale for adults. If it touches us, then it is* because *Fellini's voice, as it tells the tale, is almost troubled. It is fairly evident that Fellini, finding in these ancient personages the projection of his own human and artistic doubts, is led to wonder if the universal and eternal condition of man is not actually summed up in the frenzied realization of the transience of life which passes like a shadow. These ancient Romans, who spend their days in revelry, ravaged by debauchery, are really an unhappy race searching desperately to exorcise their fear of death. In this sense, Satyricon, developing the lugubrious accents of Toby Dammit, is an important step in Fellini's journey towards a form of existential doubt which, grafted on Catholicism, has taken the place of former optimism. . . . "*

Giovanni Grazzini, CORRIERE DELLA SERA, *Milan, 5 September 1969.*

" . . . *Everything seems to be aimed at making the viewer feel ill at ease, at giving him the impression that*

" . . . an immense effort to transform into figuratively powerful images something mysterious and unknown . . ." wrote Angelo Solmi.

Encolpius comes to grips with a coarse, savage, unfamiliar world (Martin Potter).

he is watching for the first time scenes from a life he never dreamed could have existed. This is why Fellini has described Satyricon as 'science fiction of the past,' as though the Romans of that decadent age were being observed by the astounded inhabitants of a flying saucer. Curiously enough, in this effort of objectivity, the director has created a film that is so subjective as to warrant psychoanalysis. It is pointless to debate whether the film proposes a plausible interpretation of ancient Rome, or whether in some way it illustrates Petronius; the least surprising parts are those which come closest to the original text, or which have some vague historical significance. But the author's imagination runs wild in the grotesque marriage of Alain Cuny dressed in woman's clothes, or in the battle scene with the fake Minotaur. The atmosphere is almost always morbid, claustrophobic and nocturnal. . . . "

Tullio Kezich, PANORAMA, Milan, 18 September 1969.

" . . . Prompted by a morbid delight in the physical and moral antics of a race living at the very limits of vulgarity, Fellini has assembled a dazzling array of ephebes, slaves, nobles, matrons, Romans, barbar-

ians, youths, obscene women, bloated aristocrats, parasites and plebians, in his quest for physical peculiarities capable of provoking more than just immediate pleasure in the unusual or horrible. . . . The result is an unequal mixture, which sometimes loses itself in excessive characterization, sometimes becomes truculent without reason, and which lacks the malicious and crafty frivolity pervading Petronius's work. But the mixture is exceptional just the same for its visual and figurative originality. . . . "

Claudio G. Fava, CORRIERE MERCANTILE, Genoa, 5 September 1969.

" . . . Each image, each symbol, each color, each pictorial expression rings of Fellini, his world, all he loves or hates, all he believes in, or believed in, or no longer believes in and, above all—with the same feeling of terror as that awakened by creative impotence in the hero of 8½—of the anguish he feels at impotence of any kind, which means death, fear of death. Death, the end, annihilation are the themes of this film, its dramatic and esthetic message: a single note—a dismal one, a single color—a spectral one, a single mood— that of total destruction. . . . "

Gian Luigi Rondi, IL TEMPO, Rome, 5 September 1969.

" . . . Fellini-Satyricon is a film that contains all the bitterness and anxiety of our time and at the same time, by virtue of the road it has chosen to take, goes beyond them, a film which challenges the cinema of the past and seeks to find a new one; a film that renounces itself and proclaims a new season which, in preceding films . . . was suggested only visually; a faint and 'private' message, made universal in Satyricon. . . . The basic material of the film is totally visual, carrying the same importance as musicality in a Verdian melodrama. Fellini is, first and foremost, a 'cinematographic man': the succession of images overcomes all else, even more successfully than in Juliet of the Spirits. . . . "

Mario Verdone, BIANCO E NERO XXX, 9–10, Rome, September–October 1969.

" . . . The parts which shock the most in this film are those which are the most human, too human. For Fellini, sin exists. Fellini-Satyricon celebrates the feasts of sin. Pessimism becomes metaphysical. Man is a puppet pledged to the putrefaction of death, but who is already tainted before death comes. . . . Fellini-Satyricon is the contemplation of a steaming cesspool. Nonetheless, we are spellbound, as we contemplate, by the stark horror of it all. Fellini himself is fascinated, and because he is, he touches this horror with his magic wand, and the magic immediately rings forth. Fellini's magic, his secret, is that for him beauty is nurtured by the beasts created by his dreams. Everything in the film is monstrous, terrible, horrible, turbid, and yet at the same time beautiful. The more monstrous the subject, the more beautiful Fellini's representation of it. . . . This is the film of a painter. Fellini-Satyricon is like a museum that is no longer imaginary, but animated by a sweeping movement such as that of a river, but tortured as though that river were studded with rapids and whirlpools. . . . "

Jean Louis Bory, LE NOUVEL OBSERVATEUR, Paris, 15 December 1969.

A lascivious, proudly corrupt Rome through which Fellini moves like a derisive archeologist.

" . . . The film is like a supersonic journey beyond morality; nothing in this ancient story prefigures the coming of Christianity, there is no sense of guilt over sin, no hint of cynicism. Fellini places his story in an area where literally everything is allowed, where murder, vice, incest are little more than points of reference, milestones in the evolution of mankind. The film is not only a chaos of languages, but also of ideas and concepts. Ascyltus and Encolpius are continually meeting people who talk in an unknown tongue and who, originating from Babel, have much to say in a senseless murmur. But this small mystery leads to another, greater one: that of intentions and principles. And this is what makes Satyricon superior to Fellini's two preceding films."

Robert Benayoun, POSITIF 111, *Paris, December 1969.*

"Perhaps [Fellini] didn't do it himself, build the great black barges or light the extraordinary sets that have an unearthly El Greco glow, or the `classic bareness of a Chirico, but he caused it to be done: the way those oars rise and fill the screen, or a gigantic cliff rises to the sky from the sea, or an orgy takes place and a belch is analyzed for prophecy while a nameless face, all eyes, looks questioningly into the camera, and beyond, into your eyes. . . [he] brings [his characters] to life with amazing vigor, so that they live in your own mind.

"This makes of the Fellini-Satyricon a film of classic background and powerful contemporary parallel. It is so beautifully composed and imagined that you would do yourself a disservice if, for any reason, you allowed yourself to miss it. Even the fact that it may occasionally have the effect of wearing you down with its repetitive visual opulence, or could make you weary with its far-wandering failure to achieve point, should not discourage anyone who seeks beauty, art or film complexity of experience."

Archer Winsten, NEW YORK POST, *March 12, 1970.*

"Fellini lingers lovingly on every conceivable kind of perversion, cruelty and corruption in this film, which takes even cannibalism matter of factly. To convey the depths of decadence to which Rome had sunk under Nero's reign, he uses a gallery of grotesques that people the screen with nightmare visions. . . . It is a self-indulgent series of tableaux vivants for Petronius's classic on the moral decay of ancient Rome . . . but there is no redeeming insight in this film, which Fellini supposedly made to illustrate the parallels between ancient Rome and the world today."

Louise Sweeney, THE CHRISTIAN SCIENCE MONITOR, *March 11, 1970.*

"The acting skills of an immense cast are unusually advanced, the color photography is magnificent, the material is beyond all belief and the result is another grandiose Fellini shocker, something for the strong-hearted to relish and, above all, a film that will surely become a classic."

Alan Branigan, THE NEWARK EVENING NEWS, *March 12, 1970.*

Hiram Keller (Ascyltus) and Martin Potter (Encolpius) battle with the thief (Gordon Mitchell, in the center).

THE CLOWNS

Produced by Elio Scardamaglia and Ugo Guerra for RAI-Radio Televisione Italiana and Compagnia Leone Cinematografica (Italy)/ORTF (France)/Bavaria Film (W. Germany). Director: Federico Fellini. Screenplay: Federico Fellini, Bernardino Zapponi, from a story by Federico Fellini and Bernardino Zapponi. Photography (Technicolor): Dario Di Palma. Camera operator: Blasco Giurato. Music: Nino Rota. Conductor: Carlo Savina. Costumes: Danilo Donati. Editor: Ruggero Mastroianni. Assistant editor: Adriana Olasio. Assistant directors: Maurizio Mein, Liliana Betti. Continuity: Norma Giacchero. Makeup: Rino Carboni. Special effects: Adriano Pischiutta. Hair styles: Paolo Franceschi. Set decoration: Renzo Gronchi. Mixage: Alberto Bartolomei. Production manager: Lamberto Pippia. Distribution in Italy: Italnoleggio. Running time: 93 minutes.

CAST

Themselves: Liana, Rinaldo, Nando Orfei, France Migliorini, Anita Ekberg. The Clowns: Billi, Scotti, Fanfulla, Reder, Valentini, Merli, Rizzo, Pistoni, Furia, Sbarra, Carini, Terzo, Vingelli, Fumagalli, Zerbinati, I 4 Colombaioni, I Martana, Maggio, Janigro, Maunsell, Peverello, Sorrentino, Valdemaro, Bevilacqua; Fellini's Troup: Maya Morin, Lina Alberti, Alvaro Vitali, Gasparino; The French Clowns: Alex, Bario, Père Loriot, Ludo, Charlie Rivel, Maiss, Nino; and with Pierre Etaix, Victor Fratellini, Annie Fratellini, Baptiste and Tristan Rémy, Pipo and Rhum, Buglioni the lion-tamer, Hugue, former ringmaster.

SYNOPSIS

The film opens with a boy being awakened by the raising of a circus tent. The appearance of the clowns reminds him of people from real life: a crazy midget nun, the village idiot who likes to play at war, a comic and self-important little station-master who is the butt of everyone's practical jokes, a Fascist officer who absurdly goes round and round in his motor-cycle sidecar, a crowd of village loafers. The action shifts to the present day. Fellini is conducting a television documentary; he is searching for the clowns of yesterday. After a visit to Liliana Orfei's circus, Fellini and his troupe move on to Paris, where they interview a writer who specializes in the history of the clown: Tristan Rémy. Together, they trace the few surviving clowns. With them, Fellini organizes a gigantic parade around the circus ring, but it has only the atmosphere of a funeral.

The wide-eyed astonishment of the "White Clown."

The ritual make-up, as fascinating as that of the Maoris or the Zulus, makes the clown's face look like some incredible artist's palette (above, behind the white mask, is the face of Fanfulla, who was a well-known pre-war variety theatre artist, and who has made several screen appearances in post-war years).

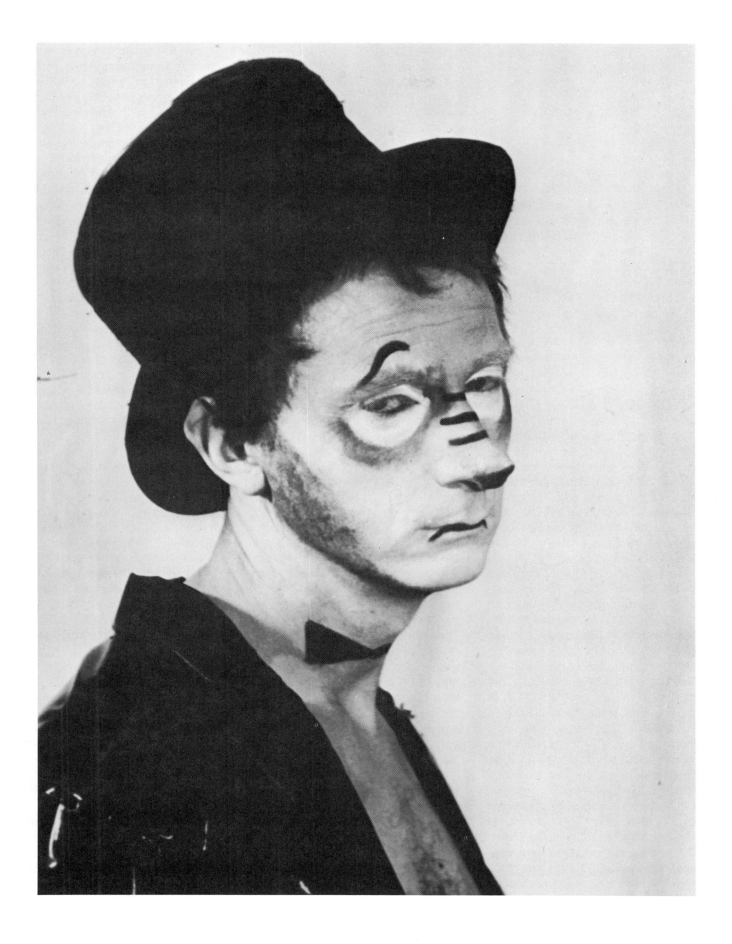

The typical intercourse of colors in the clash between two clowns.

NOTES

A story in the form of an enquiry, and an enquiry "disguised" as a story, *The Clowns* is unmistakable evidence of Fellini's innate fascination for the world of the circus, with its explicit "falseness," its painted faces, its mechanical fairytale air, its papier mâché tightrope dancers arousing the desires and dreams of young and old alike. The circus is one of the most openly liturgical of all forms of organized entertainment, on a par with certain traditions of Japanese theatre. Everything is meticulously planned right down to the last detail: the entrée of the acrobats, the horses, the elephants, the ostentatious salute of the lion-tamer and the jugglers. And, of course, the clowns, the White Clown and the Auguste, whose seemingly improvised act is as rigidly tied to a precise pattern of amusement as those of the rest of the circus players. As we said before, a liturgical pattern, a mingling of highly skilled athletes and histrionic court ceremonials, as might also be said of classical ballet.

In one of his interviews Fellini, after having given a lengthy account of his plans for the future, explains how he had come to make (in collaboration with the RAI—Italian television and radio company) a film about clowns and the circus. (Let's make a film about clowns, "the ambassadors of

my profession," had been the initial proposal.) The interview originally appeared in the book about the film published by Cappelli. So typical is it of Fellini, that one is tempted to quote it all, but for lack of space I shall select a few of Fellini's more significant comments: " . . . In the beginning my intention was to make a serious documentary. I completed my enquiry, but I somehow felt awkward. In truth, I don't know how to ask questions, and even when I do manage to ask an intelligent question, I find I am not really interested in the answer. And so, during the course of the enquiry, I spoke of this handicap . . . the only testimony one can give in making an enquiry, is that of one's own tactlessness, one's insolent curiosity. With the result that my enquiry was decidedly satirical, and in this way I was able to endure it. I repeat, the only documentation one can possibly give, is a documentation of oneself. 'The only true realist is the visionary,' who said that? The visionary, in fact, gives testimony of events that belong to his reality, in other words the truest reality of all. . .

"And now I must make an embarrassing confession: I really know nothing about the circus at all; I feel I am the last person on earth qualified to talk about it. Moreover, I must confess that I have been to very few circuses during my life, even though my admission might dishearten the

many, many friends I have in the circus, and who always meet and greet me as though I were one of them: an old horserider or sword swallower, for instance. But then again, why shouldn't they? Even though I know nothing about the circus, I really know everything, even its innermost secrets. I have always known. Right from the very first time, I have felt totally at one with all the hubub, the deafening music, those disquieting apparitions, the threat of death even . . . this sense of elation, excitement and emotion, this feeling of being at home was immediate, the very moment I entered the Big Top . . . though it was empty. There was a haunting silence all around, no sound could be heard except the distant singing of a woman going about her daily chores, and the whinnying of a horse somewhere. I was captivated, suspended, like an astronaut abandoned on the moon who suddenly finds his spaceship. . . ."

How clear then is the aimiable, complacently intellectual, subtly poetical attitude with which Fellini approaches and evokes the circus (a place endowed with a sort of familiar magic, with its absurd, grotesque, disrespectful, bungling clowns). The final result, full of interest from start to finish, does have a certain affectation about it, because of the juxtaposition of invention and "documentary," but it is also a testimony to the director's inability to manipulate reality dispassionately, that is to say without transfiguring it, recreating it, enriching it with all manner of embellishments, in a never-ending, desperate, astute skirmish with his own boundless imagination.

(c.g.f.)

REVIEWS

" . . . In developing such a typically Fellinian theme as the clowns, Fellini has been unable to resist the temptation and risk of recreating himself. In this sense, The Clowns is again an autobiographical film, and autobiographical in a visceral way; once again Fellini has not been searching for other people or other things, but for himself alone;

and once again he is not doing it in order to understand himself, but rather to parade himself...."

Giovanni Raboni, L'AVVENIRE, Milan, 1 September 1970.

"...We should take care when discussing **The Clowns**, a film made by Fellini for television, ninety minutes divided quite clearly into three parts: childhood, life and death. We should not be fooled by the schematism and mannerism of the 'progressive' critic, but rather limit ourselves to pointing out that clowns are an integral part of all Fellini's cinema, the conclusion being that this new film is repeated repertoire...."

Paolo Valmarana, IL POPOLO, Rome, 1 September 1970.

"...The film is rich in poetry and intelligent, a worthy creation of the ingenious clown that Fellini is basically, and not so basically... There is a bit of everything in this film. Sometimes crammed in by force, like the feline apparitions of Anita Ekberg among the cages of the Orfei Circus. But it is also full of Fellini: all the constants of his creative talent, his charm, his malice, his effusions, his beliefs and his skepticism...."

Guglielmo Biraghi, IL MESSAGGERO, Rome, 31 August 1970.

"...It is not that Fellini transfigures the circus, but rather that he tries incessantly to do so (as he has in earlier films) and he is not always successful. His talent sparkles frequently ... but it is held in check, channelled into more modest dimensions, by an underlying sense of artifice, the autobiographical reiteration of hackneyed themes; there is nothing new to say, nor is it said any better than in the past."

Ugo Casiraghi, MILANO, 31 August 1970.

"...The most enchanting part of the film is the first, in which Fellini, with admirable pureness of image and inimitable figurative power,

"... absurd, disrespectful, grotesque, bungling clowns ..." were the words of Fellini.

unites in his memory his admiration for the people of the circus and his amazement for the oddities of his home province.... In the second part, which takes place in Paris, there are some gaps, although the author does make up for a certain lack of expressive figures by inventing some exhilerating 'clownesque' exhibitions. The film takes off again as it nears the end, thanks to an uproarious summary of circus follies, concluding with a symbolic funeral; a burlesque and nostalgic apotheosis of a world dear to Fellini, with all its melancholy ghosts, its blatant sham and its confusion...."

Giovanni Grazzini, CORRIERE DELLA SERA, Milan-Rome, 31 August 1970.

"...Fellini the solitary prophet again seems to prefer to retire into himself and to live with his own ghosts, who talk of death, and of the absurdities, monstrosities and wonders of life, rather than to reflect rationally and solemnly on the end of civilization. Ever since **La Dolce Vita**, he has, it seems, worked in total and well-deserved liberty to express the doubts and fears of a person who has found the most disparate of images in order to represent himself on the screen. With **The Clowns**, though continuing the same introspective quest, he has managed to overcome the limits of a film 'made to order.' We might almost hope that he is faced with similar restrictions in the future. Anyway, Fellini has shown that he had nothing to lose, and possibly everything to gain, in facing and overcoming the obstacles deriving from 'external dictations.' "

Frédéric Vitoux, POSITIF, 129, Paris, July–August 1971.

" . . . We are all aware of Fellini's interest (obsession almost) in clowns. We have already been introduced, in La Strada and 8½, and even The White Sheik and Satyricon, to the violent and startling masks of this monstrous race of mortals which inhabits Fellini's world. But his return to the past here, is different from the baroque style which has sometimes undermined this director's work. First and foremost, we are dealing with an author who poses himself some historical questions on the themes he employs and on his ghosts. Certainly, he enjoys doing it, but it is interesting to note how Fellini tries to keep away from the spectacular, even though his aim is to create a spectacle born of the spectacular. This apparent contradiction is not surprising (we are reminded of La Dolce Vita and I Vitelloni); indeed, it is the author's catalyst.

"Fellini, who often plays with paradox, is dealing here with a microsociety built entirely on dualism: White Clown/Auguste; acrobats/clowns; spectators/spectacle; past/present. Sometimes this is very evident, as when the three Fratellinis perform in front of their doubles who tenderly imitate them. All this takes us back to the main historical point of Fellini's cinema: Christianity. In the clowns' act, Fellini reconstructs only Manichean violence, the apparent transgression of certain taboos, the representation of sexual blocks. . . . In brief, he continues to narrate Satyricon, but he does it more shrewdly and with less redundance. . . . "

N.S. (Noël Simsolo), LA REVUE DU CINÉMA—IMAGE ET SON, 252–253, Paris, September–October 1971.

" . . . The film . . . is totally and solely Fellinian; and it is so thanks to the kaleidoscopic presentation of the circus world, thanks to the style of editing, thanks to the gaudy choice of colors, alive and rich with chromatic variations. Fellini's enjoyment in his creation makes The Clowns a film to be watched from start to finish. And by ignoring the problem of interdependence and dissimilarity between the language of cinema and the language of television, it is equally a film for television and for cinema. The finale is full of motifs dear to 8½, with the funeral, the troupe leaving the ring and the appearance at the end of the old clown playing the trumpet. It is full of Fellini. It is full of torment for the end of a childish innocence. And it has the final touch of a director who never gives in to easy sentimentalism, but rather, when he sees that a tear is welling, quickly turns it into a subdued laugh."

Francesco Dorigo, IL PICCOLO, Trieste, 31 August 1970.

"In the clowns act, Fellini reconstructs only Manichean violence, the apparent transgression of certain taboos, the representation of sexual blocks . . ." wrote Nöel Simsolo.

ROMA

ROMA ITALY/FRANCE 1972

Produced by Turi Vasile for Ultra Film (Rome) and Les Productions Artistes Associés (Paris). Director: Federico Fellini. Screenplay: Federico Fellini, Bernardino Zapponi, from a story by Federico Fellini and Bernardino Zapponi. Photography (Technicolor): Giuseppe Rotunno. Camera operator: Giuseppe Maccari. Assistant camera operators: Pietro Servo, Roberto Aristarco, Michele Picciaredda. Music: Nino Rota. Conductor: Carlo Savina. Art director: Danilo Donati, with scenery sketches by Federico Fellini. Assistant art directors: Giorgio Giovannini, Ferdinando Giovannoni. Costumes: Danilo Donati. Assistant costumers: Romano Massara, Rita Giacchero. Set decorator: Andrea Fantacci. Editor: Ruggero Mastroianni. Assistant editor: Adriana Olasio. Assistant directors: Maurizio Mein, Paolo Pietrangeli, Tonino Antonucci. Special effects: Adriano Pischiutta. Makeup: Rino Carboni. Hair styles: Amalia Paoletti. Continuity: Norma Giacchero. Mixage: Renato Cadueri. Choreography: Gino Landi. Frescoes and portraits: Rinaldo Antonelli, Giuliano Geleng. Production manager: Lamberto Pippia. Production supervisors: Alessandro Gori, Fernando Rossi, Alessandro Sarti. Distribution in Italy: Italnoleggio. Running time: 119 minutes.

CAST

Peter Gonzales (*young Fellini*), Fiona Florence (*Dolores, the young prostitute*), Marne Maitland (*guide in the catacombs*), Britta Barnes, Pia De Doses (*princess of black aristocracy*), Renato Giovannoli, Elisa Mainardi, Paule Rout, Paola Natale, Marcelle Ginette Bron, Mario Del

A story of bedside-lamp cardinals, illuminated by the phosphorescent imagination of Fellini and Danilo Donati, during the ecclesiastical fashion parade.

The film rings of the author's familiarity with a slipshod, falsely "archeological," diligently retrospective Rome, characterized by a noticeable indifference towards the past and a deep affection for the present.

Vago, Alfredo Adami, Stefano Mayore, Gudrun Mardou Khiess, Giovanni Serboli, Angela De Leo, Libero Frissi, Dante Cleri, Mimmo Poli, Galliano Sbarra (*music-hall compère*), Alvaro Vitali (*tap dancer imitating Fred Astaire in music-hall*), Norma Giacchero (*Mastroianni's interviewer*), Federico Fellini (*himself*). Interviews with Marcello Mastroianni, Anna Magnani, Gore Vidal, John Francis Lane, Alberto Sordi. (Note: Sordi and Mastroianni were cut from the version distributed outside Italy.)

SYNOPSIS

*Rimini, the 1930s. A small boy from a Catholic boarding-school learns about the Capital, but only through the classicist rhetoric of his teachers and the arrogant grandiloquence of the Fascist regime. As far as he is concerned, Rome belongs to another planet, a place depicted in films and pho-*tographs, or imagined when listening to the Pope's Sunday blessing on the radio. Then it is 1939, and the young man of twenty leaves for Rome, which he finds to be quite different from the picture he has been taught: the dreary individuals with whom he shares a boardinghouse; the customers he meets in the taverns; the children playing in the streets; the prostitutes on the Appian Way.*

*The action moves forward to 1972, portraying a savage and apocalyptic traffic jam on the Rome freeway. Fellini is filming in the heart of a city populated by tourists and students who criticize him for his political indifference. The present mingles with the memory of a noisy audience in a small suburban variety hall, forced to flee because of an air raid warning. Next, our present-day film crew descends into the tunnels of the underground, where work is called to a halt when an important arche-*ological ruin is unearthed. The hippies of Piazza di Spagna summon up memories of the heterogeneous human fauna which frequented the brothels of the 1940s. An ecclesiastical fashion parade in a palace, attended by Pius XII, contrasts with a lively get-together of film stars and foreign writers in a Trastevere restaurant. There is confusion everywhere: the police bludgeon hippies and a group of motorcyclists roars through the silent vestiges of a distant and indifferent past.*

NOTES

Prior to all other considerations, it should be said that this film, if not actually Fellini's best (and this is a matter of opinion), is unquestionably his most "inevitable." A film which, sooner or later, he had to make, I think, rather like *8½* or *La Dolce Vita* (two films on the inability to create, whether by pen or picture). In reality, *Roma* is a sort of compendium of Fellini's relationship with the "exterior," the "rest" of the world. A world that begins in Rimini, stops for a while in Florence, and ends in Rome.

Fellini's life and career are both inexorably tied to his decision to go to Rome when still a young man, and to face adult life in a vague but peremptory way (he liked the journalists of American films, with their hats pushed back on their heads and their ready replies to everything).

Fellini's decision was the decision of his generation. Probably, if he had been ten years older, he would have gone to Milan. And had Fellini gone to Milan (Milan was the Paris of all the Rastignacs of northern Italy born before the First World War), his entire life would probably have been completely different. It is unlikely that he would have come into contact with the film industry (or perhaps he would have after all, via Milan, as did Zavattini, to give one example). What might he have become in Milan? A journalist? A novelist? A humorist, writing in that familiar, involuntarily surrealist style popular at that time? (And typical of such magazines as the Roman *Marc'Aurelio* for which the young Federico wrote several sketches; his style was provincial and immature, but delightfully promising.) But Federico went to Rome.

To explain just why he inevitably went to Rome, Fellini made a film, as indeed he always does when he wants to tell us something about himself. According to Bernardino Zapponi (Fellini's scriptwriter and editor of the customary book published by Cappelli on the making of the film), *Roma* developed from two basic ideas: ". . . I want to do some shooting from a helicopter; I want to see from up there, how the clouds form over Rome, film these huge multicolored masses as they form, fuse and break up . . ." and then ". . . The Ponentino. How is this famous westerly wind born? Where does it come from? I should like to see where it begins, follow it as it makes its way towards Rome, film people as they feel it blowing past them, in all sorts of different places, in cafés, in bed, in the street. . . ." From that moment the

Work on the subway, which looked as though it was going to become Rome's Loch Ness monster, but which in the end was completed. Fellini and Zapponi actually descended into the bowels of the earth to see what it was all about.

The salon of a low-price brothel (center photo).

Another shot from the ecclesiastical fashion parade.

search was on, the customary on-the-spot exploration: the Law Courts, the so-called "*Palazzaccio,*" closed for mysterious restoration work; the subway which, at the time the film was made, looked as though it was never going to be finished. (But which, for once, was not only finished, but actually works! Efficiently too! This just goes to show that things do get finished in Rome—sometimes.) Fellini's and Zapponi's descent into the bowels of the Eternal City, in the company of the famous "Talpa," is reminiscent of Victor Hugo.

The finished film is a combination of delightful, unreserved "invention" and a marginal, not always successful, attempt at documentation (for instance, the students or the famous actors who are interviewed in the film, among whom is Marcello Mastroianni, who is not only a friend of long standing, but also a sort of "mascot.") Besides, the documentary—in a literal sense, that is—with its need for wide open spaces, direct sound, etc., is a medium in which Fellini is not at his best, preferring as he does to reconstruct his chosen environment in the film studios (the best part of his career has been spent at Cinecittà), where he can give full rein to his imagination, and use dubbing to recreate sound. The now classical episodes of the brothel (one of the most successful attempts in Italian cinema to recreate a tradition of the past), the ecclesiastical fashion parade (one of the most satirical representations of Catholicism by a director who is Catholic *all'italiana,* that is to say basically atheist, vaguely Christian, but profoundly aware of the essence of Catholic ritual), and the little variety theatre during the war, are magnificently revealing. They highlight the Italy, and in particular the Rome, of that epoch.

Fellini's Rome, engendered from his childhood daydreams (at a time when "Romanity" was instilled in children—rather like German at the Berlitz school of languages before the war—by way of total immersion!) and from later experiences, and exemplified by three different characters: the young child who watches the train leave his hometown for the capital; the young man arriving in Rome; Fel-

Somewhere in the past of Fellini's characters there is always a fragment of gloomy, oppressive provincial life.

lini himself. The difference between the Rome depicted in books, sumptuous and imperial, and the real Rome—which for Fellini is the Eternal City of pre-war years, in essence a provincial, uncultured, lower-middle-class city of simple pleasures—is obviously the key to the film, although many failed to fully appreciate this (perhaps one has to be from the north of Italy, and Roman only by adoption, to understand it). We cannot help but feel the deep affectation Fellini nurtures for this city which has become his stage; it was here, in fact, that he approached the world of cinema, became inexorably part of it. Even his use of the Romanesque slang—for instance, the variety theatre episode with its arrogantly vulgar, uncontrolled audience—is strongly emphatic. But then it often happens that when an adult learns a foreign dialect or language he ends up by mastering it better than many "natives," or perhaps it is that he is always conscious of speaking and listening to it, as though it were flowing from some independent voice, whereas his mother tongue is embodied in his very being. Fellini observes his Roma with a ruthless eye, but he cannot hide his love for her: it is unlikely he could live anywhere else. There can be no fur-

ther doubt that, for Fellini, living and making films are one and the same thing.

(c.g.f.)

REVIEWS

" . . . The task Fellini set himself was immense and difficult. He threw himself into it with splendid recklessness, knowing that even if he were to lose control of his portrayal of the Eternal City, it would still be left with the values of a Fellinian self-portrait. In other words, we should not just be looking for Rome in this film, but above all for Fellini himself: Fellini of today. . . . The Fellinian Muses here are memory (the re-evocation of Rome during the war) and distortion of reality (the great freeway envisaged as the antechamber of hell). These episodes overflow with Fellini's immense talent, his power to evoke and represent through modification. Here, Fellini's reality . . . takes the place of reality, becomes reality. Chronically sordid, eternally transient, going to rack and ruin: this is Rome. . . . The film, built on a subjective and anti-rational perspective, appears before our eyes like some multi-storied, irregular

construction, full of gradients and stairways, antechambers leading nowhere, beautiful salons, fantastic views, never-ending corridors. . . .

"Roma is a film that proceeds in stops and starts, sometimes slowing to a standstill, at others rushing forward at break-neck speed. . . . Fellini fails to amalgamate these fragments, they escape his grasp and fall into place on different planes. The greater the director's efforts to coordinate, the more these efforts seem artificial and pointless. We would do much better to follow the film, independently from Fellini's endeavors, as a series of separate episodes, leaving it up to each individual viewer to find a unifying current. The film actually gains from this type of approach. We must let it break up into a myriad of rivulets, because, after a while, we can perceive the tension unifying this apparent disorder. . . ."

Sergio Frosali, LA NAZIONE, Florence, 17 March 1972.

" . . . Autobiographical as in all his films—which here he 'quotes' one by one with obvious enjoyment by way of allusive images—Fellini once again relates his story in the first person, as a direct witness, appearing under three distinct guises: the child watching the trains leave from his native Rimini for the capital; the young man . . . arriving in Rome where he hopes to become a journalist . . . ; Fellini himself, present as in The Clowns with a fake film crew, in the episodes representing Rome today. Mingling as he does with the action, though never becoming pleonastic . . . , the director gives us a picture of the Eternal City which is univocal, passionate, deformed, grotesque, but one hundred per cent Fellinian, and what is more, the most authentic Fellini possible. . . . "

Dario Zanelli, IL RESTO DEL CARLINO, Bologna, 17 March 1972.

" . . . Aside perhaps from a greater abandon and correlative inconti-

nence, Fellini's film on Rome is exactly what anyone, who had laid little store by the Messianic signals which generally accompany the making of his films, would have imagined it to be: a clearance sale of satirical remnants, left-overs from Fellini's workshop on the subject. This long film, more burlesque than 'committed,' is a toast to the memory of La Dolce Vita (which said almost everything there was to say), to many vestiges of 8½ and a few of Satyricon and The Clowns. It also rings with echoes of all the writings, cinema and music on Rome that have appeared in recent years, the intention here being to deconsecrate it all, and in so doing get to the essence of it. . . . "

Leo Pestelli, LA STAMPA, Turin, 17 March 1972.

" . . . The film is really a long, passionate, painful contemplation of

death suggested, once again, by the more striking and vital aspects of life. As with the classical Rome of Satyricon, so this Rome, stretching from 1939 to the present day, is only emblematic, however vital it may seem, only the starting point for a dream, the basis for a nightmare, the visualized and entirely external projection of some terrible inner torment. . . . It goes without saying that Fellini is as masterful as ever in giving form to it all. Episodes such as the freeway, the brothel, the ecclesiastical fashion show are cinema in its purest state. His style, which mixes invented news with invented memories, comes very close to poetry at times. At others, it becomes vigorously baroque, ideal for portraying the kitsch, the deformed, the horrible; and even though Fellini might have sought for better balance here and there, he always achieves the desired result: an ex-

The three comedians, singing a typical "couplet" of that era, in a reconstruction of wartime variety theatre in Rome: it is one of the most garish and ruthless episodes of the film.

travaganza alternating the nightmares of Bosch, the horrors of Goya and the scathing drawings of Grosz. . . . "

Gian Luigi Rondi, IL TEMPO, Rome, 18 March 1972.

" . . . From a stylistic point of view, the film is fairly complex (but thanks to the finely gauged editing, memory and dream slide harmoniously into one another): the traffic jam on the freeway reminds us of the brutality of Weekend, the roving camera's eye of Godard. The appearance of the tanks recalls Bergman's The Silence, while in Rotunno's abstract photography there is a distinct search for innovation. . . . "

Alberico Sala, CORRIERE D'INFORMAZIONE, Milan, 17 March 1972.

" . . . But the account is not disciplined. There are too many digressions where the author seems to take delight in the anecdote and in superfluous description. For instance, an obvious obsession with the flesh leads to a disproportionate insistence on brothels, where women are always envisaged as indecent and monstrous. This excessively personalized theme becomes boring after awhile, despite the figurative acrobatics and the pretext of a metaphysical game of mirrors. The fact is that Fellini is becoming too preoccupied with perfecting his ability to express his own personal obsessions, and therefore makes no further progress. He astonishes us but does not convince us, and he is prisoner of a mannerism he would do well to shake off. . . . "

Domenico Meccoli, EPOCA, Milan, 19 March 1972.

" . . . Images are overpowering and visceral, incongruous and vacuous. . . . The 'monsters' of childhood, magnified by experience and withered by age . . . are again the starting point for a sui generis raid on Rome, the pretext for figurative efflorescences . . . , startling effigies, neuroses of the past and present, marked by a glowing and excited fantasy which, reluctant to seek man, goes no further than the ghosts and putrid monsters. . . . "

e.c. (Ermanno Comuzio), L'ECO DI BERGAMO, Bergamo, 19 March 1972.

" . . . For those of us who love Fellini the visionary, the wizard of scenography, the master of deception, Roma might be a slight disappointment. It is not Satyricon. The fusion between the semi-documentary nature of The Clowns and the lyrical symbolism of La Dolce Vita is, however, achieved with considerable ingenuity, in this

Veils, skulls, sumptuous drapes, motionless priests, walls hung with ominous pictures: Fellini's Catholicism is all here, a mixture of derision and devotion.

recapitulation of canonical themes. *Certain self-quotations from Variety Lights and 8½ seem fresh and new, and there is such a wide range of tones, with frequent jumps from parody to pathos, from elegy to comedy, from oppression to exuberance, that the film has something for everyone. . . . "*

Giovanni Grazzini, CORRIERE DELLA SERA, *Milan-Rome, 17 March 1972.*

"It is altogether typical of Fellini that he should film his Roma, his tribute to a great city, mostly indoors on a sound stage. When he does go outside, he treats the very streets as a sound stage, with unreal lights and shadows playing over the façades . . . what matters is not the face itself, but the sense of wonder that Fellini not only offers but shares, as if that were why he makes movies in the first place. I suspect that is why there are so

many journeys of discovery—a short ride, a walk into the past or another world—in Fellini's work; and why Roma, which is almost wholly a journey of discovery, seems so richly to epitomize his career."

Roger Greenspun, THE NEW YORK TIMES, *October 16,1972.*

"Fellini's Roma is the creation of an imagination at once extravagant and strictly directed. Nightmare breaks in when the camera crew drive along the raging, wreck-strewn highway which links the city with the outside world. Fond extravagance is there when the young man who represents the Fellini of thirty years earlier arrives in Rome and dines in an uproar of Romans, all carrying on in the warm-hearted, quarrelsome way which Italians like to think typical of Italy. . . . Fellini shows a Rome

which reflects his own feelings and experiences, in short himself. The film is a huge dream, an offshoot of his Satyricon, grotesque, horrible, beautiful. But where can he go next? For a director who has reached the extremes of fantasy, there seems no way forward along the same track. One longs to see him take a new direction—back, perhaps, to that mysterious organism, more complex than Rome itself, the human being."

Dilys Powell, THE LONDON SUNDAY TIMES, *January 14,1973.*

"Even the moments that are personal—the memories—seem contrived, strained, without human warmth—as if someone had set out to do a grotesque caricature of some of the fine moments [in prior Fellini films]."

Howard Kissel, WOMEN'S WEAR DAILY, *October 16,1972.*

The Eternal City "invaded by coach loads of football fans," say the newspapers. A typical facet of Italian life which Fellini could not miss.

AMARCORD

Produced by Franco Cristaldi for FC Produzioni (Roma) and PECF (Paris). Director: Federico Fellini. Screenplay: Federico Fellini, Tonino Guerra, based on a story by Federico Fellini and Tonino Guerra, from an idea by Federico Fellini. Photography (Technicolor): Giuseppe Rotunno. Camera operator: Giuseppe Maccari. Assistant camera operators: Massimo Di Venanzo, Roberto Aristarco. Music: Nino Rota. Conductor: Carlo Savina. Art director: Danilo Donati, with scenery sketches by Federico Fellini, and collaboration by Antonello Massimo Geleng. Costumes: Danilo Donati, with collaboration by Mario Ambrosino. Assistant costumers: Rita Giacchero, Aldo Giuliani. Architect: Giorgio Giovannini. Editor: Ruggero Mastroianni. Assistant editor: Adriana Olasio. Sound: Oscar De Arcangelis. Continuity: Norma Giacchero. Assistant directors: Maurizio Mein, Liliana Betti, Gerard Morin, Mario Garriba. Makeup: Rino Carboni. Special effects: Adriano Pischiutta. Hair styles: Amalia Paoletti. Set decorator: Andrea Fantacci. Scene-painter: Italo Tomassi. Production manager: Lamberto Pippia. Production supervisors: Allessandro Gori, Gilberto Scarpellini. Production secretaries: Fednando Rossi, Giuseppe Bruno Bossio. Distribution in Italy: Dear International Running time: 127 minutes.

CAST

Bruno Zanin (*Titta Biondi*), Pupella Maggio (*Maranda, Titta's mother*), Armando Brancia (*Aurelio, Titta's father*), Stefano Proietti (*Oliva, Titta's brother*), Giuseppe Ianigro (*Titta's grandfather*), Nandino Orfei (*"Il Pataca," Titta's uncle*), Ciccio Ingrassia (*Teo, the mad uncle*), Carla Mora (*Gina, the maid*), Magali Noël (*"Gradisca"*), Luigi Rossi (*lawyer*), Maria Antonietta Beluzzi (*tobacconist*), Josiane Tanzilli (*"Volpina"*), Domenico Pertica (*blindman of Cantarel*), Antonino Faà di Bruno (*Conte di Lovignano*), Gennaro Ombra (*Bis-

Short pants for a cold winter day and a snowball fight.

cein, the liar), Gianfilippo Carcano (*Don Balosa*), Francesco Maselli (*Bongioanni, the science teacher*), Dina Adorni (*Miss De Leonardis, the math teacher*), Francesco Vona (*Candela*), Bruno Lenzi (*Gigliozzi*), Lino Patruno (*Bobo*), Armando Villella (*Fighetta, Greek teacher*), Francesco Magno (*Zeus, the headmaster*), Gianfranco Morrocco (*Conte Poltavo*), Fausto Signoretti (*Madonna, the coach driver*), Donatella Gambini (*Aldina Cordini*), Fides Stagni (*fine arts teacher*), Fredo Pistoni (*Colonia*), Ferruccio Brembilla (*Il Gerarca*), Mauro Misul (*philosophy teacher*), Antonio Spaccatini (*Il Federale*), Aristide Caporale (*Giudizio*), Marcello De Falco (*Il Principe*), Bruno Scagnetti (*Ovo*), Alvaro Vitali (*Naso*), Ferdinando De Felice (*Ciccio*), Mario Silvestri (*Italian teacher*), Dante Cleri (*history teacher*), Mario Liberati (*"Ronald Colman," proprietor of the Fulgor*), Marina Trovalusci and Fiorella Magalotti (*"Gradisca's" sisters*), Vincenzo Caldarola (*Il Mendicante*), Mario Milo (*photographer*), Cesare Martignoni (*barber*), Mario Jovinelli (*2nd barber*), Costantino Serraino (*Gigino Penna Bianca*), Amerigo Castrichella and Dario Giacomelli (*"Pataca's" friends*), Giuseppe Papaleo (*dandy*), Mario Nebolini (*Segretario Comunale*), Bruno Bartocci (*"Gradisca's" husband*), Clemente Baccherini (*proprietor of the Café Commercio*), Torindo Bernardo (*priest*), Marcello Bonini Olas (*gym teacher*), Marco Laurentino (*mutilated war veteran*), Riccardo Satta (*Il Sensale*).

SYNOPSIS

The film is essentially an evocation of the magic of the seasons. In an imaginary town on the Adriatic coast, Borgo, during the 1930s, young Titta is growing up within the confines of a Catholic education, Fascist rhetoric and an oppressive family atmosphere. The family is composed of Aurelio, the father, a small time building contractor who is always quarrelling with his wife Miranda, an hysterical, disconsolate woman; "Il Pataca," Titta's uncle, who lives off his relatives; Teo, the mad uncle, who is

As can be seen from the initials of the "T" shirts, the O.N.B. (Opera Nazionale Balilla) had not yet become the G.I.L. (Gioventù Italiana del Littorio). But the ritual of the military gym parade was there already.

in a mental hospital; the self-centered grandfather, who still likes chasing the maid despite his age; and a mischievous, undisciplined little brother. The end of winter is signalled by the "manine" of early spring flowers wafting in the air.

In order to celebrate the new season, an enormous bonfire is

erected in the main piazza. Scolded by his father because he has not yet found a job, Titta is taken by his mother to confession. When the priest asks him if he masturbates, Titta pictures in his mind all of the women of Borgo: the provocative Gradisca, a hairdresser who dreams of one day marrying Gary

Cooper; Volpina, who surrenders herself to every man in sight; the gigantic tobacco shop owner. The summer is marked by the passage of the **Rex,** *a huge transatlantic liner.*

The story is punctuated by a gallery of characters observed in a variety of different environments (the school, the Church, the Fascist meetings, and local celebrations): members of the end-of-term school photograph, the stupid priest, the aristocratic family, the cinema proprietor, the "Gerarca" (leader), the pompous lawyer, the mad Giudizio, Biscein the liar, the exhibitionist motorcyclist and many other "products" of this petty, provincial world. Autumn brings with it the **Mille Miglia,** *but also the death of Titta's mother. For Titta himself it means the end of adolescence. His dreams dissolve, just as those of Gradisca, who marries a* **carabiniere** *instead of her beloved Gary Cooper.*

NOTES

1973 was also the year of the book *Amarcord* written by Fellini and Tonino Guerra and published by Rizzoli-Milano, which contains, in narrative form, chapter by chapter, the basic story of the film: the adventures of Bobo (who becomes Titta in the film); Gradisca; the outsized owner of the tobacconist's shop, who gets hoisted up by the hero as in a weight lifting contest; the Giovane Italiane and Avanguardisti at the gym display; the appearance of the "*manine*" in March, precursors of a new season,"floating in the spring air like down or cottonwool . . . transparent spheres rising and falling, in an unending dance as though they had a life and impulse of their own . . ."; the confessional. An entire library of memories of the 1930s, influenced inevitably by the recollection of the life and customs of a small provincial town in Romagna.

A monument to Fellini's past and present, *Amarcord* is all of this and more besides. As always, he gives his own particular explanation of the film. After having revealed that at one point he wanted to entitle it simply *Viva l'Italia,* he says, ". . . but I thought that this would have been too mysterious or too didactic. Another title I wanted to give it was *Il Borgo,* in the sense of a medieval enclosure, a lack of information, a lack of contact with the unheard of, the new. . . ." He then explains: ". . . One day, in a restaurant, scribbling little sketches for the title, this word came to me: Amarcord, but I continued to say: be careful, Amarcord doesn't mean *mi ricordo* [I remember] at all, and to have viewed the film with an autobiographical 'key' would have been a grave error. Instead Amarcord is a kind of cabalistic word, a word of seduction, the brand of an aperitif. Anything, except the irritating association with *Je me souvien.* A word intended to be the synthesis, the reference point, the

There is always a father (Armando Brancia) chasing a son (Bruno Zanin) to give him a scolding, in the backwoods of Fellini's memory . . . .

The weightlifting contest with the tobacconist (Bruno Zanin and Maria Antonietta Beluzzi).

reflection almost of a mood, an attitude, a way of thinking at once ambiguous, contoversial, contradictory, the fusion of two extremes, the marriage of two opposites, such as indifference and nostalgia, innocence and guilt, refusal and assent, tenderness and irony, irritation and torment. It seemed to me that the film I wanted to make represented precisely this: the need to break away from something that once belonged to you, in which you were born and grew up, something that conditioned you, afflicted you, mistreated you, a place where everything is emotionally and dangerously confused, a past we want to remember without bitterness and which must, therefore, be freed from all entanglements, ambiguities and ties, a past to be treasured as part of ourselves and of our story, to be assimilated so that we are better able to face the present and the future."

Once again we would like to quote more of Fellini because, besides telling us a great deal about himself, he is a born writer with a special gift for

finding just the right adjective, just the right noun with an amazing, almost acrobatic dexterity. As far as I know no one has ever analyzed Fellini's style of writing: his comments are always of an enviable clarity, which is unusual in a country where most film directors speak and write like accountants or para-sciologist fortune-tellers.) Take, for instance, his dialectic ability with the word Amarcord, which means "I remember" but then again means anything but that. In the end it becomes a sort of hieroglyph, a fragment of a secret code, a hint, an incentive, a note from the past. There is no doubt that the film is autobiographical, whatever Fellini may think or say to the contrary. But it is not an autobiography in the sense of a succession of events from Fellini's life, but rather the taunting, mocking transfiguration of an entire setting in which to place that mixture of true and false hidden in the deepest recesses of the mind. Even the reviews, however enthusiastic or however reserved, emphasize the extremely "personal" outlook of the film, Fellini's

inevitable habit of using the screen as a sort of public confessional.

(c.g.f.)

REVIEWS

"Amarcord, orthographic fusion of the expression, in Romagnol dialect, a m'acord (mi ricordo—I remember), is not just the title of the film, but also the poetical refrain of Federico Fellini the director. That autobiographical background of childhood and adolescence in Rimini that he describes in almost all his films—from I Vitelloni *to* La Dolce Vita, *from 8½ to* Clowns *and* Roma—*is portrayed here as an end unto itself; it is no longer just the framework, or an interjection, but the very structure of the film. It is an album, and in some places a notebook, of recollections from domestic and public life in the Fascist 1930s, in which Rimini metaphysically becomes* il borgo *(recreated in Cinecittà) and where the Fellinian ego is identified in the*

person of Titta and in that of a local know-all whose didactic ramblings are generally given the bird. In other words, from now on, anyone wishing to seek Fellini through his films, will no longer have to jump from one to the other, it is all there, in Amarcord. Recapitulation is always a little superfluous, but this does not necessarily mean that it is boring. In brief, Fellini's film, though perhaps a little too long, is highly enjoyable; a film which, seen today, is both amusing and conforting. . . ."

Leo Pestelli, LA STAMPA, *Turin, 20 December 1973.*

". . . Amarcord *is a sort of compendium of Fellini's entire film career, and at the same time its culmination, in that the author, who has lived through two equally successful creative periods, the one representing the optical and intimate distortion of the other (for instance,* 8½, Fellini-Satyricon *and* Roma *in comparison with* La Strada, I Vitelloni *and* The Nights of Cabiria), *has managed here to combine these two periods harmoniously. He has tempered the plaintive tenderness which 'retrospection' conferred on his earlier works and at the same time the*

grotesque distortion imposed by "reality" on his later films. Amarcord *is a well-balanced, clean-cut, gentle film, even though the provincial world it portrays, with its passions, its deaths, its celebrations, its inevitable superstitions, is viewed with detatchment by the author, who loves it, but with an affection that is no longer morbid. Consequently the grotesque, although it still exists, is no longer aggressive, is almost ingrained in man, in this society of circus puppets acting out their role in this world of ours. . . ."*

Gisa Di Gianni, POLITICA, *Rome, 13 January 1974.*

"Amarcord *is Fellini's simplest, most defenseless, least aggressive film for years; and that is why we like it. . . . The new symmetry achieved here by the director has a delicate and modest quality, something we cannot resist, especially as it is so unexpected from someone like Fellini. The witchdoctor has finally discarded his habitual magniloquent spells in favor of a sort of magical underground realism, where the magic, although dulling reality a little, gives us a picture that is less shocking, more subtle and deeper*

The crazy uncle (Ciccio Ingrassia)

Magali Nöel ("Gradisca") and Maria Antonietta Beluzzi (the tobacconist) are two typical female figures of the Fellini world.

Ugo Casiraghi, L'UNITA, *Milan, 19 December 1973.*

". . . Composed like a rhapsody, weaving episodes and figures with a thread of astonishment, Amarcord is the work of an adult, more refined Fellini, in which the auto-*

A rural life of bygone days, with its scent of new-mown grass and pudgy priests (Bruno Zanin and Torindo Bernardo).

...he fabled elegance of luxury living . . .

...ographical content, as was al-ready evident in 8½ (though the ...lm also recalls The Clowns), ...ows greater insight into histori-...l fact and the reality of a gen-...ation.... It is a liberating exor-...sm and an assembly, in the ...asms of the mind racked by ...bs. It is the fear of a past which ...roustian rhetoric fails to subli-mate; it is a desperate search for impossible regeneration through grimace, sarcasm and the marvel of death. Almost all of Amarcord is a macabre dance against a cheer-ful background, punctuated by moments of absorbed ecstacy and bitter descents into hell where childhood nurtures our obses-sions. Emotion and fantasy, inven-tion and absolute mastery of the trade go hand in hand in a spec-tacle void of all intellectuallism, where nothing is true because it has been recreated (even the sea); but where reality has weight and depth as never before; it attracts and disgusts, holds and frightens, as does life itself..."

Giovanni Grazzini, CORRIERE DELLA SERA, Milan-Rome, 19 December 1973.

"... A first viewing of this film leaves a remarkable impression; each image is created with consid-erable invention (the appearance of the transatlantic liner, the Fas-cist parade, the early morning walk full of mist and visions, the crazy uncle in the tree, the peacock in the snow). The colors, and above all the light, are beautifully con-trolled and they succeed in arous-ing our enthusiasm, making Amar-cord a fascinating film.... But a second viewing of the film leaves a different impression. Those spe-cial moments remain, but the sur-prise has gone. Every now and then we are aware of repetition.... The caricaturing borders on mania, be-coming more of an expedient than a fundamental necessity, an obs-ession almost.... However, if Amarcord goes a step further in comparison with Satyricon and Roma, it is because Fellini every now and then rediscovers the force he once had, thanks above all to the character of Gradisca, superbly played by Magali Noël...."

J.C.G. (Jean-Claude Guiguet), LA REVUE DU CINEMA—IMAGE ET SON, 288–289, Paris, October 1974.

"Fellini strains every tale beyond the ludicrous, as they would be by old-timers spinning yarns and feel-ing no accountability to be any-thing but entertaining. Amarcord may not satisfy everyone who

A universe of chubby, sniggering boys in plus-fours, watching the unattainable "Gradisca" prancing beneath the protective gaze of Gary Cooper (Alvaro Vitali, Bruno Zanin and Magali Nöel).

wants movies to mean, as well as be. But even the discontented can marvel at Fellini's magnificent theatricality . . . [it] is a recollection of things past and in that it resembles but is much more significant than the flock of films that are described as being nostalgic. Fellini manifests what none of those other directors has—a true sense of sadness that, as he says in some notes he wrote for the film, 'there is no more purity, no one is genuine and no one dreams any longer.' "

Jerry Oster, THE NEW YORK DAILY NEWS, *September 20, 1974.*

"Amarcord is honestly a letting-go movie for Fellini; more good humor, more joy of life, and more small-scale observations about everyday life creep into it than any other Fellini film of the last decade. In its ribald earthiness and larger-than-life strokes, Amarcord most resembles The Apprenticeship of Duddy Kravitz among recent films, even though Fellini's flow-of-life tableau lacks tight themes or a narration that ties up loose strings. Despite the dwarves and other grotesqueries, one has good reason to believe that Maestro Fellini, the orchestrator of total movies of the mind, is turning back to humanism after a long, arid stretch of misanthropy."

Tom Allen, NEW YORK, *September 23, 1974.*

"This is another of those autobiographical rambles Fellini just gets away with, largely by haunting u with bits of his old imagery an shocking/amusing us with a ne gallery of grotesques. As per tr dition, the pattern is cyclic: a yea in the life of a coastal village, wit due emphasis on the seasons, an the births, marriages and deaths. is an Our Town or Under Mil Wood of the Adriatic seaboar concocted and displayed, with th latter-day Fellini's distaste for re stone and wind and sky, in the R man studios. The people, howeve are real, and the many non-acto among them come in all the shape and sizes one cares to imagin without plunging too deep into To Browning freak territory."

Russell Davies, THE LONDC OBSERVER, *September 29, 197*

he town band, the newsstand advertising Corriere della Sera *and* Il Resto del Carlino, *and the sports shop provide the background for "Gradisca" and her sisters (Fiorella Magalotti, Magali Nöel and Marina Trovalusci).*

Casanova

IL CASANOVA DI FEDERICO FELLINI   ITALY   1976

Produced by Alberto Grimaldi for PEA. Director: Federico Fellini. Screenplay: Federico Fellini, Bernardino Zapponi, freely adapted from *Histoire de Ma Vie* by Giacomo Casanova. Photography (Technicolor): Giuseppe Rotunno. Camera operator: Massimo Di Venanzo. Assistant camera operators: Wolfango Soldati, Bruno Garbuglia. Music: Nino Rota. Conductor: Carol Savina. Songs: "*La Grande Mouna*" by Tonino Guerra, "*La Mantide Religiosa*" by Antonio Amurri, "*Il Cacciatore di Württemberg*" by Carl A. Walken, lines in Venetian dialect by Andrea Zanzotto.

Art direction: Danilo Donati, with scenery sketches by Federico Fellini. Costumes: Danilo Donati. Assistant costumers: Gloria Mussetta, Raimonda Gaetani, Rita Giacchero. Architects: Giantito Burchiellaro, Giorgio Giovannini. Assistant art director: Antonello Massino Geleng. Editor: Ruggero Mastroianni. Assistant editors: Adriano Olasio, Marcello Olasio, Ugo De Rossi. Assistant directors: Maurizio Mein, Liliana Betti, Gerald Morin. Set decorator: Emilio D'Andria. Choreographer: Gino Landi. Assistant choreographer: Mirella Agujaro. Sound: Oscar De Arcangelis. Assist-

ant sound technicians: Franco an Massimo De Arcangelis. Continuity Norma Giacchero. Makeup: Rin Carboni. Donald Sutherland's make up: Giannetto De Rossi. Hair styles Vitaliana Patacca. Assistant hair sty ists: Gabriella Borzelli, Paolo Borzell Vincenzo Cardella. Special effects Adriano Pischiutta. Production mar ager: Lamberto Pippia. Productio assistants: Alessandro Von Normani Maria Di Biase. Production secre taries: Titti Pesaro, Luciano Bonom Distribution in Italy: Titanus. Runnin time: 170 minutes.

Peppino Rotunno is virtually unequalled at rendering the "misty," dream-like inventions of Fellini.

CAST

Donald Sutherland (*Giacomo Casanova*), Tina Aumont (*Henriette*), Cicely Browne (*Madame d'Urfé*), Carmen Scarpitta, Diane Kourys (*the Mistresses Charpillon*), Clara Algranti (*Marcolina*), Daniela Gatti (*Giselda*), Margaret Clementi (*Sister Maddalena*), Mario Cencelli (*Dr. Mobius, the entomologist*), Olimpia Carlisi (*Isabella, the entomologist's daughter*), Silvana Fusacchia (*entomologist's other daughter*), Chesty Morgan (*Barberina*), Adele Angela Lojodice (*mechanical ballerina*), Sandra Elaine Allen (*giantess*), Clarissa Mary Roll (*Anna Maria*), Alessandra Belloni (*princess*), Marika Rivera (*Astrodi*), Angelicca Hansen (*hunchback actress*), Marjorie Bell (*Countess of Waldenstein*), Marie Marquet (*Casanova's mother*), Daniel Emilfork-Berenstein (*Du Bois*), Luigi Zerbinati (*the Pope*), Hans Van Den Hoek (*Prince Del Brando*), Dudley Sutton (*Duke of Württtenberg*), John Karlsen (*Lord Tallow*), Reggie Nalder (*L'Intendente*), Vim Hiblom (*Edgard*), Harold Innocent (*Count of Saint-Germain*), Masha Bayard (*tailor*), Nicolas Smith (*Casanova's brother*), Donald Hodson (*Hungarian captain*), Dan Van Husen (*Viderol*), Gabriele Carrara (*Count of Waldenstein*), Marcello Di Falco (*Captain de Bernis*), Sara Pasquali (*young theologian*), Mariano Brancaccio (*dancer*), Veronica Nava (*Romana*), Carlì Buchanan (*depraved aristocrat*), Mario Gagliardo (*Righetto, the coachman*).

SYNOPSIS

Now old and tired, Giacomo Casanova, working as secretary and librarian to Count Waldenstein, looks back over the loves and adventures of his life. In Venice, during carnival time, Casanova agrees to demonstrate his sexual prowess with Sister Maddalena, intending at the same time to gratify the "voyeuristic" tendencies of her lover, the French ambassador, with whom Casanova hopes to gain favor. But he is arrested by the Inquisition for practicing black magic. Having escaped from Venice, Casanova goes to Paris, where he frequents the salons of Madame d'Urfé who hopes to learn from Casanova the secret of immortality. But his stay in Paris is short-lived.

Casanova sets off on his travels again. He is guest at the banquet of a homosexual nobleman, Du Bois, and, in Parma, he has a delightful amorous interlude with Henriette, a young French girl. Henriette's sudden departure throws Casanova into a fit of depression, similar to the distress he felt in London when he contracted syphilis from two prostitutes and even considered committing suicide, until his old lust for

A furiously dissipated, sad and angry Casanova (Donald Sutherland).

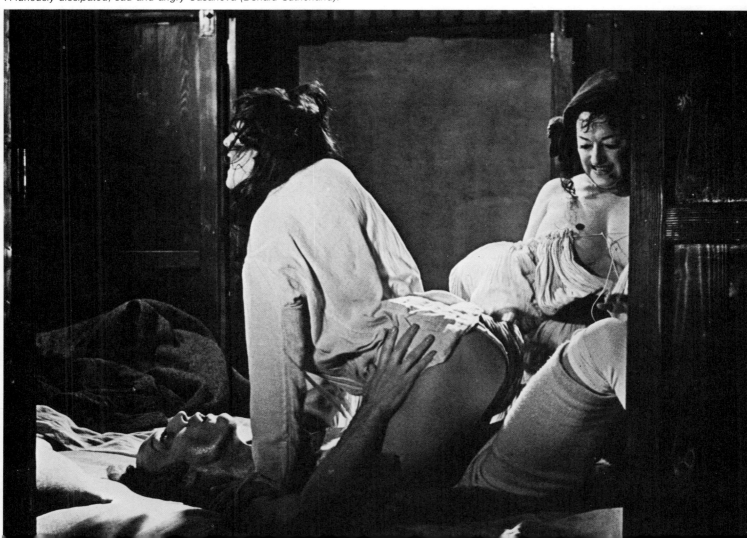

"An emotional example of dreamlike art . . ." wrote Tullio Kezich.

*Count of Waldenstein's offer.
Treated with contempt by the other
servants of the house, he consoles
himself by dancing with a mechanical doll, a frigid reminder of years
gone by.*

NOTES

Casanova brought Fellini and Bernardino Zapponi together again for
the screenplay (after the "all-Rom-
agna" experiment with Tonino Guerra
for *Amarcord*). Tangible hints of a
Fellini Casanova first began to circulate in 1974, but it was almost three
years before the film actually reached
the screen, in December 1976. It
goes without saying that the making
of the film was marked by the customary see-saw of events; for instance, the usual succession of producers: De Laurentiis (who, at all
costs, wanted Robert Redford for the
leading role), then Andrea Rizzoli
followed by Alberto Grimaldi of PEA
with whom an agreement was finally
reached.

Filming began on 21 July 1975, but
was suspended in December of the
same year due to trade union action
and controversy in general. The film
crew was fired, new personnel were
hired, the dispute was settled and
filming began again in late March
1976. The next setback was the theft
of a substantial quantity of film material from the studios during the customary close-down for the mid-Au-
gust holidays. Part of this material
was later found in a Cinecittà studio
in May 1976. A further problem was
the choice of the star: Alberto Sordi,
Michael Caine, Jack Nicholson and
Gian Maria Volonté were all considered for the role before it was finally
offered to Donald Sutherland.

Even for Fellini, the difficulties
were considerable, and they did not
end there: from the very first announcement of his intention to make
a film about Casanova to after the release of the film, there was wide-
spread criticism of the way in which
he had interpreted the person of
Cavalier Giacomo. There is evidence
of this in the reviews, in which the difference in tone assumed by the critics
is considerable. For instance, Carlo
Laurenzi says: ". . . the most man-

*life was restored by another amo-
rous adventure.*

*His adventures continue. In
Rome he accepts Lord Tallow's
challenge to make love eight times
in a row with one of the guests of
his evening orgy. In Berne he becomes ill and is taken care of by
Dr. Mobius, whose daughter Isabella he later tries to seduce. In
Naples he has a love affair with the
daughter of one of Ferdinando I's
mistresses. In the meantime, he*
*has the opportunity of meeting the
Pope, he is introduced to Voltaire,
who insults him, and he also sees
his mother again, although she
shows little interest in her son's
fate.*

*As Casanova ages, his charm
fades and the courts of Europe begin to forget him. He goes to Württemberg, but the Duke is indifferent
towards Casanova's plans for the
fortification of his castle. Casanova
has no choice but to accept the*

The Cardinals and the Pope (Luigi Zerbinati).

teristic and in a certain sense the most irritating of Fellini's films . . . ," while Morando Morandini remarks: ". . . perhaps Fellini's best film after 8½, probably the least Fellinian, and certainly the most unified and compact. . . . But then Fellini himself has made some very interesting remarks on the subject. He has always been inundated by interviews and requests for interviews; he is intelligent, a good speaker (which is not necessarily the case with film directors) and enjoys answering questions, which he does so at length and often with a delightful touch of irony. As regards Casanova, a character whose *Memoires* have probably been read by few, but whose name is universally known, here is an interesting "visual" document in the television "special" edited by Liliana Betti and Gianfranco Angelucci, "E il Casanova di Fellini?"

broadcast by the RAI (Italian radio and television company) on 6 May 1975, and an almost unlimited quantity of written interviews from which to choose. Many of these are quoted in the book edited by Betti and Angelucci and published by Cappelli. Two in particular drew my attention.

The first is the interview by Aldo Tassone published in the magazine *Gente* on 1 September 1975. Among other things, Fellini remarks: ". . . Who knows what Casanova was like? We are evaluating the character of a book. And the character is detatched, he becomes a point of reference upon which people project themselves. To me, he seems like a boring writer who has spoken to us about a loud, annoying, despicable character, a courtier who calls himself Casanova, an ill-bred man bedecked with plumes who stinks of sweat and face powder,

a man who possesses the stupidity, the arrogance and the bumptiousness of the barracks and the church, a man who always wants to be right. And it even seems that he always was right, because he knows about everything. But in a manner that is so impersonal as to get on your nerves. He is a man who does not even allow you to be ignorant, he superimposes himself upon everything; he is also six feet four inches tall and recounts that he can make love eight times in succession so that competition even here becomes impossible. He translates from Latin and Greek, knows mathematics, recites, acts, speaks French very well, and has known Louis XV and Madame Pompadour. How can one stand being around a big turd like this?"

The second is an excerpt, again selected by Betti and Angelucci, from

Valerio Riva's reportage/interview which appeared in *L'Espresso* on 26 May 1976: "... What was I hoping to achieve with this film? To get, once and for all, to the very essence of cinema, to get to what I believe is the total film. To create a picture out of a reel of film ... if you stand before a picture, you get complete and uninterrupted enjoyment from it. If you watch a film, no. The picture contains everything, and all you have to do is to look at it to discover all this. A film is an incomplete picture; it is not the spectator who is looking at the film, but the film which reveals itself to the spectator, according to a scheme and rhythm alien to that spectator. The ideal would be to make a film with a single image, eternally and endlessly rich in movement. With Casanova I wanted to get as close to this as possible: an entire film made up of fixed pictures. *Satyricon* came pretty close to this. But what was so good about Casanova, was that the character himself was ideal. Who is Casanova? A puppet watching the world through eyes of stone. There is no story in his film, apart from that minimum which the cinema obliges us to create for the sake of convention, and which no director could eliminate completely. Nothing happens around Casanova, all that is to be seen in the film, is what Casanova sees within, and not outside, his stony eyes. And so I did all I could to make Casanova the only character in the film to have his own wooden individuality; no other character does. In other words, Casanova is a sort of Pinocchio, but a Pinocchio who never grows up."

When he theorizes, Fellini might sometimes seem a little obscure, but his reaction to his characters is always rich in subtle invention. We sense the enjoyment he derives from stating things precisely, and at the same time the irritation of the creator who is later called upon, with calculated pedantry, to justify what he has done. But this need to "justify" or analyze himself in some way, inevitably pushes him into paradox: a bizarre little spirit hovers above him, and out comes the old Federico, the humorist, the cartoonist, the script writer; his films become an instrument for invention, in part ironical, in part

serious. The error of many critics and journalists is to take Fellini seriously, in a literal sense, without realizing that Federico inevitably uses his films to give vent to the bizarre, almost childish, dreams and humors of a fertile imagination.

It is interesting to note that in *Casanova* Fellini is once again working with a professional actor, after one or two experiments with little known actors. For instance, Martin Potter, Hiram Keller and Max Born of *Satyricon,* are as little known as Peter Gonzales, the young Fellini of *Roma.* The technical crew is as close-knit as ever. Peppino Rotunno, director of photography, Ruggero Mastroianni, film editor (Fellini's freindship with the two Mastroianni brothers is longstanding) and Danilo Donati, art director, worked with Fellini on many films during the 1970s, and this confirms Fellini's tendency to keep the same collaborators wherever possible, as was the case during the early years with Otello Martelli, Piero Gherardi and a few other names.

(c.g.f.)

REVIEWS

"... The Casanova depicted here has nothing to do with the Casanova emerging from historical notes and from the man's own writings.... But then Fellini was never even minimally interested in Casanova as he really was. What Fellini sees here is another of his ghosts, the projection of a dream, in other words the things that always inhabit his imagination. A monster among the monsters crowding the reveries of an artist brought up on a religious education in a provincial town on the Adriatic coast, who at an early age made his home in Rome, a city that has always 'spoken' to him as the privileged residence of an ecclesiastical society and tradition....

"If Fellini has been guilty of the 'disloyalty' of which 'Casanovians' accuse him, it does not lie here. If anything, he has been unloyal towards the enlightened, libertine, 'Voltairian' 18th century.... This century is nowhere to be found among the obsessions Fellini has inherited from his youth. The century is instead part of an ideological and intellectual problem of a former student of the Scolopi fathers. A problem which, in the film, never reaches a tone more responsible than that one would expect to find in a discussion between adolescents.... Of course, one should not deny such a freely creative artist as Fellini his total freedom. And the images in his film abound in freedom: always there is a press of objects, colors, scenographic extravaganza, visual inventions, which bear witness to the director's great imaginative power. But any controversy over his film has nothing to do with this aspect; it concerns the portrayal of a character in whom not one moment of joy is to be found...."

Mauro Manciotti, IL SECOLO XIX, Genoa, 22 December 1976.

"... Fellini does not narrate; he lumps together, he proceeds by analogies, lingering when he recognizes or recreates the emblems of his traditional myths. Casanova is the most manneristic and in a certain sense the most irritating of Fellini's films. It lacks rhythm, and excessive analogy leads to obscurity. The splendor and subtlety of certain figurations are more baroque than 18th century; but the visionary power of certain symbols ... is not sufficient to keep this bizarre parade afloat...."

Carol Laurenzi, IL GIORNALE, Milan, 11 December 1976.

"... the images in his film abound in freedom: always there is a press of objects, colors, scenographic extravaganza, visual inventions which bear witness to the director's great imaginative power," wrote Mauro Manciotti.

The frenzied, troubled loneliness of Casanova (Donald Sutherland).

"... The narrow provincial-Catholic world of the Rimini suburbs has been dangerously extended by Fellini to include a bit of Rome, a bit of Italy, and a bit of our age. Now Fellini attempts the impossible: he stretches this narrow world of private and provincial problems to cover the entire world and our entire age. Naturally, his private-intimate-dream repertoire crumbles in his hands: this is not a film, it is a heap of rubble."

Ferdinando Camon, IL GIORNO, Milan, 7 January 1977.

"... Basically, Fellini's Casanova is a disappointing film. Far from realizing that Casanova is a character in appearances the opposite, but in reality complementary, to Sade ..., Fellini has emphasized the mosaic of childhood traumas, anxieties, terror and fantasies which, in his opinion, is at the basis of Casanova's eroticism. But childishness and anxiety, terror and fantasy are represented in the film in such a limited manner that the discourse rarely goes beyond the premise, and underlines Fellini's imprisonment within his subject matter, rather than the prison of his 'Eros,' which is what he is trying to represent...."

Lino Miccichè, AVANTI!, Rome, 11 December 1976.

"... This universe, in its advanced stage of disintegration, does not ring with heartfelt anxiety, but collapses on itself forming a turbid pool from which rises the sumptuous trash of a spectacular mental effort pushed beyond the point of no return.... In reality, with Casanova Fellini has taken a step backwards, towards the apocalyptic atmosphere of his Satyricon. In the earlier film, however, he was aided by the lure of ancient ruins emerging from the mists of the past. Whereas here, the ruins are modern and the apocalypse is not announced by mystical horsemen, but by some anomalous tribade whose 18th century costume fails to hide more recent Roman or Romagnol origins...."

Guglielmo Biraghi, IL MESSAGGERO, Rome, 11 December 1976.

"... Fellini denies him everything: talent, fantasy, irony, curiosity, spirit of adventure and even luck in love. Casanova seems less involved in a delirium of the senses than in a sports contest, an exhibition of gymnastic prowess, a series of exhausting free-style exercises, though perhaps 'free' is not quite the right word, laced up as he is in corsets and knickerbockers. And it also seems as though Casanova, far from chosing his 'blossoms,' is chosen by them.... If this is Fellini's Casanova, and it most certainly is, then the film does not lend itself to some mysterious interpretation, and we are therefore led to wonder if it was really worthwhile telling this character's story, and whether the emptiness of his existence could produce anything but further emptiness. It goes without saying that Fellini adorns this void with a thousand incantations, a thousand ingenious inventions and a hundred thousand marvels. Federico's virtuosity and technique, precisely because they are based on nothing, are as eloquent as ever in displaying the extraordinary repertoire of Fellinian mannerism...."

Paolo Valmarana, IL POPOLO, Rome, 11 December 1976.

"... The deep sense of desolation

pervading the film arises from the desperation of Casanova's case and the ambiguity of the person himself, as he searches for some measure of dignity; he is at once a plunderer and a victim, so lacking in sensuality that he is not sensual even when he is 'starved.' . . . Although we find here the familiar Fellinian world of monsters, of the circus, of the extraordinary, both real and imaginary, the tone is entirely new. . . . The film is expensive, immense, demanding, ruinous and outrageous, but had it been anything else but this, it would not have been at all. True, not all the episodes are equally successful: we are bored at the entomologist's house, and we are hardly astonished at the Dresden theatre, or with Signor Du Bois, in Parma. But this is a film that Fellini had to make in order to get to the very bottom of his fears, and to the bottom of what he wishes to demonstrate, honestly. . . ."

Mireille Amiel, CINÉMA 77, 218, Paris, February 1977.

". . . Rich, multiform, varying in tone, not without the occasional break in rhythm, Casanova arouses our admiration above all in those episodes where the hero, as he grows older, acquires a certain touch of humanity which, in the beginning, he was denied; at this point we cannot but become involved. . . ."

Dario Zanelli, IL RESTO DEL CARLINO, Bologna, 19 December 1976.

". . . Casanova is perhaps Fellini's best film after 8½, it is probably the least 'Fellinian' and certainly the most unified and compact . . . as regards richness and originality of figurative inventions, narrative style, skill in tempering the horrible with the tender, the fabulous with the ironical and the ability to pass from caricature to visionary. This has always been one of the cardinal points of Fellini's talent, but here, despite occasional repetition, an especially high degree of uniformity is achieved and maintained; in addition to this, there is

A tortured world of gentlemen and ragamuffins (Donald Sutherland).

The pleasure of recreating everything in Cinecittà, like an immense toy that can be dismantled and reassembled, thanks to Rotunno's masterful photography, and Danilo Donati's transformation of Fellini's ideas.

a particularly suggestive sound track and admirable color harmony in Rotunno's photography...."

Morando Morandini, IL GIORNO, *Milan, 11 December 1976.*

"Fellini has kept the color—indeed, heightened it, but drained away the life. He seems to have fastened on the legend only to repudiate it. Seen through his hostile lens Casanova is a chilly fop whose salon manner is alternately tongue-tied and bombastic. How such a creature manages to charm so many women into the bedroom remains a mystery. Nor, once he gets them there, is it easy to see how they can derive much fun from the groaning calisthenics he puts them through. This is a film that earns its R rating not by making sin enticing but by making it repellent.... Here Ca-

sanova does not move against the rich backdrop the historical period offers but drifts through the bizarre misty regions of Fellini's own imagination. The episodes do not make up a narrative of Casanova's life but a sort of meditation on it."

Christopher Porterfield, TIME, *February 21, 1977.*

"It's hard to be enthusiastic about a puzzle you haven't put together. That's the problem any viewer will have on seeing [Casanova]. There's a lot to [the film]. Too much to be completely understood in one sitting. But the question is, what do you go to the movies for? A game or a good time. If the latter is your thing, this flick is not."

Nelson George, THE AMSTERDAM NEWS, *February 19, 1977.*

"Federico Fellini has created another revel of a movie—spectacular but singularly joyless—that has the effect of celebrating the absolute end of romance and eroticism. There's nothing left but sex, and sex is a terminal disease. Love is a placebo.... I don't know how else to interpret this strange, cold, obsessed film, which I find fascinating, because I find the man who made it fascinating, a talented mixture of contradictory impulses, and as depressing as an eternal hang-over. Other people, less convinced of the Fellini genius, may be driven up the wall ... the production is gigantic, but the ideas and feelings are small."

Vincent Canby, THE NEW YORK TIMES, *February 12, 1977.*

"... the deep sense of desolation pervading the film arises from the desperation of Casanova's case and the ambiguity of the person himself, as he searches for some measure of dignity; he is at once a plunderer and a victim, so lacking in sensuality that he is not sensual even when he is 'starved' ...", wrote Mireille Amiel.

PROVA D'ORCHESTRA

Produced for Daime Cinematografica S.p.A. and RAI-TV (Rome) and Albatros Produktion G.M.B.H. (Munich). Director: Federico Fellini. Screenplay: Federico Fellini, with the collaboration of Brunello Rondi. Based on a story by Federico Fellini. Photography (Technicolor): Giuseppe Rotunno. Camera operator: Gianni Fiore. Music; Nino Rota. Conductor: Carlo Savina. Art director: Dante Ferretti. Set decorator: Nazzareno Piana. Editor: Ruggero Mastroianni. Assistant editor: Adriana Olasio. Special effects: Adriano Peschiutta. Costumes: Gabriella Pescucci. Assistant directors: Maurizio Mein, Christa Reeh, Giovanna Bentivoglio. Music consultant: Carlo Savina. Dubbing manager: Carlo Baccarini. RAI production delegate: Fabio Storelli. Distribution in Italy: Gaumont-Italia. Running time 70 minutes.

CAST

Baldwin Bass (*conductor*), Clara Colosimo (*harpist*), Elisabeth Labi (*pianist*), Ronaldo Bonacchi (*contrabassoon*), Ferdinando Villella (*vio-*

The scene of the disaster to come, with its rows of docile music stands and air of impending disaster.

The equivocal attitude of the conductor (Baldwin Bass).

loncello), Giovanni Javarone (*tuba*), David Mauhsell (*first violin*), Francesco Aluigi (*second violin*), Andy Miller (*oboe*), Sibyl Mostert (*flutist*), Franco Mazzieri (*trumpet*), Daniele Pagani (*trombone*), Luigi Uzzo (*violin*), Cesare Martignoni (*clarinet*), Umberto Zuanelli (*copyist*), Filippo Trincia (*orchestra manager*), Claudio Ciocca (*trade unionist*), Angelica Hansen, Heinz Kreuger (*violins*), Federico Fellino (*interviewer's voice*).

SYNOPSIS

The action takes place inside a large, bare and ancient auditorium, where an orchestra is rehearsing a symphony. The members of the orchestra arrive in small groups and take up their places, each before his skeletal music-stand. In a corner is a group of trade unionists. A journalist from the television interviews the musicians. Each speaks of his or her own instrument and experiences with obvious narcissism. The conductor arrives, calling the musicians to order in a voice with a strong German accent. The rehearsal begins quietly enough, but it is soon interrupted as the members of the orchestra rebel against the orders imparted by the conductor. The conductor retires

to his dressing room where he is interviewed by the journalist.

In the meantime, a revolution breaks out in which the musicians totally reject the concept of authority, even the authority of music; disorder reigns and the walls of the oratorium are soon covered with slogans. The building begins to tremble. The walls begin to crack under the blows of a giant hammer which, in the end, comes crashing through the cement killing the harpist who is buried under a mountain of rubble. Confusion, fear and screaming. Suddenly silence returns, and the rehearsal starts again amist clouds of dust and debris. Submissively, the musicians follow the orders given by the conductor, who speaks in a tone of voice which is both neurotic and dictatorial.

NOTES

This to me is one of Fellini's most revealing films, if for no other reason than that it is his first and, in a certain sense, only "political" film. It is as though the Great Illusionist, having reached the age of sixty, had suddenly decided to show people that he had really lived like they had, had understood what was going on

around him, had perceived all the blemishes, faults, cacophony, discord, provocation and incomprehensible insinuations that seemed to be interwoven into the fabric of Italian life during the last decade.

In fact, Fellini has never taken much interest in the "present" as such; he has always preferred to use the whims of his memory in order to invent the realities of the past. In a different way *Variety Lights,* and *I Vitelloni, La Dolce Vita* and *8½,* are profoundly retrospective in their evocation, at least as much as are *Satyricon* and *Casanova* by way of their place in time. And even when Fellini does portray the present, he tries to keep away as much as possible from an interpretation of our day and age as a reality, even a "political" one (for instance, *Amarcord* and most of *Roma*). Besides, allegory is congenial to Fellini only to the extent in which it refers to a sort of realism totally detatched from reality, though ringing with realistic echoes.

And so *Prova d'Orchestra* seems almost an exception (as is *Città delle Donne,* in a certain sense). This is perhaps one of Fellini's least successful films, if we consider the result as a whole, but it is certainly one of his most ambitious, if we take into account the way in which he has tried to detach himself from the more interesting of his traditional methods of exprssion in order to "parody" them. But it proves just how much Fellini must have felt, as indeed we all did, that air of fragility characteristic of Italian society during the late 1970s and early 1980s. There seemed to be a deep mistrust of words, faces, promises, attitudes; an entire nation in which everyone seems to be wearily and unimaginatively acting out a part, where actions no longer corresponded to words, where one and all seemed to be telling lies, but so blatently that no one would ever dream of accusing them of not telling the truth. They seemed to be saying: "Look, we're lying, so don't take us seriously."

The film is typically Fellinian, especially as it affords him the opportunity to take full advantage of his delight in "faces": The cast is made up entirely of all-round actors and su-

The anonymous faces of the orchestra members, faces capable of unleashing the mysteries of music, but also all the vulgarity of our society.

pernumeraries, who make no secret of not knowing how to play their instruments, but who have very obviously been hand-picked by Fellini, from one of the vast "photo-kits" put together for each film, with that uncanny ability of his to single out from the crowd faces of unusual eloquence, faces bearing the signs of banality, corrosion or of the most ferocious and merciless "normality."

The film is concise, detatched, mysterious and yet explicit, and illustrates the deep, almost savage, sensitivity with which Fellini lives his life. As long as things seemed to be deteriorating at an acceptable average rate, Fellini was content to follow his dreams; after all, they are the most important part of each one of us. But when the situation reached danger level (an entire nation troubled by ten years of tragic events, intrigue, conspiracy and bribery, empty words, political jargon drummed into one's mind so forcefully as to become part and parcel of everyday speech), back to life came the spirit of Federico of the past, which evidently continues to live on within the body of this sumptuously Romagnol personage, who might well be likened today to some influential elder of a provincial town.

The futile, inept nostalgia of the copyist (Umberto Zuanelli).

The result is *Prova d'Orchestra,* with its slovenly, lifeless players, its clear allegory, its message, so explicit and provocatory as to become practically obscure in a country that has built its existence upon mutual deceit. The wide difference of opinion over this film is simplified in the customary selection of reviews. From these, it appears that not everyone appreciated the undisguised irony of the film, nor its equally transparent allegorical tone. In actual fact, there are few such examples in the history of Italian cinema. And where a similarity is to be found, it is generally the work of a much younger director. But with Fellini, besides a disparity in versatility and and talent (so overwhelming as to leave little room for comparison), we can perceive the importance of an age difference, which permits a very different mental outlook. (Fellini was both *ballista* and *avanguardista,* as a young man he learned the weight of a formal, organized type of rhetoric, liturgically structured according to an explicit code which was both banal and absurd, and it is evident therefore that he would inevitably react towards any style of rhetoric with a sort of amused, irritated sufferance that others would not feel.) There is also his very special delight in irony, sharpened not only by his nutural talent, but also by years of intellectual exercise.

We have the impression, watching his films, that Fellini has crossed this long and troubled post-war period rather like an ingenious sleepwalker, who is nonetheless aware of the noises, words, customs and habits around him and responds to them accordingly, but in a highly individual manner. Moreover, we again have an indication of just how great is his ability to assimilate the echoes of his time and to reproduce them later, at leisure, as a sort of grand dreamlike ballad.

(c.g.f.)

The gigantic hammer has struck: the world of Fellini and of the members of the orchestra is about to collapse. But it will be rebuilt again, as is always the case with Fellini.

REVIEWS

"... Fellini the dreamer, the visionary, incorrigible narcissist, indefatigable autobiographer, averse to any form of obligation, has come out of himself for once to have a look around outside, to observe the reality about us, and the result is a disturbing portrayal of modern Italy. We are all in agreement over one point: **Prova d'Orchestra** is a reflection of the chaos in which we live, and from which we do not know how to escape. It is not a political film, if anything it is an 'ethical allegory,' says the director: an ethical allegory born of a sense of uneasiness, of fear, of dismay and which contains perhaps, as do all ethical apologues, a warning: if we do not stop and think for a moment, try to understand just what we are doing, just how far we have gone, then the worst will be inevitable, with ugly consequences for all of us. ..."

Costanza Costantini, IL MESSAGGERO, *Rome, 12 November 1978.*

"... A bitter, almost desparate, disturbing allegory, this latest film of Fellini's. Certainly, if shown on the small screen, in the evasive placenta of the darkened rooms of thousands of TV viewers, and not only Italians at that, this film cannot but shock anyone who is genuinely concerned about the world in which we live, about the state of this **Prova d'Orchestra** of ours, our daily reality. ..."

Giorgio Strehler, CORRIERE DELLA SERA, *Milan-Rome, 14 March 1979.*

"... Only a great author could permit himself such ideological ambiguity and still appear stimulating and therefore fertile. It is astonishing: this strange oratorio, a moral environment rather than a physical setting, transcends in secret eloquence its excited populace, and the wind which blows across it at the moment of destruction has its own freezing esoteric power, rather like the wind which, in **Roma**, erased the underground frescoes, unearthed by hideous modernity. Not to mention the superb episode of the interview with the conductor in which all the traditional Fellinian irony really comes into its own. However much he might resemble Hitler, he is definitely a character. ..."

Guglielmo Biraghi, IL MESSAGGERO, *Rome, 23 February 1979.*

"... The possibility of instrumentalizing or condemning the moral of the story, interpreting it as merely a 'call to order,' has diverted attention from the authentic values of this film. Like all of Fellini's television work, from **A Director's Notebook** to **The Clowns**, it has a lightness of touch and capacity to synthesize that would be hard to find in a longer film. In portraying the members of the orchestra, Fellini's talent for caricature is once again evident, while the conductor provides Fellini with the opportunity for a brief autobiographical note on the one hand, and on the other for self-criticism which is almost paradoxical. ... Taken as a whole, the film, handled with great skill, is an ingeniously contradictory essay: it is amusing and sad, positive and desperate, captivating and irritating."

Tullio Kezich, PANORAMA, *1979.*

The dust of disaster settles on the violins.

"W il giradischi" *(long live the record player) reads one of the graffiti on the wall, where an era of graphomania in Italy is splendidly summed up.*

". . . Our impression is, that of all the ideas grouped together here by the scriptwriters, of all the designs assembled in Prova d'Orchestra, *the real Fellini is not the one who peeps at the fears and murmurings of society and brandishes trite symbols around, but the other one, the showman, the cinematographer, the storyteller who, confronted by the limits reached by man (and what if the gloomy muttering that precede the disaster were a travesty of death?) is forced to admit that the desire to dream is indestructible, thanks to the mediation of art. . . ."*

Mino Argentieri, RINASCITA, *Rome, 9 March 1979.*

". . . Prova d'Orchestra *is a film about affliction, anxiety, confusion and suffering. It is characterized by a series of insoluble contradictions, its purpose being not to provide answers, but rather to raise problems, such as the relationship between the individual and society, for instance. . . . So, making use of allegory and metaphor with characteristic virtuosity Fellini, in* Prova d'Orchestra, *offers a compendium of all our doubts. And it is also excellent entertainment."*

Jean A. Gili, ECRAN, *80, Paris, 15 May 1979.*

". . . It seems more apt to us to underline the pessimistic note in this film. In La Dolce Vita *. . . there was indignation, but there was also hope. In* Prova d'Orchestra *hope has died. We are spectators to the death of music, to the clash between two parties—the members of the orchestra and the conductor—both of which are losers. Moreover, they are not fighting over the notes of Bach or Beethoven, which would have been worth the effort, but over a clumsy score composed with a zeal equal to the ability (it takes ability to write even ugly music) of Nino Rota. Behind* Prova d'Orchestra *there is not just* La Dolce Vita, *but the same lugubrious vision of the world expressed in* Casanova. . . ."*

Callisto Cosulich, PAESE SERA, *Rome, 23 February 1979.*

". . . Prova d'Orchestra *is manifestly a film-allegory; it demands interpretation and makes symbol-hunters out of the critics. Besides possible political, moral and social interpretations, there is another, equally valid interpretation, which sees the film as a large metaphor for the relationship between cinema and television, or rather the history of the advent of cinema in TV.*

"The film . . . relates an esthetic event, a concert, which has difficulty in getting going. Rather like the film they are trying unsuccessfully to make in 8½. *But here, the reason for all the difficulty is not the author (the conductor) with his human and creative crisis, but the entire production apparatus. . . . The temple of art has been violated by daily reality, by the causality of life, and uncontrolled behavior. Hand in hand go music and commedy* all'italiana, cinéma vérité *and political metaphor, daily news and artistic performance. The television documentary has turned everything into television, the language of contemporaneity, heterogeneity and of the final disappearance of the 'aura.' . . . But at a certain point, when total degradation is reached (and this is expressed in terms of structure and not of aesthetic values) the giant hammer appears, announcing the advent of a new order.*

"A Revolution, a Restoration, Providence? No, it is only a symbol of itself, a symbol of the symbolic. Just as everything is about to come adrift, when all codes have been destroyed, the hypothesis of a return to the order of the symbolic, to the language of certitude, to the solidarity of the work of art, appears on the horizon. Together with the hammer, it is the cinema which is brought to television, with

its special effects, its clouds of smoke, its settings, its fantasy, its emotions, everything the cinema can do that television cannot. It is cinema 'for' television, it is the orchestra beginning to play again. . . ."

Alberto Farassino, LA REPUBLICA, *Milan-Rome, 15 March 1979.*

"Regardless of the many details illustrating Fellini's civic irks and social fears, he really takes over the podium for a long view, with the help of Nino Rota's ironic score, to issue a solemn warning over the masses' heads that democracy and violent discord are incompatible, leaving society a helpless prey to dictatorship. . . . While Fellini's social posture is open to debate and the ending subject to individual interpretation, there can be little or no quibbling with the creative depth of this exercise—intensified, if anything, by Giuseppe Rotunno's

ingenious lensing, the stark pace . . . and the sardonic notes of Nino Rota's score."

Werb, VARIETY, *March 7, 1979.*

"If the picture had a life of its own, if we really felt the musicians as characters, rather than figures in a carefully schematized pattern, the not-very-subtle political message might not be so tiresome. But more disturbing than the preachiness of [the film] is its lifelessness. Fellini's films generally teem with life. . . . But here, though there are a few typically amusing physiognomies, the musicians serve merely as a pretext for a lecture. One can understand why the current situation in Italy has politicized Fellini, but the cinematic result is not a happy one."

Howard Kissel, WOMEN'S WEAR DAILY, *August 15,1979.*

"As you may have heard, all of this is intended as a 'metaphor' for the collapse of European civilization. Dear God, give me a break. First of all, the music in question is by the late Nino Rota, a wonderful film composer but not quite Beethoven or Schubert, so at the literal level the unraveling of the rehearsal hardly amounts to a tragedy. Watching the film, which I though inane, it occurred to me that it was made by people who probably cared little for classical music and were quite content to see the rehearsal go smash. Indeed,the monkeyshines are staged gleefully, rather like an evening with Spike Jones, and in any case Fellini has always been more at home with chaos than with order."

David Denby, NEW YORK, *September 3,1979.*

The members of the orchestra, resigned and bungling protagonists of a collective, in some ways involuntary, rebellion, have assumed all sorts of strange positions: one is asleep, others play on regardless, while another one strips. On the wall, a mysterious warning: "Violino si nasce, direttore si muore" (Born a violin, died a conductor).

THE CITY OF WOMEN

LA CITTÁ DELLE DONNE   ITALY/FRANCE   1980

Produced for Opera Film Produzione (Rome) and Gaumont (Paris). Director: Federico Fellini. Screenplay: Federico Fellini, Bernardino Zapponi, with the collaboration of Brunello Rondi, from a story by Federico Fellini, Bernardo Zapponi. Photography (Technovision-Colore): Giuseppe Rotunno. Camera operator: Gianni Fiore. Music: Luis Bacalov. Conductor: Gianfranco Plenizio. Songs: "Una Donna Senza Uomo É," words and music by Mary Francolao, "Donna Addio," lines by Antonio Amurri. Dance: Mirella Aguiaro. Choreography consultant: Leonetta Bentivoglio. Art director: Dante Ferretti, with scenery sketches by Federico Fellini. Assistant art director: Claude Chevant. Architect: Giorgio Giovannini. Set decorators: Bruno Cesari, Carlo Gervasi. Assistant architect: Nazzareno Piana. Sculptures: Giovanni Chianese. Paintings and frescoes: Rinaldo and Giuliano Geleng. Costumes: Gabriella Pescucci. Assistant costumers: Maurizio Millenotti, Marcella De Marchis. Marcello Mastroianni's wardrobe: Piatelli. Assistant directors: Maurizio Mein, Giovanni Bentivoglio, Franco Amurri. Second unit director: Jean-Louis Godfroy. Special effects: Adriano Pischiutta. Sound: Tommaso Quattrini, Pierre Paul Marie Lorrain. Makeup: Rino Carboni. Editor: Ruggero Mastroianni. Assistant editors: Bruno Sarandrea, Roberto Puglisi, Adriana Olasio. Executive producer: Franco Rossellini. Production manager: Francesco Orefici. Second unit production manager: Philippe Lorain Bernard. Distribution in Italy: Gaumont-Italia. Running time: 145 minutes.

CAST

Marcello Mastroianni (*Snàporaz),* Anna Prucnal (*his wife*), Bernice Stegers (*woman in the train*), Ettore Manni (*Dr. Sante Katzone*), Iole Silvani (*fat peasant-motorcyclist*), Donatella Damiani (*Donatella, the soubrette*), Fiammetta Baralla ("*Ollio*"), Marcello De Falco (*homosexual at Katzone's party*), Gabriella Giorgelli (*fishwife*), Alessandra Panelli (*housewife with child in arms*), Rosaria Tafuri (*second soubrette*), Carla Terlizzi (*feminist*), Jill and Viviane

A giant padlock for a traditional female myth.

The legendary "homo fellinianus," custodian of adolescent dreams and family harems, is finally captured (Marcello Mastroianni).

Lucas (*twins*), Mara Ciukleva (*85-year-old woman*), Mimmo Poli (*guest at Katzone's party*), Nello Pazzafini (*appears in the final scene in the stadium*), Armando Parracino, Umberto Zuanelli, Pietro Fumagalli (*the three old magicians in the memory sequence*), Helene G. Calzarelli, Catherine Carrel, Silvana Fusacchia, Dominique Labourier, Stephane Emlfork, Sylvie Mayer, Meerberger Nahyr, Sibilla Sedat, Katren Gebelein, Nadia Vasil, Loredana Solfizi, Fiorella Molinari, Sylvie Wacrenier.

Anna Prucnal is dubbed by Valeria Moriconi.

SYNOPSIS

Snàporaz, a distinguished-looking gentleman in his early fifties, is dozing in the compartment of a train as it makes its way through the country. The appearance of a buxom stranger attracts his attention. He follows the unknown girl along the corridor to the toilet and, when she takes advantage of an unexpected stop and gets off the train, Snġaporaz decides to follow. She leads him across the fields and woods of a mysterious landscape. Finally, Snàporaz reaches the Grand Hotel Miramare, where a gigantic convention of feminists from different countries and of all ages is being held. Still searching for his traveling companion, Snàporaz mingles with the women. He is mistaken for a journalist and is about to be beaten up when a soubrette comes to his rescue.

Snàporaz tumbles down some stairs and finds himself in the cellar. Here he meets a corpulent female in charge of the boilers, who offers to give him a lift to the nearest station on her motorcycle. But when they reach the open country, she stops and tries to rape him. Snàporaz is on the run again, with two cars full of excited females close on his heals.

Night falls and he takes refuge in the villa-stronghold of Dr. Sante Katzone, an old school friend. Katzone and some friends of his are orgiastically celebrating his ten thousandth erotic conquest amidst audio-visual relics of his career as a libertine. It is here in this grotesque gallery that Snàporaz meets his drunken wife, who insults him; he also meets the soubrette again. The feminists break into the villa and Snàporaz escapes on a merry-go-round, where he relives his childhood years in Rimini and, especially, his initial awakenings to female charm.

Snàporaz is captured by the feminists and brought to trial. Hav-

The erotic corridor of Dr. Katzone (Marcello Mastroianni).

A gallery of pictures reminiscent of a style fashionable in the 1940s and 1950s (Marcello Mastroianni).

ing been sentenced to freedom, he then goes off to search for the ideal woman, portrayed as a Montgolfier balloon in the shape of a female. He climbs aboard, but is hit by shots from a machine-gun fired by the soubrette. At this point Snàporaz wakes up to find himself in the same train compartment with his wife sitting before him. He closes his eyes, just as the train goes into a dark tunnel.

NOTES

Città delle Donne is yet another of those films with a long story behind it. It was many years ago that Fellini first began to jot down sketches of characters and possibilities for a film that corresponded more or less to what we find here. In this film, Fellini the author is deeply sensual, with an adolescent, homely, hauntingly obsessive type of sensuality, as he evokes the brothels and variety theatres of yesterday. He depicts a kind of femininity which is at once rich and worn, warm and ironical and in a certain sense voluptuously "antiquated" in comparison with modern society's way not of considering, but describing, analyzing it.

Fellini irresistibly takes us back to the "Federico" of *Marc'Aurelio* days, to the young man who wrote those vague, unadorned little stories—so out of character with the vigorously impudent, romanesque tone of the rest of the magazine—about his ex-periences as a young student. (I remember one episode in which he tells of a date he had with a maid. "What does one say to a maid?" Federico asked himself, as he described the mixture of embarrassment, anxiety, shyness and pride he felt as he waited for his date to arrive, "What words should one use, so as not to frighten that young, plump, humble body of hers, all dolled up for the occasion?")

Now, many years later, Snàporaz's astonishment at the sight of those rebellious females, is like the young Federico's ultimate reply to his long-standing queries. Perhaps the answers are to be found in the familiar features of Marcello Mastroianni. In actual fact Fellini and Mastroianni have worked together in only a few films, but they are all significant in one way or another: *La Dolce Vita, 8½, Città delle Donne*; they all belong to moments in Fellini's career in which he has felt the need for an ostentatious, available, divinatory "alter ego." And the fact that the result aroused some perplexity even among hardened Fellini fans is not necessarily a matter for concern. On more than a few occasions Fellini's films have been received with contrasting views. But in the end he has always been mysteriously proved right, with his very special style of cinema in which the "studio" and the "set" are fundamental: fun and games among the familiar settings of Cinecittà, an enormous and at the same time minute circus, which he seems to have created somewhere between the kitchen and the reception room, as in one of those middle-class Rimini households he knew so well.

(c.g.f.)

REVIEWS

". . . Fellini the director has (luckily for him and for us) finally reached a splendid maturity which permits him to lavish his treasures upon us for the simple pleasure of doing so. Behind the festival of images and colors we can feel his delight in making this film, delight which, from the very first scene, becomes ours too, and it is something we have not felt for a long time. . . . We

The famous shell-shaped bed of male dreams (left to right, Donatella Damiani, Marcello Mastroianni and Sara Tarufi).

let ourselves be carried away by the cavalcade of inventions and are left breathless (like a young child going to the cinema for the first time) by every sequence, every shot. And if Città della Donne *lacks suspense in its story (we care little what happens to Snàporaz or Katzone, because we know that sooner or later Rimini and those bosomy extras will appear on the scene), there is suspense in the images and in the scenic inventions (we guess that Fellini is going to invent something, but we can never guess just what he is going to do it, or when he is going to do it). . . ."*

Giorgio Carbone, LA NOTTE, *Milan, 29 March 1980.*

". . . In Città delle Donne *Fellini is really only playing games. But then we would hardly expect from Fellini a deep analysis of the nature of woman. . . . It is a game with occasional gaps . . . and, more fre-*

quently, inventions which rejuvenate an all too familar, all too hackneyed subject. A surprising serenity predominates. . . . La Città delle Donne is a film with a tragic vein, which in the end proves to be lighthearted and occasionally amusing."

Francesco Bolzoni, L'AVVENIRE, *Milan, 29 March 1980.*

". . . It is a catalogue of emotions, sometimes grotesque, sometimes farcical, which provides some caustic jibes against the destruction of femininity by aggressive feminism. . . . We liked it enough. We found some imbalance in the quality of the images—the kernel seemed a little 'soft,' so to speak, and threatened here and there by some inattentive narrative and unintelligible dialectic form; from a stylistic point of view it is less homogeneous than usual. But other parts of the film are delightful. For instance . . . when fantasy is used

to create types of people rather than caricatures—in this sense Fellini, having abandoned his gallery of monsters, becomes more prosaic. Or when the ambiguity of certain characters—an excellent example is the soubrette played by the charming Donatella Damiani—provides a touch of grace and bitchiness; or when the film becomes almost a musical; or when paradox becomes surrealist, such as during the party and the hurricane at the villa of Katzone, who is in despair because his favorite dog has been killed. . . ."

Giovanni Grazzini, CORRIERE DELLA SERA, *Milan-Rome, 29 March 1980.*

". . . La Città delle Donne, *after the ominous* Prova d'Orchestra, *takes us back to the old Fellini, to the director who never seems in the slightest bit worried about repeating the same film over and over again.* La Città delle Donne *is a disappointing and melancholy dis-*

play of a style of cinema which has lost its script and plays by memory, without any particular aim in view. . . .'"

Natalino Bruzzone, IL LAVORO NUOVO, Genoa, 3 April 1980.

". . . What can we say, except that we have seen another typically Fellinian film, turgid, characterized by visionary opulence, harrowed by some examples of poor taste, but underscored by a palpable anxiety and by strange omens? . . . ."

Carlo Laurenzi, IL GIORNALE, Milan, 29 March 1980.

". . . Once again, as usual, or almost, Fellini appears as the Madame Bovary of his adolescence, and he revels in the enjoyment he feels at working with an experienced crew, side by side with faithful stage technicians who simulate trains on the move, or the sea washing the shores of the inevitable Romagnol beaches, as

though they were working on the set of Méliès [famous French fantasist who made A Trip to the Moon in 1902]. But then, again and again, Fellini has shown us that he is the greatest and most ingenious of Méliès' heirs. . . . Only the magic does not always work. And the temptation in Città delle Donne to fuse a sort of astonished confession of amused impotence before the 'new' woman of today, together with a feeling of nostalgia for the 'old' woman of yesterday, . . . despite Fellini's extraordinary virtuosity, rarely achieves the harmony of inspiration, order, strip-cartoon phantasmagory, and irony which has been inciting the author's imagination for years. . . ."

Claudio G. Fava, CORRIERE MERCANTILE, Genoa, 4 April 1980.

Though the film is overlong, even for a Fellini aficionado, it is spellbinding, a dazzling visual display that is part burlesque, part satire,

part Folies-Bergère and all cinema. As Snàporaz is haunted by the phantoms of all the women he has known, or wanted to know, from childhood on, Mr. Fellini in City of Women is obsessed by his own feelings toward women, by his need for them, his treatment (mostly poor) of them, his continued fascination by them and his awareness that (thank heavens) they'll always be different. . . . Though City of Women is about a libertine, it's anything but licentious. Mr. Fellini's licentiousness suggests a profound longing for some kind of protective discipline if not complete chastity. As such discipline would destroy Snàporaz (the leading male character) it would make impossible the conception and production of a film as wonderfully uninhibited as City of Women."

Vincent Canby, THE NEW YORK TIMES, April 8, 1981.

A multitude of candles, beautiful girls on display, smiling roller-skaters: it is all too much for Snàporaz, with his deeply-rooted, traditional beliefs.

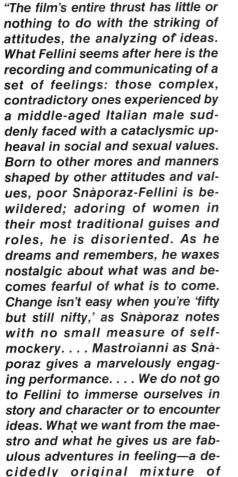

"The film's entire thrust has little or nothing to do with the striking of attitudes, the analyzing of ideas. What Fellini seems after here is the recording and communicating of a set of feelings: those complex, contradictory ones experienced by a middle-aged Italian male suddenly faced with a cataclysmic upheaval in social and sexual values. Born to other mores and manners shaped by other attitudes and values, poor Snàporaz-Fellini is bewildered; adoring of women in their most traditional guises and roles, he is disoriented. As he dreams and remembers, he waxes nostalgic about what was and becomes fearful of what is to come. Change isn't easy when you're 'fifty but still nifty,' as Snàporaz notes with no small measure of self-mockery. . . . Mastroianni as Snàporaz gives a marvelously engaging performance. . . . We do not go to Fellini to immerse ourselves in story and character or to encounter ideas. What we want from the maestro and what he gives us are fabulous adventures in feeling—a decidedly original mixture of

nostalgia, poignancy and joy that is unmistakably Fellini's own."

Joh Gould Boyum, THE WALL STREET JOURNAL, *April 17,1981.*

"Doesn't Fellini ever tire of being Fellini? Many artists, as they grow older, develop a simpler, more concentrated style—they discover the dramatic power of plainness. But Fellini has grown more wildly surreal-baroque as he has aged, and this style now dominates every subject he takes up. With the exception of Amarcord, which had

*long passages of limpid beauty, the
movies of the past twenty years
have presented one version or another of the Fellini carnival, the
Fellini banquet of life, the Fellini
combination of the pathetic and
the grotesque. In* City of Women,
*Fellini has got hold of a new sub-
ject—the way feminist ideas have
changed women—and he digs into
it entertainingly for a few scenes,
but then he retreats into the all too
recognizable world of his personal
mythology. Women's Lib stimulates
him to reveal the range of his feelings about women—which turn out
to be the same feelings he's revealed before."*

David Denby, NEW YORK,
April 13,1981.

ANd THE SHip SAils ON...

roduced by Franco Cristaldi for IA—Italian Radio-Television Rome), Vides Production (Rome), aumont (Paris). Director: Federico ellini. Screenplay: Federico Fellini, onino Guerra. Photography: (Technicolor-Panavision) Giuseppe Rounno. Cameraman: Gianni Fiore. ssistant Operators: Gian Maria Marana, Luigi Bernardini. Music: ianfranco Plenizio. Lyrics to the opras: Andrea Zanzotto. Singers: Mara ampieri (Ildebranda Cuffari), Elizaeth Norbrg Schulz (Ines Ruffo Saltini nd first Serbian Soprano), Nucci

Condó (Teresa Valegnani), Govanni Bavaglio (Fuciletto), Carlo Di Giacomo (Sabatino Lepori), Boris Carmeli (Ziloev), Bernardette Lucarin (second Serbian Soprano), Bruno Beccaria (Serbian Tenor). Scenography: Dante Ferretti. Costumes: Maurizio Millenotti. Choreography: Leonetta Bentivoglio. Paintings and frescos: Rinaldo and Giuliano Geleng. Scene Painter: Italo Tomassi. Sculptor: Giovanni Giannese. Effects: Adriano Paschiutta. Consultant for the reproduction of the battleship: Valeriano Trubbiani. Architects: Naz-

zareno Piana, Massimo Razzi. Interior design: Massimo Tavazzi, Francesca Lo Schiavo. Assistant to the costumer: Barbara Mastroianni. Editor: Ruggero Mastroianni. Assistant to the editor: Adriana Olasio, Leda Bellini, Rosanna Landi. Director's Helper: Giovanni Arduini. Assistant to the director: Andrea De Carlo. Editing secretary: Norma Giacchero. Mixing: Fausto Ancillai. Dubbing director: Riccardo Cucciolla. General organizer: Pietro Notarianni. Production director: Lucio Orlandini. Manager of production: Roberto Mannoni, Mas-

Lady and Sir Reginald Dongby (Norma West and Peter Collier). He is an English nobleman voyeuristically jealous of his nymphomaniac wife.

simo Cristaldi. Associate producer: Aldo Nemni for SIM. Origin: Italy-France. First Italian distribution: Gaumont. Length: 132 min.

CAST

Freddie Jones *(Orlando, the journalist)*, Barbara Jefford *(Ildebranda Cuffari)*, Victor Polette *(Aureliano Fucilletto)*, Peter Cellier *(Sir Reginald J. Dongby)*, Norma West *(Lady Violet Dongby)*, Elisa Mainardi *(Teresa Valegnani)*, Paolo Paoloni *(Albertini, the orchestra director)*, Sarah Jane Varley *(Dorotea)*, Fiorenzo Serra *(The Grand Duke of Herzock)*, Pina Bausch *(The Princess Lherimia)*, Pasquale Zito *(The Count of Bassano)*, Fred Williams *(Sabatino Lepori)*, Philip Locke *(the prime minister)*, Antonio Vezza *(The Executive Officer of Gloria N.)*, Francesco Maselli *(the guardian of the rhinoceros)*, Gino Costa *(the funeral home director)*, Liliana Palmero *(the gypsy)*, Umberto Barone *(the director of "La Scala")*, Pasquale Esposito *(the boatswain)*, Domenico Postiglione *(the stoker)*, Antonio Stumpo *(the wireless operator)*, Pasquale Filippelli *(a waiter)*, Radames Roccati *(another waiter)*, Salvatore Esposito *(a grave digger)*, Salvatore Di Stasio *(a sailor)*, Linda Polan *(Ines Ruffo Saltini Ione)*, Jonathan Cecil *(Ricotin)*, Maurice Barrier *(U.O. Ziloev)*, Elizabeth Kaza *(the movie producer)*, Colin Higgins *(the police chief)*, Umberto Zuanelli *(Maestro Rubbetti 1)*, Vittorio Zarfati *(Maestro Rubbetti 2)*, Domenico Pertica, Claudio Ciocca, Alessandro Partexano, Christian Fremont, Marielle Duvelle, Helen Stirling, Janet Stirling, Janet Suzman-The portrait of Edmea Tetua.

SYNOPSIS

July 1914. The steamboat Gloria N. is getting ready to leave pier number 10 in Naples' harbor. The ashes of Edmea Tetua, the opera singer, are brought on board. The goal of the cruise is to scatter the last mortal remains of the "diva" off Erimo Island, where she had been born. Orlando, a journalist, takes part in the funeral voyage. He tells the public tales and pieces of gossip, and presents the various characters with their little stories and ridiculous manias. An array of various human types is represented in the little crowd of singers, producers, voice teachers, orchestra directors, noble admirers. Ildebranda, a soprano, wants to discover the secret of Edmea's voice. The Russian singer makes chickens fall asleep with his deep voice. The Italian Count locks himself up in his cabin, which he has transformed into a votive temple in memory of the late Edmea. The comedian travels with his mother and seduces sailors. The jealous English nobleman spies on his nymphomaniac wife. The Prussian Grand Duke Harzock travels with a little entourage and his blind sister, who is also a seer and plots with her lover, the prime minister, to dispossess her brother.

Stench comes up from the ship's hold, where there is a huge rhinoceros in pain and in love, perhaps. The ship's company pulls it up and washes it. The third day of the voyage, the steamship/hearse takes on board a group of shipwrecked Serbians who have escaped from their country after the assassination at Sarajevo. The array of humans aboard the Gloria N. is thus enriched by elements of colorful and popular folklore. The Grand Duke's men lead people to believe that the newcomers are dangerous anarchists. The latter are then isolated in a corner of the deck. It is there that the Serbians improvise a dance. The group of gentlemen is infected for a while by its joyfulness.

The flagship of the Austro-Hungarian fleet arrives: the shipwrecked men must immediately be handed over. The Captain of the Gloria N. refuses. The Grand Duke insists that the cruise keep going undisturbed till the memorial service is held. Edmea's ashes are dispersed in the wind near the Island of Erimo. The shipwrecked people are then put in a lifeboat and delivered to the Austrians, a young Serbian throws a bomb towards the Austro-Hungarian battleship, which answers back with its guns. The Gloria N. starts sinking. The passengers of the steamboat keep singing under the direction of Albertini, the director.

The attempts to get the people aboard the lifeboats begin. In a cloud of black smoke, the battleship explodes. The lifeboat that transports the Grand Duke gets involved in the violent blast and is engulfed. A backward tracking shot reveals all of the crew for the movie working in a studio in "Theater 5" at Cinecitta in order to carry out the special effects for the Gloria N. tragedy. The camera then tracks forward to focus on Orlando, the journalist. He is wearing his swimming trunks and is wrestling with the long oars of a big lifeboat. He says that many people among those on the Gloria N. did manage to save themselves. Then, he adds, "Did you know that a rhinoceros gives very good milk?" The rhinoceros is well placed at the lifeboat's prow and quietly ruminates on some grass, while Orlando, laughing and amusing himself, forcefully handles the oars and gets lost on the horizon of a huge sea made of plastic.

NOTES

And the Ship Sails On . . . was presented at the 1983 Venice Festival, out of competition, of course, as was *Fanny and Alexander* by Bergman, which was shown in the unabridged television version. These were sumptuous moments, out of competition in a double Six Days of Cinema. This movie competition has taught something to the entire world: Often the participants are so superior that it would be unthinkable to have them on the same starting line as the others. If they agree to take the tour of honor, they do so during a special intermission. Such breaks are thus charged with a tension often unknown during the competition itself.

There was the usual drama with a happy ending with Fellini's arrival. There was the announcement of a press conference, but, old observer of Fellini as I am, I knew it would not take place. Nevertheless, Fellini had let me know that in case it should happen, he wanted me near him on the stage. That was an undeserved honor, which flattered me very much, all the more since I was sure that I would never stand on that stage. This is because Federico is horrified of press conferences and the endless liturgy of absurd or sharp questions and generic or pertinent answers that those questions implicitly carry within themselves. Especially if the subject is a movie and the exchange is with the director, to whom almost always are addressed questions that sound as if they were taken from a textbook on the conversation of the absurd for the sheer pleasure of the surrealists.

From the first Venice showing, it was very clear what the reaction of the critics would be. You might say that the response could be drawn along ethnic lines: The Italians were delighted but intimidated and perplexed at times. The French, of all types, enthusiastic (in that lucid and feverish way in which the French are enthusiastic, especially for Italian things—with the same air as a missionary or a lover being forced every now and then to return *in partibus infidelium* to rearrange the liturgies messed up during his absence). I cite the French since they are typical and because they are the foreign critics most aware of the Italian cinema; but the reaction was largely "national," exactly of this kind.

Once again Federico was too Italian to really seduce his countrymen. Italians, as we know, are often sensitive to another kind of "Italianism" in the movies. The kind, for example, exhibited by Visconti, full of hard languors for revolt and minutely noble leopards. *And the Ship Sails On . . .* appears to be an allegory of the natural "falsity" in making movies, to the point that it provokes a sense of subconscious resistance in many people. (Always in the most truly Fellinian version, and often in other cases, this requires the natural "corrup-

The rhinoceros tied up in the hold is ready to be pulled up on the deck. "The doctor said it needs fresh air."

tion" of the "set" and physiologically implies the mediation of machines, lights, bulkheads, veiled lenses, blurred focuses and other means to an end. All of the above is paraphernalia worthy of Cagliostro or Meliés, of whom Italian critics often get bored, since they tend to prefer the "realistic" and the "social.") The ending, with that camera which joyfully reveals the "gimmick," the ship mounted on wonderful suspension joints similar to those found in airplane factories or "Bergmanesque" circuses, is an open present offered by Fellini not only to the world of cinema but to his beloved Theater 5 at Cinecittá, where he nests his movies for years as if he were a huge cat that continuously purrs among packages of photos and a chain of visitors.

Fellini has such a happy talent for making wry faces, such a clear taste for provocation, that the festival almost ended up in an argument over the right of some people even to exhibit. To many, it was as if he were saying: "This is the truth, I don't know what to give you more than that. This is cinema, the ship is cinema. We wonder where it really sails. We must remember that the water is made of paper, that the storm is made of squeaking studs and nails. All is true, and all is fake, as in the silent documentary that at the beginning shows us the passengers boarding." Many critics often forget that they attend festivals to see "fake" things, professionally fake: the movies. They end up judging them, loving and hating them, as if they were extraterrestrial objects, not man-made, but wonderful alien objects, fantastic asteroids that

arrived in front of their eyes, jumping straight from their childish desires to see tales materialize.

We shouldn't wonder at the enor mous number of reviews devoted to *And the Ship Sails On . . .* It is the most "Fellinian" movie that could ex ist, because of its zeal for self-quo tation, its mischievous, almost child like mockery, and, always, the self effacing, serious reflections. The re views tried to balance the differen kinds of reactions: All of those who wrote about the movie (whethe completely for or somehow against it felt that they were dealing with some thing that someone else couldn't o wouldn't know how to make—o wouldn't want to in the first place.

In other words, they were pre sented with a way of making movies that proved to be once again the gi

antic projection of the crepuscular
and impudently sophomoric moods of
Romagna. Fellini has been in Rome
on a school trip for fifty years. *His*
Rome, with its baroque skies, its fat
women, its dishes of pasta
"all'amatricana," its wonderfully silent churches, its noisy streets with
wild cars, its barbaric and genial
crews," its faded and gloomy government employees, its cinema, and,
above all, its studios, its great damp
wombs where cinema is created,
where immense ships made of cardboard are constructed, where endless
floors made of wood and iron are
built, where dreams are photographed. . . .

REVIEW

*". . . And the Ship Sails On . . .
is a genial movie, although a bit
discontinuous. What is genial, for
example, is the intuition that the
European society of the "Belle
Epoque" had empited itself of all
its contents, except for the artificial
and exhaustive formalism, making
it look then like a continuous,
cheap melodrama. The other genial
intuition is that of the fundamental
unity of the world back then, completely bourgeois or, rather, totally
involved in the bourgeoisie. That
can very well be seen in the beau-*
*tiful scene where the singers per-
form leaning over the engine
room. . . . After this illuminating
scene, the film goes through a
much less inspired part. From there
it gains height in the ironically appalling passages of the shipwreck,
where the tables and the piano
slide on the floors and the luggage
floats in the corridors filled with
water. . . ."*

*Alberto Moravia, L'ESPRESSO,
Roma, October 30, 1983.*

**"Federico Fellini counts And the
Ship Sails On as his 18th feature
film and he has launched a vessel**

Lady Dongby (Norma West) and the ship's second officer. While boarding the ship, the passengers all sang: "Let's follow the waves, the hardest
path of joys and mourning, let's follow the ship that sails on."

that is chock-full of his best gags, visual fun and love of cinema as artful technique. Ship's journey, however, is a long one, and since there is not much in the direction of spiritual cargo, it also occasionally proves a tedious one and dangerously close to foundering in shallow waters. The whole production is magnificently mounted . . . audiences not happy with all the fun may rather be angered and will certainly be missing the haunting poetry, this time only sketched in cautiously, of the Maestro's best work."

Kell, VARIETY, *September 14,1983.*

"One may find it harder to justify Fellini's relentless pursuit of the polymorphous and the perverse in the service of a career-long anti-eroticism. It is hard to see why no one in the operatic cortège looks straight and uncomplicated. This may be the trap of excessive expressionism. Could Fellini have been cruising for easy laughs through the campy posturings of his pseudo-characters? More likely, he has lost whatever vestigial feeling for narrative he ever possessed, and is reduced to groping for profound meanings with an ever-wandering camera but without the psychological core, anchor and axis provided in the past by the eloquently introspective Mastroianni. . . . [The film] is too much a work of the pure imagination with the result that the audience is cast adrift on a styrofoam sea without a lifeline to any kind of recognizable reality."

Andrew Sarris, THE VILLAGE VOICE,
February 7,1984.